His Mission and Ministry

Teacher Advisory Panel

Sharon A. Abler
Dowling Catholic High School
West Des Moines, IA

Maria D.S. Andrade Johnson
Santa Margarita Catholic High School
Rancho Santa Margarita, CA

Philip R. Drey
Xavier High School
Cedar Rapids, IA

Kathryn A. Ladd
St. Pius X High School
Houston, TX

Kathleen S. Legg
Bishop Feehan High School
Attleboro, MA

Barbara SchwabKlaco
Bishop Ready High School
Columbus, OH

Maria F. Steen
Archbishop Chapelle High School
Metairie, LA

Michael J. Wielgopolski
St. Francis de Sales High School
Toledo, OH

Susan Wilkinson
Peninsula Catholic High School
Newport News, VA

His Mission and Ministry

Michael Pennock

The Subcommittee on the Catechism, United States Conference of Catholic Bishops, has found this catechetical text, © 2011, to be in conformity with the *Catechism of the Catholic Church.*

Nihil Obstat: Reverend Monsignor Michael Heintz
Censor Liborum

Imprimatur: Most Reverend Kevin C. Rhoades
Bishop of Fort Wayne-South Bend

Given at: Fort Wayne, Indiana, on 1 July 2010

The *Nihil Obstat* and *Imprimatur* are official declarations that a book or pamphlet is free of doctrinal or moral error. No implication is contained therein that those who have granted the *Nihil Obstat* or *Imprimatur* agree with its contents, opinions, or statements expressed.

Founded in 1865, Ave Maria Press is a ministry of the United States Province of Holy Cross.

Engaging Minds, Hearts, and Hands for Faith® is a trademark of Ave Maria Press, Inc.

www.avemariapress.com

ISBN-10: 1-59471-186-0 ISBN-13: 978-1-59471-186-2

Cover and text design by Andy Wagoner.

Photography credits listed on page 310.

Printed and bound in the United States of America.

Engaging Minds, Hearts, and Hands for Faith

"An education that is complete is one in which the hands and heart are engaged as much as the mind. We want to let our students try their learning in the world and so make prayers of their education."

—Bl. Basil Moreau
Founder of the Congregation of Holy Cross

In this text, you will find:

knowledge about how God reveals himself—especially in the Three Divine Persons of the Trinity—and how we respond to God's self-revelation in faith.

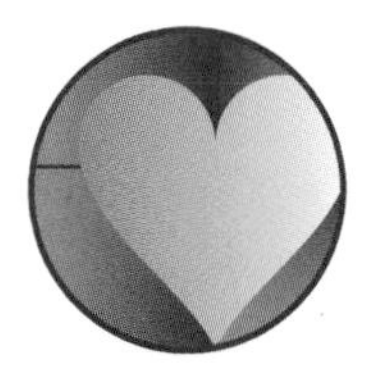

deeper ways to reflect and pray about the mystery of the Incarnation, Jesus Christ fully God and fully man.

projects and activities to encourage faith-based service in the Lord.

Contents

GOD'S REVELATION AND OUR RESPONSE

Let us be sober, putting on the breastplate of faith and love and the helmet that is hope for salvation. For God did not destine us for wrath, but to gain salvation through our Lord Jesus Christ, who died for us, so that whether we are awake or asleep we may live together with him. Therefore, encourage one another and build one another up, as indeed you do.

—1 Thessalonians 5:8-11

- ## A Definitive Victory
  Christians have faith that their lives are headed for eternal life and ultimate happiness in the Lord.

- ## The Existence of God
  It is natural for all human beings to wonder about the existence of an all-powerful God and Creator.

- ## Divine Revelation
  God shares the mystery of his divine plan through self-communication that the Church calls Divine Revelation.

- ## Scripture, Tradition, and the Deposit of Faith
  God's revelation is shared in the Deposit of Faith—the saving truths Jesus gave to his Apostles—in Scripture, and in Tradition—the living transmission of the Gospel handed on through Church teaching, life, and worship.

- ## Faith: Our Response to Revelation
  Our religious faith in God is a response to Divine Revelation, the way that God generously shows us his redemptive plan.

- ## The Catholic Church and Faith
  Jesus left behind the Church and commissioned her leaders to carry on his work of sharing the Good News about the Kingdom of God.

A Definitive Victory

There is a die-hard sports fan who digitally records all the games of his favorite teams that he is not able to watch when he is away from home. When he eventually has time, he turns on his recorder and skips to the end of the game to discover who won or lost. If his team lost, he deletes the event. But if his team won, he starts at the beginning, pours himself a cool beverage, munches on his favorite snacks, and watches the whole game.

A friend told him that this way of watching sports is lame. The man replied, "It's just the opposite. I like it because no matter how bad things look for my team, I can relax and not worry because I know the end of the story."

The attitude of this sports fan is one you can apply to your own life. You have your whole life in front of you with its ups and downs, its twists and turns. Thinking about your future can make you nervous and anxious. But because the Holy Spirit has endowed you with the gift of faith, you do not have to worry. You know how things will turn out if you stay close to Jesus Christ. His Death and Resurrection have won eternal life for you, and for all who believe in him. The Blessed Trinity shares this definitive victory of our Lord with everyone who is part of Jesus' team. No matter how bad things might look at certain points of your life, do not let worry drag you down. You know the end of the story: Jesus Christ has triumphed!

Your Image of God

People have different ways of thinking about God. However, there are two major perceptions. One stresses God's being *beyond* this world. This is known as God's **transcendence**. Another focuses on God's being *in* the world, or God's closeness to his creatures. This is known as God's **immanence**.

Read through and reflect carefully on these ten statements about God. Then write the statements in your journal or notebook. For each number, mark a **T** or an **I** to indicate whether that statement expresses God's transcendence or his immanence.

1. God is all-powerful, all-knowing, almighty.
2. To know Jesus Christ is to know God.
3. God is a stern judge.
4. God is a friend, a constant companion who walks beside me.
5. God is Abba, "Daddy."
6. God gets "angry" when people sin.
7. You can know God by experiencing true love.
8. God forgives and rarely shows anger with people.
9. God is the omnipotent creator of Heaven and earth.
10. God is like a loving mother who is willing to sacrifice all for her children.

This chapter begins the second course in our study of the most important person in human history: Jesus Christ, our Lord and our Savior. He is God's Living Word and the Second Person of the Blessed Trinity. May your study of him help you know him better and learn from him what you are called to be—a true champion who will take his Good News into the world for other people.

 **For Reflection**

How would you feel if you knew the exact day of your own death?

The Existence of God (*CCC*, 27-49)

Did you ever talk to a three-year-old? It seems every other sentence out of the child's mouth begins with the word *Why*. Try to explain the simplest concept to the little one and you get the question "Why?" "Why are things the way they are?" "Why do I have to do this?" "Why can't I do that?" "Why, why, why?"

From the time we start speaking and formulating our ideas into words, we begin to question things. It seems to be a most natural and human thing to do. And many of our questions are important and profound. Why am I here? Who am I? Where am I going? Why do people have to suffer and die? Is there life after death? Does anyone really love me? Is there a God?

People have always asked questions like these. To be human is to ask questions. We want to know the why of things. We want to know if everything makes sense. We need to know if there is someone who cares for us and who can make life meaningful.

On deeper reflection, we see that our questions not only come from our searching minds but also from our restless hearts. We sense a deep longing in our hearts for something more. We need and desperately want to be understood and loved. Sure, we may be lucky enough to experience the love of parents, family members, and friends. We may count our blessings that there might be someone in our life who understands us and accepts us. But, to tell the truth, we are never satisfied. We always want more understanding, more love, and more satisfying answers to our questions for meaning.

Where do these questions come from? Why will they never go away? Why is your heart always restless, always searching for more love and understanding?

Simply put, Christians believe that the God who made us created us with intellects that need to search for truth. We also have hearts that ache for love. The truth and love that we search for can never be totally found in other creatures. They can only be found in God himself who is Truth and Love. In other words, God has implanted in our hearts a hunger and longing for him. He is the only one who can satisfy our unquenchable thirst for meaning, for love, for happiness.

transcendence
The teaching that God, by nature, is beyond this world and beyond the comprehension of human beings.

immanence
A trait of God that refers to his intimate union with and total presence to his creation, whereby he upholds and sustains all creation in its being.

Only when we find him will we find true happiness. St. Augustine, a fifth-century Church Father, expressed it in his autobiography, *The Confessions*, when he wrote, "You have made us for yourself, and our heart is restless until it rests in you" (quoted in *CCC*, 30).

What St. Augustine is telling us, very simply, is that when you find God, you will find meaning. Meaning is not found in money, power, popularity, sex, or athletic achievement. These things pass away. They are finite. They change and are elusive. God is infinite. God is unchanging in his love. Only God can satisfy our yearning hearts.

Finding God in Creation

One way to find God is in his beautiful creation. By opening our eyes and minds to the beautiful world God created, all humans can perceive the One who made it all and keeps it in existence. St. Paul knew this so well when he wrote in his letter to the Romans, "Ever since the creation of the world, his [God's] invisible attributes of eternal power and divinity have been able to be understood and perceived in what he has made" (Rm 1:20). The Psalmist said it this way, "The heavens declare the glory of God; the sky proclaims its builder's craft" (Ps 19:2).

God speaks to us in the awesome universe he has created and keeps in existence by his Word, the Son, and his Creator Spirit. Its intricate laws keep nature's seasons transforming our earth in a stunningly beautiful pageant, year after year. All around us we see harmony and beauty. Then, contemplate the earth itself with its perfect size; its orbital speed and correct distance from the sun; and its perfect blend of gases to sustain plant, animal, and human life. Think about the intricacies of the human brain, an organ that can process more than a million messages a second. The brain enables you to reason, to dream, to experience feelings, to motivate you to act, to love. Where did this unique creation come from if not a Grand Designer who made it and made it capable of discovering him?

Finding God in the Human Person

The peak of God's creation is the human person. This unique creature has tremendous abilities. We humans can think and we can reason. We are open to truth and beauty. We have a sense of moral goodness and can recognize evil that seeks to harm us. We have freedom and treasure it. We also can use it to love others . . . or not. We have a conscience, a voice that calls us to do good and to avoid evil. All of these abilities of the human person are spiritual in nature. They do not come from the material world. They help us to acknowledge that we have a soul,

atheist
A person who denies the existence of God.

agnostic
A person who asserts that he or she does not know whether there is a God or not.

that is, a spiritual nature that shares in God's own eternal nature.

For thousands of years, people have come to acknowledge God's existence. By nature, humans are religious. Most people who have walked this earth have recognized the existence of a Superior Being, one we call God. This explains the existence of so many religions down through the ages with their various prayers, sacrifices, rituals, sacred writings, and rules of behavior. Humans, using their God-given intellects reflecting on the world, know that there is a God. This is why the Church understands that human reason can know with certainty that God exists. He is the beginning and end of all things.

What about Nonbelievers?

Yet, some people do not believe in God. For example, **atheists** deny that God exists. They are (and have been) numerically much smaller than those who accept the existence of God. Why don't they believe? Some deny God's existence because they only accept material reality and do not buy the concept of spiritual realities like love or a human spirit. Others look at human suffering and will not accept the existence of a God who would permit it. Some atheists simply will not believe in a God because, if they did, they would have to change their behavior. Still others are simply indifferent, or too busy, or too lazy to think through the big questions that lurk in the back of their minds.

Other people, known as **agnostics**, simply say they do not know if there is a God or not. In effect, agnostics refuse to take a stand on the question of God's existence. Yet, when agnostics refuse to believe one way or another, the end result makes their mind-set a lot like that of atheists.

Still other people will not believe in a God because they see the scandalous or unloving behavior of religious people who preach a message of love. Or worse, they see religious people engaging in holy wars to force their beliefs on others or killing those who might disagree with their particular beliefs.

Despite all the reasons, it's only a minority of people that does not believe that God exists. The vast majority has faith in some sort of divine reality. People recognize that God has implanted in the human heart a longing for the infinite, a longing for union with him. Our hearts and minds can indeed lead us to God and know of his existence. Fortunately, though, God does not let our search for him rest with our own limited intellects. Though humans can discover God's existence, he wants more for us. God himself wanted to speak to humans directly in a way that we could understand *who* he truly is. God is so beyond us and so holy, so infinite and eternal, that our unaided human minds can never fully know who God is or how great and wonderful he really is. We need God himself to tell us who he is and to enlighten our minds on how to live in relationship to him and others. God's communication with us is known as Divine Revelation. And we turn to this topic next.

For Review

1. What did St. Augustine mean when he wrote in *The Confessions*, the story of his conversion to God, "our heart is restless until it rests in you"?
2. Name some reasons why atheists do not believe in God.
3. What is the difference between atheists and agnostics?

Believing or Not Believing

Interview two teens and two adults about their belief in God. Ask them to explain their major reason for believing—or not believing—in God's existence. Share the results of your research with your classmates. Then tally the most common reasons on either side of the question.

4. Why is the human person the peak of creation?

For Reflection

Write about a time when you saw God in creation—in the beautiful world around you. What were your thoughts and feelings about this scene or event? How did you react?

Divine Revelation (*CCC*, 50-73)

Human reason can discover that there is a Creator, a God who watches over our world and keeps it in existence. It can also study the handiwork of this personal God and say some things about him. For example, anyone observing the vastness of the universe must come to the conclusion that the one who made it must be an all-powerful, infinite being, one who is not limited. Or when we notice that there are intelligent beings in the universe, like human beings, then we must conclude that the One who made these creatures must possess intelligence to an infinite degree. He who created a universe with intricate laws that govern it must be all-knowing, the source of human intelligence, and way beyond human comprehension.

Certainly, when we think of the qualities that God must possess we will conclude that God is perfection itself. He is not in any way limited like we are. He goes beyond his creatures. But here human thinking reaches its limit. It is clouded because God is essentially a mystery. God's ways are not our ways. God's thoughts are above our thoughts (see Isaiah 55:8). Our limited human minds can only perceive so much about God. This is one of the reasons there have been so many different religions throughout human history. People know there is a divine being, but they are confused as to what or who he actually is. So they create limited and imperfect images of God. However, these images of God are not the same as the incomprehensible, invisible, infinite God.

Is the lot of humans, then, to know that there is a God but not to really know *who* he is? Is God to remain hidden behind a veil, unknown by humans and unapproachable?

Christians, of course, answer a resounding "no" to these questions. We believe that out of his infinite love and goodness, God freely chose to reveal himself and give himself to human beings. The literal translation of *revelation* is "unveiling." The God of mystery, the One who is beyond human understanding, freely stepped into human history. God revealed the mystery or plan of his loving goodness by speaking to us through the Law and the prophets in the Old Testament, and by inviting us into a deeper relationship by sending his only Divine Son, Jesus Christ. As the Second Vatican Council put it:

> It pleased God, in his goodness and wisdom, to reveal himself and to make known the mystery of his will. His will was that men should have access to the Father, through Christ, the Word made flesh, in the Holy Spirit, and thus become sharers in the divine nature. (*Dogmatic Constitution on Divine Revelation*, No. 2, quoted in *CCC*, 51)

Divine Revelation refers to the gift of God's self-communication by which he makes known the mystery of his divine plan. God's self-communication took place gradually. It involved both deeds and words, which are bound up with each other. The various stages of God's *supernatural* Revelation culminate in the person and the mission of Jesus Christ. Divine Revelation is "supernatural" because humans, who are God's creatures, do not have a natural right to intimate friendship with him. God's self-disclosure is something we do not naturally deserve. God's invitation to a deeper life of love in union with Jesus Christ is a pure gift on God's part. It is the great news of our faith and gives our personal life and human history meaning.

Salvation History

Divine Revelation, the story of God's self-communication, tells about his saving love, his saving acts in human history. The account of God's saving activity for humanity is known as **Salvation History**. The story of God's generous love for his creatures began with the creation of our first parents and the beautiful world in which we live (see Genesis 1–2). Unfortunately, Adam and Eve disobeyed God and committed the Original Sin. Through their own free decision, they turned away from God's love and fell out of intimate friendship with him. The story could have ended here, but God refused to abandon his sinful creatures. Rather, from the very beginning, God promised to redeem us and gave the hope of Salvation and eternal life to the human race.

We learn through the story of Salvation History of the gradual Revelation of God's care for those special creatures—human beings—whom he made in his image and likeness. Through a series of covenants, God bound himself to humans forever. A **covenant** is a solemn agreement, an open-ended contract of love, in which God commits himself totally to human beings. In return, humans are to keep the terms of the covenant, for example, by worshiping only the one true God and observing the Law, including the Ten Commandments. In the Old Testament, we learn of God's promise to be faithful to us forever while humans were to remain faithful to him. Through the covenants God made with the Chosen People, we learn of his promise of Salvation, Redemption, and eternal life.

In Sacred Scripture, the inspired word of God and the written record of Revelation, we read about the various covenants God established with humans. Among the most important covenants are these:

- *The Covenant with Noah* (Gn 8–9). After the Flood, God made a covenant with Noah, his descendants (that is, all humans), and with "every living creature" (Gn 9:10) that was with Noah on the ark. God promised that a flood would never again destroy life on earth. The sign of this covenant for all future generations was to be the rainbow.
- *The Covenant with Abraham* (Gn 12–17). A profound event in Salvation History was God's covenant with Abraham, the Father of Faith for the Jewish people and our spiritual father because of our shared ancestry with the Jews. Although Abraham was an old man with an elderly wife, God promised him that he would become the father of a great nation with many descendants. These descendants of Abraham were also to receive a land of their own. The sign of the covenant was male circumcision. This was a sign that would set apart Abraham's descendants for God.
- *The Sinai Covenant* (Ex 19, 20). In the book of Exodus, we learn how God formed Israel as his special people when he freed them from slavery in Egypt at the time of the Exodus. He made

Divine Revelation
The gift of God's self-revelation by which he makes known the mystery of his divine plan.

Salvation History
The account of God's saving activity and intervention on behalf of humanity.

covenant
A solemn agreement or contract of love between God and his people.

YHWH
A name for God that God himself revealed to Moses and the Chosen People on Mount Sinai. The word means "I Am Who Am" and led to Israel's understanding that God is the one, living, and true God.

the children of Israel a kingdom of priests and a holy people. On Mount Sinai, God revealed his name—**YHWH** ("I AM WHO AM")—to Moses and, through him, gave the Chosen People the Law, including the Ten Commandments. The Law taught Israel to acknowledge YHWH as the one, living, and true God. However, the Law did not offer a means of Redemption. Through the prophets who came after Moses, God gave Israel hope for Salvation. They proclaimed a New Covenant to be written on human hearts.

- *The Covenant with David* (2 Sm 7). God established David as the rightful king of Judah. From the Davidic line would come the future Messiah, Jesus Christ, the Son of God.
- *Jesus Christ, the New Covenant* (Heb 1:1–2). The Book of Hebrews states it eloquently: "In times past, God spoke in partial and various ways to our ancestors through the prophets; in these last days, he spoke to us through a son, whom he made heir of all things and through whom he created the universe" (Heb 1:1–2). The climax of Salvation History was the coming of Jesus Christ, God's Son, the fullness of God's Revelation. Jesus did not come to abolish the Sinai Covenant; in fact, he brought it to fulfillment by revealing the depth of its meaning and redeeming offenses against it. Jesus is God's final and total Word. Jesus is the Word made flesh, God's Son. He lived among us. He taught us in word and deed about God. He completed the Father's work of Salvation. Through the life, Death, and Resurrection of Jesus Christ, God completed his revelation. Since Christ is God's final, definitive word, there will be no further revelation after him. To see Jesus is to see the Father.

God Reveals Himself as Love and Truth (CCC, 214-221, 231)

God revealed himself to Israel as "abounding in steadfast love and faithfulness" (*CCC*, 214). These qualities are much in evidence in the history of the Jewish nation. For example:

- God chose the Hebrews and made them a people (Gn 12:1–2).
- God freed the Israelites from Egypt (Ex 3:8).
- God established a covenant with the Israelites, making them a holy nation. God gave them the Law through Moses to help them recognize and serve the one living and true God, the one caring Father and just Judge (Ex 19:5–6).
- God gave his Chosen People a land (Jos 1:11).
- God established the kingdom of David (2 Sm 7:8–16.)
- God sent prophets to guide the Jews (2 Kgs 17:13).
- God sustained the Chosen People in Babylonia and restored them to Israel (Is 40:1–2).

For Review

1. What is Divine Revelation?
2. What is Salvation History?
3. Define the word *covenant*. What did covenant mean to the Chosen People?
4. What is Sacred Scripture?
5. Describe three of the covenants God establishes with his Chosen People that are described in the text.
6. What name for himself did God give to Moses and the Chosen People? What does it mean?
7. What are some of the ways that God revealed himself in love and truth to Israel?

For Reflection

- In your journal, create a new name for God for a new generation of believers. What is the name? What does this name mean?
- Which covenant described in the text is most inspiring for you? What appeals to you about this intervention by God into human history?

Scripture, Tradition, and the Deposit of Faith

God's Revelation reached its climax in the coming of Jesus Christ, his Son and our Savior. But Jesus lived, died, and rose from the dead almost two thousand years ago. This raises a couple of questions: How do we who are living today learn about God's Revelation? How was and is the story of Salvation History transmitted to future generations?

Preaching the Good News

At the end of the Gospel of Matthew, Jesus instructed the Apostles: "All power in heaven and on earth has been given to me. Go, therefore, and make disciples of all nations, baptizing them in the name of the Father, and of the Son, and of the holy Spirit, teaching them to observe all that I have commanded you" (Mt 28:18–20). This passage tells how Jesus wanted the Apostles to proclaim the Good News about the Kingdom of God everywhere so that all people would hear about his work of Salvation, justice, forgiveness, and love.

The Apostles obeyed Jesus' command. Strengthened by the Holy Spirit, they bravely went forth to proclaim the Gospel to the world. An example of the early apostolic preaching about Jesus appears in the Acts of the Apostles. We learn that the Holy Spirit, promised by Jesus, descended on the Apostles on Pentecost Sunday, a day that has been described as "the birthday of the Church." The Spirit empowered the Apostles to go forth and preach the Gospel of Jesus Christ. On that momentous day, Acts tells us how Peter preached to the Jews who were gathered in Jerusalem for the Pentecost feast.

Peter reviewed the events of Salvation History and explained how the prophecies about the Messiah were fulfilled in the life, Death, and Resurrection of Jesus Christ. He proclaimed that Jesus is both the Lord and the Messiah. Because this is true,

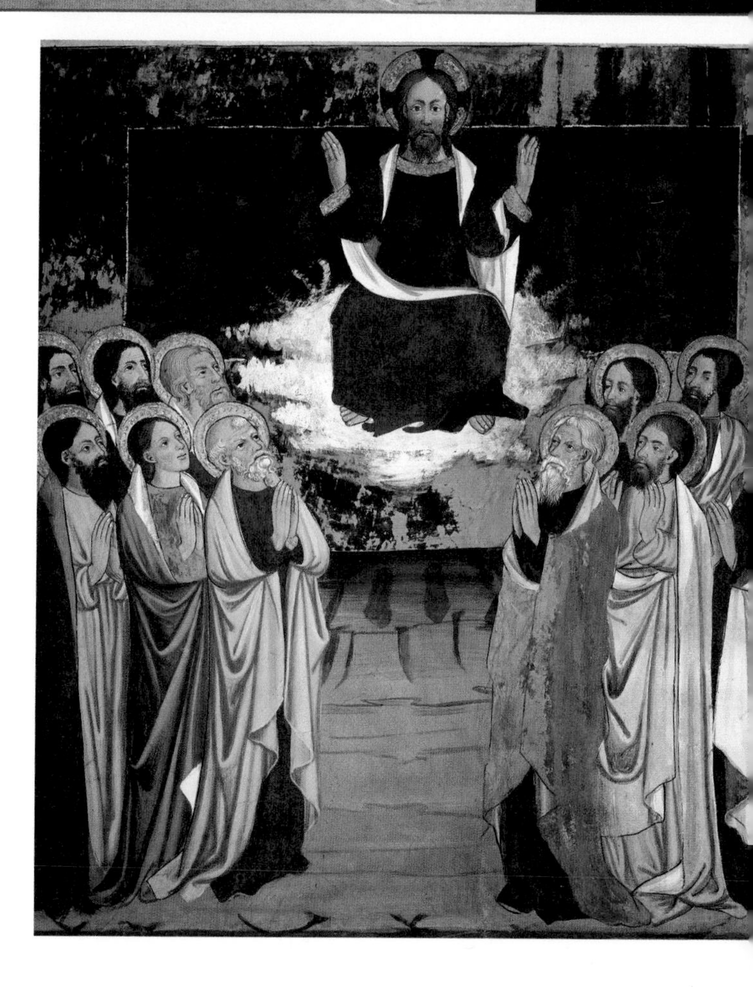

Peter challenged the people to believe in Jesus, to repent of their sins, and to accept Baptism in order to receive the gift of the Holy Spirit. Once baptized, the new believers were invited to live as a Christlike community, a family that celebrates the Eucharist and shares generously with the poor. (See Acts 2:14–47.)

The Apostles, like Peter, at first preached the Good News by spoken word. Later, they proclaimed the Good News in written form. Both their words and their writings were supported by the way they imitated Jesus. In fact, so courageous and loving was the witness of the Apostles that all, with the exception of John, the son of Zebedee, were martyred for teaching others about Jesus Christ. God had other plans for John, who was later exiled to the Greek island of Patmos in the Aegean Sea. John died of natural causes as a very old man.

Magisterium
The official teaching authority of the Church comprised of the Pope and bishops who are successors of Christ and his Apostles.

Deposit of Faith
The body of saving truths and the core beliefs of Catholicism that are faithfully preserved by the Magisterium.

Sacred Scripture
The inspired Word of God; the written record of God's Revelation.

canon of the Bible
The official list of inspired books in the Bible. Catholics list forty-six Old Testament books and twenty-seven New Testament books in their canon.

Sacred Tradition
The living transmission of the Catholic faith through the teaching, life, and worship of the Church.

dogma
A central truth of Revelation that Catholics are obliged to believe.

All the Apostles appointed successors, called bishops, to guarantee that the Good News of Salvation would be proclaimed authentically to future generations. This is a very important point. The bishop of the Church of Rome, the Pope, is the successor to St. Peter, the first Pope whom Christ chose to lead and govern his Church. Today, the Pope is "the head of the college of bishops, the Vicar of Christ and Pastor of the universal Church on earth" (*CCC*, 936). The bishops, in communion with the Pope, are the direct successors of the Apostles. They are known as the **Magisterium** (from the Latin word for "teacher"), the official teaching authority of the Church. They ensure that the "Deposit of Faith" is faithfully handed on through the generations.

> The task of giving an authentic interpretation of the Word of God, whether in its written form or in the form of Tradition, has been entrusted to the living, teaching office of the Church alone. (*CCC*, 85, citing the *Dogmatic Constitution on Divine Revelation*, No. 10)

Sources of God's Revelation

God's Revelation is found in the **Deposit of Faith**, that is, the body of saving truths that Jesus Christ gave to the Apostles and that is handed on and faithfully preserved by the Magisterium. The Deposit of Faith is one divine wellspring of Christ's truth. It contains two modes of transmission: Sacred Scripture and Sacred Tradition.

Sacred Scripture (the Bible) is the written record of Revelation. It is the inspired word of God. "*Sacred Scripture* is the speech of God as it is put down in writing under the breath of the Holy Spirit" (*CCC*, 81, quoting the *Dogmatic Constitution on Divine Revelation*, No. 9). The Bible is a library of divinely inspired writings in which God used human authors and their unique talents to put into writing what he wanted written, and nothing more. The word *Bible* means "books." "The books of the Scripture firmly, faithfully, and without error teach that truth which God, for the sake of our salvation, wished to see confided to the Sacred Scriptures" (*CCC*, 107, quoting *Dogmatic Constitution on Divine Revelation,* No. 11). This last point means Sacred Scripture is inerrant; that is, it contains no error.

As you learned in a previous course, the Bible is made up of forty-six Old Testament books and twenty-seven New Testament books. It is important to note that the Church existed before any of the books of the

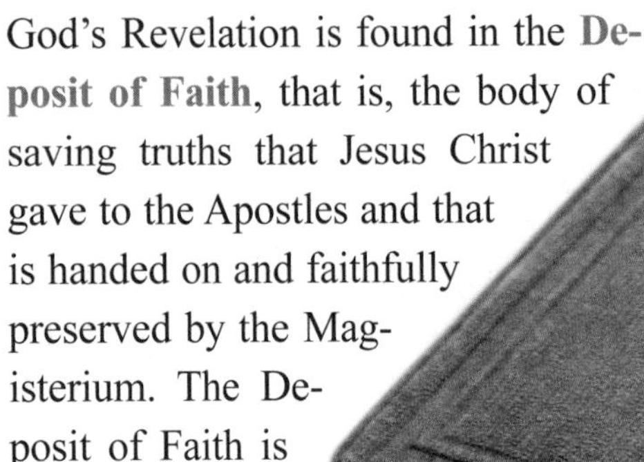

New Testament were written down. For example, the oral preaching of the Apostles came before the writing of the New Testament. This means that the Church, under the inspiration of the Holy Spirit, created the books of the New Testament, not the other way around.

It was the responsibility of the Magisterium to determine which books of the Bible belonged on the official list (**canon**) of inspired writings. The process of determining the canon of Sacred Scripture took some time. For example, the official canon of the New Testament was not decided until the Council of Rome in AD 382, which met under the authority of Pope Damasus I. The decision made at that time was reaffirmed later at the local Councils of Hippo (393) and Carthage (397). In 1546, the Council of Trent solemnly declared that all seventy-three books found in the Catholic Bible were inspired in their entirety.

Sacred Tradition is the living transmission or "handing on" of the Church's Gospel message. (*Tradition* means both "handing on" and "that which is handed on.") We find Tradition in the Church's teaching, life, and worship.

> Now what was handed on by the Apostles includes everything which contributes toward the holiness of life and increase in faith of the peoples of God; and so the Church, in her teaching, life and worship, perpetuates and hands on to all generations all that she herself is, all that she believes. (*Dei Verbum,* 8)

Recall, again, that the Apostles entrusted to their successors—the Pope and bishops—the task to "faithfully preserve, expound, and spread . . . by their preaching" (*CCC*, 81, quoting *Dogmatic Constitution on Divine Revelation*, No. 9) the Deposit of Faith entrusted to the Church. With the guidance of the Holy Spirit, the Magisterium teaches with Christ's own authority. This is especially true when the Magisterium defines a **dogma**, that is, a central truth of Revelation that Catholics are obliged to believe. The infallibility of the Magisterium "also extends to all those elements of doctrine, including morals, without which the saving truths of the faith cannot be preserved, explained, or observed" (*CCC*, 2035). Keep in mind that the Holy Father and the bishops are not above the Word of God. They are its servants. Their Christ-given task is to help us understand God's word and put it into practice by living holy lives.

The Holy Spirit also helps believers to understand, appreciate, and accept the faith that is passed on to us. The Holy Spirit dwells in the Church and attracts the faithful to believe the treasure of faith that has been passed on to us. He helps us recognize, accept, and live the word of God that comes down to us.

Tradition, Scripture, and the Magisterium are all intimately related. Tradition and Scripture flow from the one font of Divine Revelation, which makes up the Deposit of Faith. Guided by the Holy Spirit, the Magisterium teaches and properly interprets what Christ wants us to know for our Salvation. Finally, the Holy Spirit helps us, the faithful, to open our hearts and minds to accept and live the truth that we are privileged to hear.

Catholics and Sacred Scripture

We believe that God is the author of Sacred Scripture by inspiring the human authors to communicate the truths he wanted to reveal. God used the unique talents, skills, and styles of the human authors to communicate his message. Thus, there are many literary forms in the books of the Bible that convey God's truth.

The two major divisions of the Bible are the Old Testament and the New Testament. We consider the Old and New Testaments as a unity because they reveal God's loving plan of Salvation. Christians read the Old Testament in light of Christ but also see in it the gradual unfolding of God's revelation of himself in human history.

The books of the Old Testament consist of the Pentateuch (the first five books), which contain the Law and treat God's covenant of love with the Israelites. Next come the sixteen historical books that recount the story of God's saving activity in the history of the Jews, the Chosen People. These books are followed by the seven wisdom books made up of prayers, poems, and commonsense advice on how to live a good and faithful life. The final books of the Old Testament are the eighteen prophetic books, which repeatedly call the Chosen People to repentance and fidelity to God's covenant. We find in the prophetic books many prophecies about the coming Messiah.

The New Testament consists of twenty-seven books. The most important books are the four Gospels, accounts of the life and teachings of Jesus Christ. *Gospel* means "Good News." This term not only applies to Jesus himself, who is the Good News of Salvation, but also to the early preaching about him and the four written versions about the life of Christ: the Gospels of Matthew, Mark, Luke, and John. Written for different audiences, each of the four Gospels provides a true picture of Jesus Christ while emphasizing different theological themes.

The Acts of the Apostles is a history of the early decades of the Church. The twenty-one epistles, or letters, follow. Fourteen of them have been traditionally attributed to St. Paul. He was the Apostle to the Gentiles who became a zealous Christian after the Lord appeared to him. In general, apostolic pastors wrote the epistles to early Christian communities or individuals to give further instruction in the Christian faith and guidance on how to live as followers of Christ.

The last book of the Bible is the Book of Revelation or the Apocalypse of John. A highly symbolic work, it encourages its readers to remain faithful to Christ during a time of persecution. It assures us of the Lord's final triumph at the end of time. It is also the last book of the Bible and ends with the following words: "Amen! Come, Lord Jesus! The grace of the Lord Jesus be with all" (Rv 22:20–21).

The Writing of the Gospels

The four Gospels are the heart of the New Testament and of Sacred Scripture itself. They are the principal source of information about the life and teaching of Jesus Christ. They came about in three stages:

1. *The life and teaching of Jesus.* Jesus lived between 4–6 BC and AD 30/33. The Church teaches that the Gospels are historical documents that faithfully hand on what Jesus did and taught for our eternal Salvation.

SURVEYING THE BIBLE

The Bible is a rich library of stories about people of faith and great acts of faith. Read the following Scripture passages and answer the corresponding questions.

Covenant with Abraham (Gn 17)

1. How old was Abram when God made the covenant with him?
2. What did God promise Abraham?
3. What was the sign of the covenant?

Exodus from Egypt (Ex 12:43–14:31)

1. How long did the Israelites spend in Egypt?
2. List two Passover regulations.
3. What did Moses take out of Egypt? Why?
4. How did the Lord lead the Israelites?
5. How did the Israelites escape?

Giving of the Ten Commandments (Ex 19:1–20:26)

1. How did the Lord appear to Moses?
2. What is the most important command the Lord gave to the people?

2. *Oral tradition*. The Apostles preached what they witnessed about what Jesus said and did. Because they experienced the events of Jesus' life, including his Death, Resurrection, and Ascension, and were enlightened by the Holy Spirit, the Apostles were able to bring a deeper understanding of the meaning of Jesus Christ to the audience to whom they preached.
3. *The written Gospels*. Near AD 65 (for Mark's Gospel), the four evangelists committed to writing four reliable accounts of Jesus' life. They selected elements from Tradition, either what they preached orally or put in written form, and composed orderly accounts that would appeal to the various churches for which they were writing. But they did so under the inspiration of the Holy Spirit, always relating the honest truth about Jesus Christ.

For Review

1. When did the Apostles of Jesus first begin to share the Good News as Jesus had instructed them to?
2. What is the Magisterium? How is the Magisterium of the Church related to Jesus and the Apostles?
3. What is the Deposit of Faith? What are its two main modes of transmission?
4. What is Sacred Scripture and how is it organized?
5. Briefly describe the history and the content of the Catholic canon.
6. What is Sacred Tradition? How is Sacred Tradition a part of Revelation?
7. Describe the three stages in the development of the four Gospels.

For Reflection

- In your journal, imagine that you live in Galilee in the days of Jesus. Picture yourself as a younger brother or sister of one of the Apostles. Listen as Jesus directs them to go out, teach, and baptize. What are your reactions as you see how happy your brother is to follow Jesus? You can see, however, that your brother will be leaving home to go out into a frightening and violent world.
- Briefly look through the Old and New Testaments. Identify one book in each testament that you would like to read and know more about. Describe these two books and what attracts you to read them.

Faith: Our Response to Revelation (*CCC*, 26, 91-100, 142-197)

In common use, the word *faith* has to do with trust and belief. For example, when your friend says she will go to the game with you on Friday night, you believe she is telling you the truth. You trust that she will follow through on her word. You have faith in your friend and in your friendship. Your past experience has proven to you that she is dependable.

In a similar way, when you turn on your computer, you believe that the operating system will fire up and your opening program will appear on the screen. You trust that electricity (which you cannot see) will provide power to your computer and that all systems will perform as expected. You have faith in your computer.

In our daily life, we rely on faith in many different circumstances. You believe the alarm clock will go off on time, that your toilet will flush, that your toaster will work, that your ride to school will appear on time, that your friends will greet you when you arrive in homeroom, and so forth. We could not live our daily lives without belief and without trust.

Religious Definition of Faith

In a similar way, we cannot live our life with God without the virtue of faith. The theological definition of faith is deeper than our ordinary experience with the word. Simply put, faith, in a religious sense, is our positive response to God's Revelation. Out of his great love, God comes to us and addresses us as his friends in order to share his life with us. God's Revelation to us is an invitation—an invitation to accept his love and eternal life given to us through his Son, Jesus Christ, in the Holy Spirit. This invitation is a gift from God; our response is faith.

> By faith, man completely submits his intellect and his will to God. With his whole being man gives his assent to God the revealer. Sacred Scripture calls this human response to God, the author of revelation, "the obedience of faith." (*CCC*, 143)

Faith Is a Theological Virtue

Faith is both a gift and a **virtue**. The *Catechism of the Catholic Church* defines virtue as:

> an habitual and firm disposition to do the good. . . . Human virtues are firm attitudes, stable dispositions, habitual perfections of intellect and will that govern our actions, order our passions, and guide our conduct according to reason and faith. They make possible ease, self-mastery, and joy in leading a morally good life. (*CCC*, 1803–1804)

Christian theology recognizes two categories of virtues: the **cardinal virtues** and the **theological virtues**. The cardinal virtues include prudence, justice, fortitude, and temperance. They get their name from the Latin word *cardo,* which means "hinge." Many of the other moral virtues derive from these four.

Faith, however, is one of the theological virtues: faith, hope, and charity (*CCC*, 1812–1828). The theological virtues are gifts from God that are "infused" into our souls. Because they are virtues, they give us certain capabilities or powers. Specifically, because they are "theological" (from the Greek word for God) virtues, they draw us to God and enable us to live in relationship to the Blessed Trinity. Their origin, motive, and object are the one, Triune God. These virtues are called "infused" (conferred on us rather than earned) because the Lord gives them to us as gifts. We cannot earn these gifts, the theological virtues.

- ***Faith***. Conferred on us in Baptism, this theological virtue enables us to believe in God and all that God has said and revealed to us. It also helps us to accept what the Church proposes for

Who Is God for Me?

Take some time to consider your image of God more deeply. In your journal, write two to four paragraphs that describe who God is *for you*. You might also describe your earliest ideas or images of God. Do your own images or concepts of God emphasize God's immanence or closeness to you and his other creatures?

our belief, because God is truth itself. Christians must cultivate their faith, but also proclaim, bear witness to, and spread it to others.

- *Hope.* Hope enables us to desire Heaven and eternal life. It helps us trust in Christ's promises and rely on the help of the Holy Spirit and his graces, not our own strengths and abilities. Hope keeps us from getting discouraged as we live the Christian life. It keeps us going when times get tough and lonely. It makes it possible for us to strive for true happiness and live the life of Jesus' Beatitudes.
- *Charity (love).* This greatest virtue of all empowers us "to love God above all things for his own sake, and our neighbor as ourselves for the love of God" (*CCC*, 1822). Charity enables us to observe the commandments and love everyone, even our enemies, because it transforms us into God's own children. This key virtue helps us practice all the other virtues. It uplifts our human ability to love, raising it to the perfection of divine love.

More about Faith

In a certain sense, faith is our lifeline to God. It is a God-given gift that enables us to respond to God's Word and unites us personally with the Father, Son, and Holy Spirit. It is an essential gift, one necessary for Salvation. "Believing in Jesus Christ and the One who sent him for our salvation is necessary for obtaining that salvation" (*CCC*, 161).

Faith is first shared with us in the Christian home, called the "domestic Church," where parents and children worship God, receive the Sacraments, and witness to Christ and the Church by living lives of holiness, self-denial, and love. The result of the reception of this gift of faith is **religion**. Our Catholic religion flows from our Christian faith, a faith that enables us to give ourselves totally to God in Jesus Christ, to accept him and his message as it comes to us through his Church.

Christian faith unites us with a specific community of faith, the Catholic Church, which professes belief in Jesus Christ as Lord. Jesus founded the Catholic Church, which is the Body of Christ in the world. Because of God's love for us, those who call themselves Catholics are baptized into Christ's Body, the Church. We have become members of a family of faith, a community of believers in the Lordship of Jesus Christ who lives in our midst. An important obligation the gift of faith requires of us is to extend to the whole world God's invitation to believe in, accept, and dedicate our lives to Jesus Christ.

Faith is both personal and communal. You can personally say, "I believe in God" and gratefully enter into a personal relationship with the Father, Son, and Holy Spirit. But as a member of the Church, you also routinely say, "We believe." We are members of Christ's Body, the Church. Because we are part of the Church, the faith of our fellow Catholics helps to strengthen our own faith.

virtue
Moral excellence and righteousness; an inclination and habitual preference for the good.

faith
One of the theological virtues. Faith is an acknowledgment of an allegiance to God.

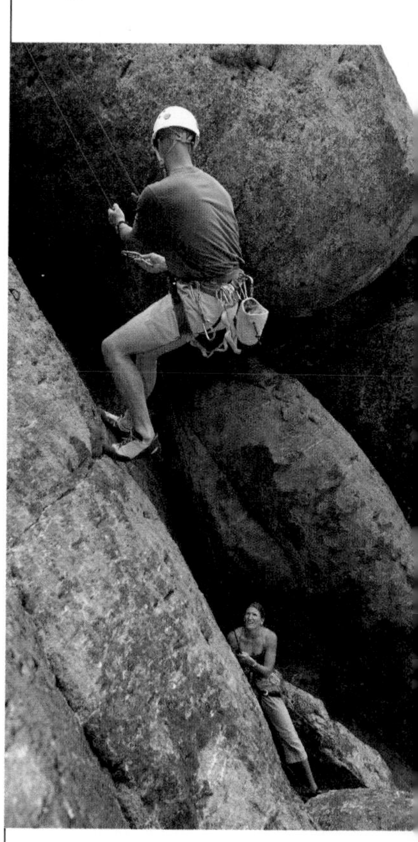

religion
A set of beliefs, values, and practices that binds believers in a relationship with God and with other believers.

This is especially true when we gather to celebrate the Eucharist. At Mass we profess our common faith and receive the Lord Jesus in Holy Communion in order to take him and his message of Salvation into the world of daily living.

Once again, faith is our response to God's Revelation, God's gift of self-communication. Faith, a gift of the Holy Spirit, enables us to commit ourselves to our loving God totally, both our intellects and our wills. In sum, essential qualities of faith include the following:

- *Faith makes it possible for us to accept Jesus as Lord.* Because of faith, we can believe God's revealed truths because God himself has revealed them to us. It helps us recognize and accept Jesus Christ as the Son of God who died to save us from our sins. It leads us to discipleship, to become his followers. It gives us the ability to imitate Christ's life of loving service both for members of the Catholic faith community and for all people. Most fundamentally it leads us to new life in the Holy Spirit and allows us to become children of God. This adoption allows us to follow the example of Christ and be more like him. In union with Jesus, we can reach the perfection of love. Our moral life grows as eternal life and reaches its fulfillment in the glory of Heaven.
- *Faith allows us to partake of the life of the Holy Spirit who testifies to us who Jesus is.* Christian faith proclaims belief in one God who is a Trinity of Persons: Father, Son, and Holy Spirit. Christian faith brings us into relationship with the Blessed Trinity.
- *Faith is a gift, but our response must be free.* No one can be forced to embrace faith against his or her will. Thus, faith is also a free human act in which our hearts and minds cooperate with God's gift of grace.
- *Faith is reasonable.* Faith is not blind. In revealing himself to us, God gave external proofs that support the internal helps of the Holy Spirit. Signs like the following help support the faith in God's Revelation that the Church invites us to accept: the miracles of Jesus Christ and the saints, prophecies, the growth and holiness of the Church, and the great good the Church has accomplished since her founding by Jesus Christ almost two thousand years ago.
- *Faith is certain* because it is founded on the Word of God who cannot lie.
- *Faith seeks understanding*. Faith always wants to grow in knowledge of the loving God and to understand better what he has revealed. So growth in faith is a lifelong task. As we grow in knowledge of God, our faith will become even stronger.
- *Faith does not conflict with science.* The truth of Revelation does not contradict the truth of science. The same God who made things that human reason can discover is the same God who reveals himself and gives us the gift of faith. God does not deny himself. The truths that can be discovered in the natural world cannot contradict the truths that God reveals. "Consequently, methodical research in all branches of knowledge, provided it is carried out in a truly scientific manner and does not override moral laws, can never conflict with faith" (*CCC*, 159).
- *It is possible to lose the gift of faith.* Through sinfulness and neglecting the dictates of conscience it is possible to weaken and even lose the gift of faith. To live, grow, and persevere in faith until the end of our lives requires listening to the Word of God, asking for God's help to strengthen our faith, staying close to the faith of the Church, and living lives of charity.

- *Catholics also believe that faith is an act of the Church.* As a gift from God, it comes before the faith of the individual. But it gives life to and supports and nourishes the individual Christian. If we cooperate with faith, we are on the path to eternal life. If we ignore it, we are subject to God's disapproval.

  > Whoever believes in the Son has eternal life, but whoever disobeys the Son will not see life, but the wrath of God remains upon him. (Jn 3:36)

- *Abraham and Mary are two important models of faith.* Abraham, the Father of Faith, obeyed God by leaving his homeland to become a pilgrim in a Promised Land. Because of his faith, God created a people through Abraham and prepared the way for the Messiah. Mary, the Mother of Jesus Christ, lived her entire life as a resounding "yes" to God's work. Her fidelity helped fulfill God's plan of Salvation through her Son, Jesus Christ. (See Chapter 2 for more information about the Blessed Mother as a model of faith.)

For Review

1. What is faith? How is faith a response to God's invitation?
2. How does the *Catechism of the Catholic Church* define virtue?
3. What are the theological virtues? How do we acquire these virtues?
4. What does it mean to say that faith is both personal and communal?
5. Define *religion*. In your own words, describe how religion is different from faith.
6. Why are both Abraham and Mary ideal models of faith for us?

For Reflection

- Tell about a person in whom you have great faith. Was your faith in this person always as strong as it is now? Was your faith in this person ever tested or threatened?
- Faith should be both personal and communal. Name three ways that communal faith—the faith of your family and Church—strengthens your own personal faith.

The Catholic Church and Faith (*CCC*, 763-766, 787-795)

Jesus Christ came into the world to accomplish the Father's plan of Salvation. He, the Word of God, is God's total self-communication. That means that Jesus shows us who God is. He ushered in the Kingdom of God. His works and his very presence signaled the coming of God's Kingdom. His Death, Resurrection, and Ascension accomplished for all time the Salvation of the world. And, when the Kingdom of God comes in its fullness, the righteous will live forever with Christ, glorified in body and soul.

During his time on earth, Jesus established a community to carry on his work in his name after his Ascension into heaven. He founded this community, "the seed and beginning of the Kingdom . . . a little flock" (*CCC*, 764), to continue his mission of bringing all people to eternal Salvation. Christ founded

Body of Christ
A rich image for the Church from St. Paul who wrote that the Church is like a body for which Christ is the head. Paul taught that the members of the Church are like the members or parts of the body, drawing direction from the head and life from the rest of the body.

the Church on the Apostle Peter. We learn in the sixteenth chapter of Matthew's Gospel how Simon Peter answered Jesus' question about Jesus' true identity. Simon Peter's response to Jesus' question set the stage for the Lord's foundation of the Catholic Church. Peter said, "You are the Messiah, the Son of the Living God" (Mt 16:16). In reply, Jesus said to Peter,

> Blessed are you, Simon son of Jonah. For flesh and blood has not revealed this to you, but my heavenly Father. And so I say to you, you are Peter, and upon this rock I will build my church, and the gates of the netherworld shall not prevail against it. I will give you the keys to the kingdom of heaven. Whatever you bind on earth shall be bound in heaven; and whatever you loose on earth shall be loosed in heaven. (Mt 16:17–19)

Simon Peter was able to state clearly the identity of Jesus because God revealed it to him. Jesus gave Simon a new name—Peter—meaning "Rock." On the Rock of Peter, Jesus established his Church. The *Catechism of the Catholic Church* tells us:

> The Lord Jesus endowed his community with a structure that will remain until the Kingdom is fully achieved. Before all else there is the choice of the Twelve with Peter as their head. Representing the twelve tribes of Israel, they are the foundation stones of the new Jerusalem. The Twelve and the other disciples share in Christ's mission and his power, but also in his lot. By all his actions, Christ prepares and builds his Church. (*CCC*, 765)

Christ gave to Peter and the Apostles—and their successors—the responsibility to preach the Gospel down through the ages. As noted before, a prime task of the Magisterium

is to hand on the Deposit of Faith, the truths that have been revealed, and to see to it that Divine Revelation is accurately, authentically, and completely presented to the people of the world. This authority comes from Jesus himself. This is why the teaching of the Magisterium comes from Christ himself. Our official teachers are the voice of Christ. They ensure that the truths of Divine Revelation are presented accurately for our benefit and for our Salvation.

The Body of Christ (CCC, 787-795)

St. Paul gives us a rich image of the Church when he teaches that the Church is the **Body of Christ** in the world. Jesus is the Head of the Body; we are its members. Faith in Jesus Christ and the Sacrament of Baptism incorporate us into the Body of Christ, the Church, by power of the Holy Spirit. St. Paul writes:

> As a body is one though it has many parts, and all the parts of the body, though many, are one body, so also Christ. For in one Spirit we were all baptized into one body, whether Jews or Greeks, slaves or free persons, and we were all given to drink of one Spirit. (1 Cor 12:12–13)

This quote emphasizes the dignity of each member of Christ's Body. We are members of the Church, each united with Christ and *each other*. Each member of Christ's Body is important and has a role to play in bringing Christ into the world. Each of us must use the gifts God gave us to build up the Church and to serve other people. In 1 Corinthians 13, Paul writes that the Holy Spirit has given each member of Christ's Body the gift of charity or love, the greatest gift of all. In this passage, Paul elaborates the various qualities of love, for example, patience, kindness, and humility. By putting these into action, Christians bring Christ into the world and let his Good News shine forth for all people.

Marks of the Church

Also in 1 Corinthians 13, St. Paul emphasizes the unity intended for Christ's Body, the Church. Unity is one of the traditional Four Marks of the Church. These traits are characteristics that point to the essential features of the Church and her mission. These Marks—one, holy, catholic, and apostolic—build up the faith of Catholics. They can also help attract nonbelievers to the Church. A brief explanation of each mark follows.

- *One* (*CCC*, 812–818; 822). The unity of the Church is rooted in the mystery of the unity of the Blessed Trinity, Father, Son, and Holy Spirit. Unity derives from the Head of the Church, Jesus, and the soul of the Church, the Holy Spirit. Charity—love—"binds everything together in perfect harmony" (Col 3:14 quoted in *CCC*, 815). The unity of the Church becomes visible in her acknowledgment of one Lord, her profession of one faith, her belief in one Baptism, and by the granting of her life by the one Holy Spirit.
- *Holy* (*CCC*, 823–829). Jesus Christ sacrificed his life to make the Church holy. He also sent the Holy Spirit to help the Church grow in holiness. All members are called to holiness, and Christ has given the Church "the fullness of the means of salvation," especially the Seven Sacraments, to help each member grow in holiness. Charity is the soul of the holiness to which everyone is called (*CCC*, 826).
- *Catholic* (*CCC*, 830–835). The *Catholic* Church is universal (*catholic* means "universal") in two ways: First, Christ is present in the Church, which receives from him the fullness of the means of Salvation: correct and complete confession of faith (doctrine), full sacramental life, and an ordained ministry that succeeds from the Apostles. Second, the Church is Catholic because Christ sends the Church out on missions to all people in all places until the end of time. No one is excluded from hearing the message of the Good News of Salvation.

- *Apostolic* (*CCC*, 857–865). Christ founded the Church on the Apostles. Guided by the Holy Spirit, it is the teaching of the Apostles that the Church faithfully hands on through the centuries. Through accomplishing this missionary mandate of Christ, the Church becomes the "universal sacrament of salvation" (*CCC*, 849). Finally, the Church is indestructible. She continues to be taught, made holy (sanctified), and upheld infallibly in the truth by the college of bishops, whom Christ appointed to succeed the Apostles. The Pope and the bishops can trace themselves in an unbroken line of succession to the Apostles.

When we talk about faith in Divine Revelation, then, we must also think of the Church. Christ lives in his Church so completely that "Christ and his Church thus together make up the "whole Christ" (*Christus totus*). The Church is one with Christ (*CCC*, 795). Faith in Jesus Christ naturally should lead the believer to Christ's Church, the Catholic Church, which he founded and in which he lives. As we profess in the Nicene Creed at Mass each Sunday: "We believe in one, holy, catholic, and apostolic Church." Why? Because in the Church we find Christ, his Good News of Salvation, and all the means Christ left us to grow in holiness.

"God is love, and he who abides in love abides in God, and God abides in him" (1 Jn 4:16). These words express most beautifully who God is and what he has done for us in Jesus Christ: "For God so loved the world that he gave his only Son, so that everyone who believes in him might not perish but

What Love Can Do

Read 1 Corinthians 13:1-13. Then examine how you are building up the Body of Christ, that is, the Church. How are you are using that gift of love in your life right now? Rate yourself on a scale of **1** to **10** how you are living some of the qualities of love discussed by St. Paul. A score of 1 would say: "There's absolutely no evidence of this in my life." A score of 10 would say: "I put this into practice very well."

- *patient:* I am willing to bear hardship without complaint; I defer to others.
- *kind:* With others, I am generous with time, talent, and treasure, not expecting anything in return.
- *not jealous:* I rejoice in the good fortune of others.
- *not pompous/not inflated:* I am humble and thank God for all my gifts and talents.
- *not rude:* I am courteous, gentle, and treat others as individuals to be respected.
- *not quick tempered:* I easily forgive others, recognizing that they are not perfect.
- *rejoices in truth:* I live by the code that "honesty is the best policy."
- *never fails:* I don't put conditions on my love; I am dependable.

Tally your score for all eight situations. Be willing to share and discuss your "score" with classmates. Talk about what this activity can teach about "what love can do."

10
9
8
7
6
5
4
3
2
1

might have eternal life" (Jn 3:16). Christ lives in his Church. His love can be found there.

For Review

1. Where in the Gospels does Jesus designate Peter as the head of the Church? Briefly describe this Gospel account.
2. Explain and describe St. Paul's comparison of the Church to a living body in 1 Corinthians.
3. Name the Four Marks of the Church. Give a brief explanation of each of these Four Marks.

EXPLAINING THE FAITH: HOW CAN WE KNOW THAT GOD REALLY EXISTS?

Other courses may have examined this question in some depth. But for now, we can briefly note several ways that can help us know that God exists: reason, personal experience, and trust in others.

We Can Know through Reason

Many brilliant thinkers have put forth logical and convincing arguments for the existence of God. St. Thomas Aquinas, for example, presented the famous five "proofs" or demonstrations for the existence of God. For example, one demonstration shows how everything has a beginning. Logically, there must be a Being who was not caused by anything else, a First Cause or a Prime Mover, who started everything off.

Related to this argument is the assumption that everything that exists or has being must come from Being itself (God). It is interesting that God revealed to Moses that his name was YHWH ("I Am Who Am"), a name that stresses that God is the Perfect Being from whom all other beings come.

Yet another demonstration for God's existence is the order to be found in the universe. There are laws and patterns in creation that seem to reflect Supreme Intelligence, a Supreme Being we call God. There are other rational proofs, too. In most ways, however, these are related to St. Paul's observation that God's "invisible attributes of eternal power and divinity have been able to be understood and perceived in what he has made" (Rm 1:20).

We Can Know through Ordinary Experience

Common human experience also leads us to conclude that there is a God. Earlier in the chapter we noted how our restless hearts, which yearn for total happiness, cannot be satisfied by any created reality. How can we explain this apparent homing device implanted in our human heart unless a loving Creator put it there to help us find him? Or how can we explain spiritual qualities like justice, love, beauty, or religious experience? They cannot come from any material reality. Does it not seem much more convincing to conclude that these are rooted in a Great Spirit—God—who is the measure of justice, beauty, and love itself?

Where does human intelligence come from? The human will? The human desire to live forever? Our existence as intelligent beings endowed with free will only seems to make sense if there is an intelligent, absolutely free being who made us in his own image.

We have certainly been created in freedom with the ability to make our own free choices, whether good or bad. This is a function of our human conscience: to provide us with the opportunity to discern good and avoid evil and to make concrete choices, approving those that are good and rejecting those that are bad. The morality of human acts depends on three basic sources: the object chosen, the end or intention for which the choice was made, and the circumstances of the moral act. Morality and making good choices depend on a source outside the human heart, an absolute standard of what is right and good and true. It is God himself who is the Supreme Good and Absolute Truth and who provides us with the standard for making good choices. Our actions are good when they conform to God and lead us to Heaven.

The Witness of Those We Trust

The vast majority of people believe that God exists. It is reasonable to believe that they are right. Further, Christians believe that God has revealed himself throughout human history. Human beings have received the Revelation of God and witnessed God's direct action in human history. The story of Salvation History appears in Sacred Scripture. We also have the testimony of many heroic and holy witnesses, including the saints and martyrs. Their intelligence, credibility, holiness, and willingness to die for their faith in Jesus Christ as God's only Son are inspiring and a strong support for belief in God.

Good, holy people living today also believe in God. Our Pope, bishops, priests, deacons, sisters and brothers, your parents and grandparents, friends, your parish community, and countless other people who love and support you believe in God. Their witness can be a strong support for your own belief in God. People outside our faith-community also believe in God. Many different religions attest to humanity's correct conclusion that there must be and is a God who made this universe of ours. Creation did not happen by chance.

For those of us who believe, our faith can help us to grow in knowledge of God given to us in his Son, Jesus Christ. By staying close to him in prayer, by living moral and loving lives, and by receiving him in the Sacraments (especially the Eucharist), we can experience more deeply and personally the reality of God, a God who lives, loves us, and sustains our very own existence.

For Review

1. What saint developed the famous "five proofs for the existence of God"?
2. Describe one of these five proofs for the existence of God.
3. What are some common everyday human experiences that suggest that God truly exists?
4. Explain why the witness of holy or martyred believers is also strong testimony that God really exists.

For Reflection

Name and tell about a famous person—past or present—who had the kind of faith in God that you admire and would want to imitate. Explain your choice.

Main Ideas

- The transcendence of God is the understanding that God is beyond this world and beyond human understanding. God's immanence refers to his presence in the world and his closeness to us. (pp. 2–3)
- Asking whether God exists is an intrinsically human and ancient question. (pp. 3–4)
- St. Augustine describes human curiosity about the existence of God as a restlessness of heart that only God himself could answer and quiet. (pp. 3–4)
- Human beings can and do find God in nature and in other human beings. (pp. 4–5)
- Atheists are people who do not believe in the existence of God. (p. 5)
- Agnostics report that they do not know whether or not God exists. (p. 5)
- Divine Revelation is the gift of self-revelation or disclosure that God gives to humanity. (pp. 6–8)
- Salvation History is the continuing story of God's generous love and interventions to save his sinful children. (pp. 7–8)
- God established many covenants with human beings to offer the promise of Salvation and continue his relationship with them. Among them were covenants with Noah, with Abraham, with Moses and the Chosen People, and with David. (pp. 7–8)
- God reveals himself to humanity through Scripture, the Sacred Tradition of the Church, and through the Deposit of Faith. (pp. 9–13)
- Jesus commissioned his Apostles and their successors to proclaim the Good News about the Kingdom of God that he had come to share. (pp. 9–10)
- At first, the Apostles simply preached the Good News, but later the stories of Jesus and his ministry and words were written down. (pp. 10–11)
- The Magisterium is the official teaching authority of the Church and is made up of the Pope and the bishops who are successors of Christ and his Apostles. (p. 10)
- The Deposit of Faith is the body or sum of saving truths that Christ gave the Apostles that have, in turn, been handed down to the Magisterium. (p. 10)
- Sacred Scripture, or the Bible, is the written record of Revelation. (p. 10)
- Sacred Tradition is the transmission or handing down of the Gospel message as it is expressed in Church teaching, life, and worship. (p. 11)
- Tradition, Scripture, and the Magisterium are all intimately related. (p. 11)
- The two major divisions of the Bible are the Old Testament, which contains forty-six books, and the New Testament, which contains twenty-seven books, including the four most important books, the four Gospels. (pp. 11–13)
- The writing of the Gospels developed after AD 65 and began with the Gospel of Mark. The Holy Spirit inspired the writing of the Gospels and the rest of the Bible as well. (p. 13)
- Faith is our positive response to God's Revelation. (pp. 13–17)
- The theological virtues are faith, hope, and love, and these virtues are infused into our souls. (pp. 14–15)
- Love (or charity) is the greatest of all virtues because it transforms us into God's children and helps us to embrace all other virtues. (p. 15)
- Faith has both a personal and communal dimension. (pp. 15–16)
- Before the Ascension of Jesus, he established a community to carry on his work. This community is the Catholic Church and its head, the Pope, is the successor of Peter. (pp. 17–18)

- The Body of Christ is a rich image for the Church presented by St. Paul in 1 Corinthians. This imagery emphasizes the vital, life-sustaining connection we have with Jesus. (p. 19)
- The Four Marks of the Church describe the Church as "one, holy, catholic, and apostolic." These are beliefs we have about the nature of the Church that we profess in the Nicene Creed that we recite at Mass. (pp. 19–20)
- St. Thomas Aquinas, the brilliant thirteenth-century Dominican theologian and Doctor of the Church, developed five proofs for the existence of God. One of these proofs suggests that there had to be a First Cause, a Being who was not caused by anything else. (pp. 21–22)
- Another compelling "proof" for God that we can identify is the witness of martyrs who gave their lives for Christ and the Gospels. (p. 22)

Terms, People, Places

Choose the italicized term in parentheses that best completes each sentence.

1. The (*Magisterium/Deposit of Faith*) is the name for the body of saving truths and core beliefs of Catholicism.
2. A (*creed/covenant*) is the name for a solemn agreement between people and God.
3. An (*atheist/agnostic*) is a person who does not know whether there is a God or not.
4. (*Faith/Dogma*) is one of the theological virtues.
5. The term (*immanence/transcendence*) refers to God being in the world and close to his creatures.
6. (*Sacred Scripture/Sacred Tradition*) is the living transmission of the Catholic faith through the teaching, life, and worship of the Church.
7. (*Religion/Virtue*) refers to a set of beliefs, values, and practices that bind believers in a relationship with God and with others.

Primary Source Quotations

Finding God

The contemplation of God is promised to us as the goal of all our acts and the eternal consummation of all our joys.

—St. Augustine of Hippo

Every little glimpse that can be gained of God exceeds every pain and every joy that one can conceive without it.

—St. Catherine of Genoa

The Creator God

If God had drawn the world from pre-existent matter, what would be so extraordinary in that? A human artisan makes from a given material whatever he wants, while God shows his power by starting from nothing to make all he wants.

—St. Theosophilus of Antioch

The same loving hand that has created you has created me. If he is your Father he must be my Father also. We all belong to the same family. Hindus, Muslims, and all people are our brothers and sisters. They too are the children of God.

—Blessed Mother Teresa of Calcutta

Take some time to ask God to be known in your life. Then write a short prayer asking God to grant you knowledge of him.

Ongoing Assignments

1. Research and report on St. Thomas Aquinas's five proofs for the existence of God.
2. Create your own PowerPoint presentation on faith. View the following video for some ideas on how to create your presentation: www.interviewwithgod.com/faith/

index.htm. Use a Bible Concordance to find other quotations on faith.

3. Interview ten people on their beliefs about Jesus Christ. Report on common beliefs people hold.
4. Create a PowerPoint presentation that depicts God's majesty reflected in his creation.
5. With several classmates, debate the question of the existence of God. Share the debate with others.
6. If possible, spend some time with a child two or three years of age. Engage the child in conversation. Note how many "Why" questions he or she asks. Record how you answered them.
7. Locate the following New Testament passages on faith. Transcribe them. Write a short paragraph describing what these verses are saying about faith. Be sure to account for all the elements in all the passages. Share your paragraph with your classmates.
   - Hebrews 11:6
   - Hebrews 11:1
   - Galatians 5:6
   - Acts 16:31
   - James 2:26
8. Beauty can lead us to God. Choose a piece of art, a photo, or a musical selection that points you to absolute beauty, that is, to the Creator God. Prepare a PowerPoint presentation to share with your classmates that explains what qualities of God you find in the piece you select.
9. Report on the life of your patron saint or a favorite saint. Explain how the person put into practice the virtues of faith and charity.
10. Write some questions you would like to ask your peers about their faith life. Choose three different peers: (1) a close friend, (2) an acquaintance, and (3) a person you do not know well. Videotape an interview with each using the questions you have prepared. Edit the interviews into one presentation and play the presentation for your class.
11. Research and report on the history of the Apostles' Creed: www.newadvent.org/cathen/01629a.htm.

Prayer

A creed is a statement of belief. The word *creed* comes from the Latin word *credo* ("I believe"). When you recite a creed, you are making a personal act of faith. Two important Christian creeds are the Nicene Creed, which we recite at Mass, and the Apostles' Creed. The Apostles' Creed is firmly rooted in an early baptismal creed used in Rome in the second century. This is significant because Peter, the first of the Apostles and the Christ-appointed leader of the Church, came to Rome to establish the Church there. Thus, the great authority of the Apostles' Creed goes all the way back to the theological formulas that arose during the time of Peter (the first Pope) and the Apostles.

The Apostles' Creed is simple, short, logically ordered, and prayerful. It highlights the essential Christian doctrine of the Blessed Trinity by proclaiming faith in

- the first divine Person (the almighty and eternal God) and the wonderful work of creation;
- the second divine Person (Jesus Christ, God-made-man) and his marvelous work of Redemption;
- the third divine Person (the Holy Spirit), who is the origin and source of sanctification that comes to us through Christ's

one, holy, catholic, and apostolic church
(*CCC*, 190).

Recite the Apostles' Creed slowly, reflecting on each of the phrases.

The Apostles' Creed
I believe in God,
the Father almighty,
creator of heaven and earth.
I believe in Jesus Christ
his only Son, Our Lord.
He was conceived by the
power of the Holy Spirit
and born to the Virgin Mary.
He suffered under Pontius Pilate,
was crucified, died and was
buried.
He descended into hell.
On the third day he rose again
He ascended into heaven
and is seated at the right
hand of the Father.
He will come again to judge
the living and the dead.
I believe in the Holy Spirit,
the holy catholic Church,
the communion of saints,
the forgiveness of sins,
the resurrection of the body,
and the life everlasting.
Amen.

- *Reflection*: Which articles of the Creed mean the most to you? Why?
- *Resolution*: Memorize the Apostles' Creed and recite it daily for the next two weeks.

WHO IS JESUS CHRIST?

I am the way and the truth and the life.
No one comes to the Father except through me.

—John 14:6

The Power of Words

Jesus Christ is the most important Word ever spoken, the Word of God.

The Incarnation of Jesus

The fundamental belief of all Christians is that Jesus Christ, the Son of God, took on human nature, became man, and was born of the Virgin Mary by the power of the Holy Spirit.

Learning about Jesus

We learn about Jesus in history and through the inherited teachings of the Apostles that come to us in Scripture and the Church.

Jesus, Resurrected Lord

The Risen Lord remains present to us in the Church—in Scripture, Sacraments, Prayer, and in the lives of Christians.

The Mysteries of Christ's Life

Just as there are many mysteries about God the Father, there are also mysteries about Jesus, the Son of God.

Jesus Proclaims God's Kingdom

Jesus came to proclaim the Kingdom of God where all are welcome, especially the poor and the lowly.

The Power of Words

The ability to create and use words to communicate is part of what makes us human. Language sets us apart from other creatures. We learn this truth in the Bible when God gave Adam the authority to name all the other marvelous creatures he had made (Gn 2:19–20).

Words can do so much good. Think of the words we use to express our love for someone. Consider the power in words we choose to tell the truth. The book of Proverbs puts it this way: "Pleasing words are a honeycomb, sweet to the taste and healthful to the body" (Prv 16:24).

But words can also do great harm. As the Irish statesman Edmund Burke (1729–1797) said, "A very great part of the mischiefs that vex this world arises from words."

Among the many sayings about words that are worth pondering are these two:

> "As a person grows wiser, he talks less and says more."
> "A major part of self-control is mouth-control."

This last point suggests that we consider very seriously the advice of this famous saying:

> Watch your thoughts, for they become words.
> Watch your words, for they become actions.
> Watch your actions, for they become habits.
> Watch your habits, for they become character.
> Watch your character, for it becomes your destiny.

Another anonymous author has the secret recipe for human relationships when he tells us what are the most and least important words of all. His advice:

> The six most important words:
> "I admit that I was wrong."
> The five most important words:
> "You did a great job."
> The four most important words:
> "What do you think?"
> The three most important words:
> "Could you please . . ."
> The two most important words:
> "Thank you."
> The most important word: "We."
> The least important word: "I."

This chapter begins with a reflection on words because it focuses on the most important word ever spoken—the Word of God, that is, Jesus. The Word of God became man in Jesus Christ. Everything about this unique Person reveals something about God because Jesus Christ is the Lord God. All events of his life are worthy of reflection and imitation.

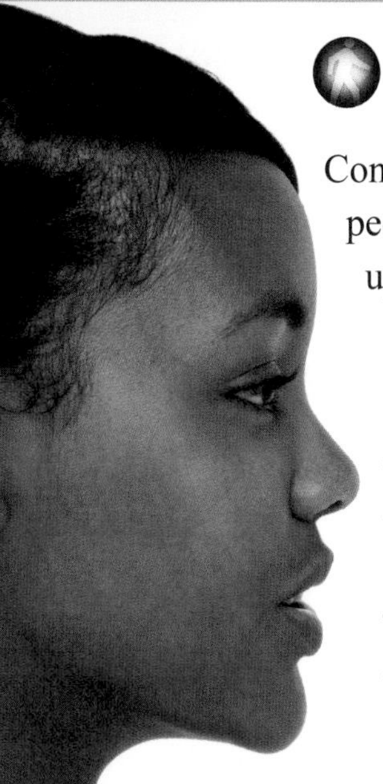

What about My Own Words?

Consider the important words discussed earlier by applying them to your own life. Identify people to whom they might apply. Then, in your journal, write a concrete plan for following up on your plans for the following important words.

1. *"I admit that I am wrong."* Which person needs to hear your honest confession? How will you go about asking for his or her forgiveness?
2. *"You did a great job."* Which person most needs your praise right now?
3. *"What do you think?"* Whose advice do you need right now? On what topic will you seek his or her opinion?
4. *"Thank you."* Who needs your gratitude? Why?
5. *"We."* Which ten people in your life would you include in the word *we*? Choose one of them and tell him or her how special he or she is to you.

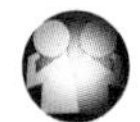

For Reflection

How do you describe the power of words?

The Incarnation of Jesus (*CCC*, 456-463)

Christians are Christians precisely because they believe that Jesus Christ is both God and man. Jesus is the unique Son of God. At the same time, he is the fully human son of Mary whom we call the Blessed Mother. This teaching about Jesus is known as the doctrine of the **Incarnation**. It is the distinctive and defining belief of Christianity. This doctrine teaches that Jesus Christ, the Son of God, "assumed a human nature in order to accomplish our salvation in it" (*CCC*, 461). The Word of God took on human flesh from his mother Mary by power of the Holy Spirit. Thus, Christians believe that Jesus Christ is both fully God and fully human.

Scriptural Background: The Gospels of Luke and Matthew

In the Gospel of Luke, we learn of the **Annunciation**. At the Annunciation, the angel Gabriel announced to Mary that she would become the mother of the Son of God through the power of the Holy Spirit. Mary was to name this child **Jesus**, a name that means "YHWH is Salvation" or "Savior." A sign that God was at work in this great event was that Mary's distant relative, Elizabeth, had conceived a child in her old age. Elizabeth, who had been barren, conceived a child because "nothing will be impossible for God" (Lk 1:37).

With great faith, Mary, who was already betrothed to Joseph, said

Incarnation
The teaching that God became flesh through the birth of Jesus Christ, the Son of God and the child of the Virgin Mary.

Annunciation
The announcement by the angel Gabriel to the Virgin Mary that God wanted her to be the Mother of the Savior, Jesus Christ.

Jesus
A word that means "YHWH is Salvation" or "Savior."

"Yes" to God's messenger. She freely entered into God's plan of Salvation. She replied to Gabriel, "Behold, I am the handmaid of the Lord. May it be done to me according to your word" (Lk 1:38). Mary's simple and humble response to God is a model for all believers. She did not know what would happen. But Mary's cooperation allowed God's divine plan of Salvation to move forward.

Mary was not living with Joseph when she conceived Jesus through the Holy Spirit. Joseph, an upright man, knew that the child was not his. But, he did not want to expose Mary to public shame. So, he decided to divorce her quietly. In a dream, however, Joseph saw that Mary's child was divinely conceived. In his dream, an angel told Joseph not to be afraid. Joseph was to take Mary as his wife. He too was told to name this child "Jesus." Matthew wrote that all these events took place to fulfill an old prophecy in Isaiah 7:14: "Behold, the virgin shall be with child and bear a son, and they shall name him Emmanuel" (Mt 1:23).

The **Nativity**, or birth of Jesus Christ, took place nine months after the angel's announcement to Mary and Joseph. This feast day, the day of our Savior's birth, is celebrated on Christmas Day. The newborn Jesus was wrapped in swaddling clothes and laid in a manger in the town of Bethlehem in Judea. Every circumstance related to his birth had been foreseen. The prophet Micah had predicted (5:1):

> And you, Bethlehem, land of Judah,
> are by no means least among the rulers of Judah;
> since from you shall come a ruler,
> who is to shepherd my people Israel.
> (Mt 2:6)

Today, we associate Christmas with gift giving, and it should be. On that first Christmas, God gave humanity the greatest gift of all—his Son, Jesus Christ. Too often this greatest of all gifts is almost forgotten in the busy, commercial "holiday" season. Christians should try to remember the slogan "Jesus is the reason for the season." We should never forget what we celebrate at Christmas. The Son of God was born into the human family. He became one of us so that we might share in his life and in the life of the Trinity. Jesus Christ became man so that we might know and love God and live with him forever.

Joseph

The New Testament does not tell us too much about Joseph, the husband of Mary, and foster father or legal father of Jesus. In fact, it does not record a single word spoken by this important man in the life of Jesus.

Reportedly, Joseph lived for some periods of his life in Nazareth in Galilee but took his pregnant wife Mary to Bethlehem where Jesus was born. Joseph then rushed his family away to Egypt when King Herod the Great ordered the killing of all male infants in Bethlehem. Later, after the death of Herod, Mary and Joseph and the very young Jesus returned to live in Nazareth. Joseph was a descendant of King David (see Matthew 1:6 and Luke 3:31) and he worked as a carpenter, a trade he also taught his son, Jesus. The Gospels (for example, Matthew 13:55, Luke 3:23, and John 6:42) confirm that Jesus was known to the people of his time as the son of Joseph, the carpenter.

Joseph and Mary traveled with Jesus to Jerusalem for the Passover feast when Jesus was twelve years old. On this occasion, Mary and Joseph lost contact with Jesus and frantically searched until they found the boy Jesus in the Temple. Jesus was teaching the elders who "were astounded at his understanding and his answers" (Lk 2:47). The Gospels do not tell us about the death of Joseph. But, it's likely that Joseph died before Jesus began his public ministry. Mark's Gospel hints at this. When the people of Nazareth would not accept Jesus' teaching in the synagogue, they identified him as the carpenter, "the son of Mary" (Mk 6:3). This identification suggests that Joseph had already died.

Although Joseph did not utter a single word in the Gospels, his presence is strongly felt. A man of tremendous faith, he raised Jesus in the Jewish faith and trained him in a trade—carpentry. Joseph also taught Jesus to be a *gentle* man. Surely, Jesus also saw the great love Joseph had for Mary. Joseph must have been a tremendous example for the boy, and then, the young man entrusted to his care. Much credit must go to Joseph when we see that Jesus was a loving, graceful, manly, hard-working, prayerful, and courageous man. The Church recognizes Joseph as the patron saint of workers and celebrates his feast day on March 19.

Scriptural Background: John's Gospel

The Prologue to the Gospel of John provides a beautiful theological description for the Incarnation.

> In the beginning was the Word, and the Word was with God, and the Word was God. He was in the beginning with God. All things came to be through him, and without him nothing came to be. What came to be through him was life, and this life was the light of the human race; the light shines in the darkness, and the darkness has not overcome it. And the Word became flesh and made his dwelling among us, and we saw his glory, the glory as of the Father's only Son, full of grace and truth. (Jn 1:1–4; 14)

The author of John's Gospel used the expression "the Word became *flesh*" to state emphatically that Jesus took on human nature and became man. He did so to counteract a first-century heresy known as **Docetism**. This heresy taught that Jesus only "seemed" to be a man. (*Docetism* comes from a Greek word meaning "to seem.") People who believed in Docetism could not believe that God would demean himself by becoming like us in all our weakness and humanity. For Docetists, Jesus was a ghostly figure who *appeared* to instruct us about godly things.

The danger of Docetism was that if Jesus only seemed to be human,

Nativity
The birth of Jesus Christ, the Son of God and of the Virgin Mary.

Docetism
A first-century heresy that taught that Jesus only seemed to be human.

then he only *seemed* to die and rise from the dead. These key events—Christ's Death and Resurrection—are the basis of our Salvation. If they are only phantasms and appearances, then we have not really been saved. Added to that, there is no more hope for our own resurrection from the dead.

The author of John's Gospel used the Greek word *sarx* to declare that Jesus really was one of us. This word *sarx* was like the Latin word *carne,* which is translated as "flesh." Obviously, a person cannot be a human being without having a human body.

So, the word *incarnation* means "God becoming flesh, or human." Jesus is truly God. He is the Word of God who was always with God. But Jesus is also truly man with the body of a man. Jesus is God-man. (Chapters 4–7 discuss in greater depth the theological meaning of Jesus as God and man.)

The Purpose of the Incarnation

Catholics understand that the Incarnation of God's Son, Jesus, brought about many blessings for all human beings.

- First, the Word became flesh to reconcile us with God. Because of the Original Sin, humans inherited a fallen nature and were prone to sin, ignorance, sickness, and death. Christ's great and loving sacrifice heals our human nature. Jesus also overcame sin and won everlasting life for us.
- Second, as God's Son, Jesus clearly showed God's love to us.
- Third, as God-made-man, Jesus became the perfect model of holiness. He is "the way and the truth and the life" (Jn 14:6) who teaches that the path to holiness is for us to give ourselves to others in imitation of him. "Love one another as I love you" (Jn 15:12).
- Fourth, by becoming human, the Word of God made it possible for us to share in God's nature. "For the Son of God became man so that we might become God" (St. Athanasius quoted in *CCC*, 460).

These blessings convince us that it is good to learn all we can *about* Jesus. Moreover, it is extremely important to know Jesus himself. Jesus is the living Lord who calls each of us by name.

For Review

1. What is the Incarnation?
2. What does the word "Jesus" mean?

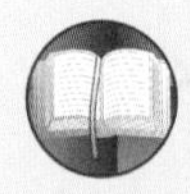

Quotations about Christ

Do an Internet search on the topic, "Quotations about Jesus Christ." Read at least fifty quotations. Then transcribe five of your favorite quotations. Display them on an attractive poster board for posting in your classroom or study area at home. Here are three sample quotations to get you started:

How sweet, the presence of Jesus to the longing, harassed soul!
It is instant peace, and balm to every wound.
—St. Elizabeth Seton

Invisible in his own nature God became visible in ours.
Beyond our grasp, he chose to come within our grasp.
—St. Leo the Great

What good is it having someone who can walk on water
if you don't follow in his footsteps?
—Author Unknown

3. What is the Feast of the Annunciation?
4. What was Docetism and why does the Church see it as a heresy?
5. Name three blessings for all human beings that result from the Incarnation of Jesus.

For Reflection

- Choose a character that interests you from the "Christmas passages" in the Gospels of Matthew and Luke. Expand on the Gospel story and write a short "eyewitness" account of the birth of Jesus from the point of view of one of these characters—for example, Joseph, Mary, a shepherd, one of the Magi, a villager from Bethlehem. Later, share this Bethlehem story with your classmates.
- Write a sixty-second public service essay for a radio station on the real meaning of Christmas—God's gift to humanity. Consider sending it or an audio recording of it to a local radio station that welcomes essays from local writers.

Learning about Jesus (CCC, 422-426)

Who is the *real* Jesus? Where do we learn about him? Where do we find him? The answer to all of these questions is in some ways simple. The Jesus we read about in the Bible is the real Jesus. The Jesus we meet in the Church is the real Jesus. The Jesus we receive in the Eucharist and the other Sacraments is the real Jesus. We also learn certain basic facts about Jesus from history.

Many Ways to Know Jesus

Think about your own knowledge of Jesus. You probably learned what you know about Jesus from your parents; teachers; retreats; priests who spoke about Jesus in homilies; or from television programs, films, books, and articles about Jesus.

But where did those people get their information about Jesus? They learned about Jesus from other people who came before them and from the bishops and Popes who made sure that what was passed on was accurate and faithful teaching.

Where did all of that knowledge about Jesus come from?

If you follow this process all the way back, you will find that what we know about Jesus came from the Apostles. Those twelve Galileans had direct contact and experience with Jesus. They knew him as a teacher and as a healer who walked with them over the dusty roads of Palestine. The Apostles were witnesses of his arrest and condemnation as a criminal. Most important of all, they saw Jesus after his Death—after he had been raised in power and glory.

These first followers of Jesus experienced the power of the Risen Lord in their own lives. At Pentecost, they were transformed from frightened cowards into bold people who boldly proclaimed the Good News (Gospel) of Jesus Christ. These men were so convinced of the truth of their message that they didn't hesitate to surrender their own lives in order to preach the simple message, "Jesus is Lord!"

As explained in Chapter 1, the testimony of the Apostles about Jesus Christ comes down to us through the Tradition of the Church and through the writings of Sacred Scripture, especially the Gospels. Both are part of the Deposit of Faith. Both are accurate sources of knowledge about Jesus Christ. Tradition and Sacred Scripture preserves the authentic message about Jesus. Knowledge of the Bible, especially the Gospels, is essential for anyone who wants to "know" Jesus Christ.

The Jesus of History

Historical records verify that there was a real man known as "Jesus, the Carpenter," "Jesus, the son of Joseph," and "Jesus of Nazareth." More information about the historical accounts of Jesus will be presented in Chapter 3. This Jesus lived most of his life in Nazareth in Galilee and learned the trade of carpentry from his foster father, Joseph. Jesus actively practiced his Jewish religion. He was a circumcised man. He studied the Old Testament writings, faithfully worshipped on the Sabbath, and recited his daily prayers and the psalms. He also celebrated the great religious feasts in the Temple and kept the precepts of the Mosaic Law.

Around AD 28, Jesus was baptized by John the Baptist, an itinerant preacher and prophet. After that, Jesus withdrew to a nearby desert to prepare for his own public ministry. After forty days, Jesus emerged from the desert and preached through the countryside. His message was about repentance, the coming of God's Kingdom, and the need to put one's faith in the Gospel.

Adopting "Kingdom Attitudes"

Jesus taught that God's Kingdom had already come. He said that this Kingdom calls people to a new way of living both as individuals and as communities. God's Kingdom brings Salvation from sin and a share in God's life. God's Kingdom is truly Good News because it brings love, justice, compassion, and forgiveness for all people. We know that this Kingdom of God or Reign of God is only partially experienced here on earth. We see that there is still pain and violence, sickness and death, all around us. It will be fully realized only in heaven. Nonetheless, Jesus wanted all of his followers to know that in the Kingdom of God, peace, justice, and joy would abound for all people. In this Kingdom, everyone would see that all people are sisters and brothers, children of God.

Take a few minutes to quietly consider your life and your relationships—family members, friends, teammates, classmates, and neighbors. It's true that no one can "download" the Kingdom of God into our lives and culture today. But, you can cultivate "Kingdom Attitudes" in your own life. You can encourage others to do the same.

In your journal or notebook, list and describe three "Kingdom Attitudes" you can adopt and make a part of your life.

"This is the time of fulfillment. The kingdom of God is at hand. Repent, and believe in the gospel." (Mk 1:15)

The Miracles and Ministry of Jesus

Besides preaching about the coming of God's Kingdom, Jesus also performed wonderful works and miracles. These miracles supported the claim Jesus made that God's Kingdom had already broken into human history. Jesus cured lepers and restored sight to blind people and hearing to deaf people. He fed the crowds with a few loaves of bread, and exorcised demons from the possessed. He also called his Apostles to witness firsthand his life, his teachings, and his miracles. Jesus also commissioned his Apostles and all of his followers to carry on his work when he was gone. In addition to his twelve Apostles, Jesus gathered many other disciples around him.

The Humanity of Jesus

Without a doubt, Jesus was a man who truly experienced human pain, fatigue, and a variety of emotions. The Gospels report his experience of hunger (Mk 11:12), thirst (Jn 4:7), and weariness (Jn 4:6). He showed anger at the moneychangers (Mt 21:12–13) and experienced deep sorrow (Mk 14:34) and heart-wrenching distress that led to tears at the death of his friend, Lazarus (Jn 11:34–35). He suffered great physical and emotional pain during his Passion and Death (Mt 27:50). Moreover, he exhibited great compassion and love for everyone he met, especially those who were suffering. "At the sight of the crowds, his heart was moved with pity for them because they were troubled and abandoned, like sheep without a shepherd" (Mt 9:36).

Obviously, Jesus had a strong and charismatic personality. Those who met him had to decide what to do about his challenging message. Jesus made statements about how life should be lived that couldn't be ignored. For example, he said that everyone would have to decide whether or not they would turn from their sins and accept God's love. Those who heard Jesus had to make an important decision about believing in him. The way Jesus preached and his actions led some people to think of him as a great prophet. But not everyone agreed with this. Even some of his relatives thought that Jesus was crazy or unstable (Mk 3:20–21).

Some of the things Jesus did and some of his teachings threatened and angered the authorities. He spoke with a unique authority and didn't quote other Jewish teachers to verify what he said. Then, he associated with prostitutes and tax collectors. That horrified and distressed many people. Jesus also gave novel interpretations of the Law. He claimed to speak for God.

Eventually the Jewish authorities conspired to have Jesus arrested. One of his followers betrayed him for money. The other Apostles abandoned him. Some Jewish officials tried Jesus and found him guilty of blasphemy because he claimed to be God's Son. They turned him over to Pontius Pilate, the Roman prefect, who sentenced him to the cruelest form

of capital punishment—crucifixion. This execution took place either in AD 30 or 33. It was alleged that Jesus claimed to be "King of the Jews," a crime interpreted under Roman law as sedition against the Roman Emperor Tiberius.

These basic facts present historical information about the life of Jesus and provide evidence that he is the most compelling human to walk the face of the earth. As the famous British writer, H. G. Wells (1866–1946), put it,

> I am a historian, I am not a believer, but I must confess as a historian that this penniless preacher from Nazareth is irrevocably the very center of history. Jesus Christ is easily the most dominant figure in all history. Christ is the most unique person of history. No man can write a history of the human race without giving first and foremost place to the penniless teacher of Nazareth.

For Review

1. Where did knowledge about Jesus originally come from?
2. How have Catholics received the testimony of the Apostles about Jesus?
3. Name several facts that are known about Jesus from historical records.
4. What was the central theme of Jesus' teaching?
5. Name some deeds done by Jesus that verified that the Kingdom of God had come.
6. How did the actions and teachings of Jesus anger Jewish authorities?

For Reflection

- Think about the many people who have helped you to learn about Jesus. Describe at least two of those people and tell what you learned about Jesus from them.
- Imagine that you are a Jew living in the time of Jesus. You have heard of his miracles and teachings. What would convince you that the Kingdom of God he talked about really was beginning? Would it be the healing of a blind man? Would it be a miraculous multiplication of bread and fish? Or would it simply be his compassion? Share your thoughts.

Jesus, Resurrected Lord (*CCC*, 427-429)

Jesus is much more than a famous and influential person who lived long ago. The Church's teaching on the Incarnation leads us to believe that Jesus is the Son of God. Jesus came to save us by dying and then rising from the dead. We believe that Jesus is alive now. Like belief in the Incarnation, belief in the Resurrection of Jesus is a fundamental belief for every Christian. The **Resurrection** is the rising of Jesus from the dead on the third day after his Death on the cross.

God raised his own Son, Jesus, from the dead. The Resurrection and glorification of Jesus reveal his true identity as God's Son, a Son who fully shared the Father's superabundant life and glory. Moreover, with his Father, the Risen Christ sent the Holy Spirit to live in the hearts of believers. That empowered them to live lives of love and service in imitation of Jesus.

The "real Jesus" of Christian faith is the resurrected Jesus, a living person whom God has revealed as both Lord and Christ (Acts 2:36). This real Jesus lives in his Body, the Church (see also Chapter 1). Through the Church, he continues to live in the world.

This Jesus you have heard about is the same as the Jesus of history who lived on this earth over two thousand years ago. When all is said and done,

Christian faith is a response to a living God. This God is powerfully at work in his Church, and among its members, through the resurrected Jesus Christ.

Meeting Jesus Today

Because Jesus is alive as Risen Lord, we can meet him today. *You* can meet him today!

You can meet Jesus in the Bible, the written record of Revelation. Remember, Revelation is God's self-communication to us. You can especially meet Jesus in the New Testament writings, most notably in the four Gospels. They record many of the important deeds that Jesus performed. They also contain many teachings that guide us toward loving service for others. The Gospels and other New Testament writings would never have been written if Jesus had not been raised from the dead, and if the Spirit had not later come to the disciples of Jesus. The Gospels were written under the inspiration of the Holy Spirit. The evangelists set down a written record of the Good News about Jesus Christ, Son of God. The Gospels were written to build and support our faith:

> But these are written that you may (come to) believe that Jesus is the Messiah, the Son of God, and that through this belief you may have life in his name. (Jn 20:31)

Besides in Scripture, there are several other ways to meet and know Jesus today. These are covered in the next sections.

Jesus in the Sacraments

The Risen Lord left his Church seven visible signs of invisible grace called Sacraments. Sacraments are "efficacious" signs, meaning they bring about the spiritual realities to which they point. Christ instituted the Sacraments and made them "of the Church" because they are "by her" and "for her." As the *Catechism of the Catholic Church* puts it:

> The sacraments are "by the Church," for she is the sacrament of Christ's action at work in her through the mission of the Holy Spirit. They are "for the Church" in the sense that "the sacraments make the Church," since they manifest and communicate to men, above all in the Eucharist, the mystery of communion with the God who is love, One in three persons. (*CCC*, 1118)

Resurrection
The rising of Jesus from the dead on the third day after his Death on the cross. Jesus was able to conquer death because he is God.

In the Sacraments of the Church, Jesus comes to us in very special moments in our life:

- when we are initiated into the Church (Baptism);
- when we need the special strength of the Holy Spirit to live the Christian life (Confirmation);
- when we receive—even daily if we choose—the sign of love we call the Holy Eucharist;
- when we are sick and in need of spiritual and physical healing (Anointing of the Sick);
- when we have sinned and need to be forgiven and welcomed back into the Church (Penance);
- when we are called to serve God as special ministers to the Church (Holy Orders);
- and when we commit ourselves to a lifetime of sharing life and love with a spouse (Matrimony).

These Seven Sacraments are powerful signs of Christ's love. They are guaranteed encounters with the Risen Lord.

Jesus in Prayer

We can also meet the living Lord in prayer. We can talk to him whenever we want. In our hearts, we can talk to Jesus as we would talk to any friend. We can meet him when we assemble with other believers, especially in the Liturgy of the Eucharist. As Jesus said, "Where two or three are gathered together in my name, there am I in the midst of them" (Mt 18:20).

Jesus in the Body of Christ

In addition to all that, Jesus lives in the Body of Christ, the Church. Jesus is the Head of this Body. And by the power of the Holy Spirit, he lives in each member of this Body. Because God became man in Jesus Christ, all of humanity has tremendous dignity. That is, we have tremendous value and worth. *You* are indeed precious in God's eyes. However, that also means that we have a great responsibility to serve other people—just as Jesus did.

In a very particular and memorable way, Jesus identified himself with the lowly, the outcast, and the marginalized. He warned that we shall be judged on how we have welcomed the stranger, fed the hungry, given drink to the thirsty, and visited the sick and imprisoned.

> He will answer them, "Amen, I say to you, what you did not do for one of these least ones, you did not do for me." And these will go off to eternal punishment, but the righteous to eternal life. (Mt 25:45–46)

Jesus reminded his followers that when we respond to the least of these, we are responding to him. He is in every one of us, especially the poor.

For Review

1. Why is belief in the Resurrection of Jesus a fundamental belief for Christians?
2. What are three different ways that we can meet Jesus in the Church?
3. What part of the New Testament is the best place to meet Jesus?
4. Why does the text call the Sacraments "guaranteed encounters" with Jesus?
5. How did Jesus put himself into the story in Matthew 25, a story about caring for the poor and outcast?

For Reflection

- Describe how Easter, the greatest of feasts, could be celebrated in new ways by your family, your school, your parish, and your community.
- Different ways to meet Jesus are listed in the text. What way works best for you? Do you prefer to meet Jesus through the Scriptures, the Sacraments, or in other people, that is, in the Body of Christ?

The Mysteries of Christ's Life (*CCC*, 512-570)

A **mystery** is a truth about God that will always be beyond human understanding. God's greatness, his eternal omnipotence, and all of his other perfections are beyond our grasp. We will never really comprehend these realities, even when we ourselves are in Heaven. The word (*mysterion* in Greek) also refers to God's saving plan that was gradually revealed in human history.

We also use the term "mystery" when we talk about Christ's life. Jesus is the link between God and his saving plan. Human beings saw God most fully when he became man in Jesus Christ. Because Jesus is the Son of God who came to redeem us, "Christ's whole earthly life—his words and deeds, his silences and sufferings, indeed his manner of being and speaking—is *Revelation* of the Father" (*CCC*, 516). It is in Christ's whole life—from the Incarnation, through his total sacrifice on the Cross, and in the final victory of the Resurrection—that we are redeemed.

Jesus said, "Whoever has seen me has seen the Father" (Jn 14:9). *Every* aspect of Christ's life, no matter how seemingly insignificant, is related to his mission of Redemption. Jesus redeemed us once and for all by his Death on the Cross. His whole life, however, paints a picture of God, Our

mystery
A truth about God and his saving plan that will always be beyond human understanding.

Epiphany
The celebration of the manifestation of God in human form; the manifestation of Jesus to the Gentiles or non-Jews.

Presentation in the Temple
The presentation of the infant Jesus by Mary and Joseph in the Temple took place forty days after his birth. This ritual observed the Law of Moses and marked the end of forty days of purification for the mother after childbirth. This presentation also completed the "redemption" of a firstborn son with a ritual offering.

Father, and his infinite love and mercy for us.

Consider the following fact. Through the Incarnation, the Almighty God became poor, small, and vulnerable by becoming one of us. This great act of humility greatly enriched us because it made it possible for us to share in his life. In quiet submission to Mary and Joseph, Jesus modeled perfect humility and obedience for us. Later, through his public life of preaching and teaching the Word of God, Jesus shouldered even more of our sad human realities. When he healed and cast out evil spirits, as the Scriptures tell us, "He took away our infirmities and bore our diseases" (Mt 8:17). Finally, in his Resurrection, he justified us (see *CCC,* 517).

In summary, Jesus Christ is the perfect man. On earth, he lived his life for us. He is our model. He teaches us how to be humble, how to pray, how to serve others, how to endure suffering, how to love. Reflecting on the various mysteries in Christ's life as they are revealed in Scripture teach us how to be his disciples.

Read the suggested Scripture passages named in the following sections in their entirety. Then, you will begin to see how a particular mystery in the life of Jesus reveals God's love.

The Birth and Infancy of Jesus

In Matthew 2 and Luke 2, we find the "Christmas stories" that are so familiar. Jesus, these Gospel passages tell us, was born in poverty. He came into the world as one of the lowly and poor.

The first to see him after Mary and Joseph were the shepherds. Pious Jews referred to this lowly group as "the people of the land." Because they were constantly herding sheep, shepherds could not faithfully observe religious rituals required by the Law. Yet, these simple, earthy people who were more or less despised by the Jewish establishment were among the first to see the Redeemer.

The Magi from the East who visited Jesus were not Jews. The story of their coming appears only in Matthew. Traditionally, we remember these Magi as "the three kings." However, they were probably from the priestly caste of Zoroastrianism. The manifestation of Jesus to non-Jews reveals that Jesus came as the Savior of all people. This is the message and meaning of the **Epiphany**.

In the **Presentation in the Temple**, we read that Joseph and Mary presented the infant as Jewish law required. Jesus was seen as a firstborn son for this couple. A firstborn son, in Jewish thinking, belonged to God. In the Temple, the aged prophets Simeon and Anna recognized Jesus as the long-awaited Messiah. They thanked God for allowing them to see this promised Savior. They predicted his future Death on the cross and warned Mary of future sorrows ("the sword of sorrow that will pierce Mary's heart").

The Flight into Egypt and the Slaughter of the Innocents are also part of this Christmas story. These events

PROPHECIES ABOUT THE MESSIAH

Check the following eight Old Testament prophecies about the Messiah. Then read the New Testament "fulfillment" of the prophecies. In your notebook or journal, briefly tell about each Old Testament prophecy, and how Jesus fulfilled it through his birth, life, ministry, and Death.

Old Testament Prophecy	New Testament Fulfillment
1. Genesis 3:15	1. Galatians 4:4
2. Deuteronomy 18:15-19	2. Acts 3:22-23
3. Psalm 2:7	3. Luke 3:22
4. Psalm 16:10-11	4. John 20:11-16
5. Psalm 22:8	5. Luke 23:11, 35-39
6. Psalm 41:10	6. John 13:18
7. Jeremiah 23:5-6; 33:15-16	7. Luke 1:32-33
8. Isaiah 35:5-6	8. Matthew 11:3-6

took place because of the jealousy of the worldly ruler, Herod the Great. Herod was an extremely brutal Jewish king. The Holy Family's forced flight into Egypt took place because Herod ordered the killing of infant and toddler boys in Bethlehem.

The forces of evil were at war against Jesus from the very beginning of his life. These events also show how God protected his Son. Jesus needed to grow into adulthood to accomplish his mission of saving all of humanity.

The Hidden Life of Jesus

The "hidden life of Jesus" refers to his life as a child, adolescent, and young adult in Nazareth. The response of Jesus to his parents and other authorities was one of respectful obedience. We can easily see a contrast here with Adam's disobedience to God. This obedience of Jesus to Mary and Joseph shows us how the Fourth Commandment should be observed. Jesus showed what it means to "honor your father and your mother." His obedience to his earthly parents reflected his perfect obedience to his heavenly Father. All throughout these hidden years of formation, Jesus also grew in knowledge of his Jewish faith.

Scripture makes it clear that Jesus regularly attended religious festivals in Jerusalem. During one of these pilgrimage journeys to the Holy City, the twelve-year-old Jesus was separated from his parents and their companions. Later, Mary and Joseph found Jesus addressing teachers in the Temple. These educated men were astounded at the wisdom of this boy from Nazareth. Even as a boy, Jesus was already totally consecrated to his mission as God's Son. His growth and development in a remote Galilean village was quite ordinary in most respects, though in others it was extraordinary. Jesus was both God and man. His growth was also full of wonderful mystery.

The Baptism of Jesus (Mt 3:1-17)

The public life of Jesus began with his baptism by John the Baptist. John's mission was to prepare the way for Jesus. John preached a baptism of repentance for the forgiveness of sins. Jesus was without sin and did not need to be baptized for that purpose, which John immediately recognized. However, by freely submitting to baptism, Jesus accepted and launched his mission to be God's Suffering Servant. When Jesus humbly submitted to John's baptism, he was showing solidarity with all human beings who *do* need forgiveness. On his shoulders, Jesus bore the guilt of humanity and took it down into the waters of the Jordan River.

The identity of Jesus as the Messiah, the promised Redeemer, was revealed at his baptism. The Holy Spirit appeared above Jesus as a dove, and a heavenly voice proclaimed, "This is my beloved Son, with whom I am pleased" (Mt 3:17). This baptism pointed to our Christian Baptism. In the Sacrament of Baptism, we go down into the water with Jesus in order to rise with him. We are reborn in water and the Spirit. We become a new child of the Father and can then "walk in newness of life" (*CCC*, 537).

The Temptations of Jesus (Mt 4:1-11)

After he was baptized, Jesus retreated into the desert for forty days of prayer and fasting. This desert time helped Jesus prepare for his ministry. In the desert, Satan tempted Jesus three ways. The first temptation challenged Jesus to satisfy his hunger by turning rocks into bread. The second asked him to use his divine powers and throw himself from the Temple parapet. Angels could catch Jesus and many adoring followers would be won over to him. The third temptation promised Jesus worldly power if he would just worship Satan.

Jesus refused all three of Satan's temptations. Instead, he gave the Evil One three wonderful responses: "One does not live by bread alone, but by every word that comes from the mouth of God" (Mt 4:4). "You shall not put the Lord, your God, to the test" (Mt 4:7). And "The Lord, your God, shall you worship and him alone shall you serve" (Mt 4:10).

Jesus was tempted. But because he possessed a perfect freedom—and true freedom always chooses the good—he never succumbed to temptation. Therefore, Jesus never sinned. Think of Jesus as the New Adam, the sinless Adam before the Fall. Jesus was like Adam before he listened to and yielded to Satan's lies. By repudiating Satan, Jesus remained faithful to God. Unlike the Chosen People who often turned from God during their forty years in the desert, Jesus was always obedient.

Handling Temptations Today

What is the greatest source of temptation for people today? With a partner or in small groups, discuss these types of temptation. Along with the five temptations given, add one more that you think young people often face. Then, put these temptations in ranking order of frequency. (**1** for most commonly experienced temptation and **6** for least commonly experienced temptation.) Once you have ranked these six temptations, share your ranking with other groups in the class.

- Temptation to be dishonest
- Temptation to be greedy
- Temptation to make fun of those who are different
- Sexual temptation
- Temptation to use alcohol or drugs
- Temptation to ________________

For Review

1. What is a mystery?
2. Describe one of the mysteries in the life of Jesus.
3. What is the Epiphany? What did this event communicate about the ministry of Jesus?
4. Describe two events that took place during the "hidden life" of Jesus.
5. Why was John the Baptist surprised that Jesus came to him for baptism?
6. How did the Holy Spirit identify Jesus as God's Son at his baptism?
7. What were the three temptations presented to Jesus in the desert?

For Reflection

- What are some things you would like to ask Jesus if you could travel back in time to Nazareth during the years when he was your age?
- The temptations that Jesus faced involved food, fame, and power. What are some areas of temptation that you and your peers most often face?

Jesus Proclaims God's Kingdom (*CCC*, 543-550)

According to Matthew's Gospel, Jesus began his ministry after John the Baptist was arrested. Jesus left his hometown of Nazareth and went to live in Capernaum on the Sea of Galilee. Matthew quotes Isaiah who prophesied that the Messiah would begin his preaching ministry in Galilee. Matthew's attention to geographical detail emphasizes that Jesus really was a historical person who taught in a specific place at a specific time.

Christ's Ministry Begins in Capernaum (Mt 4:12-25)

Matthew summarizes Jesus' essential message this way: "Repent, for the kingdom of heaven is at hand" (Mt 4:17). Mark's Gospel gives a slightly fuller version of the same message, "This is the time of fulfillment. The kingdom of God is at hand. Repent and believe in the gospel" (Mk 1:15). **Kingdom of God** and **Kingdom of Heaven** are synonymous terms.

The first part of this message calls for conversion and repentance, a true sorrow and turning away from sin, with a firm purpose to sin no more in the future. The second part explains *why* this is necessary. God's power, judgment, and rule are now taking hold in human history. God's presence is active in love, forgiveness,

Kingdom of God or Kingdom of Heaven
The beginning of God's new reign on earth, which was to bring the forgiveness of sins, the healing of the sick, and the establishment of a time of peace and joyful living for all. Jesus, the Redeemer, initiated this new Kingdom.

healing, compassion, works of justice, and creative goodness. Moreover, as those who hear the words of Jesus quickly learn, Jesus himself is ushering in the Kingdom. God's ultimate and lasting victory is present in his Son, Jesus Christ.

This passage from Matthew also tells how Jesus selected his first four Apostles: Simon Peter, his brother Andrew, and the two sons of Zebedee, James and John. These men immediately left their nets and boats and followed Jesus. What an attractive and charismatic person Jesus must have been. He won the devotion of these working-class men immediately. In all, Jesus chose twelve men to be his followers. Gradually, he shared his authority with the Twelve and sent them out to preach about the Kingdom and heal the sick in his name. Jesus planned to build his Church on these twelve Apostles. He appointed Peter as their head, the rock. Peter's role was to guard the faith from false teachings. To Peter and his successors, the Popes, Christ gave the "power of the keys." That meant that they had the authority to govern the Church.

The Kingdom Is Open to All

One of the Apostles whom Jesus chose was Matthew, a tax collector. In general, the Jews despised tax collectors. Tax collectors collaborated with the Roman occupation that imposed cruel taxes on the Jews. Tax collectors then took some of those collected taxes and pocketed them. Fellow Jews despised tax collectors as traitors. When Jesus ate dinner at Matthew's house, pious Pharisees complained and wondered why he associated with such sinners. Jesus replied,

> Those who are well do not need a physician, but the sick do. Go and learn the meaning of the words, "I desire mercy, not sacrifice." I did not come to call the righteous but sinners. (Mt 9:12–13)

The Kingdom of God is open to sinners. But sinners, too, must repent. If they do, there will be great rejoicing in Heaven—just as there is great joy for

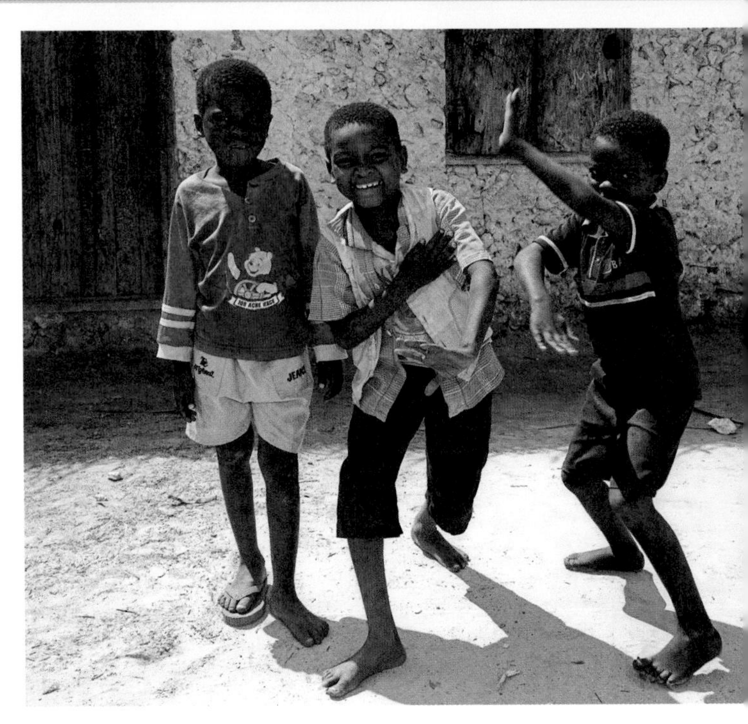

the shepherd when one lost sheep is found and returns to the fold. So great is the love Jesus has for sinners that he would sacrifice his own life "for the forgiveness of sins" (Mt 26:28).

The Poor and Lowly Are Beloved in the Kingdom (Mt 18:1-9; 19:13-14)

God's Kingdom belongs to all those who accept it humbly, like children would accept the gift of love. Jesus came to preach to the poor and declared them blessed "for theirs is the kingdom of heaven" (Mt 5:3). They are the "little ones." Jesus praised the Father for revealing the secrets of the Kingdom to those who are childlike (Mt 11:25), that is, open and accepting.

Jesus preached to the poor and to those who didn't seem to belong anywhere. He shared their lives. Especially, Jesus accepted the burdens of the poor. He also often experienced hunger and thirst. He knew what it was to be homeless: "Foxes have dens and birds of the sky have nests, but the Son of Man has nowhere to rest his head" (Mt 8:20). He taught that we should respond to the least in our midst. Those people are the hungry, the thirsty, those who are alone and abandoned. In them, we are responding to him. Active love of neighbor, and especially of the poor neighbor, is a condition for entering his Kingdom (Mt 25:31–46).

Messages about the Kingdom (Mt 13:44-46; 18:21-35; 25:14-30)

Jesus was unlike any other teacher who ever lived. He always challenged his audience with interesting messages about the Kingdom. What's more, Jesus was a wonderful storyteller. He told parables to underline important points. For example, in one of Jesus' parables, he told of a man who sold everything to purchase the field in which he had discovered a treasure. Another story was about a merchant who used his entire fortune to buy a very special pearl, a pearl of great price. What was Jesus trying to say in these stories? He was saying that we too must be willing to give up everything to gain the Kingdom. This Kingdom is worth it.

The Kingdom must also be active in our own lives. We must imitate our heavenly Father who forgives our sins. We must not be like the unmerciful servant (Mt 18:21–35) who refused to forgive his debtors. Jesus also told the Parable of the Talents to teach us not to hide the gifts God has given us. Instead, we must use them for the benefit of others.

This teaching style of Jesus also included the use of vivid images and challenging statements. For example, he taught that wealth is dangerous because it can make us think that we don't need God. Rich people sometimes believe that their money can buy them anything—even Salvation. But Jesus warned against such thinking when he said, "It is easier for a camel to pass through the eye of a needle than for one who is rich to enter the kingdom of God" (Mt 19:24).

The disciples were shocked when Jesus said this. They questioned him further, "Who then can be saved?" Jesus looked at them and said, "For human beings this is impossible, but for God, all things are possible" (Mt 19:25–26). In other words, no human effort and no human wealth can earn Salvation. Only God can accomplish that. This is why we need to be humble and childlike, admitting that without God, we are nothing.

In teaching the proper attitude to have toward God, Jesus often used a figure of speech called a **paradox**. A paradox is a statement that *seems* contradictory but contains a truth. Some people say that the more money they earn the less they seem to have. Successful business leaders sometimes admit, "Failure taught me all about success." At first, those statements don't make any sense. But there is a hidden truth when you consider them a second time. Consider the following paradoxical statements that Jesus makes:

- "Many who are first will be last, and the last will be first" (Mt 19:30).
- "Whoever wishes to be first among you shall be your servant;

paradox
A figure of speech or statement that *seems* contradictory but actually contains a hidden truth.

whoever wishes to be first among you shall be your slave" (Mt 20:26–27).

- "Whoever exalts himself will be humbled; but whoever humbles himself will be exalted" (Mt 23:12).

Jesus, God-made-man, is a perfect example of a paradox. Though he was the all-powerful Son of God, he humbled himself by becoming a man and by serving and dying for us. His love won Salvation for us. He called on those who wanted to be in his Father's Kingdom to imitate him: "The Son of Man did not come to be served but to serve and give his life as a ransom for many" (Mt 20:28).

The Miracles of Jesus (Mt 8:1-13; 9:1-7; 20:29-35)

Jesus performed many miracles to back up his words. These signs and wonders revealed that God's Kingdom really was present. They proved that he was the promised Messiah, the Son of God. These wonderful events invited people to believe in him.

Another way to look at the miracles of Jesus is to see them as signs of the Messianic age. They freed some people from hunger, injustice, illness, and even from death. However, the mission of Jesus was not to abolish all human suffering here on earth. It was to free us from the worst slavery, the slavery of sin. It is sin that keeps us from living as God's sons and daughters, and that causes all kinds of human evils.

The Church points to different types of miracles that Jesus performed.

- *Physical healings* demonstrate the power Jesus had over sin and reveal that the coming of God's Kingdom brings wholeness and true happiness.
- *Exorcisms*, that is, the driving out of evil spirits, established the power Jesus had over Satan and demons.
- *Nature miracles* (like calming the storm) attest to Jesus' power over the forces of nature, since all creation came about through him. As John's Gospel puts it, "In the beginning was the Word . . . and the Word was God. All things came to be through him, and without him nothing came to be" (Jn 1:1, 3).
- *Raising people from the dead*, and thus proving that he had mastery over life and death and was truly the Son of God.

Using Your Talents for the Kingdom

Here is a list of abilities and talents. Choose two that you are particularly good at. Or, think of abilities and talents you would add to the list. In your journal, describe how you could use one of your talents to further the work of God's Kingdom. Then follow through this week with putting this ability or talent into action.

- making friends
- teaching others
- listening
- caring
- leading
- problem solving
- working with children
- talking to the elderly
- being creative
- making music
- motivating others
- making people laugh
- helping others get a job done
- making peace
- fundraising
- showing compassion to others/empathy
- sticking to a task/persistence
- other: ________________
- other: ________________

All of the miracles of Jesus, of course, foreshadowed the great victory he was to win through his Death and Resurrection. This victory over the power of sin, Satan, and death won eternal Salvation for the rest of us.

These miracles also show us God's love, revealed again and again through his Son Jesus. For example, Jesus responded to the faith of the leper who asked him for a cure. Impressed with his faith, Jesus granted the sick man's wish. Moreover, Jesus even touched the leprous man, an act that everyone found repulsive. The sensitivity and compassion Jesus had for individuals are especially evident in this story.

Immediately after healing the leper, Jesus responded to the faith of a centurion. This was a non-Jew. This Gentile asked Jesus to cure his servant. Jesus was amazed at the faith in this soldier. Jesus told those around him that he had never found this kind of faith in any Jew. Jesus healed the centurion's servant immediately without even seeing him. In this story, it's easy to see that belief is important to Jesus. People who approach God with strong faith move him and his Father.

Faith also played a role in Jesus' healing of a paralyzed man (Mt 9:1–8). But this miracle story also had a great lesson. Before healing the man, Jesus told him that his sins were forgiven. This provoked an angry reaction from some of the scribes. They claimed that Jesus was guilty of the sin of **blasphemy**. They said that Jesus was claiming to be God. To show that he did indeed have the power to forgive sin, Jesus healed the man. In fact, Jesus was claiming to be God. He backed up his claim by performing this marvelous miracle. "When the crowds saw this they were struck with awe and glorified God who had given such authority to human beings" (Mt 9:8).

One final example of the miracles worked by Jesus was the healing of two blind men. They called to Jesus when they heard him passing by. They shouted, "[Lord], Son of David, have pity on us!" (Mt 20:30). Jesus turned back and spoke to them,

> "What do you want me to do for you?" They answered him, "Lord, let our eyes be opened." Moved with pity, Jesus touched their eyes. Immediately they received their sight, and followed him. (Mt 20:33–34)

Here again, Jesus responded to faith. A lesson for us is that Jesus wants us to tell him what we need. We must approach him and express our deepest needs. After Jesus cured these men, they followed him. Belief in Jesus is more than just words. We must put our faith to work. Our words must turn into deeds.

The Transfiguration of Jesus (Mt 17:1-13)

During the **Transfiguration**, Jesus revealed his divine glory. The event took place on a mountain in the company of Peter, James, and John. The face of Jesus "shone like the sun and his clothes became white as light"

blasphemy
Any thought, word, or act that expresses hatred or contempt for God, Christ, the Church, saints, or holy things. It is a grave sin, contrary to the Second Commandment.

Transfiguration
The glorious transformation of Jesus that manifested his divine identity for Peter, James, and John on a high mountain, probably Mount Tabor. The event, reported in all three Synoptic Gospels, also involved the appearance of both Moses and Elijah.

Paschal Mystery
The redemptive Passion, Death, Resurrection, and glorious Ascension of Jesus Christ through which Jesus not only liberated us from sin, but also gave us new life through his Resurrection.

(Mt 17:2). This special revelation of Jesus gave a foretaste of the Kingdom. Two Old Testament figures—Moses and Elijah—also appeared. Their presence symbolized that in the Law given to Israel through Moses and the prophets (Elijah was a great prophet) the sufferings of the Messiah had been announced.

The Transfiguration disclosed the divinity of Jesus. It confirmed Peter's confession of Jesus as "the Messiah, the Son of the living God" (Mt 16:16). This special vision also revealed all three Persons of the Blessed Trinity: the Father in the voice, the Son in Jesus, and the Holy Spirit in the shining cloud.

The Passion, Death, and Resurrection of Jesus (Mt 26:36-56; 27:27-56; 28:1-10)

Not long after his Transfiguration, Jesus went, for the last time, to Jerusalem. Three times, he had announced that his Passion and Resurrection would take place there in the holy city. He knew that prophets had been martyred in Jerusalem. Now his time had come. Jesus entered the city in triumph. Jerusalem welcomed him as the Son of David because he came in the name of the Lord. People asked who he was and the answer given was, "This is Jesus the prophet, from Nazareth in Galilee" (Mt 21:11).

Early in his last week, Jesus also showed courage and character when he cleansed the Temple. He overturned the tables of the moneychangers, saying, "My house shall be a house of prayer, but you are making it a den of thieves" (Mt 21:13).

On Holy Thursday, after Jesus celebrated the Last Supper with his Apostles, he went to the Garden of Gethsemane to pray. There, he experienced great agony as he foresaw the suffering and Death that awaited him. He prayed, "My Father, if it is possible, let this cup pass from me; yet, not as I will, but as you will" (Mt 26:39). Always, Jesus wanted to do his Father's will.

Peter, James, and John were the three Apostles Jesus chose to watch and pray with him. But these three men were weary and couldn't stay awake. They didn't support Jesus in his hour of agony. Jesus finally said to Peter, "The spirit is willing, but the flesh is weak" (Mt 26:41). Judas Iscariot, one of the Twelve, then led the authorities to Jesus in the Garden. Judas betrayed Jesus by identifying him with a kiss. Jesus, meanwhile, continued to refer to Judas as a friend (Mt 26:50).

Throughout the ordeal of his arrest, Jesus remained the Prince of Peace. He did not resist. He even admonished one of his disciples who drew his sword to fight back. This disciple cut off the ear of the high priest's servant. Jesus said, "Put your sword back into its sheath, for all who take the sword will perish by the sword" (Mt 26:52). Then all his disciples abandoned Jesus.

Jesus was then questioned by the high priest Joseph Caiaphas who told Jesus that he had been charged with the crime of blasphemy. The high priest turned Jesus over to Pontius Pilate, the Roman governor. Pilate then questioned, scourged, and condemned Jesus to Death.

The soldiers mocked, spat on, and forced Jesus to carry his cross. Near the cross, they divided his garments and nailed Jesus to the cross. They publicized his "crime" with a sign nailed to the top of the cross: "This is Jesus, the King of the Jews." Passing crowds reviled Jesus while some of the leaders mocked him, challenging him to save himself. Jesus endured their taunts quietly. Jesus asked his Father to forgive his persecutors because they did not know what they were doing (Lk 23:34). Finally, in great agony, Jesus died.

The Meaning of the Paschal Mystery

It's easy to see that Jesus accepted his Father's will, even if it meant that he would be killed. Jesus was the all-powerful God. He could have overpowered even ten thousand Roman soldiers who wanted to arrest him. But Jesus accepted torture, humiliation, and Death. He knew that this was not the end of the story. Christ descended to the dead to free the just who had died before him and were awaiting his redemption. And, on the third day after his Death, Jesus rose again. The Resurrection confirmed all of Christ's work and teachings. It also fulfilled all Old Testament promises and those made by Jesus himself during his earthly ministry.

By the **Paschal Mystery**, we mean the saving Passion, Death, Resurrection, and glorious Ascension of Jesus Christ. "The Paschal mystery has two aspects: by his death, Christ liberates us from sin; by his Resurrection, he opens for us the way to a new life. This new life is above all justification that reinstates us in God's grace" (*CCC*, 654).

The sacrifice Jesus made on our behalf repairs the broken relationship between God and humanity. The Paschal Mystery of Christ's total love bestows God's blessings on us. The Salvation won by Jesus Christ on the cross brings forgiveness for our sins and redeems us from sin, evil, and death. The Resurrection of Jesus and Jesus himself assure future resurrection for us.

This Paschal Mystery definitively identifies Jesus as our Savior. Hopefully, we will proclaim, as did the centurion and soldiers who witnessed his crucifixion, "Truly, this was the Son of God!" (Mt 27:54).

For Review

1. Where and how did the ministry of Jesus begin?
2. What were the two major messages Jesus gave the world when his ministry began?
3. Who were the first four Apostles? What do we know about them?
4. What is a paradox? Describe a paradox that Jesus used to teach a lesson.
5. Name and describe two types of miracles that Jesus performed.
6. What is blasphemy? Why did the Jews say that Jesus committed this sin?
7. What took place during the Transfiguration? Why did two Old Testament figures also appear with Jesus?
8. What is the Paschal Mystery?

For Reflection

- Imagine that you were with Peter, James, and John on the mountain when Jesus was transfigured. What would you ask or tell Jesus as you came down the mountain with him and the three Apostles?
- Review the parable about a camel and the eye of a needle that Jesus told in Matthew 19:24. Jesus wanted to warn people that wealth can distract us from knowing and loving God. Create your own short parable about the risks of having too much money.

Main Ideas

- Jesus is the Word of God, the most important word ever spoken. (p. 30)
- Scriptural background for the Incarnation is presented primarily in the Gospels of Matthew and Luke. (pp. 31–32)
- The Incarnation is the belief that the Word of God became flesh as Jesus Christ. (p. 31)
- Belief in the Incarnation is a distinctive belief of Christianity. (p. 31)
- The Annunciation is the angel Gabriel's announcement to the Virgin Mary that God wanted her to become the Mother of the Redeemer. (p. 31)
- The name *Jesus* means "YHWH is Salvation" or "Savior." (p. 31)
- The Nativity was the birth of Jesus Christ, the Son of God and the Redeemer. (pp. 32–33)
- Joseph was the husband of Mary and the foster father of Jesus. Joseph taught Jesus about Judaism and the trade of carpentry. (pp. 32–33)
- Docetism was a heresy that taught that Jesus only seemed to be human. (p. 33)
- Because of the Incarnation, God's great act of love, human beings can have everlasting life. (p. 34)
- We learn about Jesus through Church Tradition and Sacred Scripture; both comprise the Deposit of Faith. (pp. 35–36)
- History verifies that a man named Jesus did live and teach in Galilee and was executed near Jerusalem. (p. 36)
- The "real Jesus" of Christian faith is the resurrected Jesus. (pp. 38–39)
- Through the Seven Sacraments of the Church, the Risen Jesus remains with us. (pp. 39–40)
- We can also meet Jesus in prayer, in the institutional Church, and in other people. (p. 40)
- A "mystery" is a truth about God that human minds can never fully grasp or appreciate. (pp. 41–42)
- There are many mysteries about the Incarnation, Nativity, and Epiphany of Jesus. (pp. 41–43)
- Because little is known about the childhood and youth of Jesus, this period is called "the hidden life" of Jesus. (p. 43)
- The baptism of Jesus began his public ministry and showed his desire to be in solidarity with human beings. (pp. 43–44)
- Jesus was tempted by the devil in the desert in three different ways. (p. 44)
- Jesus began to minister and preach in Capernaum after his baptism. (pp. 45–46)
- The Kingdom of God and the Kingdom of Heaven refer to God's reign on earth and the Salvation of all through Jesus. (pp. 45–46)
- The Kingdom of God is open to all, including the poor, Jesus said. (p. 46)
- Jesus used parables, paradoxes, and vivid images in his teaching. (pp. 47–48)
- Jesus performed four different kinds of miracles—physical healings, exorcisms, nature miracles, and the raising of people from the dead. (pp. 48–49)
- Jesus was charged with blasphemy when he told a paralyzed man that his sins were forgiven. (p. 49)
- The Transfiguration revealed the divine glory of Jesus. (pp. 49–50)
- The Paschal Mystery is the saving Passion, Death, Resurrection, and glorious Ascension of Jesus Christ. (pp. 50–51)

Terms, People, Places

Match the following terms with the definitions below.

A. Annunciation
B. Blasphemy
C. Docetism
D. Epiphany
E. Incarnation
F. Jesus
G. Kingdom of God or Kingdom of Heaven
H. Mystery
I. Nativity
J. Paradox
K. Paschal Mystery
L. Presentation in the Temple
M. Resurrection
N. Transfiguration

1. ____ God becoming flesh.
2. ____ A rich image of the Church from St. Paul.
3. ____ The victory of Christ over death.
4. ____ Occurred forty days after the birth of Jesus.
5. ____ A word that means "YHWH is Salvation."
6. ____ The birth of Jesus.
7. ____ The announcement to Mary that she would be the Mother of the Savior, Jesus Christ.
8. ____ A truth about God and his saving plan that will always be beyond human understanding.
9. ____ A statement of disrespect for God's name or sacred truths.
10. ____ The Passion, Death, Resurrection, and glorious Ascension of Jesus Christ.
11. ____ A heresy that taught that Jesus only seemed to be human.
12. ____ A figure of speech or statement that seems contradictory but actually contains a hidden truth.
13. ____ The celebration of the manifestation of God in human form.
14. ____ An event reported in the Synoptic Gospels in which Jesus manifested his divine identity.

Primary Source Quotations

Our Unity with the Son of God

If Christ is with us, who is against us? You can fight with confidence where you are sure of victory. With Christ and for Christ victory is certain.

—St. Bernard

A man who was merely a man and said the sort of things Jesus said would not be a great moral teacher. He would either be a lunatic—on a level with the man who says he is a poached egg—or else he would be the Devil of Hell. You must make your choice. Either this man was, and is, the Son of God; or else a madman or something worse. You can shut Him up for a fool, you can spit at Him and kill him as a demon; or you can fall at His feet and call Him Lord and God. But let us not come with any patronizing nonsense about His being a great human teacher. He has not left that open to us. He did not intend to.

—C. S. Lewis

Welcome Christ into your lives. Without the experience of this interior meeting with Christ, life can all too easily be wasted on illusory and consumerist experiences. These obviously include the suicidal experience of drugs or the egoistic one of using our neighbor and rejecting solidarity.

—Pope John Paul II

Write down five things you believe about Jesus Christ. Rank your beliefs in order beginning with the belief you hold the strongest. Share your list with a classmate.

Ongoing Assignments

As you cover the material in this chapter, choose and complete at least three of these assignments.

1. View the film *The Nativity Story,* a film released in 2006 that stars Keisha Castle-Hughes as Mary and Oscar Isaac as Joseph. Write a film review from the perspective of how accurately it portrays the Gospel accounts of Jesus' birth narratives found in Matthew and Luke.
2. Report on some of the traditional views of the identity of the Magi. Begin your research by reading an overview of the subject in the entry found in the *Catholic Encyclopedia.*
3. Report on the Christmas customs from three different countries around the world.
4. Draw a map of the probable flight of the Holy Family into Egypt.
5. Create a PowerPoint presentation on some of the biblical sites associated with Bethlehem and Nazareth.
6. Create an illustrated lecture on St. Joseph in art through the ages.
7. Jesus always showed respect for others and was a model of obedience toward his parents and other rightful authorities. Write a letter to the editor of your local newspaper to share what you've learned from the life of Jesus about respect and obedience.
8. Write a profile of King Herod the Great. Report on some recent archaeological finds associated with him, for example, his tomb.
9. Construct a two-page newsletter—*The Bethlehem Gazette*—describing the birth of Jesus. Include articles on the shepherds, the Magi, and the political situation at the time. Include at least one graphic.
10. After reading Matthew's account of Jesus' arrest and crucifixion (Mt 26–27), retell the Passion story from the point of view of one of the Apostles or one of the soldiers who arrested, mocked, and crucified Jesus.
11. Read the following poetic Old Testament passage about honoring parents—Proverbs 6:20–23. Consider this Bible message carefully: children should show respect for their parents throughout their whole lives, especially when their parents are old, weak, and unable to care for themselves. In your journal, list five ways that you can show respect for your parents now.

Prayer

The famous Jesus Prayer, also known as the Prayer of the Heart, goes back to the fifth century. A faith-filled prayer, it invokes the power of the name of Jesus and begs his mercy. Emphasizing the humility of the one praying, the Jesus Prayer should be recited repeatedly as a form of meditation. Many Christians, especially Eastern [Catholic] Churches and Orthodox Christians, pray it often throughout the day to fulfill St. Paul's instruction to "pray without ceasing" (1 Thes 5:17).

A famous version of the Jesus' Prayer goes like this:

> Lord Jesus Christ, Son of God, have mercy on me, a sinner.

In this profound prayer, we proclaim:

- Jesus is God (Lord).
- Jesus is the Savior (the name *Jesus* means "God saves").
- Jesus is the Son of God.
- Jesus is merciful.

- We are sinners in need of our Lord's help and forgiveness.

- *Reflection*: What most needs forgiveness in your life right now? How do you most need Jesus?
- *Resolution*: Recite the Jesus Prayer slowly and thoughtfully at least twenty times. Reflect on the meaning of each word. Thank and praise the Lord for his forgiveness and love of you.

TRACING THE HISTORICAL LIFE OF JESUS

Since many have undertaken to compile a narrative of the events that have been fulfilled among us, just as those who were eyewitnesses from the beginning and ministers of the word have handed them down to us, I too have decided, after investigating everything accurately anew, to write it down in an orderly sequence for you, most excellent Theophilus, so that you may realize the certainty of the teachings you have received.

—Luke 1:1-4

- **One Solitary Life**
  Jesus' greatness did not come from any qualities that the world typically exalts, yet after more than two thousand years billions of people know and follow him.

- **Ancient Testimony about Jesus**
  Many non-Christian writers referred to Jesus, adding to objective verification that Jesus was truly a historical person.

- **The Gospels and the Historical Jesus**
  The four Gospels give us the most valid portrait of Jesus and his message. The evangelists said that Jesus not only taught the "Good News"; he is the "Good News."

- **The Reliability of the Gospels**
  The Gospels can be studied in a variety of ways through scholarly analysis that does not contradict the essential message that "Jesus is Risen" nor details between the four evangelists.

- **The Church and Martyrs**
  The dramatic witness of Christian martyrs provides further testimony of the life of Christ and the impact the Gospel had on his followers.

One Solitary Life

Here is a man who was born in an obscure village, the child of a peasant woman. He grew up in another village. He worked in a carpenter shop until he was thirty. Then for three years, he was an itinerant preacher.

He never owned a home. He never wrote a book. He never held an office. He never had a family. He never went to college. He never put his foot inside a big city. He never traveled two hundred miles from the place he was born. He never did one of the things that usually accompany greatness. He had no credentials but himself.

While still a young man, the tide of popular opinion turned against him. His friends ran away. One of them denied him. He was turned over to his enemies. He went through the mockery of a trial. He was nailed upon a cross between two thieves. While he was dying, his executioners gambled for the only piece of property he had on earth—his coat. When he was dead, he was laid in a borrowed grave through the pity of a friend.

Twenty long centuries have come and gone, and today he is a centerpiece of the human race and leader of the column of progress.

I am far within the mark when I say that all the armies that ever marched, all the navies that were ever built; all the parliaments that ever sat and all the kings that ever reigned, put together, have not affected the life of man upon this earth as powerfully as has that *one solitary life*!

You have probably read this famous mini-essay about Jesus before. By today's standards, Jesus lived far from the center of action. He certainly would not be considered one of the "beautiful people," a celebrity that media people fawn over. Yet, his life was the most remarkable one ever lived. It was life changing for all of humanity. Emperor Napoleon I of France (1769–1821) knew this when he said,

> I know men and I tell you that Jesus Christ is no mere man. Between him and every other person in the world there is no possible term of comparison. Alexander, Caesar, Charlemagne, and I have founded empires. But on what did we rest the creation of our genius? Upon force. Jesus Christ founded his empire upon love; and at this hour millions of men would die for him.

Yet, there remain those who doubt that Jesus ever existed. They claim that he was a myth invented by misguided people. Others say that although a Jewish teacher known as "Jesus of Nazareth" may have lived two thousand years ago, we can know virtually nothing about him because of the unreliability of the historical records.

These are serious charges because Christianity and Catholicism rise or fall on the actual historical existence of Jesus and the reliability of the Gospels. In this chapter we will look at the question of the historical existence of Jesus by examining several sources and related topics.

For Reflection

Emperor Napoleon had a high opinion of Jesus, even though he tried to conquer the world by force and didn't follow in the footsteps of Jesus, the Prince of Peace. Think about what you have heard or read about Jesus. What statement or evidence supports your faith in Jesus the most? Write or explain what that statement really means to you.

Statements about Jesus

Review the following ten statements about Jesus and choose five that are the most important statements for your own Christian faith. What statements might be important to someone thinking about becoming a Christian? Which statements would be unacceptable to a non-Christian?

1. Jesus is my Lord and Savior.
2. Jesus lives.
3. Jesus is both God and man.
4. I find Jesus in the Church and in my fellow Christians.
5. Jesus is love.
6. Jesus is my best friend.
7. Jesus is the Second Person of the Blessed Trinity.
8. I meet Jesus in prayer and the Sacraments, especially the Eucharist.
9. Jesus is the Messiah, the Son of God.
10. Jesus has conquered sin and death.

Ancient Testimony about Jesus

Although Jesus was a remarkable teacher, he did not leave any writings. His method of teaching was oral instruction, using memorable stories and sayings. Furthermore, we have no written records of Jesus of Nazareth that date from the years he lived, 4–6 BC—AD 30/33. However, there are many reasons why no credible historians today deny the existence of Jesus.

The Gospels and other New Testament writings date from the first century, only a few decades after the Death and Resurrection of Jesus. These writings tell us that there was indeed a unique person who inspired them. Furthermore, they refer to people (like Pontius Pilate and King Herod the Great) and events (like the destruction of the Jerusalem Temple) that other historical records can verify.

Outside the official canon of Sacred Scripture, there are numerous references to Jesus and early Christianity that date from the second century and beyond. Most of these materials come from members of the Church, and neutral observers might not consider them objective sources. This raises the question we will address in this section of the chapter: Are there any ancient historical records for the existence of Jesus that come from non-Christian sources? To put it another way, do ancient historians and writers mention Jesus?

The answer is "yes." Although these sources do not give us any detailed biographical information about Jesus, they strongly support the fact that a man named Jesus did exist during the time suggested by New Testament writings and the reports of early Christian writers. These important ancient, Roman, and Jewish writers made fascinating and important statements about the teacher from Galilee, Jesus.

Tacitus (ca. AD 56-117)

Cornelius Tacitus was a Roman senator and the greatest Roman historian. His two most important works were *Histories*, which covered the years AD 69–96, and *Annals*, an unfinished work that chronicled the reigns of four Roman emperors: Tiberius, Caligula, Claudius, and Nero. In the *Annals* (ca. AD 115), Tacitus writes of the famous "Great Fire" that broke out in Rome in the year AD 64 under the reign of the corrupt and notorious Emperor Nero. To deflect his own responsibility for the disaster, Nero blamed this fire on the Christians. He used it as an excuse to persecute them. Tacitus wrote:

> To suppress this rumor [that he had started the fire], Nero fabricated scapegoats—and punished with every refinement the notoriously depraved Christians (as they were popularly called). Their originator, Christ, had been executed in Tiberius's reign by the governor of Judea, Pontius Pilate. But in spite of this temporary setback the deadly superstition had broken out afresh, not only in Judea (where the mischief had started) but even in Rome. All degraded and shameful practices collect and flourish in the capital.

Tacitus likely checked official Roman records to compile his history. He is the only Roman historian to mention Pontius Pilate, though two Jewish writers—Josephus and Philo—tell of Pilate's harsh rule in Judea. Tacitus verified that the public ministry of Jesus took place during the reign of Emperor Tiberius. The evangelist Luke (Lk 3:12) also mentioned this important historical detail.

It's not hard to see the contempt that Tacitus had for Christianity. He described it as a degrading and shameful superstition that had made its way to Rome. He certainly was no Christian. But, neither did he deny the existence of Jesus Christ, the founder of this new religion. Tacitus also reported how Christians were arrested, mocked, and then crucified or torn to pieces by bloodthirsty dogs. He also noted that Nero soaked the corpses of Christians in oil and then burned them as torches.

Suetonius, Roman Historian (ca. AD 70-140)

Gaius Suetonius Tranquillus was a Roman writer, biographer, and friend of Pliny the Younger. In his *Lives of the Caesars*, he wrote (ca. 112) about an incident that took place in Rome during the reign of Emperor Claudius (41–54):

> He expelled the Jews from Rome on account of the riots in which they were constantly indulging, at the instigation of Chrestus.

Suetonius did make a mistake in this retelling of the Jewish expulsion from Rome in AD 49. He assumed that Jesus (whom he misnamed *Chrestus*) was there and responsible for the trouble. What most likely happened is that when the first Christians went to Rome's synagogues to preach about Jesus as the Messiah, they were met with bitter resistance and then riots. Claudius apparently believed that Christians and Jews were members of the same religious sect. Therefore, he banished them all after their public infighting.

Luke also referred to this incident in his Acts of the Apostles. He wrote of St. Paul who arrived in the city of Corinth around AD 50:

> [Paul] met a Jew named Aquila, a native of Pontus, who had recently come from Italy with his wife Priscilla because Claudius had ordered all the Jews to leave Rome. (Acts 18:2)

It's true that the writings of Suetonius did not reveal much about Jesus. But this Roman historian is important because he verifies that "Christians" were upsetting Roman authorities only a couple of decades after the Death and Resurrection of Jesus.

Pliny the Younger, Roman Historian (ca. AD 61-113)

Gaius Plinius Caecilius Secundus was the adopted son and also the nephew of the writer Pliny the Elder. He was also a senator, an important Roman lawyer, and a famous civilian administrator. He is most noted for his books of letters, many of which are literary masterpieces. The last volume of his letters was published after his death. It included his own correspondence with Emperor Trajan when he was governor of Bithynia (in modern Turkey) from 111–113.

These letters, the largest collection of administrative correspondence from Roman times, show that the author was a thoughtful governor who tried to be a good administrator. Letter 96 from Book 10 of Pliny the Younger's *Letters* includes references both to Christ and to Christians. Pliny wrote that he wasn't sure how best to deal with Christians who would not submit to Roman law and beliefs. Respectfully, he asked Trajan for advice on how Christians should be investigated, tried, and punished.

Pliny the Younger also reported that Christianity had spread so rapidly that the pagan temples had fallen into disuse. Merchants who sold sacrificial animals were in serious economic trouble. He explained that he had decided to release from prison anyone who denied that they were or had been Christians as long as they promised to worship pagan gods and the emperor. He also said that he would let go any person who reviled Christ because he heard that a Christian would never do such a thing.

Pliny did say that he was condemning to death any Christians who persisted in their Christian beliefs. He also informed Trajan that Christian practices included their worship of Christ on a determined day of the week at a celebration of the Eucharist. Pliny explained that Christians took an oath not to commit any crime, steal, commit adultery, or break promises.

Letter 96 by Pliny the Younger gave the impression that he saw Christians as foolish zealots but people who lived morally. He was concerned about the growth of what he called a "superstition" because it challenged the Roman practice of emperor worship. His letter was the first to give a non-Christian account of how Christians worship.

Trajan wrote back, reassuring Pliny that he had done well in dealing with the Bithynian Christians. The emperor confirmed that Pliny should punish any believing Christians who came to his attention, but also said that Pliny should not go looking for them. Trajan saw the Christians as potentially dangerous, but not so much of a threat that they had to be hunted down like criminals.

Josephus, Jewish Historian (ca. AD 37-101)

An important reference to Jesus comes from the important and colorful Jewish historian Flavius Josephus. Born Joseph ben Matthias in AD 37, Josephus commanded the Jewish forces in Galilee during the First Jewish Revolt (AD 66–70). The Romans captured him, but because he predicted that the commander-in-chief of the Romans in Palestine, Vespasian, would one day be emperor, his life was spared. Vespasian did become emperor in AD 69, and Josephus became his friend and a citizen of Rome.

Josephus wrote *The Jewish Wars* and a twenty-volume history of the Jews, the *Jewish Antiquities*.

These two works are a major source of historical information on life in the Holy Land under Roman rule.

In the *Jewish Antiquities*, Josephus tried to prove to the Romans and to the Jew-hating emperor Domitian (AD 81–96) that the Jews were a noble people. In the eighteenth book of the series, he mentioned John the Baptist, calling him a good man. In the twentieth book, he noted that Annas the Younger—the son of the high priest mentioned in the Gospels—put to death James the Just (in AD 62), the leader of the Christian Church in Jerusalem. He refers to this James as "the brother of Jesus who is called the Christ."

Of most interest, however, is his account of the Palestinian rule of Pontius Pilate (AD 26–36). It is a remarkable text and merits careful reading:

> Now about this time lived Jesus, a wise man, *if indeed he should be called a man*. He was a doer of wonderful works, a teacher of men who receive the truth with pleasure, and won over many Jews and Greeks. *He was the Christ.* And when Pilate, at the information of the leading men among us, sentenced him to the cross, those who loved him at the start did not cease to do so, *for he appeared to them alive again on the third day as had been foretold—both this and ten thousand other wonderful things concerning him—by the divine prophets.* Nor is the tribe of Christians, so named after him, extinct to this day.

As you probably noted, there is something strange about this passage. Scholars suspect that this passage does not come entirely from Josephus because parts of it sound as though a Christian believer wrote it. They think that a Christian copyist added certain passages to support Christian belief. Examples include the phrase, *"if indeed he should be called a man,"* references to Jesus as the Christ (Messiah), and his Resurrection. A non-believer would never have stated that Jesus was definitely the Messiah, that he rose from the dead, and that he fulfilled many prophecies. And it is certain that Josephus was not a follower of Jesus. The Church Father Origen maintained that Josephus never accepted Christianity.

Regardless of what Josephus either personally wrote or believed, he did not question the *actual historical existence* of Jesus or that Jesus was put to death at Pilate's order sometime between AD 26 AND 36. Further, Josephus stated that the followers of Jesus were very much on the scene at the end of the first century.

Thallus, Greek Historian

Another interesting tidbit of historical information is found in the writings of Thallus, a Greek historian who wrote about AD 55. His history of the eastern Mediterranean area from the period of the fall of Troy to about AD 50 has not survived. However, a passage of his writings was found in the historical writings of a third-century writer whose work, in turn, was preserved by a Byzantine historian (ca. 800).

This passage from Thallus concerned the earthquake and darkness that descended on the land when Jesus died (see Matthew 27:45). Thallus wrote that the darkness was caused by a natural eclipse of the sun. It appears that he was trying to refute the Christian belief that a miracle occurred at the time of Jesus' Death. What is interesting is that Thallus knew about Jesus and his Death and wrote about it even before any of the Gospels were written. This would make Thallus the first known ancient writer to confront some element of the Christian story in his writing.

Mara bar Serapion

Sometime after AD 73, perhaps in the second century, Mara bar ("son of") Serapion, a philosopher, wrote a letter in Syriac to his son. A version of this letter survived the ancient world and comes to us from the seventh century. In the letter, Mara talked about tyrants who made the mistake of killing their wise thinkers or rulers:

> What advantage did the Athenians gain from putting Socrates to death? Famine and plague came upon them as a judgment for their crime. What advantage did the men of Samos gain from burning Pythagoras? In a moment their land was covered with sand. What advantage did the Jews gain from executing their wise King? It was just after that their Kingdom was abolished. God justly avenged these three wise men: the Athenians died of hunger; the Samians were overwhelmed by the sea; the Jews, ruined and driven from their land, live in complete dispersion. But Socrates did not die for good; he lived on in the teaching of Plato. Pythagoras did not die for good; he lived on in the statue of Hera. Nor did the wise King die for good; He lived on in the teaching which he had given.

Scholars believe that the "wise King" refers to Jesus. Mara thought that there was a link between his death and the destruction of the Jewish nation by the Romans. He further mentioned that the teaching of this wise king lived on through the teachings he left his followers.

Lucian of Samosata (ca. AD 115-200)

Lucian was a Greek satirist. In one of his works, he mocked Christian faith and referred to some of their beliefs, including their belief in the resurrection after death. He said Christians follow the teachings of "that one," their founder and lawgiver who was crucified.

Celsus

Celsus was a late-second-century Greek philosopher who wrote a vicious attack on Christianity about AD 175. We learn of his writings from the Church Father Origen whose work, *Against Celsus*, preserves some of the false charges Celsus made against Jesus. For example, Celsus claimed that Jesus was illegitimate and that his father was a Roman soldier by the name of Panthera. Further, he claimed that Jesus went to Egypt to learn sorcery. It is clear that Celsus hated Christianity and hated Jesus Christ. However, he never denied the existence of Jesus Christ.

Babylonian Talmud

There is also a reference to Jesus in the Babylonian Talmud. That is a commentary on Jewish law that was written in the third century after Christ. One passage mentioned a certain Yeshu (Jesus) who practiced magic and led Israel away from true Jewish worship. It also reported that this man had disciples and that he was "hanged on the eve of Passover."

Collectively, these Roman, Greek, and Jewish sources do not tell us much about Jesus. But, they all acknowledge that Jesus *really* did exist. It would have been absurd for any ancient historian to make any other assertion. If there had never been a man named Jesus, how could anyone explain the movement that carried his name?

For Review

1. Give some reasons why it is important for Catholics that non-Christian sources validate that Jesus really existed.
2. Which of the resources above seems to be the most important? Why?
3. In the ancient world, some Roman emperors required people to worship them. What are some of the false gods people worship today? How are we enticed to do so?

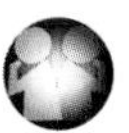

For Reflection

In your journal, write about who or what you might be willing to die for. If you were living in a setting where witnessing to your Catholic or Christian beliefs was punishable by death, would you do it?

Martyrs for the Faith

Conduct your own research and then write a one-page paper focused on those who suffer for their Christian faith. Write either about a canonized saint who died as a martyr or about Christians who are being persecuted for their faith today.

The Gospels and the Historical Jesus

evangelists
The authors of the four Gospels of the New Testament—Matthew, Mark, Luke, and John—and disciples closely associated with them.

Gospel
The "Good News," the story of the coming of the Savior, Jesus Christ, and the inauguration of God's Kingdom.

As excerpts from ancient Roman, Greek, and Jewish historians show us, references to Jesus outside the Bible do not tell us too much about him. However, they do verify that there was an actual, historical person, a man named Jesus who was put to death under Pontius Pilate during the reign of the Emperor Tiberius. These sources also verify that some Jewish leaders had a hand in the Death of Jesus. It is also clear from reading them that the followers of Jesus believed that he was the Messiah, a lawgiver, and founder of a new way of life.

Without a doubt, the New Testament gives the strongest proof that Jesus existed. It is from these writings, especially the four Gospels, that we learn the truth about him. The Gospels present a special kind of literature, that is, beautifully written faith summaries that tell how God was active in the Person of his Son, Jesus.

Though the Gospels are not biographies in the modern sense of the word, scholars do recognize in them many biographical elements that can be found in other ancient biographies. Ancient biographies were not exhaustive studies. For one thing, the length of the scrolls on which documents were written prevented long, detailed accounts of a person's life. Ancient biographies were not much interested in the youth or the physical appearance of a person. They also tended to focus on certain key events in a person's life, especially how a person died.

Retelling certain key events like this was seen as a way of understanding the character of the person. This pattern and orientation can also be seen in the Gospels. Certainly, we can conclude that the Gospel writers, the **evangelists**, wanted their readers to take as historical fact the episodes, events, and teachings that they did present in their writings about Jesus.

Gospel means "Good News." The four Gospels present the Good News of Jesus Christ. Their primary aim is to proclaim that God's Kingdom is active in the world and that Jesus Christ is God's Son and the principal agent of the Kingdom. They joyously announce that God profoundly loves us, and that Jesus died so that our sins could be forgiven and we could be saved and granted eternal life. The

ST. LUKE, THE EVANGELIST

In many ways, St. Luke, the evangelist, has written the most fascinating Gospel of the four. Luke, for instance, is the only Gospel writer to focus on Mary, the Mother of Jesus. He tells the story of Mary's Annunciation, her *Magnificat*, a timeless prayer of praise, and of her visit to Elizabeth, the mother of St. John the Baptist. Luke is also the only one who tells the tender story of the disappearance of the boy Jesus. It is also Luke's Gospel that shares the Parable of the Good Samaritan and the story of the rich man and poor Lazarus. This evangelist often focused on the faith of Gentiles (non-Jews), women, and the poor. So, his Gospel is often called "the Gospel of the poor." It was a Gospel that tried to show that God's Kingdom was open to all.

Luke himself was a Gentile, a native of Antioch, and a Greek, rather than a Jew. Some scholars also suggest that he may have been a slave who was trained as a physician. The practice of giving slaves medical training was common in the ancient world.

Luke was also a loyal companion of St. Paul the Apostle after AD 51. The Acts of the Apostles, written by Luke, includes numerous references to Paul's travels that obviously included himself.

The Gospel of Luke is also hailed for its historical accuracy and solid literary presentation. One modern historian said that Luke's Gospel and the Acts of the Apostles referred to thirty-two countries, fifty-four cities, and nine islands without making a single geographical or historical error with regard to them. Luke knew what he was talking about!

Ancient traditions suggest that Luke died at the age of eighty-four in Boetia, a city in Greece. The feast day of St. Luke is October 18. The symbol for this evangelist is the ox, often the animal of Jewish sacrifice.

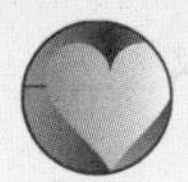

Portrait of Jesus

Although the Gospels contain no physical description of what Jesus looked like, this has not prevented artists through the ages from painting their own portrait of him. What do you think Jesus looked like? Picture him in your imagination. Imagine that you are either Peter or Mary Magdalene. Now, write a short letter (an epistle) to a friend in Rome. In the letter, describe Jesus. Tell your friend what your Master looks like and what he is like as a person. Be prepared later to share what you wrote.

Gospels also spread the message that Jesus who was put to death rose from the dead.

Jesus lives at the right hand of the Father, and has sent his Spirit to dwell in us and form us as a Church community. The Gospels tell us that Jesus himself is the Gospel, that he *is* the Good News. He reconciles us with God. He has won for us Salvation. The historical facts about Jesus in the Gospels are all given in light of the basic message of his saving activity. For all the Gospels, the Paschal Mystery—our Lord's Passion, Death, and Resurrection/glorification—is the central saving act and fact of his life story. These events take center stage in the story of Jesus.

The Writing of the Gospels (CCC, 124-127)

As you already learned, there were three stages involved in the writing of the Gospels: (1) the period of the public life and teaching of Jesus; (2) a period of oral tradition and preaching by the Apostles and early disciples of Jesus; and, finally (3) the period in which the Gospels themselves were written. Let's look at those three stages more thoroughly.

Stage 1: The Historical Jesus (4-6 BC—AD 30/33)

Jesus was born in Bethlehem in Judea between 4 and 6 BC. He lived a normal Jewish life in Nazareth in Galilee during his youth. He learned the carpentry trade from his foster father, Joseph, and probably began a public life around AD 28.

He was named *Jesus*, which we learned means "Savior." His surname might have been one of the following:

- *Jesus from Nazareth* or *Jesus the Nazarene*. It was common to identify people by their place of residence. Nazareth was a small, hilly, agricultural town in northern Palestine in the region known as Galilee. For some Jews living at this time, Nazareth was considered an insignificant and backward place. In today's way of thinking, someone from Nazareth would probably have been seen as unsophisticated. This explains Nathaniel's sarcastic remark when Philip told him that the Messiah had come from Nazareth. Nathaniel replied, "Can anything good come from Nazareth?" (Jn 1:46).
- *Jesus the Carpenter*. Sometimes people received adopted names because of their professions. In a similar way, the common English surname *Smith* designates a blacksmith or whitesmith (a trade practiced by a tinsmith or ironworker who finishes iron but doesn't forge it). Mark's Gospel informs us that Jesus worked as a carpenter before he began to preach.
- *Jesus, son of Joseph* (in Aramaic/Hebrew, *Jesus, bar/ben Joseph*). People were often known by their fathers' names. Even today, common Hispanic surnames like *Sanchez* ("son of

Sancho") and *Martinez* ("son of Martin") are derived from fathers' names. Jesus was called by his foster father's name, for example, in John 6:42 and Luke 4:22. Mark alone designates Jesus by his mother's name, "the son of Mary" (Mk 6:3), probably because Joseph had died.

During his public life, Jesus traveled the countryside and into the small towns teaching, healing, and proclaiming the coming of God's Kingdom. He made it to Jerusalem for the great feasts. But finally, after three years, the ministry of Jesus came to an end. On the fourteenth day of the month of Nisan on the Jewish calendar, the Roman prefect Pontius Pilate had Jesus of Nazareth crucified. It was done with the cooperation of some Jewish leaders who saw Jesus as a threat. Pilate affixed a sign on the cross on which Jesus was crucified that called him "King of the Jews." This took place in the year AD 30 or perhaps AD 33.

The disciples closest to Jesus were, at first, frightened and confused by his Death. But then, on Easter Sunday, they claimed to have seen Jesus after his Death and burial! They were convinced that Jesus was alive and glorified as God's Son. He had come to them by the power of the Holy Spirit. Their hearts burned with love and joy and excitement. A few weeks later, on Pentecost Sunday, they began to proclaim to the world the Gospel of Jesus Christ and the message of his Salvation.

Stage 2: Oral Tradition (AD 30-50)

The disciples began to live in the light of Christ's Resurrection. With the help and graces of the Holy Spirit, they now knew that Jesus was the Messiah, the Promised One, the Son of God, and the Lord. The Apostles remembered that Jesus had commanded them to "Go out to the whole world; proclaim the gospel to all creation" (Mk 16:15). At first, they traveled only through the Holy Land, announcing the marvelous things that God had accomplished in Jesus. Remaining pious Jews, the early Christians believed that Jesus was the very fulfillment of God's Old Testament promises. He was the New Testament—the new covenant between God and humanity. However, when their message met with resistance from their Jewish brothers and sisters, Christians began to preach throughout the Roman Empire. Their preaching took three key forms.

Kerygma

One form of early preaching by the early Christians was called **kerygma**, a preaching style that was particularly appropriate for unbelievers. The Acts of the Apostles gives us several sermons that Sts. Peter and Paul preached about Jesus. To help them in this preaching challenge, these two great Apostles spoke, referring often to a basic outline about the life of Jesus. This outline recapped the works, teachings, Death, Resurrection, and Ascension of Jesus.

In these talks, the Apostles also used many passages from the Hebrew

kerygma
A form of preaching used in the early Church that presumed an audience of unbelievers.

Scriptures to show how the prophecies made about the Messiah were fulfilled in Jesus. During this Kerygma period, the disciples slowly began to assemble collections of materials about Jesus—for example, the miracle stories, parables, and the Passion narrative. Later, the four evangelists drew on these sources to help compose their Gospels.

Didache

Another form of early preaching was referred to as the **didache** or essential "teaching" about Jesus Christ. This oral teaching approach involved further catechetical instruction for those who had already accepted Jesus. The word *catechesis* has the same Greek root and literally means to "sound down," that is, to repeat the message and explain it in greater depth. Early converts needed further knowledge about how to live a more Christ-filled life. For example, they were instructed with lists of sayings from Jesus. For example, sayings from Christ's Sermon on the Mount, which we find in Matthew 5–7, were probably assembled to help in this instruction.

didache
A word that means "teaching" that described oral teaching to those who had already accepted Jesus.

The Liturgy

The **liturgy** was still another way to "preach" the Good News about Jesus. The word *liturgy* meant "public work" but referred to the public, communal worship of Christians. The way people pray reflects their beliefs. The celebration of the Eucharist helped to shape many of the Jesus stories that the Church preserved. Certain important events, teachings, and prayers of Jesus were recalled in the early Eucharistic celebrations. Some examples of this include the words Jesus spoke at the Last Supper, the Lord's Prayer, and the story of Jesus' Passion. In some cases, some Christian communities slightly altered the wording of what was remembered. However, they always faithfully recounted the spirit of what Jesus did and said.

liturgy
The public worship and communal worship of the Church.

The Jesus material that was proclaimed, taught, and celebrated in liturgy was slowly shaped by different Christian communities. The early preachers and teachers' primary interest was to interpret the *meaning* of the key events, deeds, and sayings of Jesus. They wanted to enliven the faith of Christians. As a result, they did not set out to report a full-blown biography of Jesus. However, what they remembered, saved, and proclaimed was the heart of the message Jesus gave us. It related to the Hebrew Scriptures and was adapted to the audiences who heard it.

It is important to note, too, that although the four canonical Gospels were composed between AD 65–100, preaching about Jesus based on *oral* traditions carried on well into the second century.

Stage 3: The New Testament Writings (AD 50-ca.120)

The final stage in the process of Gospel development was the actual writing of the Gospels and other New Testament books. The earliest New Testament writings are the letters of

St. Paul. Then came the four Gospels and other writings like the Acts and the book of Revelation. When St. Luke began his Gospel, he tells us that he examined the sources, including those from eyewitnesses, and then organized the material into that beautiful literary form known as the Gospel (see the quotation on page 58).

You may wonder why it took twenty or more years before the early Christians wrote anything down. In the first century, the ordinary way of teaching and learning was through oral transmission. For his part, Jesus taught with easy-to-remember vivid stories, short sayings, striking images, poetic language, and other rhetorical devices. (See below for some examples.) Typically, ancient people had remarkable memories, especially compared to us who rely more on the printed word, computers, and visual images. But eventually the oral preaching about Jesus and his teaching had to be committed to writing for three major reasons:

1. The end of the world was not coming as quickly as the early Christians at first thought it would. The first generation of Christians believed that Jesus would come back "to judge the living and the dead" sometime in their lifetimes. And so at first, they didn't see any reason to write anything down. There were more urgent things to do, like preaching the Gospel and preparing for the Lord's return. However, they gradually saw that they were wrong about the hour of the Second Coming of Christ. Eyewitnesses began to die or, even worse, be put to death. It was soon seen that preserving the apostolic testimony about Jesus should be done in writing.
2. Distortions were setting in. This reason is related to the first. The New Testament itself gives evidence that after the Apostles preached in many communities, someone would come along and start to distort their message. A similar phenomenon was described in Chapter 2

EXPLAINING THE FAITH

What should Catholics believe about the "end of the world"?

In the Apostles' Creed, Catholics do profess the belief that Jesus "will come again to judge the living and the dead." Right before his Ascension, Jesus had reminded them, "It is not for you to know times or seasons which the Father has fixed by his own authority." He was telling them that no one on earth would know when he would return. It's clear from the Acts of the Apostles, however, that the earliest followers of Jesus assumed that this "second coming of Jesus" would come during their own lifetimes. They thought Jesus was coming soon and that the world would end with this judgment. The Church teaches that Jesus will come for the Last Judgment. Since Jesus was the Redeemer of all, he will also be the judge of all. God the Father, as the letter to the Ephesians states, "has put all things under his feet." Today, Catholics are reminded to "watch and wait" for this final stage in the establishment of God's Kingdom. We should remain prepared, ready for the return of Jesus, Our Lord and Judge. Catholic teaching also reminds us, however, that we should go on with our lives, doing the things that are expected of us each day.

when the Docetists preached that Jesus only seemed to have a body. To combat heretical teachings, early Christians needed an objective written record of their beliefs—hence, the New Testament. Even the author of John's Gospel was insistent in saying that the Word of God became flesh. He wanted his readers, and all future generations of Christians, to know for certain that Jesus was indeed both God and man.

3. More instruction was needed. It was also recognized that a written record of the Apostles' preaching could serve as a teaching device for Christians who needed more instruction. These writings could also be used in worship services. So, once the Gospels were written, the Christian community would be able to include readings from their sacred Scriptures in their Eucharistic celebrations. Finally, the Church saw that it would be able to circulate writings. Copies of St. Paul's letters, for example, could be sent to the growing Christian communities. They would provide further instruction and could help strengthen the faith of new converts.

Canonical Gospels

Based on Apostolic Tradition, the Church later developed an official list of inspired books to be included in the canon, that is, the official list of sacred books. The canon of Sacred Scripture includes forty-six Old Testament books and twenty-seven New Testament books, including the four Gospels. The Church used three major criteria for including the Gospels of Matthew, Mark, Luke, and John in the official canon:

1. *Apostolic origin.* All four Gospels were written in the first century and were based on eyewitness testimony. The evangelists all had contact with the Apostles of Jesus and preserved their testimonies about him.

WHY DO WE SAY THAT JESUS WAS BORN IN A BC YEAR?

In AD 525, a generation after the last Roman emperor was deposed, Pope John I instructed the monk-mathematician, Dionysius Exiguus (literally, Dennis the Little) to calculate the dates upon which future Easters would fall. This was a difficult task given the tradition of celebrating Easter on the first Sunday after the first full moon following the spring equinox. Dennis studied the positions of the moon and sun and produced a chart of the future Easters, beginning in 532. He calculated this new date based on the reputed birth date of Jesus Christ. His new dating was based neither on the old Roman calendar that began with the founding of Rome (753 BC on our calendar) nor on a newer Roman calendar that began in the first year of the reign of Emperor Diocletian. Diocletian had launched a bloodthirsty persecution of Christians in AD 248 on our calendar.

Instead, Dennis wanted to count the years from the birth of Jesus to promote the Good News of our Salvation in Christ. Dennis figured that Jesus was born in 754 on the Roman calendar and thus began the new Christian calendar at a year he designated as AD 1. (There was no year 0 because Roman numerals do not have a 0. Thus our calendar goes from 1 BC to AD 1. *AD* stands for *Anno Domini*—"in the year of the Lord;" BC means "before Christ.") However, Dennis got his dates wrong. Modern scholars have determined that Dennis's calculations were off four to six years. Both Matthew and Luke's Gospels claim that Jesus was born toward the end of the reign of Herod the Great. The Jewish historian Josephus tells us Herod died in 4 BC. Therefore, Jesus was most probably born around the time of Herod's death, that is, anywhere from 4-6 BC or so.

2. *Widespread acceptance.* Books to be included in the canon of the Bible also had to be circulated and accepted, the Church declared. This was true of the four Gospels.
3. *Conformity to the rule of faith.* Canonical writings needed to reflect the traditional faith of the early Church about Jesus and his teachings. These writings could not deviate from that truth by teaching something that contradicted what Jesus was known to have said. Heretical writings were both excluded and condemned because they taught something contrary to the faith and directed believers away from true teaching about Jesus Christ.

Some books that did not make it into the canon of the Bible include the so-called **apocryphal gospels**. The term *apocryphal* means "hidden." Most apocryphal writings were excluded because they were written from the second through the fourth centuries, many years after the apostolic era. They were therefore viewed as unreliable. Others were obviously fictional accounts. For example, the *Protoevangelium of James*, which attempted to fill in some details about the childhood years of Jesus, was clearly apocryphal.

The Church saw these works as fictional and not worthy of belief. Still, other writings were clearly heretical and were thus condemned by the Church. They taught things about Jesus that were clearly opposed to what the Apostles taught or believed.

Anno Domini
A Latin phrase meaning "in the year of Our Lord" used in reference to events that took place after the birth of Jesus Christ.

apocryphal gospels
A group of writings about the life and teaching of Jesus that do not meet Church criteria for inclusion in the New Testament canon. The term *apocryphal* means "hidden." Most apocryphal writings date from the second through the fourth centuries, many years after the Apostolic era.

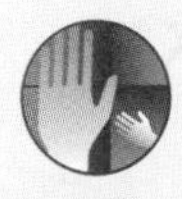

Looking More Carefully at Prejudice

When Nathaniel heard where Jesus came from, he exhibited prejudice toward Jesus (see John 1:46). *Prejudice* means "pre-judgment," that is, judging without having all the facts. Unfortunately, prejudice is an all-too-common part of the human condition. One of the first ways to overcome prejudice is to recognize that we are all afflicted with it in some ways. The next step is to try to keep an open mind about people and give them the benefit of the doubt. A third part of this approach is to counteract our prejudices by going out to meet and greet members of groups that we have prejudged. Try the following:

1. Think of a student that you have prejudged (or are currently prejudging) for one reason or another.
2. Try to identify the reason for this prejudice in you.
3. Then, make a plan to talk to meet this person.
4. Follow through on your strategy.

To Carry Your Plan Further: Create a plan to encourage students to break down social barriers that separate various groups at school, particularly during the lunch hour.

Gnosticism
A heresy from the first Christian centuries that taught that Jesus shared secret information or knowledge with only a few people who were guaranteed Salvation. Gnosticism comes from *gnosis*, the Greek word for "knowledge." Gnosticism also distrusted material creation, teaching that the human body was evil.

Synoptic Gospels
The Gospels of Matthew, Mark, and Luke that have so much content in common that they are often studied side by side. The word *synoptic* comes from the Greek word for "to see together."

An example in this category is the recently discovered Gospel of Judas. Like many other early apocryphal writings, the Gospel of Judas contained misleading teachings from a heresy known as **Gnosticism**. This heresy came from the Greek word for knowledge. Gnostic heretics believed that Jesus shared secret information or knowledge with only a few people. Having this knowledge assured a person of Salvation.

Gnosticism also distrusted material creation and taught that the human body was evil. In particular, the Gospel of Judas portrayed Judas as a hero and that he was the only Apostle to whom Jesus taught the true Gospel. These teachings, of course, contradict what the four Gospels taught about Judas and Jesus.

Perhaps the most famous non-canonical gospel is the Gospel of Thomas, an ancient writing discovered in 1945 at Nag Hammadi in Egypt. This Gnostic gospel was probably written sometime in the second century. Unlike the four Gospels, the Gospel of Thomas has no narratives about the birth, life, miracles, Passion, or Death of Jesus. It simply contains one hundred and fourteen sayings or "secret teachings" that Jesus reportedly gave to his Apostle Thomas. Some of these sayings parallel what we have in the canonical Gospels. But others claim to give secret *gnosis* (Greek for "knowledge") that guarantees immortality.

Like all Gnostic writings, the Gospel of Thomas takes a dim view of material reality and clearly contradicts teachings Jesus gave about the nature of God's Kingdom. Furthermore, it demeans the female gender, even teaching that a woman cannot enter Heaven without becoming a male. It is easy to see why the Church readily excluded such bizarre ideas and writings from the New Testament canon.

Four Gospels

The first verse of the Gospel of Mark reads: "The beginning of the gospel of Jesus Christ [the Son of God]" (Mk 1:1). This opening verse makes a very important point. It tells us that there is only one Gospel—the Person of Jesus Christ. Jesus himself is the Good News of God's immense love for us. The Church, however, recognizes four faithful expressions of this Good News, namely, the four written Gospels. These four Gospels—Matthew, Mark, Luke, and John—are the most important part of the New Testament canon because they are:

1. authentic testimonies of faith in Jesus Christ, the Son of God;
2. inspired writings;
3. written;
4. communal expressions of the Good News of Jesus.

Although these four Gospels were written for four different audiences, they all shared the same Good News about Jesus. Think of it this way. Imagine your mother, sister, best friend, and favorite teacher all writing a letter of recommendation to a prospective employer on your behalf. Each would be describing the *real* you, but each would have a unique perspective. Now imagine that they were writing not to a prospective employer, but to a relative in another state whom you had never met. Each of the letters describing your various qualities would be slanted in a different way depending on the person receiving the letter.

Something similar happened in the writing of the Gospels. The perspective of each Gospel differed because different people were composing them at different times and in different places. Each Gospel reflects the particular insights of its author. Further, each Gospel was written to and for a particular local church and was tailored to meet the concerns of that community. All four Gospels present the Good News of Jesus, but they adapt their presentation to the religious needs of the intended audience.

The more you read the Gospels, the more you will notice how closely related the first three are. For example, about 80 percent of Mark's 661 verses appear in Matthew's Gospel. About 65 percent of Mark's material appears in Luke. Scholars study these three Gospels side by side, calling them the **Synoptic Gospels**, from the Greek term *syn opt,*

EXPLAINING THE FAITH

Why shouldn't the apocryphal gospels be included in the Bible?

Some Catholics ask why the apocryphal gospels, ancient texts about Jesus, can't be included in the Bible. The Gospel of Judas, in particular, received extensive media attention. Discovered in Egypt in the mid-1970s, it was carbon dated to about AD 280. A translation of it was completed in 2006 by the National Geographic Society, which also produced a television documentary about it. This manuscript is a dialogue between Jesus and Judas in which Jesus praises Judas as the only disciple who understands him and his message. Jesus gives Judas "secret" knowledge that will assure his Salvation. According to this Gnostic "Gospel," Christ also ordered Judas to turn him over for arrest and execution. In fact, the Church views the New Testament canon as complete. Nothing new will be added. Apocryphal writings are interesting but unreliable for learning what Jesus really taught. Three criteria used by the Church to evaluate sacred texts would certainly eliminate apocryphal texts. The criteria are:

1. Apostolic origin (Can the text be traced to the Apostles who heard Jesus?)
2. Widespread acceptance (Was the text widely circulated and accepted?)
3. Conformity to the rule of faith (Does the text conform to the truth of already accepted inspired writings?)

which means "to see together." On the other hand, less than 10 percent of the Synoptic Gospel material appears in John's Gospel.

Most scholars believe that when Matthew and Luke wrote their Gospels, their primary source was Mark's Gospel. This is why so much of his Gospel appears in theirs. Matthew and Luke also have around two hundred additional verses in common. A widely accepted theory is that in addition to Mark's Gospel, they must have had a common source of sayings of Jesus when they composed their Gospels. Scholars designate this source as *Q* (from the German word *Quelle*, which means "source"). Finally, both Matthew and Luke had their own special material as a third source—usually designated *M* for Matthew's unique material and *L* for Luke's unique material. John's Gospel was the last written. It is the most highly developed Gospel theologically and did not depend on any of the other three Gospels.

Gospel	Author	Date	Audience	Theological Themes
Mark	Traditionally held to be John Mark, a traveling companion of Sts. Peter and Paul; perhaps anonymous	Shortly after the death of Peter (AD 64), perhaps between 65–70	Gentile Christians who were being persecuted for their belief in Jesus	Jesus is the Messiah but also the Son of Man who suffered; Christians should remain faithful to Jesus in their own time of suffering
Matthew	An anonymous Jewish-Christian scribe; may have drawn on an earlier work in Aramaic by the Apostle Matthew	After the destruction of the Jerusalem Temple (AD 70); most likely in the 80s	A Jewish-Christian Church probably in Antioch, Syria	Jesus fulfills Old Testament prophecies concerning the Messiah; Jesus ushers in God's Kingdom
Luke	A Gentile Christian; perhaps St. Paul's coworker and friend, Luke the physician; also wrote the Acts of the Apostles	AD 85	A Gentile Church	Jesus is the compassionate Savior who came for all people, especially the poor, Gentiles, women, the outcast; the Holy Spirit works in Jesus
John	Written and edited by close disciples of St. John the Apostle, the "Beloved Disciple"	AD 90–100	A diverse group, including Jewish-Christians who were expelled from synagogues after the Roman Revolt	(Written to strengthen faith and win converts) Jesus is superior to all prophets, including John the Baptist; Jesus is the Word of God, true God and true man, the source of eternal life

The chart on the previous page gives an overview of the four Gospels. Especially notice the intended audience and major theological themes of each of the Gospels.

For Review

1. How are the Gospels of the New Testament written in the style that ancient biographies were written?
2. What does it mean to say, "Jesus himself is the Gospel"?
3. Name and describe the three stages involved in the writing of the Gospels.
4. Explain why the Gospels have several different surnames for Jesus. How did surnames develop in the ancient world?
5. What were the kerygma and didache forms of preaching? How did they differ?
6. What were the three reasons that the Gospels were finally written?
7. What three standards did the Church use to judge sacred books?
8. What are the apocryphal gospels? Describe one of these gospels and its basic message.
9. What are the synoptic gospels? Why do scholars look at them as a group?
10. How is John's Gospel significantly different from all the rest?

For Reflection

- The Gospels deal with the Good News. Considering your life as you live it right now, what is the best news that you could personally hear? Note how your good news is in any way related to the Good News of Jesus, his love for you, and your eternal life.
- Imagine that you are a writer and committed follower of Jesus living in the early days of Christianity. You understand that your words will not be powerfully inspired as were those of the four evangelists, but you still feel called to humbly write your own "gospel" about Jesus. Focus in on a single event or period in the life of Jesus. Write about it in your journal and then share it with others.

The Reliability of the Gospels

Biblical scholars have developed many ways of studying the Gospels in a "critical" way. In this context, the word *criticism* means "the analysis, evaluation, judgment, and investigation of a written text."

Source criticism, for example, tries to determine what sources the Gospel writers used to compose their works. One of its findings is that

source criticism
The study by Scripture scholars to determine what sources the Gospel writers used to compose their works.

form criticism
A type of literary criticism used by Scripture scholars that analyzes and compares different literary forms used in the Gospels.

redaction criticism
A scholarly approach to the study of Scripture that attempts to see how each of the Gospel writers edited, or redacted, materials for that Gospel's audience.

textual criticism
Scripture study that looks to the various early manuscripts of the biblical texts.

historical criticism
An approach to Scripture analysis that tries to discover what evangelists really wanted to say when they wrote a particular text.

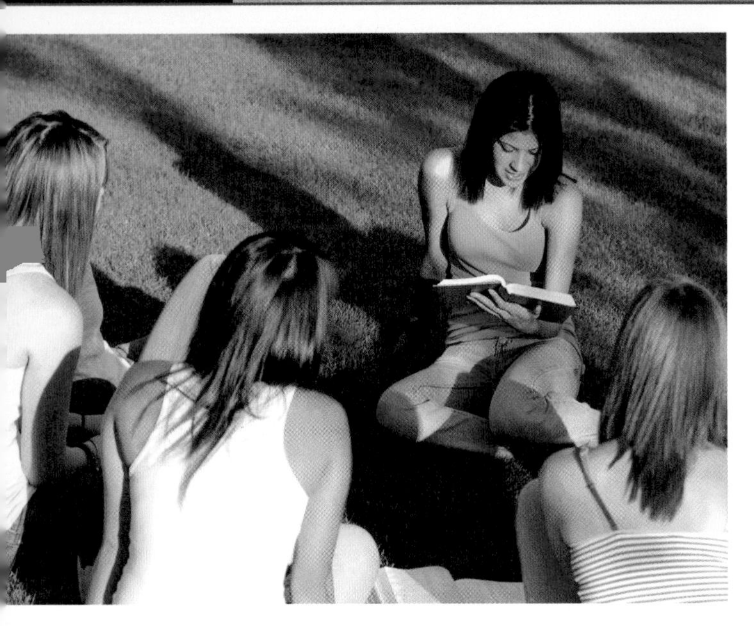

Matthew and Luke both had a common source, Q, as noted earlier.

Form criticism, on the other hand, looks to the different literary forms that are used in the Gospels. For example, it notes different forms like genealogies, prayers, and long discourses. Knowing what a particular literary unit is helps in its correct interpretation.

Redaction criticism studies how each of the Gospel writers edited (that is, redacted) his materials for his particular audience. For example, this type of scholarly study has noticed how often Matthew quotes Old Testament passages because he is writing for Christians who converted from Judaism. His audience would have been familiar with the Old Testament prophecies concerning Jesus. Matthew made a point of quoting the Old Testament to show how Jesus did indeed fulfill all the promises made to the Chosen People.

Textual criticism analyzes texts by comparing the text to various early manuscripts of biblical texts. It is interesting to note here that there are hundreds of handwritten Greek copies of the New Testament books, dating from around AD 150. In fact, there are more copies of the Gospels and other New Testament writings written near the dates of their composition than there are of any other ancient writing. Furthermore, in comparing the texts that come down to us, scholars have discovered that the differences between the vast majority of the copies are minor. These two facts alone reassure us that the Gospels have faithfully come down to us through two thousand years. They are, in fact, more reliable than *any* other piece of ancient literature known to humanity!

One other method of studying the Gospels and other biblical writings is **historical criticism**. It tries to do a number of things. For example, it attempts to discover what the evangelists really wanted to say when they wrote a particular text. This is called the literal sense of the text, that is, the determination of what the biblical authors intended and conveyed by what they wrote. Historians use knowledge of ancient languages, dating techniques, customs, traditions, archaeology, and so forth to determine the literal sense.

Historical criticism also tries to determine the probability that what the Gospels report about Jesus can indeed be traced directly to him. They have developed certain criteria like originality (the "criterion of dissimilarity"), linguistic analysis, and consistency of content to help get back to the historical Jesus. The findings of historical criticism prove beyond the shadow of a doubt that there was a unique teacher, a brilliant mind—a genius if you will—who is behind the Gospels. They definitely demonstrate that there was indeed a Jesus of Nazareth, the one we believe is the Son of God. What follows are a few scholarly findings about the historical Jesus.

The Originality of Jesus

As a pious Jew, Jesus shared many of the beliefs and customs of his people. This is to be expected. Historians would argue that if a particular saying of Jesus was also common in the Judaism of his day or resembled the beliefs of early Christians, then you cannot be certain that it actually originated with Jesus. However, if Jesus said something unique and original—something that his contemporaries could not even dream of—then a strong case can be made that it probably came directly from him alone. Here are some remarkable examples of this originality that strengthens the case that Jesus really did exist.

"Abba" Reference

Abba is an Aramaic word, a word from the language that Jesus spoke. It means "Daddy" or "Dad," but is a word that's usually translated as "Father." What is the significance of that? First, we have to realize that when the Jews of our Lord's day addressed a prayer to God, they used terms of great respect, like "Master of Heaven and Earth." They used a lofty title when praying to God because they wanted to emphasize that God was so great, so divine, that they were mere creatures compared to him. They would never think of addressing God with such an intimate, familiar term as "Daddy."

Yet, Abba is precisely the word Jesus used when he prayed to God. Only God's Son could have felt the freedom to utter such an intimate term of address. In the days of Jesus, nobody else did. No one would have dared! What is most remarkable is that Jesus invites us to also address God as "Abba," or "Daddy." We are invited to call God "Daddy" or "Father" because the Son, our brother, has revealed his Father to us. His saving acts on the cross have made it possible for us to become children of God.

Amen as an Introduction

Amen is a Hebrew word that was borrowed by those who spoke Aramaic, including Jesus. The word means "certainly." This word was always used at the end of an oath, blessing, curse, or a saying to indicate assent with the words just pronounced. "So be it" or "Yes, I agree" capture the sense of the word.

Jesus, however, used the word amen differently. He used it to introduce, not end, his own words, "Amen, I say . . ." This phrase was so new and unusual that the Gospel writers retained it when they recorded the words of Jesus. It was used fifty times in the Synoptic Gospels and twenty-five times in John's Gospel. In John's Gospel, Jesus seems to have said, "Amen, Amen" to convey the sense of "Hear ye, Hear ye." Consider this example: "Amen, amen, I say to you, whatever you ask the Father in my name he will give you" (Jn 16:23).

Nobody but Jesus taught this way. It meant that he spoke with unusual authority. He quoted no other teacher to back up his teaching. What he had to say is worth paying attention to; it is memorable and important. He is the unique source of this way of speaking.

Use of Parables

Other rabbis of Jesus' day used poetic language when they taught. But in the words of one of the

EXPLAINING THE FAITH

How do the parables of Jesus teach us lessons of faith?

As a rabbi or teacher, Jesus was apparently unique in the way he used parables. Jesus wanted people to search for and uncover parable truths. His stories forced people to stop and think about the Kingdom of Heaven and about God. Jesus told forty-one unique parables with specific lessons to share, rather than literal truths. For instance, the parable of the Prodigal Son (Lk 15:11-32) describes a reunion between a father and son. The message is about God's endless faithfulness and forgiveness. The father of the Prodigal Son, Jesus said, is like God, our Father—always ready to welcome us back. It is this kind of truth that fills the parables of Jesus and the Gospels.

greatest of all New Testament scholars, "We find nothing to be compared with the parables of Jesus, whether in the entire intertestamental literature of Judaism, the Essene writings, in Paul, or in Rabbinic literature." Jesus told forty-one unique stories known as parables to convey the Gospel message about the Kingdom of God.

Consider the story of the Good Samaritan (Lk 10:25–37) and the story of the Prodigal Son (Lk 15:11–32). They are arguably the two most famous stories told by any human being in history. They are memorable. They are touching. The message they convey is Gospel truth.

In the case of the Good Samaritan Jesus tells us that we must love our neighbor and that our neighbor includes everyone—even our enemies! This teaching is revolutionary in that it teaches how God's love is inclusive, not exclusive. It embraces every single person. And since we are children of Abba, and brothers and sisters to Jesus and each other, we must love everyone, too.

The message of the Prodigal Son is also rooted in the heart of the Gospel. It tells us of God's unlimited love for sinners. Who could ever forget the image of the loving father embracing his wayward son who had just returned to him? Who could ever forget the father's love of the older brother, telling him that "everything I have is yours" (Lk 15:31). And who could be unmoved by the father's challenge to the older son: "But now we must celebrate and rejoice, because your brother was dead and has come to life again; he was lost and has been found" (Lk 15:32)?

The parables that Jesus told were memorable, unique, and contained extremely important points of the message about God's Kingdom that he came to preach. Their existence alone proves that there was a remarkable person who created them. And the lessons they convey are so striking that they demonstrate a brilliant teacher behind them, one who had a very special relationship to God. On the other hand, Jesus also probably had many teachings that

promoted the teachings of Judaism. That was the religion in which he had been raised.

Consistency of Content in the Words of Jesus

Still another strong argument for the historical Jesus is the fact that the words of Jesus found in the Gospels have an internal consistency. In other words, there are no contradictions in the different sayings of Jesus, the miracle stories, the teachings on moral living, and the like. All of these words of Jesus are also consistent with the larger picture that arises from the Gospels. Here are three examples of this consistency:

Jesus and Love

Jesus taught his followers that they should love their enemies and pray for their persecutors. This message of inclusive love was not popular then, nor is it popular today. This theme is in several parables in which Jesus dealt with the outcasts of his day. It is also found in the Sermon on the Mount. In addition, Jesus himself lived the message he preached.

He asked his Father to forgive his executioners as he hung dying on the cross.

Sacrifice

Jesus consistently taught his disciples to sacrifice for him and for other people. For example, Jesus said, "Whoever finds his life will lose it, and whoever loses his life for my sake will find it" (Mt 10:39). Jesus not only preached this theme, he put it into practice. He consistently "walked the talk." This shows us that there was an authentic person behind the Gospel.

Forgiveness of Sin

Over and over, Jesus told people that their sins were forgiven. He also said that he was free to interpret the meaning of the Sabbath law. In so doing, Jesus was claiming to have unique authority—divine authority. He claimed the right to forgive sin and to teach on religious matters. His opponents recognized what he was doing and charged him with blasphemy. This charge ultimately was brought against Jesus and led to his Death. Yet, Jesus did not back away. This man was not simply a teacher of harmless proverbs. If he had been, Jewish authorities would not have opposed him. Those who make unique claims and challenge accepted interpretations do create controversy. There had to be someone behind the words reported in the Gospel accounts. That someone was Jesus of Nazareth, the one we believe to be the Son of God, our Savior.

Linguistic Analysis

Jesus spoke Aramaic, a rich and poetic language. Some scholars worked hard to translate all the words in the Gospel attributed to Jesus. The words were translated from Greek (the language in which the Gospels were written) into Aramaic. This study has found some remarkable patterns of speech in the words of Jesus. He was not just another rabbi (teacher) of his day. Jesus was a truly unique and creative teacher. Some linguistic studies have uncovered poetic rhythms in the teachings of Jesus. This made his words easy to remember. (Poetry is easier to memorize than prose.) His frequent use of the phrase "Kingdom of God," and the way he explained is also truly remarkable. Added to that are the puns (word plays), riddles, and striking paradoxes that Jesus used to make his presentations entertaining and profound. It's easy to conclude that Jesus was a unique teacher.

For Review

1. Define *criticism* as it is used to describe a certain approach scholars use in the study of Scripture.
2. Briefly describe the most common forms of criticism: source criticism, form criticism, redaction criticism, textual criticism, and historical criticism.
3. What do Biblical scholars mean by "originality" in the words of Jesus found in the Gospels? How can this "originality" strengthen the case for his existence?
4. What are three examples of this "originality" in the Gospel words of Jesus?
5. Explain the meaning of the Hebrew word *amen*. How did Jesus use this word in an entirely different way?
6. What interesting discoveries did scholars make when they did linguistic analysis, translating the words of Jesus from Greek back into Aramaic, the language Jesus spoke?

For Reflection

Share your own views about the difference between a father's love and a mother's love. What does it mean to you to be able to call God "Abba" as Jesus invited us to do?

martyrs
A Greek word that means "witness," referring to those who were put to death because of their religious beliefs.

The Church and Martyrs

People who deny the historical existence of Jesus Christ have a most difficult time explaining how the Catholic Church came to be. The existence of the Catholic Church makes sense because Jesus Christ established it on St. Peter and the Apostles many centuries ago. We see that Church as the Body of Christ. We also refer to it as the Bride of Christ. The two-thousand-year-old history of Catholicism can make sense only when we see that Jesus Christ founded the Church and sent his Holy Spirit to sustain it.

The earliest disciples of Jesus, like Peter, Paul, and Stephen, were so convinced about Jesus that they boldly proclaimed his story. These three and thousands of other early Christians gave up their lives while proclaiming the message Jesus left them. Only the Apostle John Zebedee died a natural death as a very old man. These first **martyrs** (a word that means "witness") actually knew the historical Jesus. They heard his teaching. They saw his miracles. They witnessed his arrest and crucifixion. They saw him after his Resurrection. They were his friends.

These brave witnesses or martyrs had absolutely nothing to gain financially, socially, or politically. They felt a burning desire to share the teaching they had received from Jesus—that God is our loving father. The sacrifices of these martyrs and of the Christian churches they founded is the greatest testimony that the Son of God came to live among us. What we see and hear today makes sense only if Jesus Christ, God's only Son, actually came among us.

For Review

1. What makes the testimony about Jesus from almost all of his own Apostles very persuasive?
2. What is a martyr? How did the earliest Christian martyrs promote the message of Jesus even further through their sufferings and death?

For Reflection

- "The blood of the martyrs is the seed of the Church," wrote Tertullian, an early Christian writer from Carthage in Africa. What was Tertullian saying about the impact that martyrs have? Do you think Tertullian was right?
- In many parts of the world, Christians are still being persecuted and killed for their faith. Compose your own prayer for religious tolerance in our world and share it with your classmates.

Main Ideas

- Despite the fact that he never had wealth, prestige, or political power, the impact of Jesus Christ has no parallel in all of history. (pp. 60–61)
- Ancient Roman, Greek, and Jewish historians wrote about the life and teaching of Jesus of Nazareth, refuting claims that Jesus never existed. (pp. 61–65)
- The Roman historian Tacitus confirmed the existence of Christians throughout the Roman Empire in his description of Emperor Nero's persecution of them after AD 64. (p. 62)
- Surprising references to Jesus as the Christ in the work of the Jewish historian Josephus suggests that a Christian secretly added material supporting Jesus. (pp. 63–64)
- The New Testament offers the strongest proof for the existence of Jesus. (pp. 66–68)
- The Gospels were written in the style of ancient biographies and do not provide much information about the early life and physical appearance of Jesus. Instead, they focus on key events in his life and the way he died. (p. 66)
- The word *Gospel* means "Good News" and is the story of Jesus Christ. Jesus himself is the "Good News." (pp. 66–68)
- There are three stages in the writing of the Gospels: (1) the period of Christ's public life and teaching; (2) the period of oral teaching by the Apostles; and (3) the period of the writing of the Gospels. (pp. 66–68)
- The kerygma style of preaching was an outreach to unbelievers while the didache approach appealed to those who were already Christians. (pp. 69–70)
- The fact that the end of the world was not coming quickly and that some teachings were being distorted prompted the writing of the Gospels. (pp. 70–73)
- The discovery of error in the calendar calculations by a sixth-century monk explains why the birth of Jesus is said to be between 4 and 6 BC. (p. 72)
- The biblical canon approved by the Church includes forty-six Old Testament books and twenty-seven New Testament books. (p. 72)
- Three standards used by the Church to evaluate sacred literature examine them for apostolic origin, widespread acceptance, and conformity to the rule of faith. (pp. 72–73)
- Gnosticism is a heresy that teaches that Jesus shared "secret knowledge" only with a few people and that this knowledge assured Salvation. It also said that the human body was evil. (p. 74)
- The apocryphal Gospels were writings focused on the life and teachings of Jesus that do not meet Church standards for the canon. These writings, including include the Protoevangelium of John, the Gospel of Thomas, and the Gospel of Judas, often include heresies such as Gnosticism. (pp. 73–74)
- The four Gospels of the canon were written for four different audiences but all contain the same Good News about Jesus. (pp. 74–76)
- The Synoptic Gospels are the Gospels of Matthew, Mark, and Luke. Because of great similarities in their content, they are often examined side by side. The word *synoptic* is from the Greek for "to see together." (pp. 75–76)
- Biblical criticism refers to a variety of scholarly approaches used to study and evaluate Scripture. Among these methods are source criticism, form criticism, redaction criticism, and textual criticism. (pp. 77–78)
- The highly unusual use of certain words like *Abba* and *amen* and the use of parables strengthens the case they originally came from Jesus himself. (pp. 78–80)

- The words of Jesus in sermons, parables, sayings, miracle stories, and moral teachings show a consistency of method and theme, and are added proof of his existence. (pp. 80–81)
- Linguistic analysis of the words of Jesus reveals that his teachings were delivered with poetic rhythms, puns, riddles, and paradoxes. (p. 81)
- The sacrifices and death of many early martyrs for their faith in Jesus is one of the strongest testimonies for his existence and teachings. (p. 82)

Terms, People, Places

Write your answers to the following questions.

1. Why were the apocryphal gospels excluded from the canon of the Bible?
2. Differentiate between form criticism, historical criticism, redaction criticism, and source criticism.
3. Explain why the Gospel of Thomas is classified under the category of Gnosticism.
4. What was the essential structure of kerygma?
5. Why are Matthew, Mark, and Luke referred to as Synoptic Gospels?

Primary Source Quotations

Jesus as a Historical Jewish Person

The book of the genealogy of Jesus Christ, the son of David, the son of Abraham. Abraham became the father of Isaac, Isaac the father of Jacob, Jacob the father of Judah and his brothers. Judah became the father of Perez and Zerah, whose mother was Tamar. Perez became the father of Hezron, Hezron the father of Ram, Ram the father of Amminadab. Amminadab became the father of Nahshon, Nahshon the father of Salmon, Salmon the father of Boaz, whose mother was Rahab. Boaz became the father of Obed, whose mother was Ruth. Obed became the father of Jesse, Jesse the father of David the king. David became the father of Solomon, whose mother had been the wife of Uriah . . . Eleazar became the father of Matthan, Matthan the father of Jacob, Jacob the father of Joseph, the husband of Mary. Of her was born Jesus who is called the Messiah. Thus the total number of generations from Abraham to David is fourteen generations; from David to the Babylonian exile, fourteen generations; from the Babylonian exile to the Messiah, fourteen generations.

—Matthew 1:1–16

Why Jesus Came

What has he [Jesus] brought? The answer is very simple: God. He has brought God! He has brought the God who once gradually unveiled his countenance first to Abraham, then to Moses and the prophets, and then in the wisdom literature—the God who showed his face only in Israel, even though he was also honored among the pagans in various shadowy guises. It is this God, the God of Abraham, of Isaac, and of Jacob, the true God, whom he has brought to the peoples of the earth. He has brought God, and now we know his face, now we can call upon him. Now we know the path that we human beings have to take in this world. Jesus has brought God and with God the truth about where we are going and where we come from: faith, hope, and love.

—Pope Benedict XVI

The Impact of the Gospels

The fourfold Gospel holds a unique place in the Church, as is evident both in the veneration which the liturgy accords it and in the surpassing attraction it has exercised on the saints at all times.

—*Catechism of the Catholic Church*, 127

Ongoing Assignments

1. View sample PowerPoint presentations on "One Solitary Life" online. Create your own PowerPoint presentation on this famous passage.
2. Reread the passage from Josephus on page 64. Keeping in mind that Josephus was not a Christian, explore this historical mystery in your journal. Do you agree with scholars that a non-believer like Josephus was probably not the author of this passage? Why or why not? Can you suggest a theory about what might have happened as this passage was recopied and passed down through the centuries? Comment on the italicized passages.
3. Listen to the *Shema* online. Copy out the first line of the prayer in Hebrew and present it in an attractive format.
4. Read Pliny the Younger's Letter 96 to Trajan and the emperor's reply. Then write a commentary on it.
5. Imagine that you could travel back in time to ask Jesus one question about his life in Nazareth. What would it be? Explore this question in writing.
6. In the Second Letter to the Thessalonians, read about a problem that had crept up in this new community of converts. St. Paul had to send a letter to scold some of his new Christians. Apparently, they had stopped working because they thought Jesus was going to return soon. Their idleness was causing dissension in the community. Read Paul's advice in 2 Thessalonians 3:11–15. What did Paul think should be done to Christians who refused to work?
7. What do you know about your name? Interview your grandparents or other family members to learn the meaning of their surnames. Ask your parents how and why they chose your first and middle names. What is your favorite name? What do you like about it?
8. The Beatitudes appear in both Matthew and Luke, and only there. Read both versions (Mt 5:3–12 and Lk 6:20–23) and write about the differences.
9. Copy the following "Amen" sayings of Jesus from John's Gospel into your journal or notebook: John 6:47, John 8:34, John 10:7, John 12:24, John 13:20. Write a sentence or two explaining the meaning and importance of each statement.
10. Read and reflect on the Parable of the Laborers in the Vineyard (Mt 20:1–16). Answer the following questions in your journal.
    - What is the main point of the parable?
    - Is the landowner a just person, that is, does he keep his contracts?
    - How is the landowner merciful?
    - Why do some of the people grumble at the landowner?
    - What is the meaning of verse 16? Can you think of an example from your life that supports the built-in truth of this verse?
    - Rewrite this parable in a modern setting. Share.
11. Present a PowerPoint presentation on Jesus as he has been depicted in art through the ages. You might begin by viewing the DVD, *The Face: Jesus in Art* (Kultur® Video).
12. Report on Veronica's Veil, the Shroud of Turin, or other images of the Holy Face.

13. Research and write a report on one of the apocryphal gospels.
14. Write a biographical sketch on an early Christian martyr. Examples might include one of the following saints: Peter, Paul, Ignatius of Antioch, Polycarp of Smyrna, Justin Martyr, or Perpetua and Felicitas.
15. Create a slideshow on at least five New Testament sites unearthed by archeological studies.
16. Report on various theories about the star of Bethlehem that guided the three Magi.

Prayer

The Shema is a central prayer to those of the Jewish faith. It affirms belief in one God. It also declares for the Chosen People and for us, their spiritual descendants, what is most important in this life. *Shema* means "listen" or "hear" in Hebrew and is the first word in Deuteronomy 6:4, "Hear, O Israel! The LORD is our God, the LORD alone!" In Hebrew, the text reads as follows: "*Shema Yisrael Adonai eloheinu Adonai ehad.*"

As a pious Jew, Jesus would have recited this prayer every morning and evening. It is the first prayer every Jewish child learns and every dying Jew hopes to have it on his or her lips at the end of life. Recite this prayer five times while concentrating on each phrase.

The entire prayer consists of three sections of the Torah: Deuteronomy 6:4–9 and 11:13–21 and Numbers 15:37–41. The first section reads as follows:

> Hear, O Israel! The LORD is our God, the LORD alone! Therefore, you shall love the LORD, your God, with all your heart, and with all your soul, and with all your strength. Take to heart these words which I enjoin on you today. Drill them into your children. Speak of them at home and abroad, whether you are busy or at rest. Bind them at your wrist as a sign and let them be as a pendant on your forehead. Write them on the doorposts of your houses and on your gates. (Dt 6:4–9)

- *Reflection*: Do you love God above everything else? How do you show it?
- *Resolution*: Think of one thing that is preventing you from loving God even more. Resolve to begin to correct it in the coming weeks.

4

JESUS CHRIST'S REVELATION ABOUT GOD

Whoever has seen me has seen the Father. How can you say, "Show us the Father"? Do you not believe that I am in the Father and the Father is in me? The words that I speak to you I do not speak on my own. The Father who dwells in me is doing his works. Believe me that I am in the Father and the Father is in me, or else, believe because of the works themselves.

—John 14:9-11

Our Father's Advice

The most important advice ever given by any father was given by God the Father for us to follow his Son, Jesus Christ.

The Mystery of the Blessed Trinity

The doctrine of the Trinity—that there are three Divine Persons, Father, Son, and Holy Spirit, in one God—is the central mystery of the Catholic faith.

God Is a Loving Father

Jesus taught us to call God "Abba" and trust in the Father's unconditional love for his creation.

Revelation about God the Son

Jesus' revelation about God the Father reveals much about his own identity as the Son of God.

Tracing Our Understanding about the Holy Spirit

The Holy Spirit's presence can be traced from the creation of the world and witnessed clearly in the life of Christ and more clearly following his Death and Resurrection.

Our Father's Advice

USA Today published an article honoring fathers and the advice they gave their children. Some of the thought-provoking nuggets of wisdom from ordinary dads include the following:

> "The man on the top of the mountain didn't fall there."
>
> "Honesty is like a trail, once you get off it you realize you are lost."
>
> "Remember who you are and where you came from."
>
> "Measure twice, cut once."
>
> "The second time you get kicked in the head by a mule it's not a learning experience."
>
> "Never be so broke that you cannot afford to pay attention."
>
> "Successful people make a habit of doing things that unsuccessful people don't like to do."
>
> "The one who quits last—wins."
>
> "If everybody else is doing it, it probably is wrong."

All of these quotes are worth mulling over. Loving fathers have much to teach their children. However, the greatest advice ever given comes from God, the Father of Jesus Christ. God has adopted us, and so he is our Father too. The most important advice for us from God our Father came at the Transfiguration.

While Peter, James, and John stood nearby as witnesses, the divine glory of Jesus was manifested. His face shone like the sun and his clothes became white as light. The voice of God was heard saying: "This is my beloved Son, with whom I am well pleased; listen to him" (Mt 17:5).

Listen to him! Listen to Jesus. Listen to Jesus who is the Son of God. With these few words, we learn who Jesus is. Moreover, we learn how we are to respond to him: Listen! This chapter considers what Jesus revealed about God the Father and how his own life more fully discloses an understanding of the Blessed Trinity.

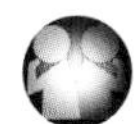

For Reflection

Which piece of advice given by the ordinary dads makes the most sense to you? Can you connect it to the advice given to us by God the Father at the Transfiguration?

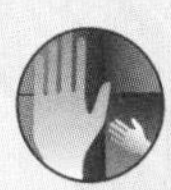

Advice for Life

Interview three adults whom you greatly admire. This could be your father, mother, grandparent, teacher, or coach. Ask each one for a one-sentence statement of the best advice they can give a young person. Share with your classmates the best piece of advice you heard. As a class, vote on and discuss the wisdom in the ten best advice statements. Post them in the classroom or school.

How Well Do You Follow Advice?

Rate how well you are listening to some of Jesus' words at this stage of your life. Read these quotes from the Gospel of Matthew. Which words of advice are easiest for you to follow? Which are most difficult?

"Stop judging, that you may not be judged" (Mt 7:1).

"Do not be afraid" (Mt 10:31).

"Do not worry about tomorrow; tomorrow will take care of itself" (Mt 6:34).

"Do to others whatever you would have them do to you" (Mt 7:12).

"Beware of false prophets, who come to you in sheep's clothing, but underneath are ravenous wolves" (Mt 7:15).

Further analyze your responses by reflecting on and answering the following questions. Write your responses in your journal or share with a classmate.

- How and why do people judge others?
- What most frightens and worries teens in today's world?
- How can faith in Jesus Christ help lessen those fears and worries?
- Who are the false prophets in our world and how do they attempt to mislead people?

The Mystery of the Blessed Trinity (CCC, 234, 237, 261-262)

At the end of Matthew's Gospel, just before Jesus' Ascension into Heaven, Jesus instructed the eleven Apostles to carry on his work. He said to them:

> All power in heaven and on earth has been given to me. Go, therefore, and make disciples of all nations, baptizing them in the name of the Father, and of the Son, and of the holy Spirit, teaching them to observe all that I have commanded you. And behold, I am with you always, until the end of the age. (Mt 28:18–20)

This passage is important for several reasons. First, it is the great commission that Jesus gave to his Apostles to spread the Good News to the ends of the earth. Second, Jesus assured the Apostles—and us—that he would remain with the Church until the end of time. Third, it told the Apostles that they were to invite others to follow Jesus by baptizing and teaching them all that he had taught them. Finally, Jesus specifically instructed the Apostles in the way they were to baptize. They were to do so in the *name* of the Father, and of the Son, and of the Holy Spirit.

This last point is especially important. It is a clear reference to the **Blessed Trinity**. The doctrine of the Blessed Trinity is a mystery and a central dogma of Catholic and Christian faith. From the mystery of the Trinity comes all other mysteries of the faith. The doctrine of the Trinity teaches that there are three Divine Persons—Father, Son, and Holy Spirit. Three Divine Persons in one God.

Recall that a mystery of faith is a truth about God that will always be beyond human understanding. The doctrine of the Trinity is one of these mysteries. With our limited human intellects, it would be impossible to see and understand God as he truly is. It would be like looking directly into the sun. We can't do that. We have to turn away because the light of the sun is too powerful, too bright, and too intense for our eyes. The sun, after all, is only a creation of God. God's light and greatness is much greater!

Human beings can never fully comprehend God's identity as the Blessed Trinity. It is a mystery hidden in God. We know about the Trinity because of the Incarnation of God's Son, Jesus Christ. Jesus

Blessed Trinity
The central mystery of the Christian faith. It teaches that there are three Persons in one God: Father, Son, and Holy Spirit.

ecumenical council
A worldwide, official assembly of the bishops under the direction of the Pope. There have been twenty-one ecumenical councils, the most recent being the Second Vatican Council (1962–1965).

creed
A statement of belief; sometimes a collection of creedal statements.

came and walked among us. He told us about who God is. We also know about the Trinity through the Holy Spirit. Through the Holy Spirit, God is revealed in three Divine Persons in one God. The doctrine of the Trinity goes beyond human reason but does not contradict it. We are only able to understand the truth of the Holy Trinity because God revealed it to us. This is why "[T]he Church confesses . . . 'one God and Father from whom all things are, and one Lord Jesus Christ, through whom all things are, and one Holy Spirit in whom all things are'" (*CCC,* 258). Through study and reflection on Sacred Scripture and on Sacred Tradition, the Church gradually defined the doctrine of the Trinity. That happened over the course of several centuries and was reflected in announcements from the first six ecumenical councils of the Church.

Belief in the Incarnation and in the Trinity is reflected in the creeds of the Church. These doctrines appear in both the Apostles' Creed and in the Nicene Creed that we recite at Mass. Another creed was composed by St. Athanasius (ca. 296–373) or those writing in his name. This bishop, Church Father, and Doctor of the Church once said: "For the Son of God became man that we might become God." St. Athanasius strongly defended the doctrine of the Blessed Trinity at the first **ecumenical council** of the Church held at Nicaea in 325.

In his creed, St. Athanasius clearly stated that "we worship one God in Trinity, and Trinity in Unity. . . . The Father is God, the Son is God, and the Holy Spirit is God, and yet there are not three gods but one God."

The next sections of this text point out exactly where in Scripture Jesus revealed each Person of the Blessed Trinity: Father, Son, and Holy Spirit. (More truths about the Blessed Trinity will be covered in Chapter 5.) For example, the Old Testament taught that there is only *one* God, a belief that's expressed in the *Shema*: "Hear, O Israel! The LORD is our God, the LORD alone!" (Dt 6:4). This belief is honored by observing the first

EXPLAINING THE FAITH

What is a creed?

According to the *Catechism of the Catholic Church*, creeds are needed to provide the Church with a common language of faith. Each creed begins with "I believe," but that statement really means, "I pledge or commit myself to what *we* believe." So, a **creed** starts with the word *I*, but it describes the beliefs of a community. From the beginning, the Apostles and their successors handed on formula statements of Christian beliefs for all the followers of Jesus. According to the *Catechism*, the Apostles' Creed and the Nicene Creed are the most important creeds for Catholics. Both are divided up into three parts. Part one speaks about God the Father as the first Divine Person and the Father's work of creation. Part two speaks of the second Divine Person, Jesus and his work of Redemption. Part three speaks of the third Divine Person, the Holy Spirit, and the Spirit's role in our sanctification.

ST. PATRICK OF IRELAND

On Holy Saturday in AD 433, Bishop Patrick and a few Christian helpers arrived at a hill near Tara in Ireland where the Irish king, Leoghaire, lived. Leoghaire had ordered that no fires be lit in his kingdom until a signal fire was first lit at Tara to call to his attention his chieftains.

St. Patrick had already begun to teach about Christ in this pagan land where he had once been enslaved. There had been stiff resistance from Druid priests. A native of Scotland, Patrick had been kidnapped as a teenager and sold to an Irish chieftain who forced the boy into the lonely life of a shepherd for six years. In those six years, as Patrick later wrote in his autobiography, *Confessio,* the young man learned to pray and hear God's call. Now, on this Holy Saturday evening, in defiance of the pagan king, Patrick ordered the lighting of the Easter fire to celebrate Christ's Resurrection. Though the pagan Druid priests rushed to Patrick's camp to douse the fire, they were unable to do so.

The next day, dressed in his bishop's robes and wearing a bishop's miter, Patrick proceeded to Tara to see the king and his chieftains. Thick, black clouds darkened the hills that day. But, according to tradition, one quiet prayer from Patrick brought bright sunlight piercing through the clouds. The leaden skies soon disappeared. Irish tradition goes on to recall that Patrick then reached down to pluck a shamrock from the earth. Holding the shamrock high, Patrick began to teach about the one true God with three Persons, the mystery of the Blessed Trinity. Patrick stayed at Tara throughout Easter week, sharing the teachings of the faith. King Leoghaire and his chieftains were soon converted. Christianity came and flourished in Ireland.

commandment: "I, the LORD, am your God, who brought you out of the land of Egypt, that place of slavery. You shall not have other gods besides me" (Dt 5:6–7). Speaking about this one God, Jesus taught that the Father is God, that the Son is God, and that the Holy Spirit is God. The commission to the Apostles is an important example of where Jesus revealed—in one single verse—that there is one God in three Divine Persons.

For Review

1. How did Jesus instruct his Apostles to baptize others?
2. What does the Church teach about the Trinity?
3. Explain the statement made by St. Athanasius: "We worship one God in Trinity, and Trinity in Unity. . . ."
4. How did the coming of Jesus change what people of faith knew about God?
5. How did Church teaching about the Trinity develop over the first six centuries?

For Reflection

- The complete text of the First Commandment in Deuteronomy 5:6-7 states: "I, the LORD, am your God, who brought you out of the land of Egypt, that place of slavery. You shall not have other gods besides me." How could obedience to this commandment reflect your faith that there is only one God?
- Catholics recite the Nicene Creed at every Sunday Mass. Is it a good idea for people to state what they believe over and over? Discuss this with your classmates.

God Is a Loving Father (*CCC*, 205-231, 238-242, 268-271)

The Old Testament tells us a great deal about God. For example, it reveals that YHWH ("I AM") is the only God. He is unique with no equal. He is the creator of the universe who made everything out of nothing. He created out of wisdom and love, and to show his glory. A loving God brought creation into existence. Creation did not happen by accident. God directs creation through **divine providence**, that is, by his loving and watchful guidance over us and over all of creation.

God also created human beings in his image and likeness. He endowed them with great dignity, and human souls that are capable of thinking, choosing, and loving. We are the crown of God's creation, a composite of body and spirit or soul. God creates the soul immediately at the time we are conceived. We are destined for eternal life. Everything God created is good. That includes the visible, material world and world of spiritual realities and invisible beings like angels.

Though tainted with sin, humans never cease to be fundamentally good. God so loved humans that eventually he sent his only Son to redeem us and invite us into a personal relationship with him. John's Gospel eloquently states this message about Jesus Christ: "For God so loved the world that he gave his only Son, so that everyone who believes in him might not perish but might have eternal life" (Jn 3:16).

The Traits of God

God's love, beauty, truth, goodness, divine providence, and life shine forth in creation. This is why intelligent human beings can look at the created world and recognize the handiwork of a Divine Being behind it all. As the Old Testament tells us, there is no one like YHWH. We learn that God has the following traits:

- *God is* ***infinite*** *and* ***omnipotent****.* God is without limits and all-powerful. God can do everything. In our creeds, we proclaim belief in "God, the Father Almighty." He created out of nothing. He saves human beings. He makes the dead rise again. As the angel Gabriel said to Mary, the Mother of Jesus Christ, "For nothing will be impossible for God" (Lk 1:37).
- *God is* ***eternal****.* God always was and always will be. God is the one being who always existed.
- *God is pure spirit and contains all things.* As a pure spirit, God is everywhere. He is not limited to space and time. God is always present to everything he makes. "In him we live and move and have our being" (Acts 17:28). Every creature that exists depends on God. God's existence sustains the universe. God's willingness to keep everything in existence reveals his love, care, and concern for his creatures.
- *God is unchangeable.* God does not change—ever. His love and concern are unwavering.
- *God is supremely holy.* Holiness is a quality of being absolutely other than creation. God is transcendent, meaning that God is totally beyond our understanding and beyond our reach. God surpasses everything and everyone. He created all that exists. He always existed before there was time. He always is and always will be. God is far beyond our human ability to comprehend him perfectly. Whatever we can say about him is limited. There is so much more to God than our minds can possibly understand. God's goodness and love are unlimited. We cannot possibly praise this gracious, good, and holy God enough.
- *God is personal.* God is alive and the source of all life. He knows all things. He loves and cares beyond limit. Time and again, the saving God revealed personal love.

This last point may be the most important trait for you to keep in mind. Our Creator is also a personal, loving God. The Old Testament tells the story of God's undying love for human beings despite their sinfulness. Our loving God made covenants with

divine providence
The sovereignty of God over events in the lives of individuals and throughout history.

infinite
A term that means extending endlessly, having no end or limits.

omnipotent
An attribute of God that he is everywhere, unlimited, and all-powerful.

eternal
A term that describes existing without a beginning and forever.

humans. He chose the Hebrews as his special people, freed them from slavery in Egypt, and formed them into a nation. Then, he gave them a land of their own. God established the kingdom of David from which the future Messiah was to come. He sent prophets to guide this Chosen People and sustained them during their captivity in Babylon. Faithful to his word, God later restored the captive people to the Holy Land.

Throughout the Old Testament, God promised the Jews that a time would come when he would send a savior. In due course, his Son was born and became one of us. It was Jesus who fully revealed to us who God is, and what his plan of Salvation was. In truth, the most loving part of this Salvation story was the Passion, Death, and Resurrection of Jesus. Through this horrendous sacrifice known as the Paschal Mystery, Jesus won Salvation for us.

God's Fatherly Love

The Chosen People saw God as a loving Father who created the world. He also fashioned various covenants with them, gave them the Law to guide them, and served as their shepherd. The Jews turned to God in times of trouble as children turn to a trusted adult to stand faithfully by them. "O Lord, hold not back, for you are our father. Were Abraham not to know us, nor Israel to acknowledge us, You, LORD, are our father, our redeemer you are named forever" (Is 63:15–16).

The Old Testament also describes God as the "father of the poor: who cared for and protected the defenseless." As Psalm 68 proclaims,

> Sing to God, praise the divine name;
> exalt the rider of the clouds.
> Rejoice before this God
> whose name is the LORD.
> Father of the fatherless, defender of widows—
> this is the God whose abode is holy,
> Who gives a home to the forsaken,
> who leads prisoners out to prosperity.
> (Ps 68:5–7)

Jesus taught that God's fatherly love for us is beyond what we can even imagine. As we know, Jesus taught us to call God "Abba" ("Daddy" or "Papa"). That teaching was unique and different. Jesus taught that the Father of the Chosen People, the Creator God who made covenants with them, was also *his* Father. God was an eternal Father for Jesus, but Jesus was the unique Son who shared God's own nature. In the Last Supper narrative in John 13–17, Jesus called God "Father" forty-five times.

To highlight his unique relationship as God's only Son, Jesus referred to "*My* heavenly Father" (Mt 15:13). But he also talked about "*Your* Father in heaven" (Mt 5:45). Jesus taught that God is eternally the Father through his relationship to the Son and vice versa. Both Persons are divine:

> No one knows the Son except the Father, and no one knows the Father except the Son and anyone to whom the Son wishes to reveal him. (Mt 11:27)

The Apostles certainly understood the unique relationship Jesus had with the Father. For example, John's Gospel begins by referring to Jesus as "the Word of God." Jesus was the very image of the invisible God. Jesus was God-made-flesh. Jesus was always in relationship to God:

In the beginning was the Word,
and the Word was with God,
and the Word was God. (Jn 1:1)

In his earthly ministry, Jesus often told of the Father's love. Jesus, God's unique Son, invites us, his disciples, to also address God as Abba too. By virtue of Christ's saving acts, and through the power of the Holy Spirit and our baptism, we have been adopted into the divine family by God, our Father. This is why we can in humility approach God and say, "Our Father who art in heaven."

Jesus tells us to pray to the Father frequently, trusting that our heavenly Father will answer us. We should never give up, but be persistent in our prayers. God knows our needs and will give us what is good for us. "If you then . . . know how to give good gifts to your children, how much more will the Father in Heaven give the holy Spirit to those who ask him?" (Lk 11:13). The teaching of Jesus revealed God's unconditional and total love. God is like the father in the Parable of the Prodigal Son who welcomed back his wayward child with open arms—no questions asked. He was like a good shepherd who went out of his way to find a lost sheep. The Father's love is immeasurable. We cannot earn his love; it is a gift showered on good and evil people alike.

Jesus, God's faithful Son, spent his whole life doing his Father's will. He asks us to pray, "Thy will be done on earth as it is in heaven." This means imitating his Father—our Father by adoption—by forgiving those who hurt us, by not judging others, by heeding his command. Jesus asks us to, "Be perfect, just as your heavenly Father is perfect" (Mt 5:48). It means trusting that our loving Father will take care of all our needs. The heavenly Father knows what we need for life. Therefore, we should "seek first the kingdom [of God] and his righteousness, and all these things will be given you besides" (Mt 6:33).

The healing miracles of Jesus revealed a compassionate God. And the sacrifice of Jesus on the cross shows us a Father who gave his own selfless

EXPLAINING THE FAITH

Can we also think of God as Mother?

"God is Father, and even more, he is Mother." That was a statement made by Pope John Paul I during his brief (thirty-three days) pontificate in 1978. The Pope's observation made headlines because viewing God as our Mother was not very common in the Judaeo-Christian tradition. Many years later, in 1999, Pope John Paul II agreed with his predecessor. John Paul II's comment came in reflections about the Parable of the Prodigal Son. The father in the parable, John Paul II said, had "all of the characteristics of fatherhood *and* motherhood." However, when the Pope considered this loving parent finally embracing the son, it seemed to the Pope that the father "shows the profile of a mother."

At times, the Bible refers to God's parental tenderness and love using the images of a mother. One beautiful reference comes from Isaiah: "As a mother comforts her son, so will I comfort you" (Is 66:13). In another passage, the prophet compares God's constant love to that of a mother, "Can a mother forget her infant, be without tenderness for the child of her womb? Even should she forget, I will never forget you" (Is 49:15). Jesus himself used feminine images when teaching about God's love. For example, he compared God to a woman who rejoiced when she found a lost coin (Lk 15:8-10). On another occasion, he said his own desire to gather the people of Jerusalem was like that of a hen who gathered her young under her wings (Mt 23:37). The Church teaches, of course, that God is pure spirit and has no sexual identity. In our mind and imagination, however, we should feel free to think of God as one who loves and protects us as a father *and* a mother.

Son for our Redemption. The Father is a saving God who redeems us through his Son, Jesus Christ, in the Holy Spirit. The Father brought his beloved Son back to life, and through him, he promised resurrection to all who believe. St. Paul assured us: "Thanks be to God who gives us the victory through our Lord Jesus Christ" (1 Cor 15:57).

For Review

1. What is the divine providence of God?
2. What are three of God's traits that the Old Testament talks about?
3. What does it mean to say that God is omnipotent?
4. Tell how is God infinite.
5. Name two ways that Jesus taught that God is our Father.
6. How did Jesus himself suggest that God is also like a mother?

For Reflection

Where do you see the Creator's hand in the world you see around you?

Revelation about God the Son (*CCC*, 240-242)

The Old Testament used the title "son of God" in a variety of different ways. Sometimes, it referred to Israel (e.g., Ex 4:22), on other occasions to a king (2 Sm 7:14), and sometimes to angels (Job 1:6). The title is used as well in the New Testament. What did it mean when Jesus was called "the Son of God"? In what sense was Jesus different from Israel, kings, and angels? How was Jesus different from other human beings? Was Jesus truly the Son of God in a divine sense? When Jesus revealed himself to be the Son of God, was he claiming to be God?

Christians, of course, believe that Jesus is "the human face of God." St. Paul's Letter to the Colossians puts it this way:

> He is the image of the invisible God,
> the firstborn of all creation.
> For in him were created all things
> in heaven and on earth. . . .
> He is before all things,
> and in him all things hold together.
> (Col 1:15–17)

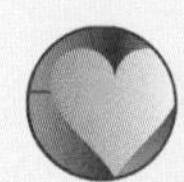

An Act of Faith

Here is a traditional prayer that expresses central Catholic beliefs, especially in the doctrines of the Blessed Trinity and the Incarnation.

> O my God, I firmly believe that you are one God
> in three divine Persons, Father, Son, and Holy Spirit;
> I believe that your divine Son became man
> and died for our sins, and that he will come to judge the living
> and the dead. I believe these and all the truths which the
> Holy Catholic Church teaches, because you revealed them,
> who can neither deceive nor be deceived. Amen.

Write your own short Act of Faith. Include in it statements (articles) of what you believe about God. Be ready to share and compare your Act of Faith with others in your class.

And in the Synoptic Gospels, Jesus did reveal himself to be the Son of God. We know that Jesus addressed God as "Abba" or "Daddy." We also learn much more about this father and son relationship. For example, right after Peter told Jesus, "You are the Messiah, the Son of the living God" (Mt 16:16), Jesus replied: "Blessed are you, Simon son of Jonah. For flesh and blood has not revealed this to you, but my heavenly Father" (Mt 16:17).

Notice how Jesus referred to God as "*my* heavenly Father." This indicates that God was his father in a totally unique way. And when the worried Mary and Joseph found the boy Jesus in the Temple in Jerusalem after a Passover feast, he told his bewildered parents, "Did you not know that I must be in my Father's house?" (Lk 2:49).

One of the most memorable examples of Jesus teaching about his unique identity as "Son of God" occurred after his disciples returned from a preaching mission. Jesus was pleased with their work and praised his heavenly Father:

> At that very moment he rejoiced [in] the holy Spirit and said, "I give you praise, Father, Lord of heaven and earth, for although you have hidden these things from the wise and the learned you have revealed them to the childlike. Yes, Father, such has been your gracious will. All things have been handed over to me by my Father. No one knows who the Son is except the Father, and who the Father is except the Son and anyone to whom the Son wishes to reveal him." (Lk 10:21–22)

Jesus had special knowledge of his Father. Clearly, there was a divine union between Father and Son. As we read the Gospels, we can see how Jesus gradually shared that special knowledge with his Apostles. Some of the ways are recounted in the following sections.

The Meaning of the Parable of the Tenants (Mk 12:1-12)

The enemies of Jesus understood that he claimed a unique relationship with God. That is why they eventually charged him with blasphemy. For the Jewish leaders, Jesus was speaking with great disrespect and irreverence when he claimed to be equal to God. This accusation against Jesus is represented in the Parable of the Tenants in the Gospel of Mark. In this story, evil tenants cheated a vineyard owner. They beat and killed the owner's servants who came to collect some of the produce of the vineyard. Finally, as Jesus tells the story, "He had one other to send, a beloved son. He sent him to them last of all, thinking, 'They will respect my son'" (Mk 12:6).

The parable is really an allegory that tells how God had sent prophets (servants in the story) to the Jews (the tenants). The prophets were abused; some were killed. Then, as the story continues, the vineyard owner decided to send someone with even more authority. This representative would be special and unique. The meaning of the allegory was clear. God decided to send his only Son into the world.

The meaning of this allegory was not lost on the Jewish leadership. Everyone who heard the parable knew that Jesus was claiming to be the beloved son of the vineyard owner—and the beloved Son of God. He was much greater than the prophets who had come before him. He was the rightful heir to the Father.

Recall that in the parable the vineyard owner's son was also killed. By telling this parable, Jesus was predicting his future arrest and death. Those who heard the story knew what Jesus was claiming. They understood that he was criticizing them. The Gospel reports, "They were seeking to arrest him, but they feared the crowd, for they realized that he had addressed the parable to them. So they left him and went away" (Mk 12:12).

The Gospel of John Teaches about the Son of God

The Gospel of John also presents Jesus as the Second Person of the Blessed Trinity. One of the most central passages that revealed that Jesus was the Son of God occurred at the Last Supper. Philip asked Jesus to show the Father to him and to the other Apostles. In reply, Jesus said,

> Whoever has seen me has seen the Father. How can you say, "Show us the Father"? Do you not believe that I am in the Father and the Father is in me? (Jn 14:9–10)

John's Gospel is also noted for the important "I AM" sayings of Jesus. In these sayings, Jesus made some remarkable claims. He used images and comparisons from the Old Testament to describe himself. In the Old Testament, these same images had referred to God himself. Jesus said:

- *"I am the bread of life" (Jn 6:35).* In the Old Testament, YHWH was the one who gave manna to the Chosen People.
- *"I am the light of the world" (Jn 8:12).* God is the author of light in the Genesis creation account (1:3).
- *"I am the gate for the sheep" (Jn 10:7) and "I am the good shepherd" (Jn 10:11).* Both of these images recall God's promise to be the shepherd of his people (Ps 23).
- *"I am the resurrection and the life (Jn 11:25).* The Old Testament reveals God as the author of life, the one who will restore life (for example, in Gn 2:7 and Is 26:19).
- *"I am the way and the truth and the life"* (Jn 14:6). Psalms 15:11 and 42:3 proclaim YHWH to be the way to life and truth.
- *"I am the true vine" (Jn 15:1).* The prophets Isaiah (5:1–7) and Ezekiel (17:22–24) use the image of the vineyard owner to describe God who planted the vine, an image of Israel.

All of these "I AM" statements revealed profound truths about who Jesus was and what he means for us. But one other statement that Jesus made truly astounded his enemies. In speaking to his listeners, he said, "For if you do not believe that I AM, you will die in your sins" (Jn 8:24). In response to Jesus, they asked him who he really was. Jesus said that they would know his true identity: "When you lift up the Son of Man, then you will realize that I AM, and that I do nothing on my own, but I say only what the Father taught me. The one who sent me is with me" (Jn 8:28–29).

These teachings became clearer to the Apostles, and to his other disciples after the Resurrection of Jesus and after the outpouring of the Holy Spirit at Pentecost. With the eyes of faith, the Church began to understand more profoundly who Jesus truly was and is. They realized that he did things that only God could do, marvelous works that revealed his identity as God's only Son. Jesus cured lepers, made deaf people hear, gave sight to the blind, made the lame walk, and drove out demons. He demonstrated his power over natural forces when he calmed the storm and multiplied the loaves and fishes. He claimed the power to forgive sins, something only God could do. He backed up his claim by performing miracles. He raised the dead to life, proving that he was Lord of life.

Jesus taught that he alone truly knew the Father, and that all that the Father had was his. He also said that the Father has given him all power, and that his words were the words of the Father who sent him. Knowing Jesus meant knowing the Father. And if we loved Jesus, both Jesus and the Father would take up their dwelling within us.

When we read the Gospels knowing that Jesus was the Son of God, then we can easily discover the many ways that he revealed himself as God. He was the Second Person of the Trinity and was one with the Father. Therefore, everything Jesus did—and said—also revealed who God is and what he does.

Matthew's Gospel Teaches Jesus Is Emmanuel

While John's Gospel often used parables to tell about Jesus as God's Son, Matthew's Gospel stated the truth simply and directly—Jesus is Emmanuel, "God-is-with-us." Jesus is God's love who came to deliver us from sin and death, and bring the eternal life that he shared with the Father. One of the greatest promises Jesus made to his Apostles is found in the last verse in Matthew's Gospel. Jesus had sent his Apostles out into the world to preach and baptize in the "name of the Father, and of the Son, and of the holy Spirit." Jesus told his friends, "Behold, I am with you always, until the end of the age" (Mt 28:20). Jesus, the Son of God, was promising that he would never abandon his brothers and sisters. He would remain as Head of his Body, the Church.

Following the Son

Jesus Christ, as God's Son, is the perfect model for how to live our own lives. In all ways, he aimed to do the will of his Father. He was humble and never abused his power. He even washed the feet of his Apostles at the Last Supper to teach his followers how to serve one another. In addition, he was obedient. As the Letter to the Hebrews puts it: "Son though he was, he learned obedience from what he suffered" (Hb 5:8). Obeying the teachings of Jesus is essential for us, his disciples. The Letter to the Hebrews continues: Jesus "became the source of eternal salvation for all who obey him" (Hb 5:9).

For Review

1. How was the term "son of God" used in the Old Testament?
2. Tell how the Parable of the Tenants, a story Jesus told, was actually about himself and his future persecution and death.
3. Why did Jesus use "I AM" statements commonly used in the Old Testament to refer to God?
4. How was Jesus comparing himself to God the Father when he said, "I am the bread of life" and "I am the true vine"?
5. What are two ways reported in the Gospels that Jesus showed obedience to his Father?

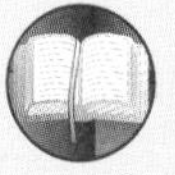

The Witness of Scripture: Jesus Is God's Son

Read at least five of the following eight New Testament passages. Reflect on these verses and write about three important things they tell us about Jesus as the Son of God.

- John 1:18, 49
- John 3:16-18
- John 5:19-26
- John 6:40
- John 11:3-4, 27
- Galatians 4:4
- Hebrews 1:2
- Hebrews 4:14

6. When did the Apostles finally realize who and what Jesus really was?

For Reflection

- Reread the Parable of the Tenants in the Gospel of Mark (Mk 12:1-12). Update the parable to tell the same story in a modern setting.
- In your opinion, what would have been the hardest truth for Jesus to communicate about his Father?

Tracing Our Understanding about the Holy Spirit (*CCC*, 243-244)

Throughout Salvation History, God the Holy Spirit's revelation of himself was ongoing if not gradual. For example, the Old Testament clearly reveals the Father and points to the coming of the Son. The Holy Spirit was always present, of course. However, the Holy Spirit seems hidden because the Spirit does not speak about himself in the Old Testament. However, it was not until after the Death and Resurrection of Christ that the disciples of Jesus began to understand the Holy Spirit as a distinct and separate Person of the Blessed Trinity.

Jesus and the Holy Spirit

In his public ministry, Jesus gradually revealed the mystery of the Holy Spirit. For example, he told the Pharisee Nicodemus that he would have to be born again in water and the Spirit (Jn 3:5–8). In his dialogue with the Samaritan woman at the well, he talked about worshiping God in Spirit and truth (Jn 4:10, 14, 23–24). In his instructions to the crowds on the Eucharist, he taught about the Spirit giving life (Jn 6:27, 51, 62–63). However, at the Last Supper, Jesus made repeated references to the Holy Spirit. There he promised to send the Holy Spirit to comfort and teach the disciples:

> I will ask the Father, and he will give you another Advocate to be with you always, the Spirit of truth, which the world cannot accept, because it neither sees nor knows it. But you know it, because it remains with you, and will be in you. (Jn 14:16–17)

Later, at that same meal, Jesus told his friends that he would soon endure suffering and a painful Death. But Resurrection would also follow. Though he had his mission to accomplish, Jesus promised to send the Holy Spirit to his disciples. It would be up to the Spirit to give them needed help and comfort:

> But I tell you the truth, it is better for you that I go. For if I do not go, the Advocate will not come to you. But if I go, I will send him to you. . . . [W]hen he comes, the Spirit of truth, he will guide you to all truth. (Jn 16:7, 13)

Finally, after his Resurrection and right before he ascended into heaven, Jesus told the Apostles:

> You will receive power when the holy Spirit comes upon you, and you will be my witnesses in Jerusalem, throughout Judea and Samaria, and to the ends of the earth. (Acts 1:8)

The Lord addressed this promise not only to his Apostles, but to all believers and followers. The Spirit of Truth, the Holy Spirit, comes to teach us the meaning of Divine Revelation. He also gives us the power and grace to understand, accept, and follow the teachings Jesus left us. Finally, the Holy Spirit gives us the gift of fortitude, that is, the courage and strength to proclaim the Gospel of Christ to the world.

The Coming of the Holy Spirit (CCC, 731–732)

The promises Jesus made to send the Holy Spirit were fulfilled on Pentecost Sunday. Pentecost was originally a Jewish harvest feast that took place fifty days after Passover. On the day that the Holy Spirit came, the Apostles were hiding in the Upper Room in Jerusalem. It was the place where the Last Supper had been celebrated. Mary, the Blessed Mother, and other women were with the Apostles who were terrified but praying for direction. In the Upper Room, the followers of Jesus were trying to make sense of his Death and Resurrection. Acts then recounts what happened:

> [S]uddenly there came from the sky a noise like a strong driving wind, and it filled the entire house in which they were. Then there appeared to them tongues as of fire, which parted and came to rest on each one of them. And they were all filled with the Holy Spirit and began to speak in different tongues, as the Spirit enabled them to proclaim. (Acts 2:2–4)

This was a world-changing event, and immediately after, the Apostles went out into the city to proclaim the Gospel to the crowds. The Apostles spoke in **tongues**. This gift from the Holy Spirit allowed them to preach in different languages to many different people gathered in Jerusalem. Although the Apostles had never

learned these languages, they were understood. At first, the crowds did not know what to think of these men. Suddenly, they were boldly testifying for Jesus and the Gospel. Some laughed and claimed that the Apostles were drunk. But Peter assured them that they were all sober; in fact, it was only nine in the morning. Peter explained that what was happening was promised by the prophet Joel who said:

> "It will come to pass in the last days," God says,
> "that I will pour out a portion of my spirit upon all flesh.
> Your sons and daughters shall prophesy
> your young men shall see visions,
> your old men shall dream dreams. . . .

tongues
A term for the practice of "speaking in tongues"; a gift from the Holy Spirit that allows a person to speak in languages that were never learned.

and it shall be that everyone shall be saved
who calls on the name of the Lord."
(Acts 2:17, 21)

So powerful was the work of the Holy Spirit that soon three thousand people believed in Jesus Christ and were baptized on that day. The Holy Spirit gave the Apostles the courage to preach the Gospel despite all kinds of obstacles. Eventually, the Spirit inspired them to preach the Good News to every corner of the Roman Empire, all by the end of the first century. The Holy Spirit remains alive in the world and in the Church. It is the Holy Spirit who brings Christ's Salvation to all people everywhere.

John's Gospel provides different insights about the Holy Spirit than found in the Acts of the Apostles. John tells us how Jesus prayed that his Apostles would receive gifts from the Spirit to help them. Appearing to the frightened and confused disciples in the Upper Room, Jesus twice offered them his greetings of peace. Then, he sent them on a great mission by saying:

> As the Father has sent me, so I send you. . . . Receive the Holy Spirit. Whose sins you forgive are forgiven them, and whose sins you retain are retained. (Jn 20:21–23)

EXPLAINING THE FAITH

What is monotheism?

Belief in one God is often called **monotheism.** The term has two Greek roots, *monos*, which means "one," and *theos*, which means "God." The concept of one God is primarily found in the "Abrahamic" religions: Judaism, Christianity, and Islam. Monotheism opposes **polytheism**, a belief in more than one god, and atheism, the belief that there is no God. In addition to belief in one God, Christians believe that the one God is in three Divine Persons, Father, Son, and Holy Spirit. Neither Judaism nor Islam teaches that Jesus Christ is the Son of God, the second Person of the Trinity.

This passage might remind us of how God breathed life into Adam and Eve at the beginning of human history. In a similar way, after his Resurrection, Jesus prepared his disciples. They would soon receive new life, the life of the Holy Spirit, a life of adoption into God's family. John's Gospel stresses how Christ's Church is to continue the work of Salvation.

The Holy Spirit in the Old Testament (CCC, 702-716)

The Hebrew word ***ruah*** is often used in the Old Testament to speak of God's mysterious, powerful, and life-giving presence. This word was used to describe the Spirit's work in creation and at work among the Chosen People. Later Old Testament writings gradually presented God's spirit in more personal terms, as a guiding and instructing presence. Typically, however, Old Testament authors saw the Spirit more as a force, power, and a presence. They lacked a clear idea of the Holy Spirit as a separate Person of the Blessed Trinity. This understanding did not develop until Jesus revealed the Holy Spirit as a distinct Person of the Blessed Trinity.

Now that the Holy Spirit has been given to the Church, she can search the Old Testament and see more clearly the Holy Spirit's active presence in Salvation History. For example, the Holy Spirit is present:

- *In creation (Gn 1:2), and in giving the breath of life to Adam and Eve (Gn 2:7), and to all human beings who bear the very image and likeness of God.* God's Spirit keeps the world in existence, but the Spirit also works in a special way through humans.
- *In the covenant with Abraham.* Our first parents sinned and left humanity weak, deprived of God's glory. But YHWH did not abandon us. He promised the aged Abraham that, by the power of the Holy Spirit, he would father a child. Through Abraham's descendants, all the nations of the world were to be blessed through the

coming of a Messiah. Filled with the Holy Spirit, this Savior would open the gates of Heaven for all.

- *In theophanies and in the giving of the Law.* A theophany is a manifestation of God who showed himself by power of the Holy Spirit, for example, as in a cloud and in fire when God called Moses and gave the Chosen People the Law. But in these visions, the Holy Spirit both revealed and concealed God's Word. God's Spirit helped the Chosen People to keep the Law. The Law later served as a teacher to lead people to Christ, but it could not save them. It made people aware of how sinful they were and that without the Holy Spirit, they would not be able to obey God's law.
- *In Israel's kingdom and the Exile.* The Spirit inspired kings like David to rule in YHWH's name. But after David's time, the Chosen People drifted away from the Law and ignored God's covenant. God's Spirit "anointed" Israel's prophets like Elijah (2 Kgs 2:9) and Elisha (2 Kgs 2:15) who spoke on his behalf by instructing people to remain faithful to the covenant. But the sinfulness of the Israelites eventually led them to being exiled in Babylonia. Then, the Holy Spirit sustained them until they could return to the Promised Land. He continually spoke through the prophets like Isaiah who called people to remain true to God and promised that one day a new king, the Messiah, would come to rule them as a Suffering Servant. They promised that God's Holy Spirit would be with this Person in a very special way. Christians, of course, recognized this promised one to be Jesus.

The Suffering Servant Songs of Isaiah revealed the Messiah's qualities. They also prophesied the Lord's Passion and his Death as necessary preludes for a fuller release of the Spirit. The last Suffering Servant Song of Isaiah tells us:

> Yet it was our infirmities that he bore,
> our sufferings that he endured. . . .
> Like a lamb led to the slaughter or a sheep before the shearers,
> he was silent and opened not his mouth. . . .
> And he shall take away the sins of many,
> and win pardon for their offenses.
> (Is 53:4, 7, 12)

It is only when Jesus Christ came that the Holy Spirit was fully and

monotheism
From the Greek words *monos* ("one") and *theos* ("God"); the belief in one, all-powerful God. Christianity, Judaism, and Islam are three great monotheistic religions.

polytheism
The belief, in opposition to Christian doctrine, that there are many gods.

ruah
A Hebrew word meaning "wind" or "breath" often used in the Old Testament to refer to God's mysterious and powerful life-giving presence.

undeniably revealed as a separate, distinct Person of the Blessed Trinity.

The Holy Spirit in the Ministry of Jesus (CCC, 717-730, 743-746)

And after his Ascension into Heaven, Jesus and God the Father did indeed send the Holy Spirit to guide the Church until the end of time. When we read the Gospels closely, we can see clearly how the Holy Spirit played an important role in the entire ministry of Jesus—from beginning to end. For example:

- *The Holy Spirit enabled Mary to conceive Jesus, God's Son, and bring him into our midst.* Jesus is Emmanuel—"God-with-us." Mary, the Blessed Virgin, is a great example of a Spirit-filled person. Graced by God from the moment of her own conception in the womb of her mother, she cooperated fully in bringing her Son into the world. She is the perfect model for cooperating with the Holy Spirit. "Through Mary, the Holy Spirit begins to bring men, the objects of God's merciful love, into communion with Christ" (*CCC*, 725).
- *The Holy Spirit helped John the Baptist to prepare people for the way of the Lord.*
- *The Holy Spirit was at the baptism of Jesus.* In fact, in accounts of the baptism of Jesus, we find one of the most important Biblical testimonies for the existence of three Persons in the Trinity. Luke's Gospel told about the baptism of Jesus this way:

  > After all the people had been baptized and Jesus also had been baptized and was praying, heaven was opened and the Holy Spirit descended upon him in bodily form like a dove. And a voice came from heaven, "You are my beloved Son; with you I am well pleased." (Lk 3:21–22)

  In this passage, the Third Person of the Blessed Trinity—the Holy Spirit—took the form of a

  dove and descended upon Jesus Christ, the Son and Second Person of the Blessed Trinity. The First Person of the Blessed Trinity, the Father, declared that Jesus was his "Beloved Son." Those who might deny that God is in three Divine Persons will have great difficulty dealing with this remarkable passage!
- *The Holy Spirit led Jesus into the desert for prayer and fasting, and sustained him there in his battle with Satan.*
- *Jesus began his preaching ministry in Nazareth filled with the Spirit's power* (*Lk 4:14*). Jesus testified that the Spirit was upon him and had anointed him to preach Good News to the afflicted, proclaim liberty to captives, give sight to the blind, and let the oppressed go free (Lk 4:1–21). The miracles of Jesus resulted in healings, the driving out of demons, the raising of people from the dead, and a display of power over all the forces of creation. All of this was done through the power of the Holy Spirit.
- Recall, also, that *Jesus gradually revealed the Holy Spirit to people like the Samaritan woman, Nicodemus, and other disciples and then promised to send another Advocate (or*

Paraclete) after his Death and Resurrection. Jesus himself is our advocate before the Father, but he promised to send *another* Paraclete—"the Spirit of truth" who would remain with us, guiding us to the truth.

- Finally, *the Holy Spirit remained with Jesus, even during his Death and Resurrection.* When a soldier stabbed Jesus with a spear, blood and water gushed from the wound. This symbolized the life and waters of the Holy Spirit flowing out into the world (Jn 19:34). Through the Spirit, God raised Jesus from the dead. Our Risen Lord has a spiritual, glorified body. As resurrected Lord, through the power and presence of the Holy Spirit, Jesus is the invisible head of his Body, the Church. And, as St. Augustine wrote, the Holy Spirit is the soul of the Church. The Spirit gives life to the Church and directs it in Christ's continuing work of Salvation.

In reflecting on the activity of the Holy Spirit in the Gospels, we learn that when the Father sends the Son, he also sends the Holy Spirit. The Son and Holy Spirit have a joint but distinct mission. It is Christ Jesus who is visible and who shows us the image of God. It is the Holy Spirit, however, who reveals to us who God is.

Gifts of the Holy Spirit (CCC, 1831)

The Holy Spirit gives us what we need to live as God's children and Christ's disciples. The Church recognizes seven gifts that the Holy Spirit showers on us at Baptism and Confirmation. The Old Testament prophet Isaiah (Is 11:2–3) said these qualities would identify the Messiah. Jesus lived each of these gifts perfectly. For example, Jesus showed *wisdom* in teaching his parables. He reflected *understanding* of the poor and sick. He showed perfect *reverence* for his Father, for other people, and for the beauty of creation. He showed great *fortitude* in following his mission.

For Review

1. How was the revelation of the Person of the Holy Spirit in Scripture different from the revelation of God the Father and God the Son?
2. When did Jesus say was the time that the promised Holy Spirit would finally come to the Apostles?
3. What is it that the Holy Spirit brings? How are believers expected to be different?
4. What were the Jewish origins of Pentecost?
5. What is *ruah* and how was this word used in the Old Testament?
6. Give two examples of the Holy Spirit's presence or involvement in Salvation History in the Old Testament.
7. Give two examples of the Holy Spirit's presence or involvement in the ministry of Jesus.

For Reflection

Imagine you were at the first Pentecost. Share your own account about the dramatic descent of the Holy Spirit.

Main Ideas

- The advice of God the Father is that we should listen to his Son, Jesus. (p. 90)
- In studying what Jesus revealed about God, it's clear that he wanted his followers to know that God is Father, Son, and Holy Spirit. (pp. 91–94)
- Jesus commissioned his followers to teach and baptize "in the name of the Father, Son, and Holy Spirit." (p. 91)
- The doctrine of the Trinity is a mystery because we can never truly understand that the three Persons of God are equal, and distinct but eternally and harmoniously united in love. (pp. 91–94)
- Catholic beliefs in the Incarnation and Trinity are reflected in the creeds and in other Acts of Faith. (p. 92)
- St. Athanasius, an early Church Father, wrote, "For the Son of God became man that we might become God." (p. 92)
- The Church developed its teaching about the Trinity in its first several centuries through six ecumenical councils. (p. 92)
- Belief in one God underlies the First Commandment: "I, the Lord, am your God; you shall not have other gods besides me." (pp. 92–94)
- Each Person of the Trinity is fully God even though the Trinity is One. As St. Athanasius put it, "God is a Trinity in unity." The Divine Persons are in relation to each other—Father to Son and Father to Spirit; Son to Father and Son to Spirit; Spirit to Father and Spirit to Son. (p. 92)
- The Old Testament reveals much about God the Father, particularly that YHWH ("I AM") is the only God. (pp. 94–98)
- God the Father is the Creator of the universe and made everything out of nothing. (p. 94)
- God cares for and watches over all of creation through *divine providence,* a loving and watchful divine guidance. (p. 94)
- God's loving care for humans is so great that he sent his Son Jesus to redeem us and invite us into a new relationship with God. (p. 94)
- In the Old Testament, we learn that YHWH, or God, is *infinite, omnipotent, eternal*, a pure spirit, unchangeable, supremely holy, personal, and loving. (pp. 94–95)
- God the Father's love for creation led to the promise of a Savior for the world. (pp. 94–96)
- It was Jesus who revealed most fully who God is and how God planned to save us. (p. 96)
- The Jews saw God as a loving Father, and Jesus himself called God "Father" forty-five times at the Last Supper in John's Gospel. (p. 96)
- Jesus invited his followers to call God "Abba" or "Daddy" and taught us to pray to God with the "Our Father." (pp. 96–97)
- Jesus preached about persistence in prayer to God our Father and talked about doing his Father's will. (pp. 96–97)
- Though Scripture often talks about God as Father, God is pure spirit and therefore neither male nor female. However, images of God as mother are also found in the Old and New Testaments. (p. 97)
- The Old Testament phrase "son of God" was used to refer to Israel, the king, and an angel. In the New Testament, the phrase was often used to refer to Jesus. (pp. 98–99)
- Jesus made it clear that he really was the Son of God, equal to his Father in divinity, and many of his parables carried this message. (pp. 98–101)
- In John's Gospel, the "I AM" statements of Jesus use the same images for God the Father in the Old Testament. (p. 100)

- After the Death and Resurrection of Jesus, the Apostles had a deeper understanding of Jesus as the Son of God. (p. 100)
- Although the Old Testament reveals God the Father and points to the coming of Jesus as Son, revelation of the Holy Spirit evolved slowly. (pp. 102–107)
- Jesus often referred to the Holy Spirit in his teaching and promised that the Spirit would come after his Death and Resurrection. (pp. 102–103)
- The Holy Spirit came to the followers of Jesus in great power on Pentecost Sunday. (pp. 103–104)
- *Ruah*, a Hebrew word that means "wind" or "breath," refers to God's mysterious and life-giving power, and often refers to the Holy Spirit's actions. (pp. 104–105)
- Through the gift of the Holy Spirit to the Church, we can witness the Spirit's presence in the Old Testament. (pp. 104–105)
- The Holy Spirit played a key role in the ministry of Jesus. (pp. 106–107)

Terms, People, Places

Match the following terms with the definitions below.

Divine Providence	Ecumenical Council
Eternal	Infinite
Monotheism	Omnipotent
Polytheism	Ruah
Tongues	Blessed Trinity

1. God is everywhere, unlimited, and all-powerful.
2. A worldwide, official assembly of bishops under the direction of the Pope.
3. A term that describes existing without a beginning and forever.
4. The central mystery of the Christian faith.
5. A term that means extending endlessly, having no end or limits.
6. The belief that there is one, all-powerful God.
7. A term meaning "wind" or "breath."
8. The sovereignty of God over events in the lives of individuals throughout history.
9. A gift of the Holy Spirit that allows a person to speak in prayer languages that were never learned.
10. A belief that there are many gods.

Primary Source Quotations

Jesus, the Only Son of God

The Gospels report that at two solemn moments, the Baptism and the Transfiguration of Christ, the voice of the Father designates Jesus his "beloved Son." Jesus calls himself the "only Son of God," and by this title affirms his eternal preexistence. He asks for faith in "the name of the only Son of God." In the centurion's exclamation before the crucified Christ, "Truly this man was the Son of God," that Christian confession is already heard. Only in the Paschal mystery can the believer give the title "Son of God" its full meaning."

—*Catechism of the Catholic Church,* 444

Augustine's Short Prayer to the Holy Spirit

O Holy Spirit, descend plentifully into my heart. Enlighten the dark corners of this neglected dwelling and scatter there Thy cheerful beams.

—St. Augustine of Hippo

An Early Church Father on the Divinity of Jesus

But he Jesus is himself in his own right, beyond all men who ever lived, God, Lord, and king eternal, and the incarnate word, proclaimed by all the prophets, the Apostles. . . . The Scriptures would not have borne witness to these things concerning him, if, like everyone else, he were mere man.

—St. Irenaeus

Write your own statement about Jesus that proclaims his divinity.

Ongoing Assignments

1. Write a two-page report on the life of one of the great defenders of the faith, St. Athanasius. Do an Internet search for "St. Athanasius."
2. Create a PowerPoint presentation showing how artists have depicted God the Father in art. Be sure to include Michelangelo's scene of creation painted on the ceiling of the Sistine Chapel.
3. Read the following passages to find out some things Jesus said about God the Father. Answer the questions that follow:
   - Matthew 18:19–20: What does Jesus tell us to do? What is the payoff?
   - Matthew 18:21–35: What is the point of this parable?
   - Luke 11:1–13: What will the Father do for us if we follow Jesus' teaching?
4. Compose a prayer to the Blessed Trinity. Address each Divine Person in your prayer.
5. Choose one of the Gospels and select seven memorable sayings of Jesus. Find pictures to illustrate the sayings. Design a display of these sayings and their illustrations.
6. Psalm 23 is beloved for its imagery of a caring, loving God who is our shepherd. Read this Psalm carefully. Then rewrite it using different imagery that still represents God's loving kindness. Create a short PowerPoint presentation with verses, appropriate background artwork, and some favorite instrumental music.
7. Create a collage illustrating the "I AM" sayings in John's Gospel.
8. Note how Psalms 8, 19, 29, 65, or 104 offer praise of God's majesty. Create a visual presentation to illustrate one of these psalms.
9. Read the following Scripture passages. Summarize how God's Spirit is represented in each of these passages.
   - Genesis 1:1–2; 2:7
   - Isaiah 11:1–3
   - Isaiah 61:1-2
   - Ezekiel 36:26–28
   - Ezekiel 37:1–14
   - 1 Corinthians 12:4–13:13

Prayer

Pray the following prayer for courage to help you to live a Christ-like life. Note how the prayer incorporates all three Persons of the Blessed Trinity.

Prayer for Courage
O gracious Father,
Source of all excellent things,
grant us strength and hope in these days of uncertainty,
finding courage through your Holy Spirit;
and give us grace so to live, not in our own weakness,
but in your unceasing steadfastness,
ever encouraged by the company of heaven;
through Jesus Christ, your Son our Lord,
who lives and reigns with you and the Holy Spirit,
one God, now and forever. Amen.

- *Reflection*: What is the greatest source of temptation in your life right now that distracts you from following Jesus?
- *Resolution*: Pray this prayer often in the coming days to gain the fortitude to live by your Christian convictions.

Chapter 4 Quick View

JESUS HELPS US TO UNDERSTAND THE TRINITY, MARY, AND THE HOLY SPIRIT

Finally, brothers, rejoice. Mend your ways, encourage one another, agree with one another, live in peace, and the God of love and peace will be with you. . . .The grace of the Lord Jesus Christ and the love of God and the fellowship of the holy Spirit be with all of you.

—2 Corinthians 13:11, 13

- **Beyond Human Understanding**
  We understand the mysteries of faith only as God reveals them to us.

- **The Inner Life of God**
  Even with our limited human intellects, we can still reflect on the Immanent Trinity, that is, the inner life of God.

- **God's Actions in Our Lives**
  Our understanding of the active and inseparable work of the Triune God—Father, Son, and Holy Spirit—in Salvation History is described by the term "Salvific Trinity."

- **The Role of Mary, the Mother of God**
  Mary, the Mother of God, is a perfect model of Christian faith, the disciple *par excellence*.

- **The Holy Spirit Gives and Renews Life**
  The Holy Spirit, the third Person of the Blessed Trinity, is the "breath" of God the Father and the guide to Jesus as he shared Good News and offered himself as a Savior for all people.

Beyond Human Understanding

There is a famous story about St. Augustine of Hippo, one of the Church's greatest theologians. One day while walking along the seashore, he was thinking deeply about the doctrine of the Trinity. He was trying to understand this great mystery so that he could explain it to believers. While deep in thought, Augustine noticed a small child playing on the beach. The child had dug a hole in the sand and was running back and forth to the ocean with a seashell. He would fill it with seawater and run back to empty the water into the hole in the sand. Amused at this impossible task, Augustine finally told the boy, "That tiny hole in the sand will never hold this immense ocean!" The boy suddenly looked straight at Augustine and replied with a seriousness way beyond his years, "And you can never hold the immense and mysterious truths of God in your small mind!"

Then, as the story goes, the child immediately disappeared.

This story reminds us that the Trinity—three Divine Persons in one God—is certainly a mystery beyond full human understanding. We are able to believe in this central doctrine of faith, however, because Jesus reveals to us this truth about God's nature. In the same way, Jesus helps us to understand

Experiencing God

Here are some common experiences that speak of God's presence. Which of these experiences led you closer to God? Write your own short journal reflection recounting a time when one of these experiences awakened in you a sense of the mystery of God.

- enjoying beauty in nature
- holding a newborn baby
- celebrating the Eucharist with friends and family
- experiencing forgiveness for something you've done wrong
- being aware of a parent's love for you
- feeling close to a best friend
- being praised by a teacher or coach
- finally figuring something out after a long struggle
- doing a good deed for someone who really needed it
- finding the courage to persevere when you wanted to quit
- seeing God in a person you greatly admire
- being rescued from a dangerous situation

the central roles the Blessed Mother, Mary, and the Holy Spirit have in our lives of faith.

This chapter allows us to further delve into these mysteries of faith. As the little boy encouraged St. Augustine, we must approach these mysteries with humility, thanking God for revealing such profound truths to us.

 For Reflection

How do you react when you encounter a deep mystery—a truth that's too big for human understanding?

The Inner Life of God (*CCC*, 232-233, 236)

This course has already pointed out that the doctrine of the Blessed Trinity is central and essential to Christianity. All of the Christian creeds highlight belief in this sacred mystery—that there are three divine Persons in one God. For example, the Athanasian Creed states:

> Now this is the Catholic faith: We worship one God in the Trinity and the Trinity in unity, without either confusing the persons or dividing the substance; for the person of the Father is one, the Son's is another, the Holy Spirit's is another; but the Godhead of the Father, Son, and Holy Spirit is one, their glory equal, their majesty coeternal. (Athanasian Creed quoted in *CCC*, 266)

One of the ways we are reminded daily of our Trinitarian belief is when we pray the most common of prayers, the Sign of the Cross. Focus on this prayer for a moment, giving it your full attention: "In the name of the Father and of the Son and of the Holy Spirit. Amen."

Just as the words do, the gestures used to pray the Sign of the Cross profess our belief in God as Trinity. As the prayer is said, the person touches first the forehead, then the chest, and finally both shoulders. We are saying that we make this profession with our minds, our hearts, and entire beings. A variation on this prayer is also prayed at times. A small sign of the cross is traced with the thumb on the forehead, then on the lips, and then over the heart. This prayer of words and gesture petitions the Triune God to bless our thoughts, words, and desires.

There is a clear connection between our Sign of the Cross prayers, our baptismal commitment, and our faith in the Blessed Trinity. This connection begins at Baptism when we become Christians. As part of the rite of Baptism, the candidate is immersed three times in the baptismal waters. Or, water is poured over his or her head three times, as the minister says, "*N*, I baptize you in the name of the Father, and of the Son, and of the Holy Spirit." We then spend our lives being more incorporated into the divine life of God in three Persons.

As the *Catechism of the Catholic Church* tells us, the baptismal ritual "signifies and actually brings about death to sin and entry into the life of the Most Holy Trinity through configuration to the Paschal mystery of Christ" (*CCC*, 1239). Christians are baptized in the *name* of the Father and of the Son and of the Holy Spirit—together.

The Immanent and Salvific Trinity

There is only *one* God, but there are three Divine Persons in this one God.

Although this a mystery, a truth of the faith that our minds can never fully understand, God has created human beings with minds that want to know the truth and are attracted to God, the source of all truth. This is why intelligent human believers, guided by the Spirit, have struggled to explain, even if in a partial way, this profound truth of our faith. Though we do not and cannot understand this mystery perfectly,

theology
The study of the existence or the attributes of God; a word taken from the Greek words *theos* ("God") and *logos* ("word").

Immanent Trinity
A focus on the inner life of God as a Trinity of three divine Persons without consideration of God's relationship to human beings or his creation work.

Salvific Trinity
The active and inseparable work of the Triune God—Father, Son, and Holy Spirit—in Salvation History.

we believe it because Christ has revealed it to us.

Theology is the study of the existence or the attributes of God, and it explores the inner life of God. Great theologians have helped us reflect more deeply on the Trinity and other doctrines. In their writings, St. Augustine (AD 354–430) and St. Thomas Aquinas (AD 1225–1274) taught two deeper truths about the Trinity. These teachings discuss the **Immanent Trinity** and the **Salvific Trinity**.

The Immanent Trinity refers to "God's inner life" or "how God exists in God." When we reflect on the Immanent Trinity, we are thinking about how and what God is, always was, and always will be. We are reflecting on God himself without human beings or any other creatures in the picture.

On the other hand, the Salvific Trinity refers to the many works God has performed to reveal and communicate his divine life on behalf of our Salvation. When we focus on the Salvific Trinity, we are reflecting on how God has interacted with us, how he has gone outside of himself to communicate with us, save us, and adopt us into the divine family.

As ways to understand the mystery of the Blessed Trinity, the Immanent Trinity and the Salvific Trinity are intimately related. When we reflect on God's saving works, we learn something about who he is. The better we understand who God is, the more clearly we see and understand all of his works. Nonetheless, our reflections and understanding can only take us so far. We must always remember that the Blessed Trinity is a profound mystery. As God said through the prophet Isaiah:

> [M]y thoughts are not your thoughts, nor are your ways my ways, says the LORD. As high as the heavens are above the earth, so high are my ways above your ways and my thoughts above your thoughts. (Is 55:8–9)

EXPLAINING THE FAITH

Why should we study theology if we imitate God best by loving one another?

"Loving God is greater than knowing him," St. Thomas Aquinas wrote. One of the most brilliant theologians of the Church understood that knowledge of God only takes us so far. And yet, theology is appropriately known as the "queen of the sciences." Theology is the study of the attributes and the existence of God. Theological thinking and reading can move us to find God's reflection in the difficult questions of life. If we find God's reflection, we know that he really exists. It is our hearts that seek and find God, the loving Creator. We learn to love him with our hearts. But our minds can also lead us a long way on this journey of the heart. What we learn and know about God enriches our love. What we discover about who God is strengthens our faith.

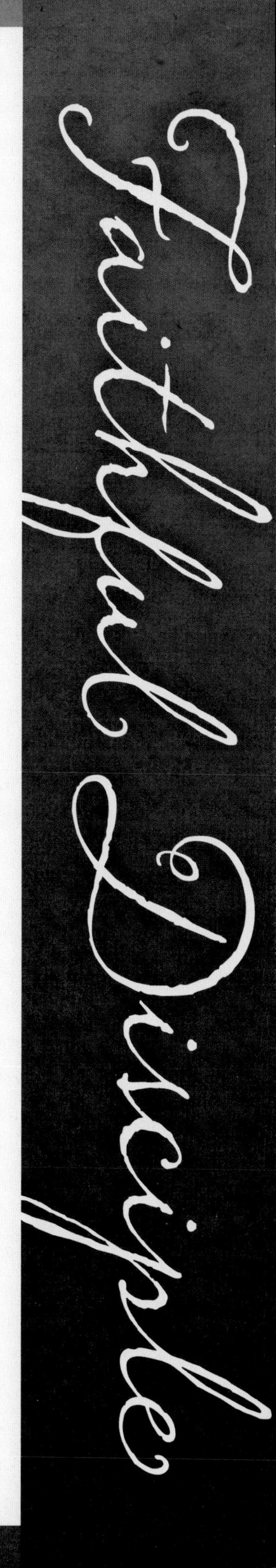

ST. AUGUSTINE
OF HIPPO

St. Augustine, one of the most important Christian theologians and writers of all times, once tried very hard to turn his back on Christianity. He was born in AD 380 in Thagaste in present-day Algeria. His mother, St. Monica, was a Christian of Berber descent. His father, Patricius, was an official in the city, and a pagan who allowed his wife to raise their son as a Christian.

It was clear that Augustine was a brilliant, creative boy, bound for great achievements. Though not particularly wealthy, Patricius insisted on the best education available for his son. Augustine abandoned his Christian beliefs when he went to study in Carthage. All around him were pagan influences. He began to lead a wild and self-indulging life. For many years, he lived with a woman who gave birth to his son Adeodatus. He also became a Manichean, a religion that taught that all matter is essentially corrupt and evil. Though grieved about her son's choices and lifestyle, Monica never quit praying that he would someday return to the faith.

In Europe in 386, Augustine happened to read a biography of St. Anthony the hermit. It touched him deeply. Gradually, he turned again toward Christ. Monica was overjoyed. Soon after that, Augustine and his son were baptized and Augustine decided to return home to Africa with his mother and son. On the voyage home, both Monica and Adeodatus died. Back in Hippo, though grieving, Augustine was consoled by his new faith. He became a priest and then later a bishop. Augustine's writings and presentation of Christian beliefs earned him the title of Doctor of the Church. His autobiography, *Confessions*, is a Christian classic and the first great autobiography in Western literature. Augustine died at the age of seventy-five in 430.

consubstantial
The quality "of one being" in the relationship between all the divine Persons of the Trinity—Father, Son, and Holy Spirit. So, the Son and the Holy Spirit have the exact same nature as the Father, the first Person of the Trinity.

The Church Teaches about God's Inner Life (CCC, 245-256, 264)

To help express Trinitarian faith, the early Church developed formulas like St. Paul's greeting to Christian converts: "The grace of the Lord Jesus Christ and the love of God and the fellowship of the holy Spirit be with all of you" (2 Cor 13:13). In addition, early Church councils and Church Fathers developed a vocabulary to help address the mystery of the Trinity. Three important terms from that era that have become part of our faith vocabulary are:

1. *Substance* means "nature" or "essence." Substance is what makes something what it is. When we say that the Father has the same substance or nature as the Son and the Holy Spirit, we are proclaiming that God is *one* divine being. All three Persons have the same divine nature.
2. *Person* refers to the distinctions among the Father, Son, and Holy Spirit.
3. *Relation* designates that the Father, Son, and Holy Spirit are distinct because of their relationships.

Using this vocabulary as background, the Church teaches the following mysterious three truths about God's own inner life:

1. *There is only one God.* The Blessed Trinity is one God, that is, one divine being that possesses a divine substance or nature.
2. *There are three distinct Persons—Father, Son, and Holy Spirit—in one God.* We should not think of the word *Person* in the same way we do when we call human beings "persons." Rather, "Person" in the Blessed Trinity refers to distinctions between the members. Thus, there are not three separately conscious or free-standing individuals in God. *There is only one divine being.* There are not three separate intellects or wills in the one God. When one Person of the Trinity acts, the other two Persons also act in communion. Each divine Person is distinct but does not act separately from the others. God is one, a "community-in-unity." The Divine Persons are inseparable in both what they do and in what they are. They love us with the same love and know us with the same knowledge.
3. *The Divine Persons have distinct relationships with one another.* Our faith is in one God with three Divine Persons who are really distinct from one another. In a mysterious way, we can say, "God is one but not solitary" (*Fides Damasi* quoted in *CCC*, 254). The Divine Persons are distinct in origin. The Church explains the relationships among the three Persons of the Trinity this way:

- *The Father.* The First Person of the Trinity is absolutely without origin. From all eternity he "begets" the Son, the Second Person of the Trinity. The Son proceeds from the Father. There was never a time when the Son did not proceed from the Father. Therefore, the Father is in relationship to the Son from all eternity.
- *The Son.* We can think of the Father's begetting of the Son as God knowing himself perfectly. The Father expresses himself perfectly to himself, and this is the Son, the Word of God. Thus, the Son is the Father's perfect, divine expression of himself. They are one, yet distinct. The Son of God is in relationship to the Father from all eternity. As the Son of God, he is true God, and is **consubstantial** with the Father. *Consubstantial* means "having the exact divine nature as the Father."
- *The Holy Spirit.* The relationship of the Father and Son is a perfect relationship. The Father and Son love each other with an eternal, perfect, and divine love. The love that proceeds from the Father and the Son is the third Person of the Trinity, the Holy Spirit. The Holy Spirit proceeds from both the Father and the Son as the perfect expression of their divine love for each other. In other words, the Holy Spirit is the Spirit of Love between the Father and the Son. The Spirit binds them into a community of unity. Since the Holy Spirit proceeds from the Father and Son eternally, the Spirit is consubstantial with the Father and the Son.

In a classic expression of faith, the *Athanasian Creed* expresses the relationships of the Three Persons of the Trinity this way:

> The Father is not made by anyone, nor created, nor begotten. The Son is from the Father alone, not made, not created, but begotten. The Holy Spirit is from the Father and the Son, not made, not created, not begotten, but proceeding. . . . The entire three Persons are co-eternal with one another and co-equal, so that . . . both Trinity in Unity and Unity in Trinity are to be adored.

In summary, the inner life of God, the Immanent Trinity, can be summarized in this way:

1. There is one God with one divine nature.
2. In this one God, there are three Divine Persons: Father, Son, and Holy Spirit.
3. The Father, the Son, and the Holy Spirit are distinct but in eternal relationship with each other.

Symbols for the Trinity

For many centuries, Christian art has used many images to try to express the mystery of the Triune God. For example, the equilateral triangle symbolizes the equality in nature of the three divine Persons. The sides unite to form one figure, suggesting the one and inseparable divine essence. Here is further information about the equilateral triangle, called the "Shield of the Trinity" and two other images:

Shield of the Trinity

The translation from the Latin reads that the Father (*Pater*) is (*est*) God (*Deus*); the Son (*Filius*) is God; and the Holy Spirit (*Spiritus Sanctus*) is God. Thus, God's unity is professed. Equality among the Persons is symbolized by the equilateral triangle. And the distinction between each Person of the Trinity is again conveyed by the Latin: the Father is not (*non est*) the Son nor the Holy Spirit; and the Son is not the Father nor Holy Spirit; and the Holy Spirit is not the Father nor Son.

Shamrock

The legendary story tells that when St. Patrick was preaching to the pagans in Ireland, he was challenged to prove how God could be one being yet three Persons. As pointed out in the feature on page 93, St. Patrick picked a shamrock and asked whether he held up one leaf or three leaves.

"If three, then why one stem? If one stem then why three leaves?" Those who questioned him could not answer. St. Patrick responded, "If you cannot explain such a simple mystery as a shamrock, how can you hope to understand such a profound one as the Blessed Trinity?"

Tree and Sun

St. John Damascene taught with two famous images for the Trinity. The first is a tree where the Father is the root, the Son the branches, and the Spirit the fruit. The substance of each (root, branch, and fruit) is all the same—that of a tree. And yet, there is distinction. So it is with the Trinity. Each Person has the fullness of the divine nature; yet, there is distinction. One God, three Persons.

The second metaphor St. John used was that of the sun. The Father is the sun, the Son is the rays, and the Holy Spirit is heat. Distinction, but all the same substance.

For Review

1. How do gestures used to pray the Sign of the Cross show as much faith in the Trinity as the words do?
2. What do theologians mean by "God's inner life" or the Immanent Trinity?
3. What are three important terms that are used to discuss the mystery of the Trinity? Briefly explain each term.
4. What does the Church mean by the word *Person* as it is used in describing the Trinity? How is this meaning different from the way it is usually used?
5. How is the Father, the First Person of the Trinity, related to the Son? And how is the Son related to the Father?
6. Briefly describe how the Holy Spirit is related to the Father and the Son.

For Reflection

To which Person of the Blessed Trinity do you most usually address your prayers? Why do you think this is so?

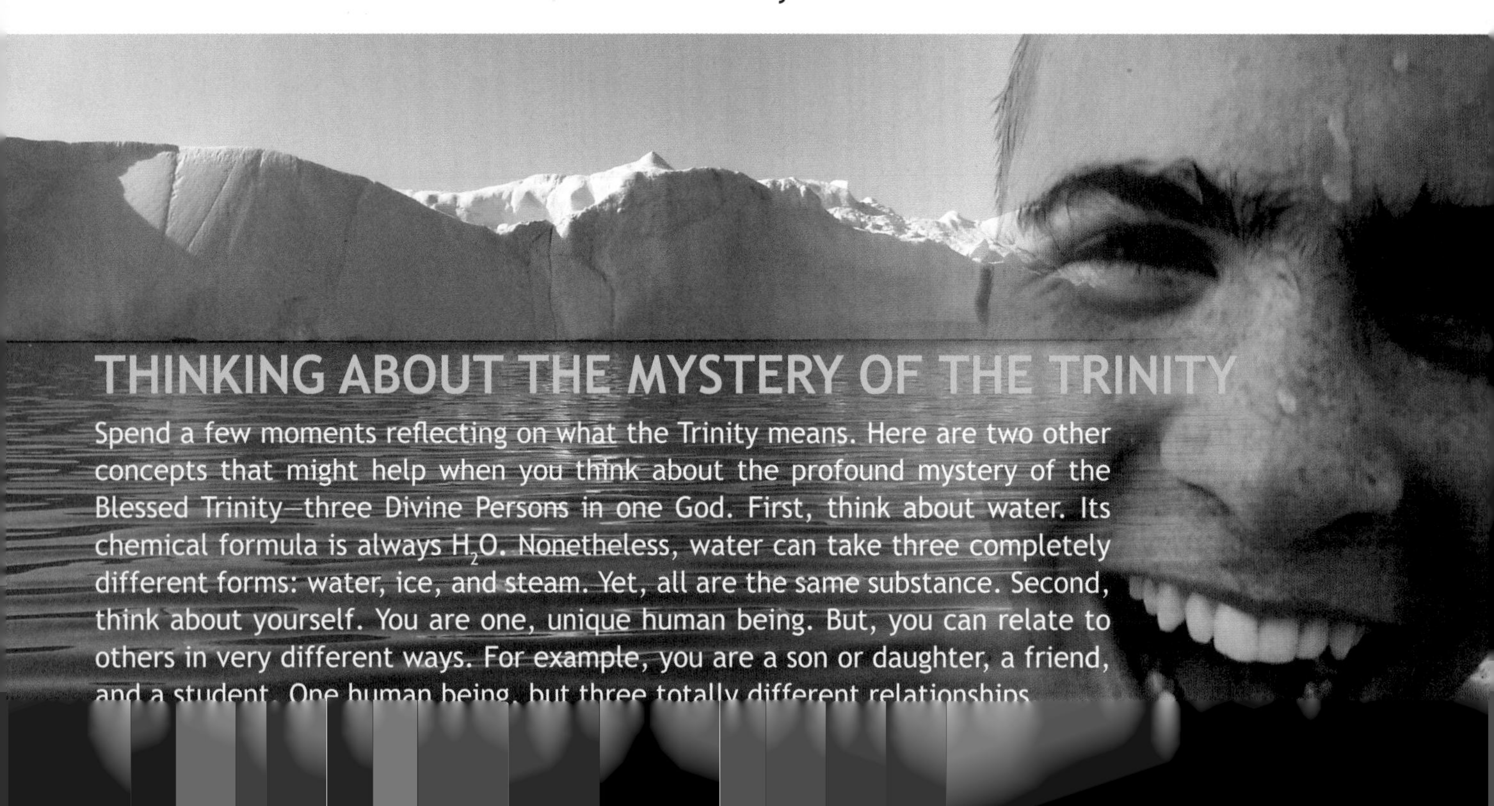

THINKING ABOUT THE MYSTERY OF THE TRINITY

Spend a few moments reflecting on what the Trinity means. Here are two other concepts that might help when you think about the profound mystery of the Blessed Trinity—three Divine Persons in one God. First, think about water. Its chemical formula is always H_2O. Nonetheless, water can take three completely different forms: water, ice, and steam. Yet, all are the same substance. Second, think about yourself. You are one, unique human being. But, you can relate to others in very different ways. For example, you are a son or daughter, a friend, and a student. One human being, but three totally different relationships.

God's Actions in Our Lives (*CCC*, 257-260, 267)

When we study the Salvific Trinity, we are reflecting on God's action in our lives and in the world. God reveals the Trinity to us through his deeds in Salvation History, but especially through Christ's Incarnation. But, there are many other ways that we encounter the work of the Holy Spirit.

For example, we meet God's work through the beauty and greatness of creation, especially through its intricate design and awesome power. God is the Creator of every galaxy, every waterfall, and every tiny hummingbird. And yet Jesus taught us not to fear this Creator, and not to consider him distant or remote. Jesus told us to call this Creator "Abba" or "Daddy." This mighty but approachable God is merciful, filled with love for us, and compassionate beyond what we could possibly hope for.

A second way that we experience God's intervention in the world is through our Redeemer. Jesus Christ is God who became flesh, or one of us. This second Divine Person is known as Emmanuel ("God-with-us"). As our Savior, he is also God "for us and with us"; he is our faithful companion. Through the teachings, actions, and miracles of Jesus, we have met God the Son. In Jesus Christ we also encounter a brother and a friend who deeply cares for each of us as individuals. Jesus Christ is God with a human face.

A third way that we experience God's work is through the Holy Spirit who lives in us. This Spirit also gives us life and showers his gifts on us. The Holy Spirit prays in us and directs us to live Christ-filled lives. He joins us to Jesus Christ who, in turn, takes us to his heavenly Father. We pray "to the Father, through the Son, in the Holy Spirit." The Holy Spirit is the love of God that Jesus promised. The Spirit is the soul of the Church, giving it life until the end of time.

God has communicated himself to humanity, and to each of us as well, in these three distinct ways. But, God's revelation as a Trinity of Divine Persons took place gradually through Salvation History. Catholic philosopher Peter Kreeft states God's progressive revelation this way:

> First as the transcendent Creator "outside" us; then as the incarnate Savior "beside" us; then as the indwelling Spirit "inside" us. The reason for this progression, first Father (Old Testament), then Son (Gospels), then Spirit (Acts of the Apostles and the Church), is found in God's very being, which is love (1 Jn 4:18), and in the purpose and motive for God's self-revelation to man, which is love. For love's aim is always greater intimacy, deeper union with the beloved; so the stages of God's self-revelation are stages of increasing intimacy with man (from "outside" to "beside" to "inside").

Our Trinity Work

Being made in God's image means that we reflect the life and works of the Trinity. We can imitate the work of the Holy Spirit, the Sanctifier, when we imitate his life, act out of love, use our minds to grow in knowledge, and use our hands to help others.

Commit yourself to a specific act of service or love in imitation of the Trinity. In the next month, perform one of the following activities. Or, do something similar to reflect the work of God the Father, God the Son, and God the Holy Spirit:

- make gifts for residents of a nursing home
- tutor younger students at an elementary school
- teach an adult computer skills
- offer to help a younger sibling with a homework project
- serve at a food bank
- help clean up a city park
- help at an animal shelter
- volunteer at your local library
- participate in your parish youth group
- cook and serve a meal for your family

Divine Missions of the Blessed Trinity

Creation, Salvation, and sanctification are known as the **divine missions of the Blessed Trinity**. Although we attribute creation to the Father, Salvation (Redemption) to the Son, and sanctification to the Holy Spirit, we must remember that all three Persons of the Trinity act as one and are fully present in all the missions. As the *Catechism of the Catholic Church* reminds us, "each divine person performs the common work according to his unique personal property" (*CCC*, 258). All three Persons share divine attributes—for example, all are eternal, almighty, all-knowing, all-loving, all-holy, transcendent and yet immanent.

> Inseparable in what they are, the divine persons are also inseparable in what they do. But within the single divine operation each shows forth what is proper to him in the Trinity, especially in the divine missions of the Son's Incarnation and the gift of the Holy Spirit. (*CCC*, 267)

The Blessed Trinity Is Love

Our contemplation of the Blessed Trinity also leads us to a fundamental truth about God and his nature: God is love! The First Letter of John states it so: "God is love, and whoever remains in love remains in God and God in him" (1 Jn 4:16). The *Catechism of the Catholic Church* explains further:

> God's very being is love. By sending his only Son and the Spirit of Love in the fullness of time, God has revealed his innermost secret: God himself is an eternal exchange of love, Father, Son, and Holy Spirit, and he has destined us to share in that exchange. (*CCC*, 221)

As a sign of our gratitude, God asks that we love in imitation of him. We were made to love, and the source of our true happiness is to love God and others. Our goal is to get to know, love, and serve God in this life, and to be united with God for all eternity. Prayer helps us reach this destiny.

We first learn love in our own families, which is a reflection of the love of God. We allow the Triune God to live in us when we reach out in love to our brothers and sisters. Jesus and the Holy Spirit have revealed that the nature of God is a family. Pope John Paul II said, "God in his deepest mystery is not a solitude but a family, since he has in himself fatherhood, Sonship, and the essence of a family, which is love."

For Review

1. Define Salvific Trinity.
2. How do we experience God's action differently through each Person of the Blessed Trinity?
3. What is meant by the term "divine missions of the Blessed Trinity"?
4. How is the Trinity like a family that we can imitate?
5. What is the fundamental essence or reality of the Trinity?
6. What does God ask of us as a sign of gratitude for our existence and our blessings?

For Reflection

- Pope John Paul II wrote that "God in his deepest mystery is not a solitude but a family." Explain what this means to you.
- Describe a time and experience when you felt as though you "met God through creation."

The Role of Mary, the Mother of God (*CCC*, 484-511, 722-724, 963-975, 2673-2677)

Mary, the Mother of God and the Mother of the Church, is the perfect model of Christian faith, the disciple *par excellence*. She is the Mother of the Savior and our Blessed Mother too. She is the greatest **saint**, that is, a holy person who lives now with God through the grace of Jesus Christ. Mary is the model for everyone who wants to live their lives for God and for others.

Mary has a unique role in Salvation History. Her "yes" to God's plan to send his Son was instrumental in fulfilling God's plan. As a young girl, Mary was probably betrothed or engaged to marry by the age of twelve or thirteen. Mary did not understand how she was to conceive a child when the angel Gabriel appeared to her. However, Mary was humble and open to God's invitation. Her "yes" of acceptance revealed that she was willing to be involved in the saving mission of her Son Jesus—from the very beginning of his life.

divine missions of the Blessed Trinity
The distinctive works of God's saving intervention in the world—creation, Salvation, and sanctification. Although creation is attributed to the Father, Salvation (Redemption) to the Son, and sanctification to the Holy Spirit, all three Persons of the Trinity act as one and are fully present in all the missions.

saint
A "holy one" of God who lives in union with God through the grace of Jesus Christ and the power of the Holy Spirit and whom God rewards with eternal life in Heaven.

Assumption
The dogmatic teaching of the Catholic Church that when the earthly life of Mary was completed, she was taken body and soul into the presence of God. Mary was granted this grace, the Church says, because she is the sinless Mother of God.

A Model of Faith and Trust: The Annunciation

The biblical account of Mary's life begins in Nazareth, a small town in the region of Galilee in Palestine. Mary must have been very frightened when the angel Gabriel greeted her and announced that God was very pleased with her. Mary learned that she was to conceive a child whose name would be Jesus, a name that means "Savior" or "God with us." The Church calls this event the Annunciation. The angel announced to her:

> The holy Spirit will come upon you, and the power of the Most High will overshadow you. Therefore the child to be born will be called holy, the Son of God. And behold, Elizabeth, your relative, has also conceived a son in her old age, and this is the sixth month for her who was called barren; for nothing will be impossible for God. (Lk 1:35–37)

As you can imagine, what the angel said—that Mary was to conceive a very special child without having sexual relations with Joseph—was too much for Mary to fully understand. But Mary was an open, loving, faith-filled person. The only goal in her young life was to obey God's will, whatever that might mean. Without hesitating, Mary responded: "Behold, I am the handmaid of the Lord. May it be done to me according to your word." Then the angel departed from her (Lk 1:38).

Mary's response—"May it be done to me according to your word"—is a powerful example for all Christians. Many times in our lives, we also don't fully understand what God is asking of us. In fact, we are not really capable of fully understanding what God wants from us. He desires our faith. Once we surrender to his will and allow him into our lives, God leads the way. Luke's Gospel tells us that the angel left Mary but God did not. Within Mary's womb, a baby was soon conceived. This child was God's Son.

An Example of Charity and Outreach: The Visitation

After agreeing to God's plan for her life, Mary immediately set off to visit her cousin Elizabeth (Lk 1:39–56). Mary's first thought was to help her elderly cousin who was also pregnant, not pamper herself as any expectant mother might do. It would have also been natural for Mary to be worried about the reaction of Joseph, her family, and her village to the pregnancy outside of marriage. But Mary held on to the angel's promise. God had a plan, and she had to trust him. Mary turned away from her own concerns and traveled to visit and help care for Elizabeth.

A Witness of Faithfulness: Staying with Jesus

Mary and Joseph raised Jesus in a loving, prayerful home. They fed, sheltered, and taught him. They looked out for all his needs. Tradition says that Joseph died before Jesus began his public ministry. But Mary remained with her Son as he began to do the work he was to do. She was a witness for his works and words and supported him completely. For example, at the wedding feast at Cana, she told people to listen to her Son (Jn 2:5). Moreover, Mary was a faithful disciple during Jesus' final hours. She stayed with him to the end, standing beneath the cross at his horrible death. And finally, she cried as a mother would do at the death of a child.

According to Acts 1:14, after the Ascension of Jesus, Mary was in the Upper Room with the Apostles on Pentecost Sunday. On that day, the Holy Spirit came in power to these followers of Jesus. Perhaps Mary had been encouraging these confused and frightened disciples to wait patiently for the Holy Spirit.

The Church is not sure if Mary, the Mother of God, physically died before her **Assumption** (see page 127). Though apocryphal Gospels talk about it, no one knows the specifics of her passage. Was she was raised from a grave like Lazarus? Was her Assumption seen by anyone? Was Mary in Ephesus during her last days on earth? Did Mary physically die before she was assumed? Early Church Fathers and theologians seem to believe that Mary did die before her Assumption. In the mind of the modern Church, however, this remains a mystery. Mary's body and soul, Pope Pius XII said, "were united as she was taken to Heaven to be with her son Jesus, the Son of God." In fact, the Assumption of Mary had been celebrated on August 15 for many centuries. The followers of Jesus believed that he would take his Mother to be with him immediately. Belief in Mary's Assumption into Heaven had been common in the Church since the seventh century. Today, the Church tells us that Mary's Assumption is a promise for all people. All of the faithful will one day be received into paradise to be with God.

Today, Mary reigns as Queen of Heaven. The Church honors her with many titles, all of which reflect our beliefs about this special person. Her greatest title is "Mother of God." Other titles are: "Our Lady," the "Immaculate Conception," the "Blessed Mother," the "Mother of the Church," "Ever Virgin," the "Queen of Heaven and Earth." As Our Blessed Mother, Mary continues to pray for us before her Son. This is also why the Church prays to Mary using titles like "Advocate," "Helper," "Benefactress," and "Mediatrix."

Because of the special role Mary plays in Salvation History, the Church teaches several important truths about her. Five important truths are discussed in the sections that follow.

The Immaculate Conception

From the first moment of her own conception as a baby in the womb of her mother, Mary was preserved from Original Sin. This also means that from the first moment of her existence, Mary was full of grace. That is, Mary was free of any alienation from God caused by sin. She was to have a special role in God's work of Salvation. Therefore, God graced her

Immaculate Conception
The dogmatic teaching of the Catholic Church that Mary was conceived in the womb of her mother without the stain of Original Sin that all other human beings inherit. This teaching was declared as an infallible teaching by Pope Pius IX in 1854.

Theotokos
A Greek term for Mary meaning "God bearer" or "birth mother of God" that was first used by the Council of Ephesus in AD 431.

infallible teaching
Catholic teachings, proposed by the Magisterium in union with the Pope, that is declared to be totally free of error. Infallibility is a gift of the Spirit whereby the Pope and the bishops are preserved from error when proclaiming a doctrine related to Christian faith or morals.

with this divine favor in anticipation of her Son's Death and Resurrection. The Church celebrates the feast of the **Immaculate Conception** on December 8, a holy day of obligation.

We also learn that Mary was so close to God that she did not commit any personal sins. She lived a blameless life, the most blessed of all human beings. The angel Gabriel proclaimed to her, "The Lord is with you" (Lk 1:28). As the Mother of God, Mary is all-holy.

The Virgin Mary

In the Apostles' Creed, we proclaim that Jesus was born of the Virgin Mary. This expresses our belief that God took the initiative in the Incarnation. God alone is the Father of our Lord and Savior, Jesus Christ. Jesus was conceived by the Holy Spirit and born of the Virgin Mary. Mary remained a virgin even after the birth of the Lord.

This conception of Jesus in a virgin is God's work. It is beyond "all human understanding and possibility" (*CCC*, 497). Only with faith can we understand its true meaning. From all eternity, God chose Mary to be the Mother of Jesus. She was a true daughter of Israel from a long line of holy women. This heritage helped prepare her to cooperate with God's plan of Salvation. Her response, "May it be done to me according to your word" (Lk 1:38), helped God's plan of Salvation.

Mother of God and Mother of the Church

The Church teaches us to call Mary the "Mother of God." The Council of Ephesus (AD 431) used the term "**Theotokos**" to express this truth. *Theotokos* means "God-Bearer" or "Birth-giver of God." Because Mary is the Mother of Jesus Christ, it is therefore proper to call her the Mother of God. This title for Mary is highest among her titles.

> The One whom she conceived as man by the Holy Spirit, who truly became her Son according to the flesh, was none other than the Father's eternal Son, the second person of the Holy Trinity. Hence the Church confesses that Mary is truly "Mother of God." (*CCC*, 495)

When Jesus was dying on the cross, he told that Mary would be our Mother too. "Behold, your mother," Jesus told John who stood at the foot of the cross with Mary (Jn 19:27). Mary is a spiritual mother for each of us and is counted as the Mother of the Church. Mary is also a "New Eve." Unlike the first Eve, Mary cooperated fully with the Holy Spirit to bring Christ into the world. We know that children imitate their mothers. By giving Mary to us as our mother, Jesus wanted his followers to learn to imitate her fidelity, obedience, compassion, love, and prayerfulness, know what great things he does out of love, and have a perfect model of faith and holiness.

The Assumption of Mary

Christians must believe in the Resurrection of Jesus. As St. Paul wrote to the Christians in Corinth, "if Christ has not been raised, then empty (too) is our preaching; empty, too, your faith." Because we believe in Christ's Resurrection, we hope that we too will one day rise from the dead as Christ promised.

After her earthly life was completed, Mary was immediately taken, body and soul, into the loving and joyful presence of God. We call this mysterious blessing the Assumption:

> Finally the Immaculate Virgin, preserved free from all stain of original sin, when the course of her earthly life was finished, was taken up body and soul into heavenly glory, and exalted by the Lord as Queen over all things, so that she might be the more fully conformed to her Son, the Lord of lords and conqueror of sin and death. (*CCC*, 966, quoting *Lumen Gentium*, no. 59)

Long before belief in the Assumption of Mary was an official dogma of the Church, Christians marked it as a feast. In Syria, the Assumption of Mary was celebrated as early as the fifth century. In 1950, Pope Pius XII declared the teaching about the Assumption an **infallible teaching**. Mary, the Pope said, "having completed the course of her earthly life, was assumed body and soul to heavenly glory." The doctrine of the Assumption of Mary connects two realities: Mary's unique role as God's mother preserved from Original Sin and the reality of our final Resurrection in Christ.

Mary was preserved from death's decay. She was the first to share in the Lord's Resurrection. The Church celebrates this feast on August 15 as a holy day of obligation. It reminds us of our own future joyous resurrection if we remain faithful to Mary's Son, Jesus Christ.

Veneration of Mary

Catholics have always had special devotion to Mary. After all, she is the Mother of God and the Mother of the Church. Venerating Mary means asking Mary to join her prayers to ours. We ask her to intercede for us, to act as a "go between" to God for us. In the "Hail Mary," we beg, "Pray for us sinners, now and at the hour of our death. Amen." Praying to and honoring her have two major benefits: They increase our love for her. They help us imitate her virtues, especially her life of total commitment to her Son, Jesus.

Giving Mary special honor is not meant to hide the role of Jesus as our mediator. Her motherly role is to help us pay attention to Jesus, the unique Redeemer. Her good qualities make her a special human being, one who directs us to her Son. All good Marian art—like Michelangelo's *Pietà*—draws our attention not to her, but to her Son and points to Mary's role in the mystery of Salvation. She gives her Son to humanity. She leads us to him. She shows us how to respond to him. She intercedes on our behalf, like she did for the young married couple in the miracle at Cana (Jn 2:1–12).

There are many devotions to Mary. The most popular is the Rosary, which includes vocal prayers

Learning about Mary in the Gospels

Read the following passages about Mary. Write your answers to the corresponding questions.

1. *Luke 2:41-52*. What do you learn about Mary in this scene, especially verse 51?
2. *John 2:1-12*. What does this passage reveal about Mary? What lesson does Mary teach us here about prayer? About service?
3. *John 19:25-27*. What does this passage tell us about Mary? What might Jesus be telling us, his disciples, about his Mother through this passage? What do you admire most about Mary?

and meditation on the mysteries of Christ's life. The most repeated prayer in the Rosary is the *Hail Mary*. Other popular Marian devotions include the Angelus, the First Saturday Devotion, the Litany of the Blessed Mother, and various novenas.

For Review

1. How is Mary, the Mother of God, both the perfect model of faith and the greatest saint?
2. What happened at the Annunciation?
3. Why does the Church see Mary's "yes" to God as a great example of faith?
4. How was Mary one of her Son's followers until the end of her life?
5. What is meant by the *Immaculate Conception*? Why does the Church require that Catholics understand and believe this teaching?
6. What is the history and meaning of Mary's title, *Theotokos*?
7. Tell what happened at the Assumption of Mary.
8. Name and describe three popular devotions to Mary.

For Reflection

- Mary was a teenager when she conceived and bore Jesus. What are five questions you would like to ask her about that experience?
- While dying on the cross, Jesus told Mary that the Apostle John would be like a son to her. Jesus then asked John to care for Mary, and according to John's Gospel, "from that hour the disciple took her into his home" (Jn 19:27). What are some ways that you have welcomed Mary into your life?

The Holy Spirit Gives and Renews Life (*CCC*, 733-742, 747, 976, 1830-1832, 1845)

It is the Holy Spirit, the third Person of the Blessed Trinity, who gives life to the Church. The Holy Spirit has the same substance (nature) as the Father and Son. He is the breath (Spirit) of the Father with whom Jesus is totally filled. Jesus promised to send the **Paraclete**, the Holy Spirit, after his Resurrection and Ascension into heaven. As we have seen, the Spirit came in all his power on Pentecost Sunday to serve as our advocate.

The Holy Spirit is the great gift that the Father and the Son give to the world. He is the Life-Giver who enables us to recognize who Jesus is. "No one can say 'Jesus is Lord,' except by the Holy Spirit" (1 Cor 12:4). The Holy Spirit guides Church leaders (the Magisterium) by teaching, directing, and strengthening them so they may serve as compassionate and wise servants of the Gospel. The Holy Spirit also lives in each believer. He is our internal teacher who leads us to Christ and showers us with many gifts to lead Christ-like lives.

The Holy Spirit is God's gift or **grace** to us. When we are baptized, the Holy Spirit comes to us. We become temples of the Holy Spirit and are justified before God. **Justification** means that our sins are forgiven and we are able to enter into a right relationship with God through faith in Jesus Christ. This justification begins a lifelong healing process, a conversion or turning to God that leads to eternal life and makes it possible to share in God's own life.

The Holy Spirit also gives life to and builds up the Church. This Church is the Body of Christ and the Temple of the Holy Spirit. The Spirit uses the Church to draw us to Christ, to reveal the good things the Lord has done for us, and to make present today the Paschal Mystery of Christ's love. One of the ways this is done clearly is through the Eucharist in which we share God's own life.

The Gifts of the Holy Spirit

The Holy Spirit showers many gifts on the Church. These gifts strengthen and build up the Church. There are seven particular **gifts of the Holy Spirit** that make it easier for us to live a Christian life. Jesus promised these gifts and said that his followers would receive them through the Holy Spirit. A special outpouring of the gifts comes at the Sacrament of Confirmation.

Here are some practical ways to think about how these gifts of the Holy Spirit can help us live as committed Christians: *Wisdom* enables us to look at reality from God's point of view. *Understanding* helps us to reflect on the deeper meaning of our faith. *Knowledge* shows us how God is working in our lives and in the world. *Counsel (right judgment)* helps us form our consciences in the light of Church teaching. *Fortitude (courage)* is the strength to follow one's own convictions. *Piety (reverence)* moves us to respect the Lord through praise and worship and enables us to respect the dignity and worth of others. *Fear of the Lord (wonder and awe)* shows concern about the reality of sin in one's life.

Charisms, Gifts That Serve the Church

St. Paul tells us about other gifts that are meant to build up the Church (see 1 Corinthians 12:4–11). There are many different gifts, Paul explained, but they come from the same Lord. Each gift, known as a **charism**, is given to benefit the person and strengthen the whole community. In this list of charisms, Paul includes wisdom, knowledge, faith, healing, miracle-working, prophecy, discernment, speaking in tongues, and interpreting tongues.

St. Paul also wrote about the **fruits of the Holy Spirit**, that is, spiritual perfections that result from the Holy Spirit living in us. These are the first fruits of eternal glory (see Galatians 5:22–23). Church tradition lists them as charity, joy, peace, patience, kindness, goodness, generosity, gentleness, faithfulness, modesty, self-control, and chastity.

All these gifts are related to one another. When we use these gifts, we show that we are united to Christ Jesus, the true vine (Jn 15:1). The Holy

Paraclete
Another name for the Holy Spirit that means advocate, defender, or consoler.

grace
God's gift of friendship and life that enables us to share his life and love.

justification
The forgiving of our sins in order to welcome us into a right relationship with God through our faith in Jesus Christ.

gifts of the Holy Spirit
Seven spiritual gifts from the Holy Spirit given to the Church and her members, especially at Baptism and Confirmation. The gifts are wisdom, understanding, knowledge, counsel, fortitude, piety, and fear of the Lord or wonder and awe.

charism
A spiritual gift given by God to individuals to help build up and strengthen the Church.

fruits of the Holy Spirit
Spiritual perfections that result from the Holy Spirit living in us. The Church lists them as charity, joy, peace, patience, kindness, goodness, generosity, gentleness, faithfulness, modesty, self-control, and chastity.

Imitating God Who Is Love

"God is Love" (1 Jn 4:8, 16) and love is his first gift, containing all others. "God's love has been poured into our hearts through the Holy Spirit who has been given to us" (Rm 5:5). (*CCC*, 733)

Reread 1 Corinthians 13 where St. Paul lists the qualities of Christian love. Identify the one quality of love that you think others would find most evident in your own life right now. Write a short reflection on how you can put this quality into even greater practice in the future.

Spirit is the Spirit of Love, God's great gift to us through Jesus.

"'God is Love'" and love is his first gift, containing all others. 'God's love has been poured into our hearts through the Holy Spirit who has been given to us'" (*CCC*, 733). God gives it to us freely. It is not something we can earn, nor do we deserve it. It is pure gift. God does not give love to us because we are good. We are good because God loves us and lives in us. If we allow the Spirit to live in us, then love in all its brilliance and goodness will shine through us. In 1 Corinthians 13, St. Paul describes certain qualities of love like patience, kindness, gratitude, humility, respect, consideration of others, mildness, forgiveness, fortitude, and other Christ-like traits. Love is the fountain from which all goodness flows. We do not learn to live until we love.

The Holy Spirit's Presence in Our World (CCC, 683-690, 742-743)

With the descent of the Holy Spirit on Pentecost, the Paschal Mystery was completed and the mystery of the Blessed Trinity was fully revealed. The Holy Spirit brings the Church into existence. As the Church's Advocate, he sustains her in so many ways. As the *Catechism of the Catholic Church* teaches (688), we find the Holy Spirit actively working in the Church in:

- the Scriptures, which he inspired;
- Sacred Tradition, witnessed to throughout the ages by the Church Fathers;
- the Magisterium of the Church, that is, in the Holy Father and the bishops whom the Holy Spirit guides in their roles as teachers and servants of God's people;
- the Sacraments, both words and symbols, which put us in contact with the Risen Lord;
- prayer, where he continually intercedes for us;
- the many gifts and ministries that build up the Body of Christ, the Church;
- the apostolic and missionary life and outreach; and
- the saints, whose lives witness to the presence of the Holy Spirit and his continuing work of Salvation.

The Holy Spirit is essential for living as a disciple of Jesus. The Holy Spirit is the Blessed Trinity's gift to us, and he is the great Gift-Giver. In Baptism the Holy Spirit gifts us with the faith to acknowledge Jesus as our Lord and Savior, adoption into God's own family, and the privilege of being able to address God as Father.

Symbols of the Holy Spirit

Becoming more familiar with the symbols that the Church uses for the Holy Spirit helps us to understand the Spirit more deeply.

Fire

One of the major symbols of God the Holy Spirit is fire. God appeared to Moses in a burning bush—a symbol of divine holiness. God led the Israelites through the desert by pillars of fire. Fire purifies to make one holy. It also punishes the wicked, as in the destruction of Sodom. Fire represents the transforming energy of the Holy Spirit.

Fire also gives light. Jesus calls himself the "Light of the World." His followers are to be light as well, leading others to him and to the truth of the Gospel. Thus, he gives the Holy Spirit to his disciples to empower them to enlighten the world. The Holy Spirit is our inner light to help us see Jesus and burn with love for him and others.

Tongues of Fire

Tongues of fire are often associated with the Holy Spirit's coming at Pentecost. Tongues, of course, enable us to speak. Jesus always spoke God's truth because he was filled with the Holy Spirit. His words forgave sin, resulted in cures, controlled the forces of nature, and brought the dead back to life.

The Spirit whom Jesus gives to his disciples also enables us to reverse the prideful confusion brought to humanity at the time of the Tower of Babel (Gn 11:19). The Holy Spirit makes it possible for us to proclaim Christ Jesus, to speak the truth, and to create community in the Lord's name.

Anointing with Oil

The New Testament associates anointing with oil to being anointed with the Holy Spirit. The title *Christ* means "anointed one." The Sacraments of Baptism, Confirmation, and Anointing of the Sick all use oil to signify that the Holy Spirit brings gifts, strength, and healing. Related to the use of oil is the teaching that in certain Sacraments—Baptism, Confirmation, and Holy Orders—there is an indelible seal or character to this anointing from the Holy Spirit. These Sacraments can therefore be received only once.

Water

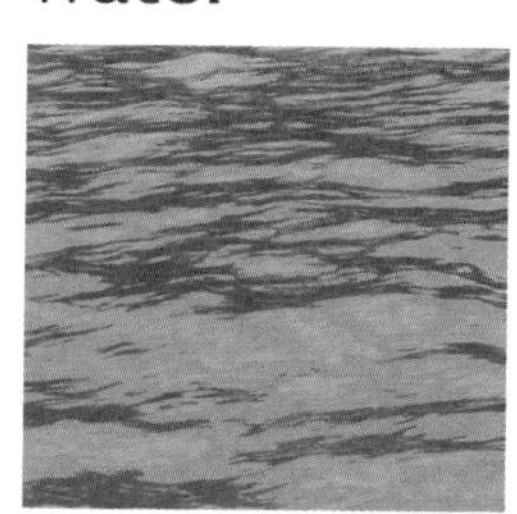

The symbol of water can represent both death and life. Too much water causes floods that lead to destruction and death. On the other hand, water is essential for life. Water symbolism associated with both death and life appears in the Bible. For example, God punished humanity in the time of Noah by sending the Flood. But God also created out of the watery chaos and sent springs of water to the Chosen People in the desert.

Jesus associated water and the Holy Spirit when he said to Nicodemus: "Amen, amen, I say to you, no one can enter the Kingdom of God without being born of water and Spirit" (Jn 3:5). This clearly refers to the Sacrament of Baptism, which brings about death to an old life of sin, and then brings rebirth to eternal life. The waters of Baptism initiate us into Christ's body, the Church, and bestow on us the gift of the Holy Spirit.

Laying on of Hands

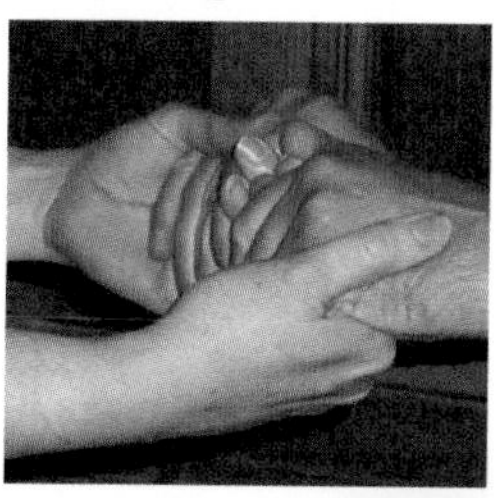

Through the power of the Holy Spirit, Jesus typically healed through touch. His Apostles healed in the name of Jesus and through the power of the

Holy Spirit. They conveyed the Holy Spirit through the laying on of hands. This sign is also used in the Sacraments (Confirmation and Holy Orders) to signify the giving of the Holy Spirit.

Dove

Throughout the Old Testament, the dove was often a symbol of the Holy Spirit. A dove released by Noah returned to the Ark with an olive tree branch to show that the floodwaters were receding. The dove is a symbol of life. In Biblical times the dove was also used as a purification offering for the poor (for example, Luke 2:24).

The Gospels say that at the baptism of Jesus, the Holy Spirit descended on him in the form of a dove. This image of a descending dove brings to mind God's hovering Spirit over the waters at creation. A dove also signifies gentleness, virtue, and peace—gifts that we receive when we are united to the Holy Spirit.

Two other symbols of the Holy Spirit mentioned in the *Catechism of the Catholic Church* are the "finger of God" that writes the divine law on our hearts and the "cloud and light," that reveal the saving God, yet veil his divine glory.

For Review

1. Name three ways that the Holy Spirit brings needed gifts to the Church.
2. What are the gifts of the Holy Spirit? Why are they given to individuals and to the Church as a whole?
3. What are *charisms?* How do these gifts help the Church?
4. Name the twelve fruits of the Holy Spirit.
5. What are two ways that the *Catechism of the Catholic Church* says that the Holy Spirit works actively in the Church?

GOOD FRUIT AND BAD FRUIT

If we live by the Holy Spirit, good fruit will show itself in our lives. If we ignore the Holy Spirit and live according to the flesh (the world's standards), then certain vices—moral deformities or bad habits—will fill our lives and distort God's image in us. What follows is a list of spiritual fruits and moral vices with a scriptural passage for each.

1. Read and copy into a notebook or journal at least five biblical verses from each category.
2. For three days check the daily newspaper or an Internet news website to find evidence of spiritual fruit in today's world, as well as evidence of the existence of vice.
3. Summarize these findings in a one-page report. Also reflect on whether you find more of a media focus on virtue or on vice? If you find a difference, why do you think this is so?

Spiritual Fruit
love (Jn 13:35)
joy (Rm 15:13)
patience (perseverance) (Rm 2:4)
kindness (2 Cor 6:6)
goodness (Rm 15:14)
faithfulness (Mt 23:23)
gentleness (1 Cor 4:21)
self-control (Acts 24:25)

Moral Vices
sexual promiscuity (1 Cor 5:1)
idolatry (1 Pt 4:3)
sorcery/witchcraft (Rv 9:21)
hatred (Rm 8:7)
jealousy (Rm 13:13)
self-seeking (2 Cor 12:20)
heresy/factions (1 Cor 11:19)
drunkenness (Lk 21:34)

6. List and briefly describe common symbols of the Holy Spirit.

For Reflection

- What contemporary image might capture who the Holy Spirit can be in the life of a twenty-first-century Christian?
- The gifts of the Holy Spirit are wisdom, understanding, knowledge, counsel, fortitude, piety, and fear of the Lord, sometimes called wonder and awe. What gift do you think you may need the most to live as a committed disciple of Jesus?

Main Ideas

- The *Sign of the Cross* is a profession of faith in the Triune God that we make with both gestures and words. (p. 115)
- Expressing our faith in the Trinity connects us with our Baptism and our baptismal commitment. (p. 115)
- Christians are baptized "in the name of the Father, and of the Son, and of the Holy Spirit"—together in the Trinity—not in the name of each Person separately. (p. 115)
- Though the Trinity is a mystery that we cannot ever fully understand, Jesus and the Holy Spirit have revealed truths about it. (pp. 115–116)
- St. Augustine and St. Thomas Aquinas, two of the most distinguished theologians of the Church, have helped the Church see the "inner life of God," or the Immanent Trinity. (pp. 115–116)
- The *Immanent Trinity* refers to how God exists and who God is, always was—and always will be—without consideration of God's creation and creatures. (p. 116)
- The *Salvific Trinity* is focused on how God interacts with and reveals himself through his creation, especially through his saving works. (p. 116)
- *Substance* means the essence of something—what it truly is. The Church teaches that all three Persons of the Trinity have the same substance. (p. 118)
- The term *Person* refers to the distinctions among the Father, Son, and Holy Spirit. (p. 118)
- *Relation* is a word for distinctions between Father, Son, and Holy Spirit because of their relationships. (pp. 118–119)
- The Church teaches three basic truths about the inner life of God: that there is only one God; that there are three Persons in one God—Father, Son, and Holy Spirit; and that the divine Persons have distinct relationships with one another. (pp. 118–119)
- The Father, the first Person of the Trinity, has no origin and "begets" the Son from all eternity. (p. 119)
- The Son, the second Person of the Trinity, is the perfect expression of the Father and is eternally in relationship with the Father. (p. 119)
- The love that proceeds from the Father and the Son is the third Person of the Trinity, the Holy Spirit. (p. 119)
- Christian art has developed symbols of the Trinity that help us reflect on this mystery of our faith. (pp. 119–120)
- We recognize God's saving actions in our lives in many ways, including through the beauty and order we see in creation. (p. 121)
- We also see God's saving actions through Jesus, the Son of God, who became man and entered human history to teach and save us. (p. 121)
- We also see God's saving actions through the Holy Spirit whom Jesus sent to strengthen, inspire, and direct us. (p. 121)
- God's revelation as a Trinity of Persons took place gradually through Salvation History. (p. 121)
- The *divine missions of the Blessed Trinity* are creation (the primary work of the Father), Salvation or Redemption (the work of the Son), and sanctification (the work of the Holy Spirit). (p. 122)
- The fundamental truth about the Trinity is that the Trinity—and therefore God—is love. (pp. 122–123)
- Prayer helps us to reach our destiny—knowing, loving, and serving God in order to be with God for all eternity. (pp. 122–123)
- The nature of God is a community of love; when we love others in our families and

communities, we imitate God. (pp. 122–123)

- Mary, the Mother of God, is the first and greatest Christian and the greatest saint. (p. 123)
- A *saint* is a holy person who now lives in the presence of God. (p. 123)
- Mary said "yes" to God's plan at the *Annunciation*, the announcement by the angel Gabriel that God wanted her to be the mother of his Son Jesus who would be sent as a Savior. (pp. 123–124)
- At the *Visitation*, Mary, who was already pregnant, traveled to visit and help her elderly cousin Elizabeth, who was also expecting a child. (p. 124)
- Mary was faithful to her son Jesus and his mission, and was with the other followers of Jesus when the Spirit was sent to them at Pentecost. (p. 125)
- The Church teaches that Mary was herself conceived in her mother's womb without the stain and consequences of Original Sin. This special grace is referred to as her *Immaculate Conception*. (pp. 125–126)
- According to Church teaching, Mary remained a virgin throughout her life. (p. 126)
- In AD 431, the Council of Ephesus declared that Mary was *Theotokos*, a Greek term for "God-Bearer," or the "Birth mother of God." (p. 126)
- The *Assumption* is a feast celebrating the teaching that Mary was taken, body and soul, into the presence of God when her earthly life was completed. (pp. 125–127)
- There are many prayers and devotions to venerate or honor Mary. The Church teaches that Catholics can and should ask Mary to intercede for them, joining their prayers to God. (pp. 127–128)
- The Holy Spirit is the greatest gift to humanity from God the Father and God the Son. (pp. 128–129)
- *Grace* is a gift or benevolence from God. (p. 128)
- Because of Jesus Christ and the Paschal Mystery (his suffering, Death, and Resurrection), the sins of human beings are forgiven through *justification*. (p. 128)
- There are seven *gifts of the Holy Spirit* that are given to the Church to help us live like Christ: wisdom, understanding, knowledge, counsel, fortitude, piety, and fear of the Lord or wonder and awe. (p. 129)
- A *charism* is a special gift given by the Holy Spirit to individuals for the building up of the Church. Among common charisms reported in 1 Corinthians 12 are faith, healing, miracle-working, prophecy, discernment, speaking in tongues, and the interpreting of tongues. (pp. 129–130)
- The Holy Spirit actively works in the Church in the Scriptures, Sacred Tradition, Magisterium, Sacraments, prayer, ministries of the Church, apostolic and missionary life, and the saints. (p. 130)
- There are several symbols of the Holy Spirit: fire, tongues of fire, anointing with oil, water, laying on of hands, and dove. (pp. 131–132)

Terms, People, Places

Complete each sentence by choosing the correct answer from the list of terms. You will not use all of the terms.

Annunciation
Assumption
Charism
Consubstantial
Divine missions of the Blessed Trinity
Fruits of the Holy Spirit
Grace
Immaculate Conception
Immanent Trinity
Infallible teaching
Justification
Paraclete
Person
Relation
Saint
Salvific Trinity
Substance
Theology
Theotokos

1. As he warned his followers that he would soon be arrested and executed, Jesus promised to send the ______ or Comforter.
2. The teaching that Mary was conceived without the stain of Original Sin was announced in 1854 and is called the dogma of the ______.
3. Given by the Holy Spirit to the Church and her members, these ______ are spiritual gifts that help us to live as followers of Jesus with more commitment and determination.
4. The teachings from the Church that are said to be completely free of error are ______ and are announced by the Pope.
5. The term ______ describes the distinctions among the Father, Son, and Holy Spirit of the Trinity.
6. Consideration of ______ reflects on the inner life of the Trinity without consideration of God's creation or his creatures.
7. A holy person who is now living in the presence of God is often called a ______.
8. A Greek term for the "God bearer" or the "Mother of God," ______ was introduced to the world at the Council of Ephesus in AD 431.

Primary Source Quotations

How We Learn to Believe
We can't have full knowledge all at once. We must start by believing; then afterwards we may be led on to master the evidence for ourselves.
—St. Thomas Aquinas

God, Our Father and Creator
If there is anyone who is not enlightened by this sublime magnificence of created things, he is blind. If there is anyone who, seeing all these works of God, does not praise him, he is dumb; if there is anyone who, from so many signs, cannot perceive God, that man is foolish.
—St. Bonaventure

The Gift of Courage
To have courage for whatever comes in life—everything lies in that.
—St. Teresa of Avila

The Gift of Wisdom
How much better to get wisdom than gold, to choose understanding rather than silver!
—Proverbs 16:16

The Mystery of the Trinity
The mystery of the Most Holy Trinity is the central mystery of Christian faith

and life. It is the mystery of God himself. It is therefore the source of all the other mysteries of faith, the light that enlightens them. It is the most fundamental and essential teaching in the "hierarchy of the truths of faith."

—*Catechism of the Catholic Church*, 234

Put yourself in the shoes of someone who knows nothing about Catholic beliefs. Which element of Catholicism would spark your curiosity the most? Write three or four paragraphs about what you know and believe about this topic. Use your textbook as a resource to support your reflection.

Ongoing Assignments

1. Create a PowerPoint presentation on how the Blessed Trinity has been represented in art. Discuss the symbolism involved in at least three different paintings.
2. Create a PowerPoint presentation on how the Blessed Mother has been portrayed in art through the ages. Include at least twenty pictures in your presentation.
3. Research and report on one of the famous apparitions of Mary. Examples include Guadalupe, Lourdes, and Fatima. Conduct your own Internet research on Apparitions of Mary.
4. Write your own Litany to the Blessed Mother. For inspiration, refer to several popular litanies:
   - Litany of Loreto
   - Litany of Mary of Nazareth
   - Litany of Our Lady of Lourdes
5. Read and report on Mary as the first disciple. See, for example, an article by Raymond E. Brown, S.S., "Mary, the First Disciple" (*St. Anthony Messenger,* May 1997).
6. Report on the icon of Mary of Perpetual Help.
7. Create a booklet with pictures to illustrate any ten mysteries of the Rosary.
8. Research and report on five feast days of the Blessed Mother.
9. Read paragraphs 40–42, the Conclusion of Pope Benedict XVI's Encyclical Letter *Deus Caritas Est (God Is Love)*. Report on five interesting things he says about the Blessed Mother. Locate articles about the encyclical by conducting an Internet search of the English or Latin title. You can find the encyclical online at the Vatican website.
10. Read each of the following Scripture passages and note which symbol of God's Spirit (fire, tongues of fire, anointing with oil, water, laying on of hands, dove) is depicted:
    - Exodus 19:18
    - Psalm 104:30
    - Ephesians 5:6–20
    - Revelation 21

11. The seven-fold flame symbol represents the seven gifts of the Spirit: wisdom, understanding, knowledge, counsel, fortitude, piety, and fear of the Lord. On your own, draw a symbol of the Holy Spirit that expresses one of the Spirit's qualities. Then write your own brief explanation of the symbol.

12. Compose a prayer to the Holy Spirit designed to help students who are preparing for a test. Share this prayer with your classmates.

Prayer

The Memorare is one of the most beloved of all Marian prayers. Its authorship is often attributed to St. Bernard of Clairvaux (1090–1153), a great theologian of the Church. Pray this prayer often, calling on Mary to intercede for your needs.

Memorare
Remember, O most gracious Virgin Mary,
that never was it known
that anyone who fled to your protection,
implored your help,
or sought your intercession was left unaided.
Inspired by this confidence,
I fly unto you,
O virgin of virgins, my Mother,
To you I come, before you I stand,
sinful and sorrowful.
O Mother of the Word Incarnate,
despise not my petitions,
but in your mercy hear and answer me.
Amen.

- *Reflection*: Reflect individually on the following question: *What is it that I need most in my life right now?* In prayer, ask Mary to pray with you to God for this need. Consider sharing this need with classmates and asking for their prayers as well.
- *Resolution*: A novena is a nine-day prayer. Make a novena with the *Memorare* by praying it at least once each day for nine days straight.

6

JESUS' LIFE REVEALS HIS MISSION

Have among yourselves the same attitude that is also yours in Christ Jesus, who, though he was in the form of God, did not regard equality with God something to be grasped. Rather, he emptied himself, taking the form of a slave, coming in human likeness; and found human in appearance, he humbled himself, becoming obedient to death, even death on a cross. Because of this, God greatly exalted him and bestowed on him the name that is above every name, that at the name of Jesus every knee should bend, of those in heaven and on earth and under the earth, and every tongue confess that Jesus Christ is Lord, to the glory of God the Father.

—Philippians 2:5-11

- **The Son of God Humbled Himself**
  The mystery of the Incarnation is that although he was Master of the Universe, the Son of God became a tiny child.

- **The Humanity of Jesus**
  Through the power of the Holy Spirit, Jesus "became flesh and made his dwelling among us."

- **By Nature, One of Us**
  As a man, Jesus experienced what every human being commonly experiences including the emotions of grief, joy, anger, compassion, and love.

- **Jesus Spoke about His Divinity**
  From his proclamation made in the synagogue at Nazareth, Jesus never tried to hide his divine identity, making it clear that he had been sent by his Father and that he was one with him.

- **Jesus Demonstrated His Divinity**
  In addition to his words, Jesus showed his divine nature with his miraculous works and actions.

The Son of God Humbled Himself

St. Paul wrote the passage that opens this chapter that tells us to imitate the humility of Jesus Christ. Scholars believe that St. Paul was quoting an early Church hymn about Jesus in this passage. This hymn tells us that Jesus, who is God, agreed to humble himself to become a man. What's more, Jesus also became an obedient servant. His sacrifice on the cross opened the gates of Heaven to us. For this, the Father has greatly exalted Jesus, who now sits at the right hand of the Father. The hymn concludes by instructing everyone—in Heaven, on Earth, and under Earth—to honor Jesus Christ. His name and his glory is above every other.

In a similar vein, the Church Father St. Gregory Nazianzen (ca. 329–ca. 389) wrote this about the way Jesus lived his life with gentle acceptance and generosity:

> He began his ministry by being hungry, yet he is the Bread of Life.
> Jesus ended his earthly ministry by being thirsty, yet he is the Living Water.
> Jesus was weary, yet he is our rest.
> Jesus paid tribute, yet he is the King.
> Jesus was accused of having a demon, yet he cast out demons.
> Jesus wept, yet he wipes away our tears.
> Jesus was sold for thirty pieces of silver, yet he redeemed the world.
> Jesus was brought as a lamb to the slaughter, yet he is the Good Shepherd.
> Jesus died, yet by his Death he destroyed the power of death.

Jesus Felt What We Feel

See for yourself how Jesus experienced the same things every other human being experiences. Choose and read four of the eight emotional or physical incidents that Scripture reports. Write a short reflection that shares how you feel knowing that Jesus experienced these human emotions.

Scripture	Jesus' Feelings
John 8:48–49	Jesus is called names.
Matthew 26:31, 37–40	Jesus is alone and deserted by friends.
Matthew 4:2; John 19:28	Jesus is hungry and thirsty.
Mark 6:1–6	Jesus is rejected by those who knew him.
Luke 13:34–35	Jesus is distressed.
Matthew 21:12–13	Jesus is angry.
Matthew 27:41–44	Jesus is mocked and made fun of.
John 4:6	Jesus is tired.
John 11	Jesus is mourning the death of a friend.

Jesus is both God and man, something that seems to be an apparent contradiction. But it is the great faith statement of Christians: Jesus Christ is truly human but also truly the Son of God. As the *Catechism of the Catholic Church* further explains:

> The unique and altogether singular event of the Incarnation of the Son of God does not mean that Jesus Christ is part God and part man, nor does it imply that he is the result of a confused mixture of the divine and the human. He became truly man while remaining truly God. Jesus Christ is true God and true man. (*CCC*, 464)

This chapter covers more about the dual natures of Jesus Christ. Jesus was and is truly God and truly human.

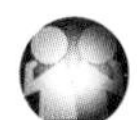 For Reflection

How do you think Jesus would have been most *like* you as a teenager? How would he probably be most *unlike* you?

The Humanity of Jesus

In the first chapter of the Gospel of John, the evangelist describes the Incarnation in beautiful and mysterious terms. Jesus, according to this description, is "the Word" (of God). Through the power of the Holy Spirit, Jesus "became flesh and made his dwelling among us."

The Incarnation—God becoming man in Jesus Christ—is a true mystery of our faith. We profess our faith in the Incarnation every time we recite the Nicene Creed: "For us men and for our salvation he came down from heaven; by the power of the Holy Spirit, he became incarnate of the Virgin Mary, and was made man."

Even if we've heard it said many times, it's good to recall why the Word of God became flesh. These are among the reasons why God became man in Jesus Christ:

> to save us by reconciling us with God;
>
> to reveal to us the depth of God's love;
>
> to serve as a model of holiness;
>
> to enable us to partake in God's divine nature. (See *CCC*, 456–460.)

This section examines more closely some of the Gospel passages that stress the true humanity of Jesus Christ. By reflecting on the humanity of Jesus, we come to know a brother who has experienced life as a human being—just as we do. As the author of the Book of Hebrews put it:

> For we do not have a high priest who is unable to sympathize with our weaknesses, but one who has similarly been tested in every way, yet without sin. (Hb 4:15)

Born into a Human Family

If you re-read Matthew 1:1–17 and Luke 3:23–38, you will be reminded that Jesus was truly born into a human family. Though he was conceived by the power of the Holy Spirit, he was born of a woman, the Virgin Mary. Jesus came into this world as a hungry, helpless little infant, the same way that each of us does. This child was dependent on his parents for food, clothing, housing, and education.

Testimony from Two Gospels—Matthew and Luke

The Gospels of both Matthew and Luke firmly rooted Jesus in the flow of human history. They provided an extensive **genealogy** for Jesus and for his family tree. Matthew, writing for a Jewish-Christian audience, showed that Jesus was part of the Chosen People who traced their lineage back to the great figures of Jewish history. Matthew called Jesus Christ, "the son of David" and "the son of Abraham" (Mt 1:1). In both cases, the word *son* meant "descendant."

Matthew made it clear that Jesus was a legal heir to the throne of King David, the long-promised

genealogy
A record or history of the ancestors or descendants of a person, a people, or a nation.

Messiah. In Jesus, God was to fulfill the promises he made to the Chosen People. The structure of Matthew's genealogy is in chronological order. It begins with Abraham and ends with Jesus. It traces the ancestors of Joseph, the foster father of Jesus.

Matthew's genealogy is particularly interesting because it includes five women—an inclusion that violated the usual pattern of Jewish genealogies. Three of the women—Tamar, Rahab, and Bathsheba—had, at one time, questionable characters. Tamar disguised herself as a harlot to seduce her father-in-law, Judah. Judah failed to

support her after she was widowed. The product of their relationship was a son, Perez. Rahab, from Jericho, was also a prostitute. However, she became a heroine to the Chosen People for hiding the spies of Joshua. She later became the wife of Salmon and the mother of Boaz. Bathsheba had an adulterous affair with King David. Later, the repentant King David married her, and she became the mother of King Solomon. Ruth, on the other hand, was a foreigner who married a Jew. When her husband died, she remained by the side of her mother-in-law, Naomi, and accompanied her to Israel. Ruth's steadfast fidelity was greatly admired. She eventually married Boaz, a relative of Naomi's. Ruth and Boaz were the parents of Obed who was the grandfather of King David.

Why did Matthew include these women in his genealogy? Perhaps he did so to show that God is a God of surprises. God's action in Salvation History does not always coincide with the preconceptions people have about how he should act. Remember that Jesus included some rather ordinary men among his Apostles, including Matthew, a despised tax collector. The fact is that God chooses whomever he wants to do his work.

This theme is supported later in the Gospel in the recounting of Jesus' ministry. Jesus also associated with the poor, with people society rejected, and with prostitutes and sinners. Jesus came to save everyone.

Luke wrote for Gentile-Christians who were less familiar with Jewish prophecy. Therefore, Luke took a different approach in his version of the genealogy of Jesus. Unlike Matthew's genealogy, Luke began his genealogy with Jesus and moved backward. He traced the lineage of Jesus all the way back to Adam, and then to God. In the last verse of the genealogy, he called Jesus "the son of Adam, the son of God" (Lk 3:38). Luke was making two important theological points here. First, he was stressing that Jesus is indeed human, a descendant of the first humans. In a sense, then, Jesus is a brother to every other human being. He is one of us. Moreover, as the Savior, Jesus came to redeem not only the Chosen People, but all people. This point of view in Luke's genealogy fit well with the theology in the rest of Luke's Gospel. Luke's Gospel makes it clear that Jesus is the Universal Savior.

Second, Luke wanted to clearly state that Jesus was, in fact, the Son of God. Significantly, Luke inserted the genealogical background of Jesus right after his baptism. At the baptism of Jesus, God said, "You are my beloved Son; with you I am well pleased" (Lk 3:22). So, Luke was making it clear that Jesus is the Son of God *and* a human being with a family tree.

If you compare the family trees in these two Gospels, you will see that many names do not agree. There are reasons for that. First of all, genealogies are not meant to be comprehensive, tracing every ancestor of Jesus all the way back to the first human being. Rather, they are abridgements, or condensed summaries. This shortening may have been done to aid in memorization. In the first decades after the Death and Resurrection of Jesus, the Good News was passed from believer to believer only through oral recitation.

Son of a Carpenter

Interestingly, the genealogies of both Matthew and Luke show that Joseph was the foster father but not the biological father of Jesus. Mary conceived Jesus by the power of the Holy Spirit. God is the true Father of Jesus. However, because Joseph was Mary's husband, he was considered to be the foster father of Jesus. And because Jesus was born into Joseph's family, he was a legal heir. Jesus had the legal right to claim himself as a descendant of King David. Luke makes this clear by stating, "He [Jesus] was the son, as was thought, of Joseph" (Lk 3:23).

Jesus was known as "the carpenter's son" (Mt 13:55) and the "son of Joseph, from Nazareth" (Jn 1:45; also Jn 6:42 and Lk 4:22). It is likely that Joseph died before Jesus began his public life. In Mark's Gospel, he was identified by those in the synagogue at Nazareth as "the carpenter, the son of Mary" (Mk 6:3). It would have been unusual to refer to Jesus by his mother's name unless Joseph had already died.

Interestingly, these passages do reveal how Jesus earned a living before he embarked on his teaching ministry. Most people must engage in gainful employment at some time in their lives. It is part of the human condition. Jesus learned carpentry from St. Joseph. There are some interesting speculations based on this knowledge. Perhaps Jesus may have helped to build boats. Seven of his Apostles were fishermen. Maybe Jesus met them while making some repairs. Certainly, Jesus used many metaphors and analogies from the carpentry trade in his teaching. He spoke about entering by the narrow gate and building one's house on rock, not on sand. In one parable, he told of a vineyard owner who built a tower for his produce (Mt 21:33). So, perhaps Jesus helped build homes, construct doorways, or erect towers. We don't know for sure. We do know that he was familiar with many of these objects that carpenters make and the tools they used. One of the most warm invitations that Jesus extended to his followers involved a yoke:

> Come to me, all you who labor and are burdened, and I will give you rest. Take my yoke upon you and learn from me, for I am meek and humble of heart; and you will find rest for yourselves. For my yoke is easy, and my burden light. (Mt 11:28–30)

In this passage, Jesus asked us to be his disciples. Rather than acting as a harsh taskmaster, he promised to provide rest for those worn down by burdens. Jesus himself must have had many days of grueling, hard, and dusty work.

Faithful Disciple

ST. HILARY
OF POITIERS

Born into a pagan household in Poitiers, France, in AD 315, Hilary often gave in to the common pleasure-seeking of the day that led people to live only to satisfy their human desires. But Hilary was troubled by this lifestyle. He knew there had to be something more to life.

His search led him to ask questions about God. He was told many things: everything from ideas that God didn't even exist, to beliefs in many gods, to notions that God did exist but had little to do with or did not care for his creation. Hilary wondered why God would create and then not care about what he had made.

His search led to the Christian Bible. When he read the verse in Exodus 3:14 where God shares his name with Moses—"I am who am"—Hilary said, "I was frankly amazed at such a clear definition of God, which expressed the incomprehensible knowledge of the divine nature in words most suited to human intelligence." Still, he pondered the meaning of God's purpose.

Later, Hilary discovered the Gospel of John and had another clear insight upon reading the words in the prologue: "In the beginning was the Word, and the Word was with God, and the Word was God" (Jn 1:1–2). Further, he had discovered Jesus Christ, coming to believe that Jesus had been sent to bring eternal life to those who believed. He also believed with his whole heart that Jesus was God's Son, one with the Creator of the universe.

Hilary was a married man with a daughter. On receiving this inspiration, he and his family were baptized. Hilary was so respected in Poitiers that his citizens soon called for his acclamation as bishop. Much of the rest of Hilary's life was devoted, along with St. Athanasius, to dispelling the heretical belief of Arianism started by the priest Arius in the fourth century. Arius accepted that Jesus was the Son of God, but he claimed that the Son was *created* by God and thus was not equal to God. In short, he denied the divinity of Jesus.

At one point Hilary was exiled by the emperor Constantius for speaking out against Arianism. While imprisoned, Hilary read and studied more about the controversy and clarified the Church's beliefs in the full humanity and divinity of the Lord. On Christ's divinity he wrote, "It is Christ dwelling in us through his flesh who gives us life." He also wrote extensively on the meaning of the Holy Trinity.

St. Hilary was proclaimed a Doctor of the Church in 1851. He is known as the "Doctor of Christ's divinity."

Raised as a Jew

Luke's Gospel also makes it clear that Mary and Joseph raised Jesus in the Jewish faith and tradition. According to Jewish law, he was circumcised on the eighth day after his birth (Lk 2:21). He was then given the fifth most common Jewish name of that era—Jesus or "Yeshua." (The name Joseph was the second most popular name for males, while Mary was the most common female name).

As was customary, Jesus was also presented as an infant in the Temple in Jerusalem (see Luke 2:22). Mary and Joseph wanted to fulfill the requirements of Mosaic Law. Two doves or young pigeons were offered in sacrifice in accord with the law (Lk 2:24). Because they offered doves rather than a yearling lamb, it's clear that Mary and Joseph were not wealthy.

Jesus grew up and lived most of his life in Nazareth. Even after he moved to Capernaum and launched his public ministry, Jesus was known as "Jesus of Nazareth" (Mt 4:13). In his day, Nazareth was off the beaten path. It was a small and insignificant rural village. The fact that Jesus was from Nazareth gave rise to that famous but insulting remark from Nathaniel. When Philip declared that Jesus of Nazareth was the Promised One, Nathaniel questioned Philip's claim. "Can anything good come from Nazareth?" Nathaniel argued sarcastically in John 1:46. But it was in this simple village that Jesus learned his Jewish faith. Here, he grew up among good, hard-working, but largely poor people.

Around the age of five or six, Jesus would have begun to learn the written **Torah** and to read and write in general. **Aramaic** was his primary language. Aramaic was an ancient Semitic language related to Hebrew the way French is related to Spanish. Jesus probably also learned to read and write Hebrew. Hebrew was the language the Jews spoke before the conquests of Assyria in the eighth century BC and Babylonia in the sixth century BC. The sacred books were written in Hebrew. Some scholars also believe that Jesus may have known some Greek. There were a number of Greek-speaking Gentiles who lived in Galilee, especially in Sepphoris, a large city that was an hour's walk from Nazareth. If Jesus found work there as a carpenter, he may have learned enough Greek to communicate with

Torah
The entire body of Jewish literature, teaching, and law.

Aramaic
A western Semitic language commonly spoken in Palestine, Syria, and Mesopotamia from the third century before Christ until AD 650. Aramaic was later replaced by Arabic.

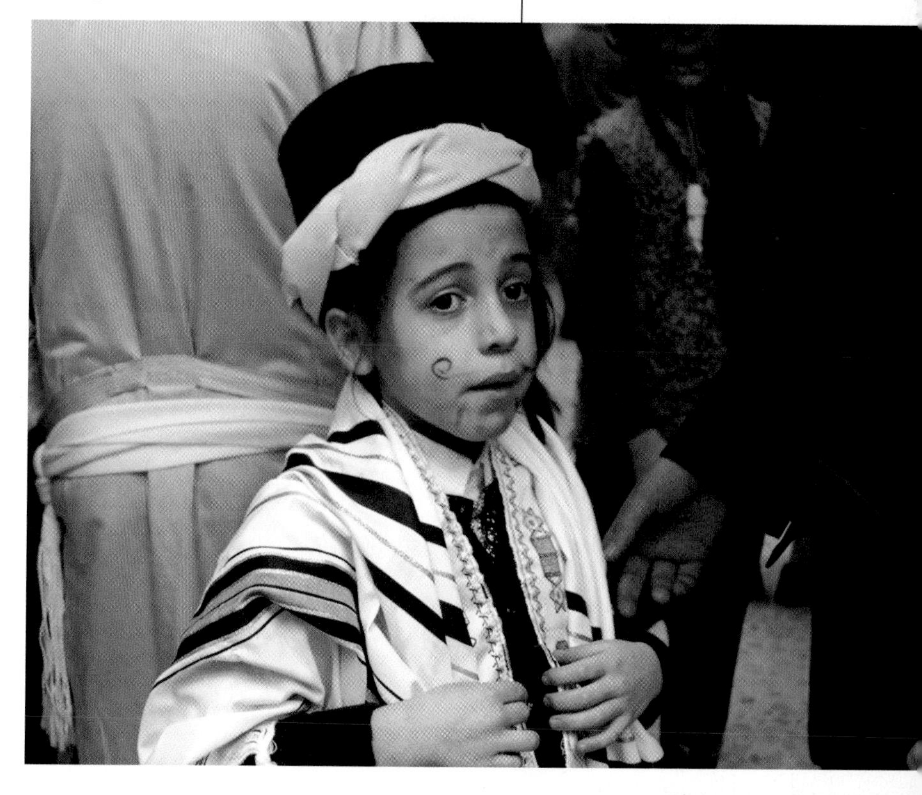

his employers. Jesus may also have talked to Pontius Pilate in Greek at his trial. In John 18:28–40 this conversation is reported. It is unlikely that Jesus spoke Latin, or that Pilate spoke Aramaic. On the other hand, it is possible that an interpreter was present during the exchange between Jesus and Pilate.

In the schooling that Jesus received tremendous emphasis would have been placed on memorization. This method of learning was typical. This helps to explain why the disciples of Jesus were able to repeat his teachings accurately for several decades before the Gospels were written. Jesus learned his Scriptures well. The New Testament is full of examples of Jesus quoting various Scripture passages from memory and then interpreting them in ways that astounded his listeners. Jesus even challenged Satan with passages from the Old Testament when Satan tempted him in the desert (Lk 4:1–13; Mt 4:1–11). Luke says that in Nazareth, the boy Jesus "grew and became strong, filled with wisdom; and the favor of God was upon him" (Lk 2:39–40).

When Jesus was twelve, Mary and Joseph took him to Jerusalem for the feast of the Passover. There, he astounded the teachers of his day with his insights and knowledge (Lk 2:46). After his parents found him in the Temple, Jesus returned with them to Nazareth. Luke's Gospel tells us that Jesus was obedient to his parents. Children owe obedience to their parents. The boy Jesus showed respect and honor to Mary and Joseph by obeying them as well. Luke concluded this episode by once again stating, "Jesus advanced [in] wisdom and age and favor before God and man" (Lk 2:52).

Simply put, Jesus grew older as all people do. He also continued to learn and became a very wise man. In all ways, Jesus "found favor" before God and man. Certainly, as God's only Son, he was beloved and would have God's favor, or loving acceptance. But, Luke tells us that Jesus also learned the social graces of his community. That made him a gracious companion, someone others would like to get to know.

For Review

1. Why did the author of Matthew's Gospel include an extensive genealogy to trace the ancestry of Jesus?
2. Who were the great figures of Jewish history that Matthew's Gospel wanted to connect to Jesus?

Researching Your Own Family History

Construct a family genealogy by interviewing several family members. A genealogy is a study of the ancestors or descendants of a person, family, or group. If possible, try to go back at least four generations on your mother's (maternal) and your father's (paternal) sides. In your research, try to find answers to these questions for each person:

1. What is the person's full name?
2. What is the person's relationship to you?
3. Where and when was this person born? If deceased, where and when did he or she die?
4. What was this person's occupation or work?
5. Was this person a Catholic? What did you find out about how he or she practiced the Catholic faith?
6. What interesting fact or facts did you discover about your ancestors?

3. Who were the women included in the genealogy of Jesus that Matthew provided? Why was this a surprising inclusion?
4. How do scholars explain the differences in genealogies found in Matthew's Gospel and in Luke's?
5. Describe three Gospel references that remind us that Jesus really worked as a carpenter.
6. Briefly tell about the education that Jesus likely had in Nazareth.
7. How do we know that Jesus was very familiar with Scripture?

For Reflection

- Because he was divine as well as human, do you think it was easy for Jesus to obey Mary and Joseph? Explain your point of view.
- Why is knowing your family history helpful?

By Nature, One of Us

In philosophy, "nature" or "substance" refers to what makes something what it is. For example, a chair has the "nature" of a chair. It is shaped and formed in such a way that it forms a seat. Although there may be a vast variety of different kinds of chairs, every chair has the same nature. That is, it possesses the "qualities of being" that makes it something that can be used to sit on.

All human beings—and there are billions of us—have a human nature. Although each individual is different, we all possess two qualities that make us human beings. These two qualities are possessing a human body and possessing an immortal or human soul. To be human, then, means having a human body *and* an immortal soul.

Jesus, Human in Body

Jesus, of course, had a human body. After his Resurrection, he possessed a glorified body (Lk 24:39). Like every human being, Jesus had the same kind of experiences that all of us do. He got very hungry, for example, when he fasted in the desert (Mt 4:2). He was so thirsty when he was dying on the cross. His throat was parched from dehydration and from gasping for breath. He uttered, "I thirst" (Jn 19:28). He also often suffered great fatigue. On a long walk through Samaria, he sat down at the well, exhausted. That was the occasion when Jesus met and talked with the Samaritan woman (Jn 4:6–29).

Jesus had few possessions and knew what poverty was like. He said, "Foxes have dens and birds of the sky have nests, but the Son of Man has nowhere to rest his head" (Lk 9:58). The only possessions Jesus had were his clothing and a pair of sandals.

After his scourging and crucifixion, Jesus died. Medical authorities say crucifixion victims of that era would have likely died of asphyxiation when they could no longer raise their chests to inhale and fill their lungs. The body of Jesus endured one of the most cruel forms of capital punishment. Despite the severe pain inflicted on him, Jesus bore it heroically. The First Letter of Peter states it eloquently:

> When he was insulted, he returned no insult; when he suffered, he did not threaten; instead, he handed himself over to the one who judges justly. He himself bore our sins in his body upon the cross, so that, free from sin, we might live for righteousness. By his wounds you have been healed. (1 Pt 2:23–24)

Jesus, Human in Spirit

The human spirit or soul has two faculties or powers: the intellect and free will. Our intellects enable us to reason, learn, and grow in knowledge and to process and reflect upon our emotions. Our wills enable us to choose between good and evil, that is, to discern what is right and wrong. Our wills also enable us to choose the good of others, that is, to act out of love. The following incidents in Jesus' life show that he had a human nature with a human spirit or soul that made him like us in everything but sin.

Jesus Was Tempted

Temptation is defined as "the inducement to sin that comes through some sort of persuasion or the promise of a good or pleasure." Temptation is not sin itself. It is a test or trial of the right use of our freedom. Every temptation leads to a choice—whether to do good or to give in to evil. Like all humans, Jesus was tempted, and not only during the forty days he was in the desert. Peter tempted him to be a worldly Messiah (Mk 8:31–33). Satan tried to turn Jesus away from his mission during the terrible time of his Passion and crucifixion. The Letter to the Hebrews tells us Jesus was "tested in every way, yet without sin" (Hb 4:15). His experience of temptation makes Jesus an understanding Savior, one who is ready to help us in our own times of temptation. "Because he himself was tested through what he suffered, he is able to help those who are being tested" (Hb 2:18).

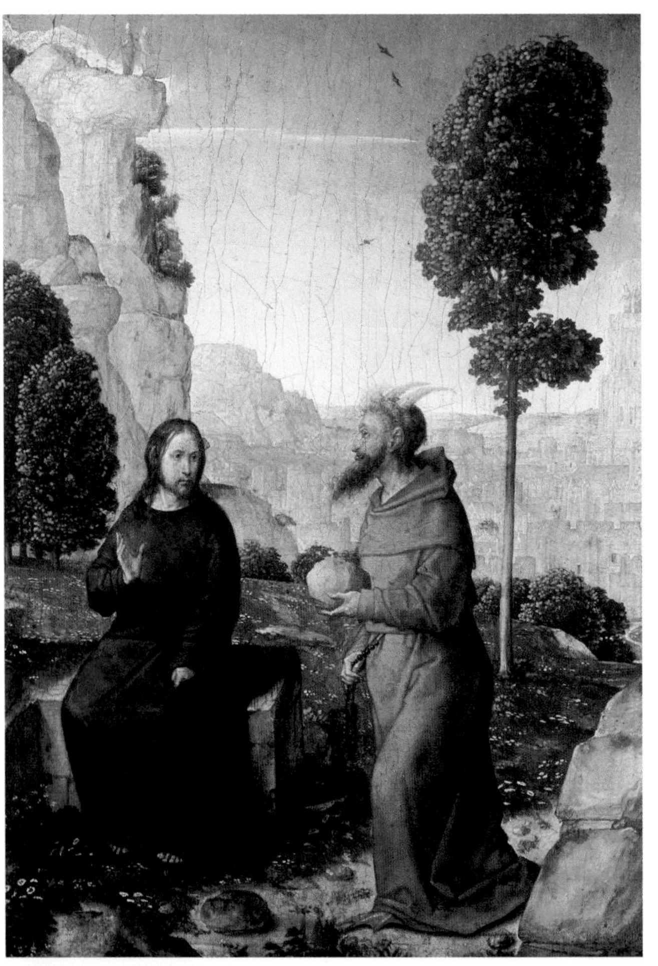

Jesus Was Endowed with a True Human Knowledge

Early in the Gospel of Luke, it is reported that Jesus "advanced [in] wisdom and age and favor before God and man" (Lk 2:52). Other references in the Gospels aid us in understanding this mysterious union of the divine and human natures in one divine Person. In the eighth chapter of the Gospel of Luke, there is a story about a woman with a severe hemorrhage. When she touched Jesus, he turned and asked, "Who touched me?" (Lk 8:45). By asking, it can be understood that he did not know who touched him. On another occasion reported in Mark 13, the Apostles asked Jesus when the world was going to end. Jesus replied, "But of that day or hour, no one knows, neither the angels in heaven, nor the Son, but only the Father" (Mk 13:32). This advice from Jesus stands good for all time: "Be watchful! Be alert! You do not know when the time will come" (Mk 13:33).

Jesus' human soul was endowed with true human knowledge that as such could not in itself be unlimited. Christ's human knowledge expressed the divine life of his Person. In his human knowledge, Jesus had immediate knowledge of the Father and of the secret thoughts of people. He also had a fullness of understanding of the eternal plan of Salvation that he came to reveal.

Jesus Loved Others and Was Loved in Return

Jesus also had an unselfish love for many people. For example, he felt love for the rich but restless young man (Mk 10:21) who did not want to give up his wealth to follow Jesus. Jesus also loved countless people who came to him for healing. There were lepers, deaf and blind people, the lame, and those who were possessed. Jesus also loved special friends like Martha, Mary, and Lazarus (Jn 11:5). The same was true of his deep and loving friendship with the Apostles and the Beloved Disciple who was likely John of Zebedee. It was this Apostle who leaned affectionately on the chest of Jesus during the Last Supper (Jn 13:25).

Jesus also showed affection for people he didn't really know. There was Nicodemus, a Pharisee and member of the Sanhedrin; and Joseph of Arimathea. Joseph was a prominent member of the Sanhedrin who later provided a grave for Jesus. And Jesus showed great love for his Mother as he was dying on the cross. He entrusted her to the care of the Beloved Disciple and to the Church (Jn 19:25–27).

Jesus Displayed True Human Emotions

Besides his genuine love for others, friends and enemies alike, Jesus also felt and acted upon other typical human emotions. Some of these are listed here:

- *Jesus wept.* Jesus showed his grief at the death of his friend Lazarus (Jn 11:35). He also wept over the holy city of Jerusalem, which he knew would not accept him as the Messiah and would be destroyed in the future by the Romans (Lk 19:41–44).
- *Jesus was joyful.* Jesus was very happy at many dinners that he shared with people. Among these was the wedding feast at Cana (Jn 2:1–11), the dinner at Matthew's house after Jesus called him to be an Apostle (Mt 9:9–10), the meal at the house of Zacchaeus (Lk 19:7), and at many other occasions. Jesus rejoiced when the seventy-two disciples came back after their mission (Lk 10:21) and at the Last Supper when he called his disciples his friends (Jn 15:11). Jesus did not require his disciples to fast while he (the bridegroom) was with them (Mt 9:15). Jesus so enjoyed himself on festive occasions that his opponents called him "a glutton and a drunkard, a friend of tax collectors and sinners" (Lk 7:34).
- *Jesus showed anger.* Anger is an emotion or a passion. As with other passions, anger is neither good nor evil in itself. What we do with them is what makes them good or bad. For example, we *should* get angry when we see an innocent person being harmed. Anger can move us to action, to help defend the innocent victim. Sometimes, Jesus was angry, but he never harmed anyone. For example, he severely reprimanded his friend, Peter, for suggesting that he should not go the way of the cross. Jesus "rebuked Peter and said, 'Get behind me, Satan. You are thinking not as God does, but as human beings do'" (Mk 8:33). Jesus was angry at his opponents who, in their stubbornness, questioned him about healing on the Sabbath (Mk 3:5). Jesus also cleared the money-changers out of the Temple because they were disrespecting God's house (Jn 2:13–17).
- *Jesus needed time alone but also enjoyed human companionship.* Throughout his ministry, Jesus frequently withdrew from the crowds and his Apostles to spend time by himself. "Rising very early before dawn, he left and went off to a deserted place, where he prayed" (Mk 1:35). But Jesus chose companions to help him in his ministry. "He appointed twelve [whom he also named Apostles] that they might be with him and he might send for them to preach and have authority to drive out demons" (Mk 3:14–15). He invited three of these Apostles—Peter, James, and John—to see him raising a young girl from the dead (Mk 5:37), to witness his Transfiguration (Lk 9:28), and to pray with him in Gethsemane (Mk 14:33). Jesus also told his Apostles at the Last Supper, "I have eagerly desired to eat this Passover with you before I suffer" (Lk 22:15).
- *Jesus was troubled, distressed, and sorrowful.* At the Last Supper, Jesus was deeply troubled at the prospect that one of his disciples was going to betray him (Jn 13:21). Later, in the Garden of Gethsemane, when contemplating his immediate future, Jesus told his Apostles, "My soul is sorrowful even to death" (Mt 26:38). Jesus genuinely feared what was to come, but he faced it with courage and put the future in the hands of his Father. "My Father, if it is possible, let this cup pass from me; yet, not as I will, but as you will" (Mt 26:39). And later Jesus

EXPLAINING THE FAITH

Did Jesus have brothers and sisters?

The New Testament does mention "brothers and sisters" of Jesus (e.g., Mt 3:31-35). The Church understands these references to be children of another Mary, a disciple of Christ. The words *brother* and *sister* may also refer to close relatives like cousins. The Church holds that Jesus was Mary's only child and that she was ever-virgin, though she is the spiritual Mother of all.

prayed, "My Father, if it is not possible that this cup pass without my drinking it, your will be done!" (Mt 26:42).

- *Jesus showed compassion.* Jesus took pity on many people, as evidenced by the many cures he performed. But he also knew human weakness. Perhaps this is why forgave the woman caught in adultery and saved her from being stoned to death by her accusers (Jn 8:1–11). Jesus said, "Let the one among you who is without sin be the first to throw a stone at her" (Jn 11:7). Jesus also revealed deep insight into human nature when he told the Apostles in the Garden, "Watch and pray that you may not undergo the test. The spirit is willing, but the flesh is weak" (Mt 26:41).

Many stories that Jesus told reveal a person who loved nature and was close to it. He talked about animals and birds, flowers in the fields, the growth and harvesting of crops, trees and good fruit and bad fruit, shepherds and sheep, farmers and vineyards. Undoubtedly, he was observant of the world around him and enjoyed the outdoors and the beauty of the natural world.

Jesus also must have been a person with an attractive aura. People flocked to see and hear him, and took great delight in his teaching (Mk 12:37). He went out to them, teaching in synagogues, boats, hillsides, fields, on the roadsides, at the dinner tables of friends and opponents alike. Children rushed to him. Sinners were drawn to him, wanting to hear his forgiving words. And even simple folk recognized him as someone special.

At the same time, some people had a negative view of Jesus. Some religious authorities saw him as a threat and criticized him openly. They were especially upset that he taught on his own authority, not quoting other rabbis, as was the custom of the day. Mark's Gospel surprisingly reports that Jesus' own relatives came to get him to come home, saying, "He is out of his mind" (Mk 3:21). Scribes and other religious figures even accused him of being possessed by the devil (Mk 3:22).

To his neighbors in Nazareth, Jesus seemed all too ordinary. When he taught in their synagogue, they were astonished and began to ask:

> "Where did this man get all this? What kind of wisdom has been given him? What mighty deeds are wrought by his hands! Is he not the carpenter, the son of Mary, and the brother of James and Joses and Judas and Simon? And are not his sisters here with

The Gospels Show How Human Jesus Was

Choose and read any five chapters of the four Gospels—Matthew, Mark, Luke, or John. In these five chapters, find specific passages that reveal the *humanity* of Christ. These verses might reveal a particular emotion or reaction, such as sorrow, compassion, joy, etc. Briefly explain how the verse reveals the humanity of Jesus. Find at least ten examples in the five chapters you choose.

> us?" And they took offense at him. (Mk 6:2–3)

It's likely that Jesus was amused but also offended by their response. He observed, "A prophet is not without honor except in his native place and among his own kin and in his own house" (Mk 6:4).

Yes, Jesus was a real human being. He grew older and taller, got hungry, thirsty, and tired as all humans do. Jesus had a human soul and experienced emotions as we do. He was sorely tempted but never sinned. Because he lived an ordinary human life and suffered greatly, Jesus Christ can and does understand us. The more we read about and reflect on the humanity of Jesus Christ, the more we can see that he was a perfect human being. His many personal virtues make him our hero and our model:

> In all of his life Jesus presents himself as *our model*. He is "the perfect man," who invites us to become his disciples and follow him. In humbling himself, he has given us an example to imitate, through his prayer he draws us to pray, and by his poverty he calls us to accept freely the privation and persecutions that may come our way. (*CCC*, 520)

For Review

1. What are the two qualities that define a human being?
2. What are two examples of anger in Jesus that can be found in Scripture?
3. What are three examples of the compassion of Jesus that can be found in Scripture?
4. Why did some religious authorities see Jesus and his teaching as threatening?
5. Did Jesus have siblings? Explain your answer.

For Reflection

In your journal, write about what you find most appealing about the human personality of Jesus. How do you think people would react to him today if they met him in person?

Jesus Spoke about His Divinity

The Gospels and the other books of the New Testament clearly teach the divinity of Christ. In the Gospels, we learn how Jesus perfectly fulfilled all the Old Testament prophecies concerning the Messiah. These include the prophecies that he would be born of the tribe of Judah (Gn 49:10), of the House of David (Is 11:1–2), in Bethlehem (Micah 5:1), of a virgin (Is 7:14), and that he would be worshiped by kings from afar (Ps 72:10) and perform great **miracles** (Is 35:5–6). His Death and manner of suffering were also foretold: he would be betrayed (Ps 41:10), sold for thirty pieces of silver (Zec 11:12–13), suffer for our sins (Is 50:6), be led like a

miracle
A deed or an event that cannot be explained by ordinary human intervention or known natural forces.

sheep to the slaughter (Is 53:7), and have his hands and feet pierced (Ps 22:17).

When you think about it, it is remarkable how Jesus fulfilled all of these prophecies. Jesus himself made prophecies that were also fulfilled. For example, he predicted that he would be condemned to Death by the religious authorities, mocked by Gentiles, betrayed by one of his Apostles, and denied three times by Peter. He also predicted the destruction of Jerusalem and the Temple, an event that took place during the First Jewish Revolt (66–70). The fulfillment of his prophecies supported his claims to be on a divine mission. As he said, predicting the betrayal of Judas, "From now on I am telling you before it happens, so that when it happens you may believe that I AM" (Jn 13:19).

The fulfillment of prophecies about and by Jesus strongly supports his divine credentials. But there are many other things that Jesus said that reveal who he is. Four of these are featured in the next sections: his use of the title "Son of Man"; his claim to be the "Suffering Servant"; his proclamation of himself as the "Messiah in Nazareth"; and Peter's confession of faith that Jesus was the "Son of the living God."

The Son of Man

Very frequently in the Gospels Jesus spoke about himself in the third person using the title "the **Son of Man**." This title and self-designation for Jesus appears fourteen times in Mark, thirty times in Matthew, twenty-five times in Luke, and thirteen times in John.

What is interesting about the title "Son of Man" is that it reveals something about the humanity of Jesus, as well as his divinity. One Old Testament meaning of the term was simply to refer to a human being in a humble way as distinct from God. The expression was used to contrast the poverty and weakness of humans compared to God's might and power. (See, for example, Isaiah 51:12 and Psalm 8:4.) Thus, in using the title, Jesus was emphasizing his ordinary human nature, his identification with us. However, this title carries more meaning than as a simple and humble expression of human nature. In Luke's Gospel, in addressing the Sanhedrin, Jesus says, "From this time on the Son of Man will be seated at the right hand of the power of God" (Lk 22:69).

And, in talking about the end of the world in Mark's Gospel, Jesus says the following: "And then they will see 'the Son of Man coming in the clouds' with great power and glory" (Mk 13:26).

Daniel 7:13–14 and the Jewish books of Enoch and Esdras help us better understand the more heavenly aspect of the title "Son of Man." In these books, the "Son of Man" is a supernatural figure, God's unique agent who will help usher in the fullness of God's Kingdom. He will also serve as the judge of all humanity. A powerful image in Daniel's vision relates:

> I saw One like a son of man coming, on the clouds of heaven; When he reached the Ancient One and was presented before him, He received dominion, glory, and kingship; nations and peoples of every language serve him. His dominion is an everlasting dominion that shall not be taken away, his kingship shall not be destroyed. (Dn 7:13–14)

This certainly highlights the divinity of the one who will serve as Judge of the living and the dead.

Jesus may have used the term "Son of Man" because he could give it the meaning he wanted it to have. People misunderstood the fact that Christ's concept of a Messiah included the traits of a "suffering servant." By using the title "Son of Man," Jesus may have been trying to emphasize that he was human like us, but also divine and sent by God.

Suffering Servant

Isaiah 52:13–53:12 contains the Fourth Suffering Servant Song. The anonymous author of these verses, designated "Second Isaiah," wrote to encourage the exiled Israelites in Babylon. His message was that Redemption comes through suffering.

Jesus took these verses and applied them to himself. He was the Messiah who was also the Suffering Servant. The Son of Man would die so that all people could have abundant life.

Jesus Proclaimed Himself as Messiah in Nazareth

In Luke's Gospel, we learn that soon after his temptation and his selection of the Apostles, Jesus returned to his hometown, Nazareth. Once there, he went to the synagogue on the Sabbath because that was his custom. It was his turn to do the reading. When handed the scroll, Jesus searched until he found this selection from the prophet Isaiah. He then read:

> "The Spirit of the Lord is upon me,
> because he has anointed me
> to bring glad tidings to
> the poor.
> He has sent me to proclaim
> liberty to captives
> and recovery of sight to the
> blind,
> to let the oppressed go free,
> and to proclaim a year acceptable to the Lord."
> (Luke 4:18–19 quoting Isaiah 61:1–2; 58:6)

Jesus then rolled up the scroll, gave it back to the attendant and sat down. His reading made a dramatic impact. Everyone was looking at him. They were waiting for him to give a homily on the reading. Jesus did so in one short sentence, "Today this scripture passage is fulfilled in your hearing" (Lk 4:21).

At first, the explanation Jesus offered amazed his audience. His townsfolk marveled at what he said. No one could miss the significance of his message. He proclaimed, in effect, that Isaiah's prophecy about the Messiah was actually coming true—right *then*, in their very midst!

But then it dawned on someone. "Isn't this the son of Joseph?" (Lk 4:23). Could Jesus really be implying that he himself was the Messiah sent by God? People were in an uproar. Jesus defended himself and pointed out that no prophet is honored in his own country. He also told two stories about how the Old Testament prophets Elijah and Elisha left Israel to minister to foreigners because of the lack of faith of the Chosen People.

No one missed the point Jesus was making. He was suggesting that God's people would reject the Messiah and that God would take his message to the Gentiles. This enraged the people of Nazareth. They rose in arms against Jesus, drove him from the synagogue, and took him to the brow of a hill with the intent to throw him off. Miraculously, though, Jesus escaped the crowd and walked away because his time to die had not yet arrived.

This incident at Nazareth teaches an important lesson about Jesus. People really wanted to accept the Messiah, and they wanted to believe that he had come. However, they were expecting a different kind of Messiah, probably a flashy, forceful

Son of Man
A title Jesus used to refer to himself. It emphasizes both Jesus' humanity and divinity. Its origins are in Daniel 7:13: "I saw . . . one like a son of man coming on the clouds of heaven."

military leader. They simply could not see how an ordinary carpenter from their own village could possibly be YHWH's Promised One. Jesus was too much like them. He was so ordinary.

However, Jesus showed us how God works. God works through the ordinary. He takes us by surprise. His ways are not our ways. He comes to us unexpectedly. The question Jesus was really asking his townsfolk was, "Are you willing to be open-minded enough to be surprised by God?" Jesus asks us the same basic question today.

Peter's Confession of Faith (Mt 16:13-20)

We studied this passage in an earlier chapter (pages 17–18), but because of its importance, it is included here among things said about the divinity of Jesus. The incident occurred midway through his ministry while Jesus and his Apostles were in the region of Caesarea Philippi. Jesus put this question to his disciples: "Who do people say that the Son of Man is?" (Mt 16:13). They answered that some thought Jesus was John the Baptist, others Elijah, still others Jeremiah or one of the prophets. All of these answers were interesting because they reveal what a tremendous impact Jesus was making. The Jews thought God was coming back to them in a special way by sending a great prophet. The people saw something very special indeed in Jesus.

Jesus then asked his Apostles what they thought. Simon Peter replied, "You are the Messiah, the Son of the living God" (Mt 16:16). Note carefully what Peter was proclaiming: the Son of Man was the Son of God! They were one and the same.

Jesus said to Peter, "Blessed are you, Simon son of Jonah. For flesh and blood has not revealed this to you, but my heavenly Father" (Mt 16:17). Jesus then gave Simon a new name—Peter, a name that meant "rock." Jesus told Peter that he would build his church on him and his rocklike faith. Jesus accepted Peter's identification of him. Jesus admitted that he was indeed the Son of God, a truth that Peter recognized because God the Father had revealed it to him.

For Review

1. Name two prophecies that Jesus himself made about his future.
2. What was the Old Testament meaning of the term "Son of Man"? How did Jesus give the title a new meaning?
3. What was the message of the "Suffering Servant" that Jesus wanted to communicate?
4. In the synagogue of Nazareth, what works did Jesus predict that he would do as the Messiah?
5. What kind of Messiah were the people of Nazareth expecting?
6. What was Peter's answer when Jesus asked his Apostles who they thought he was? How did this answer set Peter apart from the others?

For Reflection

- Write about a time in your life when God's grace took you by surprise. Explain how God's love came to you in an ordinary, unexpected way.
- Think about the proclamation Jesus made in Nazareth. Now, think about a time when you took a public stand on an important issue—even when you knew it would bring you criticism. How did you feel before and after taking this stand? Compare your feelings to what Jesus must have felt. People who had known him his whole life tried to banish and even kill him.

Jesus Demonstrated His Divinity

In addition to his words, Jesus showed his divinity by what he did. His works told the world that he was the Son of God. Jesus did wonderful works or miracles, and he forgave the sins of those imprisoned by their weaknesses and failings.

The Miraculous Works of Jesus

All the Gospels proclaim that Jesus performed miracles. By definition, the miracles worked by Jesus were extraordinary and observable events that cannot be explained by human abilities or known natural forces. They can be explained only by divine intervention. The miracles of Jesus point to who he really is:

> The signs worked by Jesus attest that the Father has sent him. They invite belief in him. To those who turn to him in faith, he grants what they ask. So miracles strengthen faith in the One who does his Father's works; they bear witness that he is the Son of God. (*CCC*, 548)

Of course, the greatest miracle of all was the Resurrection of Jesus himself from the dead! Other miracles were also an important part of his ministry. No one before, and no one since, has brought a dead person back to life as Jesus did for his friend, Lazarus. The body of Lazarus had already been decaying in his tomb for several days. The number and variety of miracles that Jesus performed are fantastic. There were physical healings, nature miracles, exorcisms (expulsion of evil spirits), and raising people from the dead. For example:

> When it was evening, after sunset, they brought to him all who were ill or possessed by demons. The whole town was gathered at the door. He cured many who were sick with various diseases, and he drove out many demons. (Mk 1:32–34)

Today, some people do not believe in miracles simply because they deny that God can intervene in the natural world. In effect, they deny God's power, and ultimately, they deny that God became man in Jesus Christ. These critics are like people described in John's Gospel who refused to believe that Jesus cured the man born blind (Jn 9:1–41). In this striking story, Jesus mixed his saliva with clay, smeared it on the man's eyes, and told him to wash himself in the pool of Siloam. The man did as Jesus instructed and was miraculously cured. His neighbors were astounded—no one blind from birth could possibly gain his sight.

When some of the Pharisees questioned the man about his cure, they simply would not believe him. The fact of the cure was plain to see. But, the prejudices against Jesus prevented these people from embracing the truth. Some even said Jesus committed evil by curing on the Sabbath. When interrogated

EXPLAINING THE FAITH

Why did Jesus use saliva and clay to help heal the blind man?

Although it's surprising for us to read that Jesus used his own saliva to help heal, it would not have been shocking or disgusting in his own day. In the ancient world, saliva was thought to be ideal for the healing of warts, spots, boils, and tumors. Jesus spat into the clay on the ground and then mixed a thick paste to rub on the eyes of the man born blind. In modern times, scientists have discovered that saliva does indeed have healing properties. One chemical in saliva, histatin, helps in the healing of wounds, which might explain why animals instinctively "lick their wounds." Other proteins in saliva also help fight infection, and still another chemical called opiorphin is up to six times more effective than morphine as a pain medication. Jesus, the Son of God, could have healed sick people with a whispered word or even with a look. But Jesus wanted to touch in healing. He often laid his hands on the sick to let those who were suffering feel the caring touch of a compassionate healer. Then, Jesus added the miraculous power of God to the "medicines" of his day to help people see, hear, walk, talk, and feel well again.

repeatedly by Jesus' opponents, the cured blind man rejected their argument that Jesus was a sinful man:

> This is what is so amazing, that you do not know where he is from, yet he opened my eyes. We know that God does not listen to sinners, but if one is devout and does his will, he listens to him. It is unheard of that anyone ever opened the eyes of a person born blind. If this man were not from God, he would not be able to do anything. (Jn 9:30–33)

The man's response so angered the Pharisees that they forcefully ejected him from their presence. When Jesus heard about the man's ill treatment, he sought him out, and asked,

> "Do you believe in the Son of Man?" He answered and said, "Who is he, sir, that I may believe in him?" Jesus said to him, "You have seen him and the one speaking with you is he." He said, "I do believe, Lord," and he worshiped him. (Jn 9:35–38)

Notice the irony! The man born blind could *see* who Jesus really was. Jesus was "the Lord," meaning God. And because the man knew who Jesus truly was, he did the right thing. He worshiped Jesus.

The vast majority of people who witnessed the miracles of Jesus knew that something spectacular was happening. They saw these miracles with their own eyes or were blessed to receive a wonderful healing. But how did they interpret what they witnessed? What was going on? Based on the question Jesus posed to the Apostles on the road to Caesarea Philippi, most people believed that Jesus was a great prophet. On the other hand, some of the opponents of Jesus could not deny these miracles. However, they said that this power of Jesus was coming from Satan.

Jesus himself told us why he performed these powerful signs: "These works that I perform testify on my behalf that the Father has sent me" (Jn 5:36).

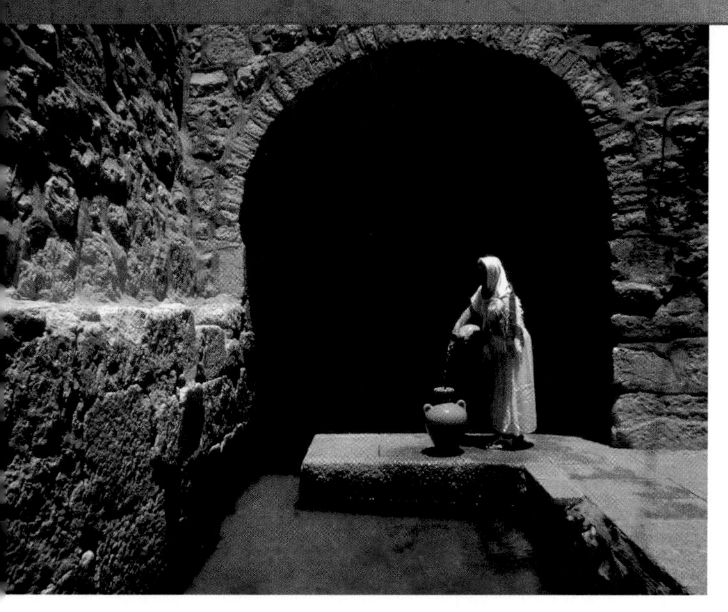

The miracles were performed for a reason: to help us conclude that Jesus is the Son of God.

Forgiving Sins (Mk 2:1-12; Mt 9:1-8; Lk 5:17-26)

By forgiving people's sins, Jesus also demonstrated his divine nature was the forgiving of sins. The physical healing of the paralytic and the forgiving of his sins took place on the same occasion. This event at Capernaum is one of the most dramatic examples of Christ's power to heal a person, body and soul. The story, reported in the three Synoptic Gospels, is worth retelling.

Early on in his ministry, Jesus returned to Capernaum, the base of his operations during his public life. Many people came to see and hear him preach there. They flocked to the small home where Jesus was staying. It became so crowded that there was no space left to get through the doorway.

Four friends of a paralyzed man wanted to bring him to Jesus. Because they could not get in through the crowded door, they ingeniously went up to the roof (probably using an outside stairs). There, they loosened either some tiles in the roof or a section of the mud-thatched roof. Then, they lowered their friend right down into the room so that he would be closer to Jesus. Jesus was deeply moved by the faith of these men. He compassionately said to the paralytic, "Child, your sins are forgiven" (Mk 2:5).

Some scribes sitting there observed what Jesus did. They began to murmur among themselves, accusing Jesus of blasphemy. By saying that the man's sins were forgiven, Jesus was, in fact, claiming to do what only God can do. From the point of view of the scribes, Jesus greatly dishonored God. They understood that he was saying that he himself was God.

Jesus knew what the scribes were thinking. He asked them a question: Is it easier to say that a man's sins are forgiven or to tell him to get up and walk? Obviously, it was easier to *say* that a person's sins were forgiven than to perform a miraculous deed. But to show that the Son of Man had the authority to forgive sins on earth, Jesus commanded the man to rise, pick up his mat, and go home. The man immediately obeyed. All present were astounded by this miracle done by Jesus. They began to glorify God, saying, "We have never seen anything like this" (Mk 2:12).

This particular Gospel account tells us that Jesus had the power to heal the inner brokenness of human beings—their sins—as well as their bodily ailments. It helps to establish in an extraordinary way that Jesus, the Son of Man, is indeed the Son of God. But the charge of blasphemy ultimately led to the condemnation of Jesus at his trial before the Sanhedrin. During the trial, Joseph Caiaphas, the high priest, shouted to Jesus,

> "I order you to tell us under oath before the living God whether you are the Messiah, the Son of God." Jesus said to him in reply, "You have said so. But I tell you: From now on you will see 'the Son of Man seated at the right hand of the Power' and 'coming on the clouds of heaven.'" Then the high priest tore his robes and said, "He has blasphemed! What further need have we of witnesses? You have now heard the blasphemy; what is your opinion? They said in reply, "He deserves to die!" (Mt 26:63–66)

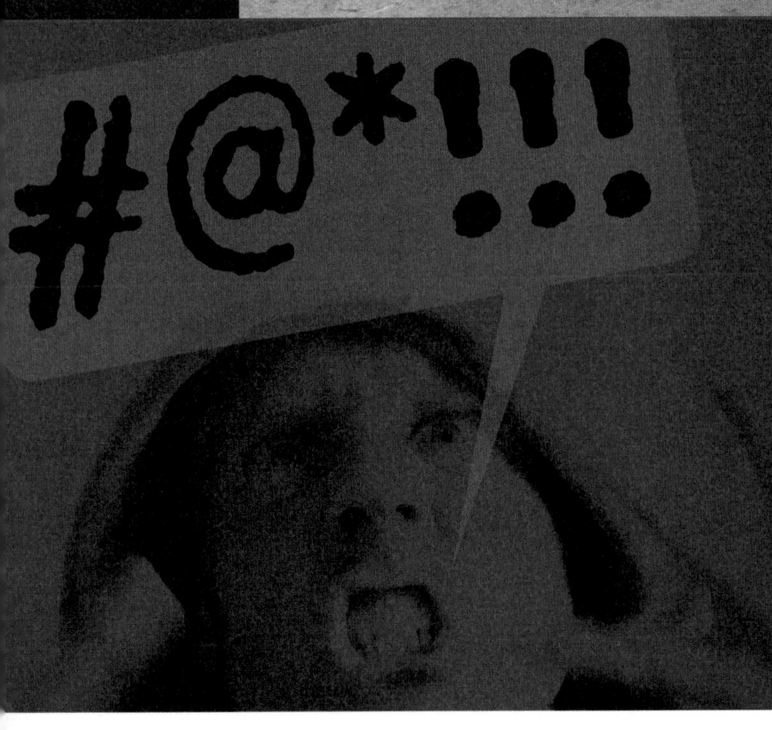

BLASPHEMY IN THE TWENTY-FIRST CENTURY: WHAT IS THAT?

According to the dictionary, blasphemy is the disrespectful use of God's name. In many cases, this "misuse" or "abuse" of God's name involves using God's name in "stress" or anger. We call that "swearing." As a class, discuss what you see as useful but contemporary guidelines for the respectful use of God's name, a respect we are also called to by the Second Commandment.

Jewish authorities sentenced Jesus precisely because they believed he was claiming what no ordinary man could claim to be. For them, the claims of Jesus were an outrage, punishable by death under Mosaic Law. Jesus, they said, was guilty of committing blasphemy. But, Jesus never said they were mistaken in their judgment. That's because Jesus himself said that he was the Son of God.

For Review

1. Which miracle, among all the miracles that Jesus worked, is the most important to the Gospel writers and to all Christians? Why is it the most important?
2. What did Jesus do and say when he healed the man born blind in John 9:1-41?
3. Why was the reaction of the scribes so negative when they witnessed Jesus healing the man born blind?
4. In his trial before the Sanhedrin, what specific crime against Jewish law led to the condemnation and Death of Jesus?

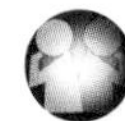

For Reflection

What is one way you will commit yourself to show more respect and love for the name of God?

Healed in Body and Spirit: A Capernaum Memory

Reflect quietly for a few moments on the story of the paralyzed man whom Jesus healed in body and spirit. Jesus changed life completely for this man. His paralysis was healed and his sins were forgiven! Imagine that you are that man a year or two after your healing. In your journal or notebook, write in his voice and in several pages the story of how "your" life changed when your best friends stubbornly lowered you through a roof into the smiling presence of the most wonderful man in the world.

Main Ideas

- Fundamentally, Jesus experienced life as a human being just as we do. (pp. 142–145)
- A genealogy is a record or a study of the ancestors or descendants of a person, people, or nation. (pp. 143–145)
- The genealogy in the Gospel of Matthew emphasized that Jesus was a descendant of Abraham and King David. (pp. 143–144)
- The genealogy in the Gospel of Luke emphasized the divinity of Jesus, the Redeemer. (pp. 144–145)
- Matthew's inclusion of women in the genealogy of Jesus was surprising because Jewish genealogy was typically traced through males. (p. 144)
- Though he was not the biological father of Jesus, as the husband of Mary, Joseph was seen as the foster father of Jesus. (pp. 144–145)
- Jesus was trained as a carpenter by his father Joseph and later earned his living at that trade. (p. 145)
- Jesus was raised according to Jewish tradition and law and practiced his Jewish faith throughout his life. (pp. 147–148)
- Jesus spoke Aramaic daily, learned to read and understand Hebrew, and may have learned Greek. (pp. 147–148)
- By nature, Jesus Christ was completely human and had both a human body and soul. Jesus was also fully divine and was the second Person of the Blessed Trinity. (pp. 149–153)
- Since he was fully man, Jesus' soul was endowed with true human knowledge that as such could not in itself be unlimited. (pp. 149–150)
- Throughout his lifetime, Jesus had the physical and emotional experiences that all humans encounter—hunger, thirst, fatigue, pain, fear, joy, grief, anger, pleasure, compassion, and love. (pp. 151–153)
- Old Testament prophecies from Isaiah, Micah, the Psalms, and Zechariah were fulfilled in Jesus, the Messiah predicted throughout the Old Testament. (pp. 153–156)
- Jesus revealed his own divinity through both his words and his deeds. (pp. 153–154)
- Jesus often referred to himself as "the Son of Man," an Old Testament term used to distinguish an individual from God. (p. 154)
- Jesus took on the "Suffering Servant" identity presented in Isaiah 52. (pp. 154–155)
- Jesus announced that he was the Messiah in the synagogue at Nazareth but was rejected by religious leaders and his fellow Nazarenes. (pp. 155–156)
- Peter called Jesus "the Son of the Living God" when Jesus asked his disciples who they thought he was. (p. 156)
- Jesus' miracles pointed to his divinity. (pp. 157–159)
- By forgiving people's sins, Jesus also demonstrated his divine nature. (pp. 159–160)

Terms, People, Places

Use all five vocabulary terms to write a brief description of who Jesus of Nazareth really is. Try to use the five terms in no more than three sentences.

Aramaic
Genealogy
Miracle
Son of Man
Torah

Primary Source Quotations

Who Was Jesus for the Early Church?
Grant us, O Lord, to hope in the name of Jesus, the beginning of all creation; open the eyes of our heart to know You, and

You alone, are the "Highest in the highest." You remain Holy among the holy. . .

Through Jesus Christ Your beloved Son, You have taught us, sanctified us, and given us honor. Be our helper and protector. Save those of us who are afflicted; have mercy on the humble; raise the fallen; show Yourself to those in need.

Let all the nations know that You alone are God, and that Jesus Christ is Your Servant, and that "we are Your people, the sheep of Your pasture."

—A Prayer from St. Clement of Rome

What the Birth of Jesus Christ Means
God's Word became human to accustom human beings to receiving God. God has begun to live with the human race.

—St. Irenaeus, Bishop

The Impact of the Birth of Jesus
Jesus was a surprise, the likes of whom no one expected.

—Pope Benedict XVI

The Works of Jesus Demonstrated His Divinity
By freeing some individuals from the earthly evils of hunger, injustice, illness, and death, Jesus performed messianic signs. Nevertheless, he did not come to abolish all evils here below, but to free men from the gravest slavery, sin, which thwarts them in their vocation as God's sons and causes all forms of human bondage.

—*Catechism of the Catholic Church*, 549

Jesus Was Fully Human
The Church was led over the course of centuries to confess the full reality of Christ's human soul, with its operations of intellect and will, and of his human body. In parallel fashion, she had to recall on each occasion that Christ's human nature belongs, as his own, to the divine person of the Son of God, who assumed it.

—*Catechism of the Catholic Church*, 470

These quotations focus on the way Jesus revealed his identity. He was the Son of God who became man—alike us in all ways but sin. Write a short response (two or three sentences) to the excerpt from Pope Benedict XVI. The Pope says that Jesus was a total surprise for the human race!

Ongoing Assignments

1. Research and study the genealogies of Jesus in more depth. Do some Internet research into the "genealogy of Jesus." Make a list of the common ancestors given in both Luke and Matthew's genealogies.
2. Read the following Scripture passages about three of the women in Jesus' family tree. Note in your journal something interesting about each person.
   - Tamar: Genesis 38:6–30
   - Rahab: Joshua 2:1–24
   - Bathsheba: 2 Samuel 11:1–27
3. Report on the methods of carpentry in the time of Jesus. What jobs did carpenters do? What products did they fashion? What raw materials were available for carpenters in the Galilean area? What tools were typically used by carpenters?
4. Research information and write a two-page report on some recent archaeological digs at Sepphoris, a town only an hour's walk from Nazareth. Do an Internet search for "Sepphoris dig."
5. Write a profile of Joseph of Arimathea. Research some Internet sites to learn about the legends associated with him. Retell and comment on this man's life and the legends about him.

6. Check a handbook to the Bible and biblical dictionaries and encyclopedias or search the Internet to prepare a report on how a young Jew would have been educated in Jesus' day.
7. Report on modern-day miracles that have taken place at the Shrine of Lourdes, France.
8. Read about the healing of the blind man in John 9:1–41. With several other classmates, build upon this reading. Write and enact a skit depicting this miracle.
9. Do a report on Joseph Caiaphas. Include information on the finding of his burial box (ossuary).
10. Read the following Gospel texts about four great works or miracles that Jesus performed. In your journal, answer the questions related to each miracle and comment on this work of Jesus. If you could choose, which miracle would you want to witness?
    - *The Man Born Blind (Jn 9:1–41)*: Why did the blind man's parents react as they did when they were questioned by the authorities? What did the man say that angered the authorities?
    - *Gerasene Demoniac (Mk 5:1–20)*: What did the people want Jesus to do after they heard about the miracle? Why did they react this way? What did the possessed man want to do? How did Jesus answer him?
    - *Raising the Widow's Son (Lk 7:11–17)*: What motivated Jesus to bring this man back to life? How did the people react to this miracle? What did they say about Jesus?
    - *Feeding the Four Thousand (Mt 15:32–39)*: What motivated Jesus to perform this miracle? What was left over after all ate?

Prayer

Prayer to Become More Like Jesus

God, our Father, You redeemed us and made us Your children in Christ. Through Him You have saved us from death and given us Your Divine life of grace. By becoming more like Jesus on earth, may I come to share his glory in Heaven. Give me the peace of Your kingdom, which this world does not give. By Your loving care protect the good You have given me. Open my eyes to the wonders of Your Love that I may serve You with a willing heart. Amen.

- *Reflection*: What human qualities in Jesus do you most admire? What surprises you the most about Jesus?
- *Resolution*: Pray the above prayer daily for the next two weeks.

7

THE CHURCH KNOWS JESUS BY MANY NAMES

For there is one God.
There is also one mediator between God and the human race,
Christ Jesus, himself human,
who gave himself as ransom for all.

—1 Timothy 2:5

- ## Knowing What the Words Mean

  To study the names and titles given to Jesus, we must study the meaning, history, and context of the words.

- ## Gospel Words to Describe Jesus

  The many words or titles used for Jesus in the Gospels give us even more insight and understanding about our Redeemer.

- ## Christian Symbols Teach about Jesus

  The Church has created many symbols to help Christians understand more clearly who Jesus is.

- ## Church Councils Clarified Teachings about Jesus

  Throughout the first five centuries of Christianity, the Church struggled to stop dangerous heresies by presenting and explaining important Christian teachings at ecumenical councils.

- ## The Nicene Creed Summarizes Beliefs about Jesus

  At the Council of Nicaea, in AD 325, the Church presented an enduring summary of the important dogmatic teachings about Jesus and the Trinity in the Nicene Creed.

Knowing What the Words Mean

Sir Christopher Wren (1632–1723) was a famous seventeenth-century scientist, mathematician, and the greatest English architect of his age. He designed fifty-two churches in London, including the famous St. Paul's Cathedral, which was rebuilt after the Great Fire of London in 1666. It took him thirty-five years to finish construction of this masterpiece. When St. Paul's Cathedral was completed, he anxiously awaited the reaction of Queen Anne. After touring his magnificent edifice, she gave her verdict: "It is awful; it is amusing; it is artificial."

How would you react if an important person you admired judged your life's best achievement this way? However, when Sir Christopher heard the queen's verdict, he was greatly pleased. He accepted her words with joy! Why did he react this way? In 1710, the English word *awful* meant "awe-inspiring" while *amusing* meant "amazing." The word *artificial* meant "artistic." Today, the words *awful, amusing,* and *artificial* have far different meanings for us than they did in eighteenth-century England. If we heard those words from Queen Anne, we would think we were being severely criticized. In Wren's day, he was being eloquently praised.

The words we use have great power to communicate or to mislead. That is why it is important to know what words mean. It is important for those who hear the words to have a common understanding of what these words mean to those who speak or write them. This lesson in history about Sir Christopher and Queen Anne reminds us that it is even more essential to understand the words that are applied to Jesus Christ in Scripture. This chapter focuses on the meaning of the words and titles used to describe Jesus. Understanding the context of the Scriptures allows us a deeper union with Jesus the Christ.

How Others Would Describe You

In this chapter we will be looking at how the early Church described Jesus. How about you? How do people describe *you*? What is your essential identity? How would you like people to see you? Here is a list of possible "identities" for you. Read through the list and pick three assessments that you think others would use to describe you. Then ask a classmate to assess you using the same word list. Compare and discuss the assessments you have for each other. How are they the same? How are they different?

good student	diligent worker	savvy survivor
faithful friend	star athlete	gutsy go-getter
awesome musician	fun companion	computer geek
dependable helper	mechanical wizard	creative artist
serious Catholic	intellectual searcher	committed disciple

For Reflection

Sometimes a person's actions tell us so much more than words can. Describe an action that you witnessed that really helped you see who and what a certain person was like.

Gospel Words to Describe Jesus

This chapter continues a study of **Christology**. The word *Christology* is derived from the Greek words for **Christ** (*Christos*) and word (*logos*). Christology, then, is that branch of Christian theology that studies the nature, Person, and works of Jesus Christ. It addresses questions like these: "Who is Jesus Christ?" "How can Jesus be both divine and human at the same time?" "What do we mean when we call Jesus the Son of God?"

In fact, the New Testament itself guides us in beginning to understand who Jesus is through the many titles it uses to describe him. We have discussed some of these in depth in previous chapters. For example, we explored:

- Jesus is *Emmanuel*—God with us (Mt 1:23).
- Jesus is the *Word (Logos) of God* who always existed with God and is God. All things, including life, came to be through him (Jn 1:1–5).
- Jesus is the *Son of Man* who is both human and God's divine agent who will usher in his kingdom (used over eighty times by Jesus in the Gospels, for example, Mk 8:31).
- Jesus is the unique *Son of God* (Mt 16:16, Jn 10:36).
- Jesus is "*I AM*" that is, God (Jn 8:58).

All of these titles reveal something profoundly truthful about Jesus Christ. But these are not the only titles for Jesus in the Gospels. Eight more titles or names for Jesus give us even more insight into the Person of Jesus. They are explored in the sections that follow.

Rabbi

The New Testament uses the term "**rabbi**" for Jesus fourteen different times. It is used most often by the followers of Jesus. For example, at the beginning of John's Gospel, two disciples address Jesus as "Rabbi" (Jn 1:38). Peter refers to Jesus as "Rabbi" at the Transfiguration (Mk 9:5). Judas addresses Jesus with this term at the Last Supper (Mt 26:25). The meaning of this term becomes clear when we see what the Pharisee Nicodemus, a ruler of the Jewish people, said to Jesus:

> Rabbi, we know that you are a teacher who has come from God, for no one can do these signs that you are doing unless God is with him. (Jn 3:2)

Rabbi is the Jewish word for Teacher. The many occurrences of the title help us to see that Jesus was thought of as something beyond a

Christology
The branch of Christian theology that studies the nature, Person, and works of Jesus Christ.

Christ
The Greek term for "Messiah." It means "the anointed one."

rabbi
A highly respected teacher of Jewish law or theology.

simple carpenter. He was known as a respected and admired teacher. In fact, the teaching style of Jesus was unique. Other rabbis often quoted other authorities to support their teaching. Jesus quoted no one. He spoke with singular authority—his own authority.

> Jesus then went down to Capernaum, a town of Galilee. He taught them on the Sabbath, and they were astonished at his teaching because he spoke with authority. (Lk 4:31–32)

The Pharisee Nicodemus tells us that the source of Christ's teaching authority was clear. Jesus came from God and performed the works that only God can perform.

Christ (CCC, 436-440, 453)

One of the most important of all titles given to Jesus is the title "Christ." Christ comes from the Greek word *Christos,* which translates as "Messiah," a Latin word for "anointed one" or savior. The name Christian comes from this title.

The Messiah was God's Anointed One, born into the lineage of King David who would fulfill all the divine promises made to the Chosen People. Many of the contemporaries of Jesus had different ideas of what and who the Messiah would be. For example, the Zealots, and many other Jews, were expecting a revolutionary, military-type Messiah who would throw off the "yoke" of the Roman oppressors through violence. The Essenes, a monastic group, many of whom who lived in the desert near the Dead Sea, were expecting two Messiahs: a priestly ruler, who would reform worship in the Jerusalem Temple, and a political king. Still others saw the coming Messiah as a prophetic figure like Moses or Elijah who would call the Jews to reform themselves morally and spiritually.

Jesus accepted the title of Messiah. But his concept of the Messiah differed from that of his contemporaries, including even his own Apostles. Consider, for example, Peter's profession of faith in Mark's Gospel (Mk 8:27–33). Peter correctly identified Jesus as the Messiah. Jesus acknowledged that he was indeed the Messiah, but then he began to talk about the "Son of Man" who would suffer and die for his people. For Jesus, the Messiah is the Son of Man who will come in glory at the end of time, but he is also the Suffering Servant as described in Isaiah 42–53. This serving, suffering Messiah would sacrifice his very life for his people.

Peter had difficulty accepting the kind of Messiah that Jesus said he would be. Peter even rebuked Jesus' arguments. Jesus saw Peter's disagreement as a temptation to take and use political and military power. Jesus immediately and strongly corrected Peter by saying, "Get behind me, Satan. You are thinking not as God does, but as human beings do" (Mk 8:33).

At his baptism, God the Father anointed his only begotten Son with the Holy Spirit. This anointing inaugurated the Kingdom of God. But

prophet
A title given to Jesus. A prophet is one who predicts the future but is also known as a representative and spokesman for God. Jesus acted as prophet in both ways but chiefly as God's representative because he was God himself.

God's Kingdom was not an earthly kingdom of power, wealth, and prestige. It was a Kingdom in which peace, love, and service were to reign. Jesus led this Kingdom by way of the cross, not by the conquering sword.

It is also interesting to point out that after Peter acknowledged Jesus to be the Messiah, Jesus told his disciples to keep his true identity quiet. Mark's Gospel reports that Jesus "warned them not to tell anyone about him" (Mk 8:30). You might think this is strange. Wouldn't Jesus want his followers to broadcast the news that he was the Messiah promised to his people for many, many generations? But, Jesus wanted his identity kept quiet for the time being. His concept of the "anointed one" radically differed from that of his contemporaries. Jesus did not want people to come to him for the wrong reason. He wanted them to approach him in faith and to accept and live his message of love, peace, and service.

Not until the Resurrection, Ascension, and glorification of Jesus would the early Christians begin to understand who Jesus really was. A major theme in the Gospel of Mark is that following Jesus means picking up a cross in daily imitation of him. Christ is the Messiah who is a Suffering Servant. Being a Christian, then, means imitating Christ and being willing to suffer for him. Walking the way of the cross with the Messiah leads to participation in his glorious Resurrection. Suffering for Christ helps lead to eternal life.

Jesus accomplished his mission of suffering service through the threefold office of Prophet, High Priest, and King. These are three other titles given to Jesus in the New Testament.

Prophet

A **prophet** is commonly thought of as one who predicts the future. Certainly this is one role of a prophet. Chapter 6 pointed out how Jesus did indeed make prophecies that were later fulfilled. One example was his prediction about the destruction of

EXPLAINING THE FAITH

Does God still send prophets to the world?

According to the Nicene Creed, the Holy Spirit has "spoken through the prophets" in times past. Throughout the Old Testament, according to the Church, God inspired many to speak his Word to Israel. Prophets have always had two roles. They predict the future, but more commonly, they speak in God's name and share his will for the present. The Old Testament prophets were Ezekiel, Habakkuk, Hosea, Isaiah, Jeremiah, Job, Joel, Jonah, and many others. John the Baptist is seen as the last prophet of the Old Testament.

At Pentecost, the Holy Spirit came in great power to infuse the followers of Jesus with special gifts called charisms. Included among these charisms was the gift of prophecy. Prophets, the Church teaches, call people to a new faithfulness to God and to the performance of deeds of justice and mercy. It may not always be easy to identify God's modern prophets. Like prophets in the Old Testament, modern prophets are often ignored or rejected. In nineteenth-century Italy, St. John Bosco seemed to issue a prophetic call for the loving care of homeless and abandoned boys and girls. Speaking about this need and serving the children became his lifelong work. Twentieth-century Catholics like Dorothy Day and Blessed Mother Teresa of Calcutta have certainly played the role of modern prophets. Echoing the Gospel, they witnessed to God's love of the poor, the homeless, the unemployed, and the unwanted. According to 1 Corinthians 14:3, prophecy is given for the "up-building and encouragement and consolation" of the Church. As long as there is faith and a commitment to hear the Gospel, there will be prophets among us.

the Jerusalem Temple. In fact, the city of Jerusalem and the Temple were completely destroyed by the Roman army led by the future emperor Titus in AD 70. The destruction of the Temple and the looting of its sacred treasures has been mourned by Jews ever since.

Another meaning for *prophet* is "a person who represents God." This kind of prophet is sent by God to speak for him and perform works on God's behalf to instruct the people.

Many people considered Jesus a prophet of this second description. For example, when Jesus entered Jerusalem during Holy Week to great acclaim, the city took notice and asked who he was. "The crowds replied, 'This is Jesus the prophet, from Nazareth in Galilee,'" (Mt 21:11). After Jesus raised the son of the widow of Nain, the people were awestruck and exclaimed, "A great prophet has arisen in our midst" and "God has visited his people" (Lk 7:16). And after he multiplied the loaves and the fishes, the people said, "This is truly the Prophet, the one who is to come into the world" (Jn 6:14).

Jesus is the very Word of God who speaks for his Father and teaches through his words and his deeds the full message of Salvation. Jesus' role as prophet involved testifying to the truth. As he told Pontius Pilate, "I came into this world to testify to truth" (Jn 18:37). It takes courage to be a prophet, especially when someone is threatening your life. Jesus—like so many prophets before and after him—was put to death because the authorities did not want to hear the truth he came to share.

Priest

One definition of a **priest** is that he is a mediator between God and humanity. Because of the Original Sin, a gulf between God and his creatures had opened. In the Old Testament, God appointed priests and anointed them to offer sacrifices to help bridge the gap that sin had caused between God and his people.

The Letter to the Hebrews calls Jesus the "great high priest" (Hb 4:14). Jesus is the Mediator between God and us. He is the Perfect Sacrifice. He offered his life for all people on the altar of the cross:

> But when Christ came as high priest of the good things that have come to be . . . he entered once for all into the sanctuary, not with the blood of goats and calves but with his own blood, thus obtaining eternal redemption. (Hb 9:11–12)

Today, Jesus the Christ, the anointed one of God, continues his priestly role at each celebration of the Eucharist.

King

When Jesus was born, the Magi from the East came to Jerusalem and asked, "Where is the newborn king of the Jews?" (Mt 2:2). At his trial, his opponents accused Jesus of claiming to be king of the Jews. Pontius Pilate asked Jesus if he were the **king** of the Jews. Jesus responded, "You say so" (Mk 15:2). By that, Jesus meant, "Yes, just as you say, I am the king of the Jews." Pilate, knowing that Jesus was innocent of any crime, had him crucified anyhow. Nonetheless, Pilate instructed the soldiers to put an inscription on the cross.

> It read, "Jesus the Nazorean, the King of the Jews." Now many of the Jews read this inscription, because the place where Jesus was crucified was near the city; and it was

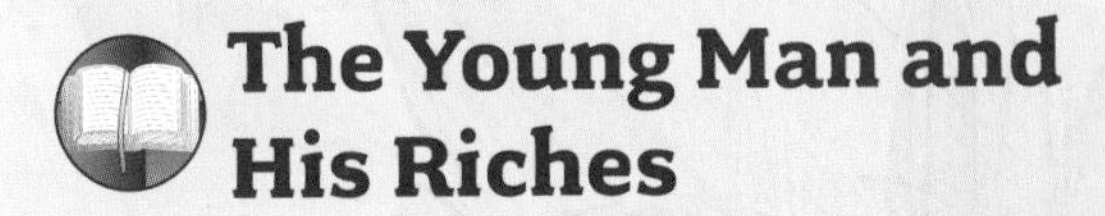

The Young Man and His Riches

Read the Gospel passage about the rich young man in Mark 10:17-31. Reflect on this story for a while. Now use your imagination and write a two-page story about what *might have happened* to this young man later in life. How did this encounter with Jesus change his future?

written in Hebrew, Latin, and Greek. (Jn 19:19–20)

Thus, Pilate advertised the crime for which Jesus was crucified, his claim to be a king. This crime was sedition and was punishable by death under Roman law because a person who was king would be in conflict

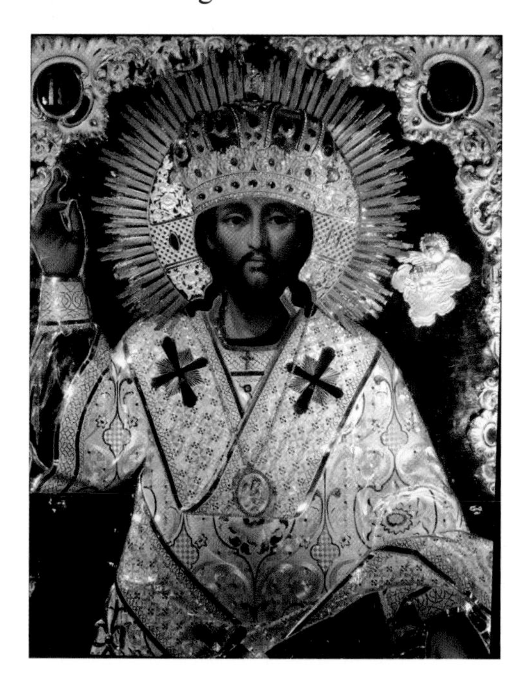

with Caesar, the Roman king. On the other hand, the chief priests were upset with what Pilate did. They asked him to change it to say that Jesus *claimed* to be King of the Jews. But, Pilate refused to change what he had written.

Jesus was not the Messiah the people were expecting. Nor was he the worldly king they wanted him to be. He had already refused Satan's offer of worldly power (Mt 4:8–10). After he multiplied the loaves and the fishes (Jn 6:15), he withdrew from the crowds when they wanted to make him king.

The truth is that Pilate did not make a mistake when he had the inscription put on the cross. Jesus was indeed the King of the Jews and, in fact, of all people. As the Book of Revelation puts it, Jesus is the King of Kings (Rv 17:14, 19:16). As the Son of God and the Word of God, Jesus Christ is the rightful ruler of the universe. But he does not lord it over others. He did not come to be served as a worldly king. He came as the Son of God to serve through suffering and dying for us to bring about our Salvation. The reign of Jesus is not one of brute power, force, or rule by fear. His reign is a rule of gentleness, compassion, and love. His method of leadership serves as our model. With the help of the Holy Spirit, Christians are called to serve and love others with compassion in imitation of the King of Kings.

Lamb of God

How Jesus saves us becomes clearer when we reflect on the history of the title "**Lamb of God**." In the Old Testament, the lamb was associated with the Passover feast. When the ancient Hebrews were enslaved in Egypt, God told Moses to tell the mighty pharaoh to "let my people go." The pharaoh refused to obey God. So, the Lord sent ten plagues to Egypt. The tenth plague was the killing of all the firstborn in Egypt. God instructed the Chosen People to kill an unblemished lamb and sprinkle its blood on the doorposts and lintels of their dwellings. Then, they were to roast the flesh of the lamb and eat it with unleavened

priest
A title given to Jesus that meant "a mediator between God and humanity." In the Old Testament, priests offered sacrifices for the Chosen People. Jesus became the priest of the New Testament, offering himself as a sacrifice for all. Today, priests are members of the order of the presbyterate and co-workers with the bishops.

king
A title given to the newborn Jesus by the Magi from the East who came to honor him. Jesus was also called a "king" at the end of his life by Jews seeking to accuse and convict him of sedition.

Lamb of God
An Old Testament title for Jesus that has roots in the Passover celebration. Unblemished lambs were sacrificed for the Passover meal. Jesus gave up his life for the redemption of all humanity and became the sacrificial lamb of the New Testament.

bread and bitter herbs. These bitter herbs symbolized their flight into the desert and the trials they would experience there. The blood on the doorposts was to be a sign to the Angel of Death who would "pass over" or skip that house. This Passover meant the sparing of the firstborn in the Israelite families.

> The blood will mark the houses where you are. Seeing the blood, I will pass over you; thus, when I strike the land of Egypt, no destructive blow will come upon you. (Ex 12:13)

The sacrificial lamb, then, was a symbol of Salvation and freedom for the Israelites. In the New Testament, St. Paul called Jesus our Paschal Lamb who has been sacrificed (1 Cor 5:7). John the Baptist also testified to Jesus this way the first time he saw him,

> "Behold, the Lamb of God, who takes away the sin of the world." . . . John testified further, saying, "I saw the Spirit come down like a dove from the sky and remain upon him. I did not know him, but the one who sent me to baptize with water told me, 'On whomever you see the Spirit come down and remain, he is the one who will baptize with the Holy Spirit.' Now I have seen and testified that he is the Son of God." (Jn 1:29, 32–34)

John the Baptist recognized who Jesus was and declared not only that he was the Lamb of God, but also the Son of God. The next day, John was with two of his disciples when he saw Jesus walk by. Once again, John proclaimed, "Behold, the Lamb of God."

One of these two disciples was Andrew who took John the Baptist at his word. Andrew immediately left John and began to follow Jesus. From that day on, Jesus invited Andrew and the other disciple to stay with him. Andrew then told Simon, his brother, that he had found the Messiah. Andrew brought Simon to Jesus. When Jesus met Simon, Jesus looked at him and said, "You are Simon the son of John; you will be called Kephas (which is translated Peter)" (Jn 1:42).

The first Apostles, it seems, were attracted to Jesus because he was pointed out as the Lamb of God. John's Gospel underscored the importance of this image. John reported that Jesus' Death on the cross took place at the exact moment when the Passover lambs were slaughtered in the Jerusalem Temple (Jn 19:28–42). The symbolism is very clear: The blood of the slain lambs saved the ancient Israelites at the time of the Passover. Sacrificial lambs were also used in other sacrifices on major feasts and for personal sacrifices like sin offerings. However, the blood of the true Lamb of God replaced the death of all other sacrificial lambs. God the Father provided the sacrificial lamb—his Son Jesus. It was through the sacrifice of Jesus on the cross that all humanity was saved. Through Jesus, our sins were forgiven. He took on the sin of the world and removed it through his death.

savior
A title given to Jesus that means "one who protects or saves from present or future danger"; a Messiah.

Lord
A New Testament title given to Jesus that meant "God." In Greek, the word was translated as *Kurios* and in Hebrew *Adonai*.

Alpha and Omega
A Christian symbol formed with the first and last letters of the Greek alphabet —Alpha and Omega. Together, these letters suggest that Jesus is the beginning and end or completion of all history.

In an unbloody manner, every Catholic Mass commemorates the sacrifice of the Lamb of God (*CCC,* 1367). Before we receive Holy Communion, the priest holds up the consecrated host. The priest then says: "Behold the Lamb of God, behold him who takes away the sins of the world."

Savior

A definition of the word ***savior*** is "one who protects us from present or future danger." Most appropriately, the name Jesus means "Savior" or "God saves."

In Luke's Gospel, an angel appeared to the shepherds in the fields and reported the great news to them: "Today in the city of David a savior has been born for you who is Messiah and Lord" (Lk 2:11). In John's Gospel, the Samaritans who went to meet Jesus enthusiastically told their neighbor, the Samaritan woman, that they now knew that Jesus was "truly the savior of the world" (Jn 4:42).

Later, New Testament writings, for example, Second Timothy, reminded early Christians that Jesus is our Savior:

> The appearance of our savior Christ Jesus . . . destroyed death and brought life and immortality to light through the gospel. (2 Tm 1:10)

Lord (CCC, 446-451, 455)

When Jesus lived on Earth, the title "**Lord**" could refer to a ruler or some powerful person. It was also used as a form of address similar to the way we use the word "sir." Some people, most notably foreigners, may have used it this way when they were talking with Jesus, and especially when they were asking him for a favor. An example of this occurs in Mark 7:28 when a Syrophoenician woman asked Jesus to drive a demon out of her daughter.

However, when Christians apply the title "Lord" to the name of Jesus, it means something entirely different. "Lord" translates the Greek word *Kurios*, which, in turn, translates the Hebrew word *Adonai*. *Adonai* was the word the Chosen People used whenever the most holy name for God—YHWH—would appear in the Hebrew Scriptures (the Old Testament).

Therefore, to give Jesus the title "Lord" is to state quite boldly that he is God. This is exactly what the Apostle Thomas did when Jesus appeared to him. Thomas said, "My Lord and my God!" (Jn 20:28). That proclamation must have burst out of Thomas when Jesus invited him to put his finger in his wounds and believe.

Jesus has the same sovereignty as God. For Christians, Jesus is the Lord in their lives. Jesus is the one who deserves their total devotion and obedience. The power, honor, and glory that are owed to God the Father are also due to Jesus.

Other New Testament Titles for Jesus

The New Testament is overflowing with titles for Jesus. For example, St. Paul called Jesus the "last Adam." As Paul said, "The first man, Adam, became a living being." Jesus, the last Adam, became "a life-giving spirit" (1 Cor 15:45). In the Book of Revelation, Jesus called himself the **Alpha and the Omega**: "I am the Alpha and the Omega," said the Lord God, "the one who is and who was and who is to come, the almighty" (Rev 1:8). St. Paul referred to Jesus as the "Image of God" (2 Cor 4:4).

Other titles for Jesus in the New Testament include:

- Advocate (1 Jn 2:1)
- Author of Eternal Salvation (Hb 5:9)
- Deliverer (Rm 11:26)
- Divine Physician (Mt 9:12–13)
- Head of the Church (Eph 1:22)
- Living Water (Jn 4:14)
- Mediator (1 Tm 2:5)
- Prince of Life (Acts 3:15)

For Review

1. What is *Christology*? What questions does it ask—and then answer—about Jesus?
2. What is the meaning of the word *rabbi*?
3. Since Jesus was often called "rabbi," what assumptions can we make about the way people viewed him?
4. What does the title "Christ" mean?
5. Describe the different concepts of "Messiah" among the contemporaries of Jesus.
6. What did Jesus himself teach about his role as the Messiah?
7. What are two different meanings of the word *prophet*?
8. How was the claim Jesus made to be a king later used against him?
9. What did the sacrifical lamb symbolize for the Israelites?
10. What did Christians mean when they used the term "Lord" in speaking of Jesus?

For Reflection

- Imagine you are beginning a blog about Jesus intended to appeal to teens. Name some creative titles for the blog that would fulfill that goal.
- List your three favorite titles for Jesus and explain why they are your favorites.

Christian Symbols Teach about Jesus

Down through the centuries, artistic symbols for Jesus Christ have helped to teach Catholics more about the Lord. These Christian symbols appear in religious paintings, in altar carvings, on the walls of catacombs, and in illustrations that decorate Bibles. Most of these symbols are rooted in a Scriptural quote or in some traditional belief about Jesus.

By definition, a symbol is an external sign of some reality. Sometimes, that reality is spiritual and invisible. Words, for example, express ideas. Words are external signs that we can hear or see. In a way, Jesus himself is a symbol, the perfect symbol of his Father. Jesus is also God's own Word. He is a visible sign of the invisible God, "an image of God" as St. Paul expressed it.

The symbols in the following section all reveal something important about Jesus and the Catholic faith.

Alpha and Omega

ΑΩ

Alpha is the first letter of the Greek alphabet; omega is the last letter. In Revelation 1:8, Jesus calls himself the Alpha and the Omega, meaning he is the beginning and end of all history.

INRI

The Roman authorities had a custom of posting the crime of condemned criminals on their crosses. The idea was to advertise the crime to thwart others from even thinking about committing something similar. In the Holy Land, Romans would have affixed a sign in three languages: Greek, Hebrew, and Latin. Visitors to Jerusalem during the religious festivals would have understood at least one of these languages.

INRI abbreviates the Latin words that would have been posted: *Iesus Nazarenus Rex Judeorum*, which translates to "Jesus of Nazareth, King of the Jews."

Jesus Christ the Conqueror

The upper left corner abbreviates the name Jesus (the first and last letters in Greek); the upper right corner abbreviates the title Christ (the first and last letters in Greek). The lower word NIKA is a Greek word that means, "to conquer" or "be victorious." Thus, taken altogether, the symbol means, "Jesus Christ is victorious" or "Jesus Christ the Conqueror."

Chi-Rho

Chi (**X**) and Rho (**P**) are the first two letters of the Greek word for Χριστος (Christos). This common symbol for Jesus identifies him as the Messiah.

Fish

The Greek word *Ichthus* means "fish." It is an anagram for the first letters of a short creed. It reads, "Jesus Christ Son of God Savior."

I — Iesous = Jesus
X — Christos = Christ
θ — Theou = of God
Y — Uios = Son
Σ — Soter = Savior

IHS

IHS are the first three letters of the name Jesus in Greek Ιησους (or Iesous).

Lamb

As discussed on pages 171–173, Jesus is the Lamb of God who takes away the sins of the world (Jn 1:29; see also Rv 5:12). A lamb standing with a banner represents the Risen Christ who has conquered death. A lamb standing with a cross and wound in its side represents Christ's Passion. A lamb seated on a throne or a book symbolizes Christ the Judge. You will sometimes find lambs engraved on the tombstones of children because lambs are gentle and innocent, just like children.

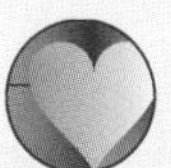

When God Touched Me

Sometimes, special people or events in our lives can act like powerful symbols. They represent and remind us of a deeper and sometimes invisible reality. Write about a time when God touched your life deeply through some event or special person. How did this event or this person influence you? Share what you wrote with your classmates.

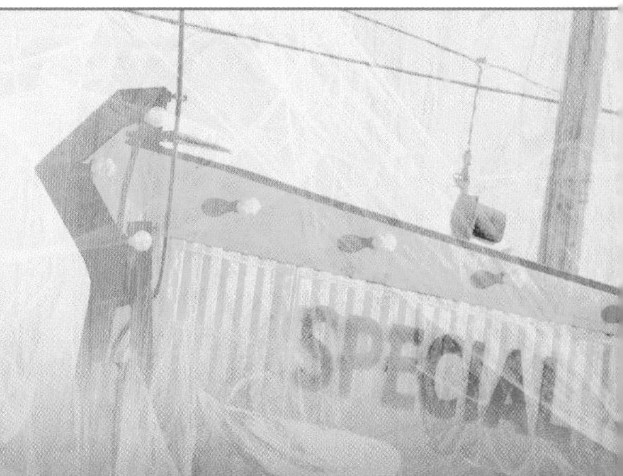

For Review

1. How did Christian symbols help the first Christians learn about their faith?
2. What is the meaning of the Alpha and Omega symbol as it relates to Jesus?
3. Describe how a fish became a symbol for Jesus.
4. Why is the lamb often used as a symbol for Jesus Christ?

For Reflection

- Describe a cross or crucifix that has been meaningful for your family or for you personally. What is it made from? How and when did you or your family obtain it?
- Non-religious symbols are also all around us. Some of these symbols help to unify us when unity is needed. If you can, identify symbols for the United States, for your city, for teens, for athletes. Explain the value of these symbols.

Church Councils Clarified Teachings about Jesus (CCC, 464-483)

Belief about Jesus Christ—who he is and what he means for us—has developed through the ages. People have always asked questions and wanted answers. This desire to know was also true in the early centuries as the Church began to evangelize the Gentile world with its pagan religions and philosophies. People wanted to know answers to questions like these about Jesus:

- Who is Jesus?
- Did Jesus always exist?
- Is Jesus equal to the Father, and therefore divine?
- How can Jesus be both human and divine at the same time?

Sometimes, people developed mistaken ideas about Jesus. These theological mistakes contradicted what the early Church and the Apostles believed and taught about him. Thus, false teachings about Jesus began to circulate. These false teachings led to heresies. A **heresy** was a denial of some truth or truths of the Catholic faith, the teachings of the Apostles, or what was written in the Gospels and other New Testament books.

Whenever false teachings challenge traditional Church teaching and mislead people, the Magisterium must clarify what Catholics should believe by issuing clear statements. The Church always knew what she believed about Jesus: He is truly the Son of God and therefore truly divine. It is the role of the Church to express these truths so clearly and precisely that every generation of believers will hold the right truths about our faith and not be troubled with doubts.

Catholics believe that Jesus lives in his Church and promised to be with us always. Jesus leads and guides his Church through the power of the Holy Spirit. Jesus appointed Peter, the Apostles, and their successors—the Pope and bishops—to lead the Church. Jesus told these leaders to hand on the truths of Revelation that he'd entrusted to them. Jesus said, "You are Peter, and upon this rock I will build my church, and the gates of the netherworld shall not prevail against it" (Mt 16:18). And later he said, "And behold, I am with you always, until the end of the age" (Mt 28:20).

These two quotes assure us that the Church will remain faithful to the truth. Jesus promised that. In an unbroken line of Apostolic succession, the Popes and bishops have passed on truthful teachings to the People of God.

During the first five Christian centuries, the Church dealt with a number of theological questions about Christ's identity and the Blessed Trinity. The Church Fathers helped clarify Church teaching in both of these areas. The **Church Fathers** were bishops, theologians, teachers, and scholars whose writings have greatly contributed to Church doctrine and practice. Among these Church Fathers were men like St. Irenaeus (ca. 130–202), St. Athanasius (ca. 297–373), St. Cyril of Alexandria (ca. 376–444), and Pope St. Leo the Great (ca. 400–461). The Church Fathers and bishops gathered in several ecumenical councils that issued dogmatic teachings about the Catholic faith. They also promulgated the Nicene Creed that we recite at Mass on Sundays. This Creed contains the most important beliefs we profess about Jesus Christ and the Blessed Trinity. Listed in the next sections are some of the questions answered by the councils.

Is Jesus Really Human?

The first set of false teachings about Jesus concerned whether or not he was truly man. Recall from page 33 that a heresy known as Docetism held that Jesus only *seemed* to be a man. It taught that though the body of Jesus appeared real, it was just an illusion. The Docetists denied the humanity of Jesus. They could not imagine how the eternal God could possibly hunger, thirst, suffer, and die for us. To this group, to be human seemed to be ungodly. The Gospel of John answered this false teaching head on. John's Gospel insisted that the Word of God became "flesh," that is, he was born a human being with a body.

The Docetist heresy was a form of Gnosticism, the heresy that falsely held that Jesus shared secret knowledge with just a few close friends. Like the Docetists, the Gnostics denied the true humanity of Jesus as well as his Resurrection. Gnosticism also denied the validity of Sacred Scripture, and the authority of the bishops to rule the Church. In *Against Heresies,* the major work of St. Irenaeus, this saint defended the Catholic faith and contradicted these Gnostic beliefs. Irenaeus defended **orthodoxy**, that is, true and established teaching. He also affirmed the importance of Christian tradition and the authority of the bishops. This Church Father taught that because the Roman Church traces her authority back to Peter, it is the true source of right teaching and belief.

heresy
An obstinate denial after Baptism to believe a truth that must be believed with divine and Catholic faith, or an obstinate doubt about such truth.

Church Fathers
Bishops, theologians, teachers, and scholars whose writings have greatly contributed to Church doctrine and practice. Among the Church Fathers of the early Church are Sts. Irenaeus, Athanasius, Cyril of Alexandria, and Pope St. Leo the Great.

orthodoxy
From the Greek word *orthodoxos*, it means having the "right" opinion or thinking; adhering to the accepted or traditional, especially in matters of religious faith.

Arianism
A heresy common during the first Christian centuries that denied that Jesus was truly God; named after Arius (AD 250—336), a priest and popular preacher from Alexandria, Egypt.

Nestorianism
A fifth-century heresy that taught that Christ exists as two persons—the man Jesus and the divine Son of God. The heresy was corrected by Church teaching that stated that Jesus has two natures (a divine nature and a human nature) in one Person. The heresy originated with Nestorius, (ca. 386—ca. 451) the Archbishop of Constantinople.

Monophysitism
A fifth-century heresy that promoted the error that Jesus had only one nature—a divine nature. In response, the Church taught that Christ has two natures, one divine and one human; from the Greek words *monos,* which means "one" or "alone," and *physis*, which means "nature."

Is Christ Really God?

Another set of false teachings came about because Arius (AD 250–336), a popular priest and preacher from Alexandria in Egypt, denied that Jesus was equal to God the Father. The heresy named after Arius is known as **Arianism**. Arius could not accept the teaching of the Incarnation, that God had become a man. Therefore, Arius taught that Jesus was God's greatest creature and an *adopted* Son of God. But Arius denied that Jesus *is* God. Arianism was a dangerous heresy because it denied the divinity of Christ, the central teaching of Christianity. If Jesus is not truly God, by what power and authority does he redeem us from our sins? Salvation would be lost.

St. Athanasius was a key figure in combating Arianism. He saw it as a divisive threat to the unity of Christian faith. The emperor Constantine agreed and called the first ecumenical council at Nicaea to counteract Arianism. The council condemned the heresy and issued the Nicene Creed. The creed was confirmed at the Council of Constantinople in 381 along with the teaching that Jesus is of the same substance or nature *(homoousios)* as God. Thus, both Councils clearly taught that Jesus is divine, the very thing that St. Thomas the Apostle recognized when he addressed the Risen Jesus as "My Lord and my God."

Arianism should have died at the Council of Nicaea, but unfortunately some emperors after Constantine tolerated Arianism. So, the heresy spread, especially in the Eastern Empire where Arian missionaries converted many of the barbarians. St. Athanasius valiantly defended the Nicene teaching of Christ's divinity. He taught that if Christ is not divine, then he could not be our Savior. Only God could restore people to communion with himself. Though he suffered and was exiled five times, St. Athanasius was known as the "Father of Orthodoxy" (true teaching), and his teaching prevailed at the Council of Constantinople.

How Many Persons Are in Christ?

Another heresy problem emerged when the patriarch of Constantinople, Nestorius, taught that there were two persons *in* Jesus—one divine, one human. Nestorius also refused to call Mary "the Mother of God." He claimed that she was mother to only the "human Jesus." St. Cyril of Alexandria contradicted Nestorius and defended Mary's title "*Theotokos*" ("God-bearer"). He said that it was perfectly correct to talk about Mary as the true Mother of God. St. Cyril also taught that Jesus was one divine Person and the second Person of the Blessed Trinity. We worship *one* Christ and Lord, not a human being along with the divine Word. The Council of Ephesus (AD 431) upheld St. Cyril's view and condemned **Nestorianism**.

CHURCH COUNCILS RESPOND TO HERESIES ABOUT JESUS

The Council	Church Teaching	The Heresy
Nicaea (325)	Jesus is "consubstantial" with the Father; he is divine.	Arianism: Jesus is only a creature; he is not equal to the Father.
Ephesus (431)	Jesus is one Person, a Divine Person. Mary is truly the "Mother of God." Jesus is both human and divine.	Nestorianism: Jesus was two persons—one human, one divine.
Chalcedon (451)	Jesus is one divine Person with both a divine nature and a human nature.	Docetism: The body of Jesus was only an illusion. God did not really become one of us. Monophysitism: Jesus only possesses a divine nature; he is not truly human.

How Many Natures Are in Christ?

Another heretic, Eutyches, made a different error than Nestorius. He claimed that the divine nature of Jesus absorbed his human nature. He said that Christ's human nature was swallowed up "like a drop of honey into the water of the sea." This teaching was known as **Monophysitism** from the Greek words for "one" and "nature." In effect, Eutyches was denying that Jesus was truly human.

Pope St. Leo the Great corrected this heresy in his work, *Tome.* Pope St. Leo's teachings were confirmed at the important Council of Chalcedon (AD 451). This Council taught the famous Chalcedon formula: *Jesus is one Divine Person with two natures—a divine nature and a human nature.* The Second Council of Constantinople (AD 553) confirmed this teaching. The Third Council of Constantinople (AD 680) also confirmed this teaching and added that because Jesus has two natures, he also possessed two wills. The human will of Jesus, though distinct from his divine will, was not opposed to it.

Summary of Key Dogmatic Teachings about Jesus

From the early ecumenical councils at Nicaea (AD 325), Constantinople I (AD 381), Ephesus (AD 431), Chalcedon (AD 451), Constantinople II (AD 553), and Constantinople III (AD 680–681), the Church formalized several official teachings about Jesus. They are summarized below:

1. *Jesus is the only Son of God.* Although Christ had a natural human mother, Mary, he had no natural human father. The Father of Jesus truly is the First Person of the Trinity, God the Father. All humans are the adopted children of God; only Jesus is the natural Son of God. Jesus shares in the very nature of God.
2. *Jesus Christ is true God.* He was born of the Father and is of one substance with the Father. This means that Jesus has the same nature as the Father. There was never a time when Jesus was not God.
3. *Jesus Christ is true God, God from God, Light from Light.* Like the Father, the Son has a divine nature. The Son, proceeding from the

Father is of one substance with the Father. Jesus Christ is true God just as light is identical to the light from which it comes.

4. *Jesus is "begotten, not made, one in Being with the Father."* The always-existing Son "proceeds" from the Father. In fact, this Son, Jesus, always proceeded and always will proceed. The Father did not "generate" the Son the same way that human fathers generate their sons. Christian faith holds that the Son is not "made" by the Father because the Son is not a created being. Rather, the Father "begets" the Son who is one in being with the Father. The Council of Nicaea distinguished between "begotten" and "created":

    The Father begets his Son and creates the world. The Son always existed in relationship to the Father from whom he proceeds. If Jesus is truly the only Son of God, then he must always have been so. As John's Gospel so eloquently states:

    In the beginning was the Word [the Son]:
    and the Word was with God
    and the Word was God. (Jn 1:1)

5. *All things were made through the Son.* Since the Son is one in being with the Father, he also shares in the creation of the world. "All things came to be through him" (Jn 1:3).
6. *There is only one Person in Christ, the Divine Person.* Jesus Christ is the Word of God, the second Person of the Blessed Trinity. Thus, everything in Christ's human nature is to be attributed to his divine Person, for example, his miracles and even his suffering and death.
7. *Mary, by conceiving God's Son, is truly the Mother of God.*
8. *There are two distinct natures in the one Person of Christ.* Jesus has a divine nature and a human nature. He is perfect in divinity and perfect in humanity. Jesus Christ is true God and true man. The union of the human and divine natures in the one Person of Jesus is so perfect that it is said that in Jesus, God truly shared in the experiences of humanity. God truly suffered, truly experienced death, and truly rose victorious over death.
9. *As a true man, body and soul, Jesus embodies the divine ways of God in a human way.*
10. *As true God and man, Jesus has a human intellect and a human will.* Both are perfectly attuned and subject to his divine intellect and will, which he has in common with the Father and the Holy Spirit.
11. *Jesus, God-made-man, is our Savior.* By uniting ourselves to his death and Resurrection through faith, we will share in the eternal life he has promised.
12. *The mission of Jesus Christ and the Holy Spirit are distinct but inseparable.* Whenever the Father sends his Son, he always sends his Spirit.

For Review

1. What are *heresies*? How did they spread?
2. Who were the Church Fathers? What role did they play in responding to heresies?
3. What was the major teaching of the heresy of Arianism? How did this false idea begin and spread?
4. Why did the Church see Arianism as a particularly dangerous heresy or error?
5. Where and when did the early Church councils that tried to correct heresies meet?
6. Who was known as the "Father of Orthodoxy"? Why was he given this title?
7. How does the Church answer the question about how many Persons there are in Christ?
8. Define *Monophysitism*. How did it develop?

9. How did Pope St. Leo the Great answer the heretical teachings of Monophysitism?
10. What are three of the dogmatic teachings about Jesus that the early Church councils presented? Briefly explain these three teachings.

For Reflection

- How does the amazing fact that Jesus is both God and man make *everything* different?
- Dietrich Bonhoeffer (1906-1945) was a famous Lutheran pastor and theologian who opposed Adolf Hitler and Nazism during World War II. He was also involved in the failed plot to assassinate Hitler. Reverend Bonhoeffer was imprisoned in 1943 and brutally tortured and hanged in 1945 right before the war ended. He once wrote, "If Jesus Christ is not true God, how could he help us? If he is not true man, how could he help us?" Write or discuss the meaning of Dietrich Bonhoeffer's observation.

The Nicene Creed Summarizes Beliefs about Jesus

The Nicene Creed, which was endorsed and expanded at the Council of Constantinople, serves as a classic and important summary of Christian belief about Jesus Christ, the Blessed Trinity, and the Catholic Church. What follows is a brief explanation of its major sections.

- *We believe in one God, the Father, the Almighty, maker of Heaven and earth, of all that is seen and unseen.*

  Our God is almighty and all-powerful. He is perfectly one. He is the Creator of everything

EXPLAINING THE FAITH

How will Jesus act as judge?

In the Nicene Creed, Catholics profess that Jesus "will come again in glory to judge the living and the dead . . ." The Apostles' Creed makes a statement that is almost identical. But what does it mean to say that Christ will be our judge of our lives? Simply put, the Church teaches that the Father has given the role of judge to his Son Jesus. Jesus is the perfect judge because Jesus has redeemed the world with righteousness and love. As the *Catechism of the Catholic Church* tells us, "Full right to pass definitive judgment on the works and hearts of men belongs to him as redeemer of the world. He 'acquired' this right by the cross." On Judgment Day, Jesus will come gloriously to secure the final and full victory of good over evil, of truth over lies. It has to be that way! The last chapter of our Redeemer's Good News must be finally and completely told. Justice must reign. Jesus, the Lord of all Creation, will weigh and examine each person's works and heart. And what will be the basis of his judgment? At the moment of our death, we will receive our eternal reckoning in a particular judgment that refers to how we lived our life like Christ. The Gospel tells us the criteria in Matthew 25:44-46:

> "For I was hungry and you gave me no food, I was thirsty and you gave me no drink, a stranger and you gave me no welcome, naked and you gave me no clothing, ill and in prison, and you did not care for me." Then they will answer and say, "Lord, when did we see you hungry or thirsty or a stranger or naked or ill or in prison, and not minister to your needs?" He will answer them, "Amen, I say to you, what you did not do for one of these least ones, you did not do for me." And these will go off to eternal punishment, but the righteous to eternal life.

In a way, each person judges himself or herself. Jesus Christ will only need to hold up a mirror. Each of us will see and recall the deeds and words of our lives and the intentions and hungers of our hearts. Judgment will come at the moment we see how we have accepted or refused the grace of Christ's redemption and how we have answered the call of God's love.

that is. Yet, Jesus revealed that we should pray to our Almighty God as our loving Father, "Abba," whom we can address with great trust. God loves us beyond what we can possibly imagine.

- *We believe in one Lord, Jesus Christ, the only Son of God, eternally begotten of the Father, God from God, Light from Light, true God from true God, begotten, not made, one in Being with the Father. Through him all things were made.*

  God so loves us that he proves his love through his Son, Jesus, through whom all things were made. This passage affirms that Jesus is both divine and the Lord of creation. He always existed as God's only Son. Jesus is indeed the Lord.

- *For us men and for our salvation he came down from Heaven.*

  Jesus came to save us from our sins. His mission was to heal the alienation caused by the Original Sin, an alienation that separates us from God, other people, and ourselves. Jesus is the Father's gift to us to rescue us from death and bring us home to the Father in heaven.

- *By the power of the Holy Spirit he was born of the Virgin Mary, and became man.*

  The mystery of the Incarnation—God becoming man in Jesus—took place when Mary said "yes" to God. Her faith in God's power to do marvelous things is an example for us today. The conception of Jesus through God's Spirit means that God's gracious activity brings forth our Salvation. Jesus represents a new beginning for the human race, a beginning started by God, not by us.

- *For our sake he was crucified under Pontius Pilate; he suffered, died, and was buried.*

  The way that Jesus preached about God's Kingdom and his call for conversion led to resistance and misunderstanding. But, Jesus did not give up. In an act of love and obedience to his Father and redemptive love for us, Jesus freely surrendered himself on the cross. He underwent a terrible death for our sake.

- *On the third day he rose again in fulfillment of the Scriptures.*

  This faith statement proclaims that Jesus is alive! Through his life, death, and Resurrection, Jesus has conquered sin and death. He has redeemed us from slavery to sin and the devil. His Resurrection is the source of our own hope for eternal life:

  > I am the resurrection and the life; whoever believes in me, even if he dies, will live, and

Applying the Teachings of Jesus

Check the teachings of Jesus on the following themes. Read and transcribe the following quotations into your journal. Then write a statement of commitment commenting on how one or more of these passages will help you to be a better disciple of the Lord.

- Possessions (Lk 12:15)
- Forgiveness (Mt 18:21-22)
- Discipleship (Lk 9:23)
- How to Live (Mt 7:12)
- Enemies (Mt 5:44)
- Humility (Mk 10:31)
- Love (Jn 15:17)
- Faith (Lk 17:6)
- Sincerity (Mt 6:1)
- Judgment (Mt 7:1)
- True Happiness (Lk 11:28)
- Prayer (Mt 7:7)
- Worry (Mt 6:33-34)

everyone who lives and believes in me will never die. (Jn 11:25–26)

- *He ascended into Heaven and is seated at the right hand of the Father. He will come again in glory to judge the living and the dead, and his kingdom will have no end.*

  This clause of the Creed affirms that the Risen Lord now lives with his Father. He intercedes for us at the Father's "right hand." That's a privileged position of special honor and influence. We also believe that one day in the future God's Kingdom will be fully established throughout the universe. The Good News from Jesus will serve as the standard for judging every creature. One day all creation will acknowledge the central fact of our faith: Jesus Christ is Lord!

- *We believe in the Holy Spirit, the Lord, the giver of life, who proceeds from the Father and the Son. With the Father and the Son he is worshiped and glorified. He has spoken through the Prophets.*

  In this statement of faith we profess that the Holy Spirit is the source of our life and gifts. He is the third Person of the Blessed Trinity. He empowers us to recognize and believe in Jesus. The Holy Spirit dwells in us and directs our hearts and minds to Jesus who draws us to his Father. The Holy Spirit helps us, the members of Christ's body, to continue the Lord's work until he comes in glory.

- *We believe in one holy catholic and apostolic Church. We acknowledge one baptism for the forgiveness of sins. We look for the resurrection of the dead and the life of the world to come.*

  In the final passage of the Creed, we acknowledge that Jesus lives in his Church. We take seriously his command to baptize in the name of the Father, and of the Son, and of the Holy Spirit. When we profess our belief in the Resurrection, we acknowledge that the Resurrection of Jesus is the source of our eternal happiness. We look to everlasting life because of our Savior and Lord Jesus Christ.

For Review

1. Which council expanded the Nicene Creed?
2. What important topics did the creed then address?
3. What does this creed say about the Holy Spirit, the third Person of the Blessed Trinity?

For Reflection

- The Nicene Creed states that all things were made through Jesus Christ, the Son of God. Name and describe two things that really remind you of Jesus. (These might be things found in nature. Or, they might be manmade inventions that are really life-giving or healing, etc.)
- What are some ways that you look forward to "the life of the world to come"? What do you think Heaven will be like?

Main Ideas

- Christology is the branch of Christian theology that studies the nature, Person, and works of Jesus Christ. (p. 167)
- The word *rabbi* means "teacher" but refers more specifically to a highly respected teacher of Jewish law or theology. (pp. 167–168)
- Though rabbis typically taught by quoting other authorities to support their own teaching, Jesus spoke on his own authority. (p. 168)
- One of the most important titles given to Jesus is "Christ," a title that comes from the Greek word *Christos*, which translates as "Messiah." (pp. 168–169)
- Though Jesus accepted the title of "Messiah," his concept was far different from the military savior or leader that most Jews expected; Jesus said he would be a Suffering Servant sort of Messiah and would die to save his people. (pp. 168–169)
- Other titles given to Jesus were "Prophet," "Priest," "King," and "Savior." (pp. 169–173)
- "Prophet," a title given to Jesus, refers to a person who predicts the future and also acts as a representative of God. Jesus was a prophet in both senses of the word, but primarily as God's spokesman, since he himself was also God. (pp. 169–170)
- Another title commonly given to Jesus is "priest," a term that means "a mediator between God and humanity." In the Old Testament, priests offered sacrifices to God; Jesus is the anointed one of God and is himself the sacrifice offered for all people. (p. 170)
- "Lamb of God" is an Old Testament title for Jesus that has roots in the Passover. Unblemished Passover lambs were sacrificed for the Passover meal. Jesus gave up his life for the redemption of all humanity and became the sacrificial lamb of the New Testament. (pp. 171–173)
- "Savior" is a title given to Jesus that means "one who protects or saves from present or future danger"; a Messiah. (p. 173)
- "Lord" was a New Testament title given to Jesus that meant "God." In Greek, the word was translated as *Kurios* and in Hebrew *Adonai.* (p. 173)
- Down through the centuries, Christians and Catholics have expressed their faith in Jesus through symbols. Among symbols for Christ are Alpha and Omega, INRI, Jesus Christ the Conqueror, Chi-Rho, fish, IHS, and the lamb. (pp. 174–175)
- Heresies or false teachings about fundamental Christian doctrines emerged often during the first Christian centuries. Especially common were heresies about the Trinity and about Jesus. (pp. 176–177)
- Church Fathers such as Sts. Irenaeus, Athanasius, Cyril of Alexandria, and Pope St. Leo the Great helped to proclaim clear teachings about Christian beliefs. (p. 177)
- The Pope, Church Fathers, and bishops of the Church gathered at ecumenical councils to confront heresies and present clear Christian teachings for the Church. (pp. 177–180)
- Among the heresies confronted by the Church in its first centuries were Docetism, Arianism, Gnosticism, Monophysitism, and Nestorianism. (pp. 177–179)
- Heresies focused on whether Jesus was really man, was Jesus really God, how many persons there were in Jesus, and how many natures Jesus had. (pp. 177–179)
- St. Athanasius, one of the fourth-century Fathers of the Church, suffered greatly for his defense of the Nicene Creed and orthodox Christian teaching. Athanasius was later known as the "Father of Orthodoxy." (p. 178)
- The Nicene Creed was endorsed and expanded by the Council of Constantinople. This creed is an important summary of Christian beliefs. (pp. 181–183)

Terms, People, Places

Complete the sentences using seven of the vocabulary words below.

Alpha and Omega
Arianism
Christ
Christology
Church Fathers
Ecumenical councils
Heresy
King
Lamb of God
Lord
Monophysitism
Nestorianism
Orthodoxy
Priest
Prophet
Rabbi
Savior

1. When Christians called Jesus __________, they were really calling him "God," which was translated as *Adonai* in Hebrew or *Kurios* in Greek.
2. A _____________ is any denial of some important truth of the Catholic faith, the teachings of the Apostles, or what was written in the New Testament.
3. The branch of Christian theology that studies the nature, Person, and works of Jesus Christ is called ______________.
4. ______________, another title given to Jesus, referred to his role as a mediator between God and humanity.
5. ____________ was a fifth-century heresy that mistakenly taught that Jesus had only one nature—a divine nature. The name of this heresy was taken from a Greek word for "one" and a Greek word for "nature."
6. Bishops, theologians, and scholars who vigorously and bravely defended and taught the Christian faith during the early life of the Church are called the ______________.
7. The word _____________ is taken from a Greek word that means "having the right opinion or thinking."

Primary Source Quotations

The Two Natures of Jesus Christ

We, then, following the holy Fathers, all with one consent, teach people to confess one and the same Son, our Lord Jesus Christ, the same perfect in Godhead and also perfect in manhood; truly God and truly man, of a reasonable [rational] soul and body; consubstantial [coessential] with the Father according to the Godhead, and consubstantial with us according to the Manhood; in all things like unto us, without sin; begotten before all ages of the Father according to the Godhead, and in these latter days, for us and for our salvation, born of the Virgin Mary, the Mother of God, according to the Manhood; one and the same Christ, Son, Lord, only begotten, to be acknowledged in two natures, inconfusedly, unchangeably, indivisibly, inseparably; the distinction of natures being by no means taken away by the union, but rather the property of each nature being preserved, and concurring in one Person and one Subsistence, not parted or divided into two persons, but one and the same Son, and only begotten, God the Word, the Lord Jesus Christ. . . .

—The Chalcedonian Creed

Defending the Faith

Virtue is nothing without the trial of temptation, for there is no conflict without an enemy, no victory without strife.

—Pope St. Leo the Great

The Compassion and Humanity of Jesus
I have read in Plato and Cicero sayings that are very wise and very beautiful; but I never read in either of them: "Come to me, all you who labor and are burdened, and I will give you rest."
—St. Augustine of Hippo

All Creation Will Acknowledge: Jesus Christ Is Lord
Have among yourselves the same attitude that is also yours in Christ Jesus,
Who, though he was in the form of God,
did not regard equality with God
something to be grasped.
Rather, he emptied himself,
taking the form of a slave,
coming in human likeness;
and found human in appearance,
he humbled himself,
becoming obedient to death,
even death on a cross.
Because of this, God greatly exalted him
and bestowed on him the name
that is above every name,
that at the name of Jesus
every knee should bend,
of those in heaven and on earth and
under the earth,
and every tongue confess that
Jesus Christ is LORD,
to the glory of God the Father.
—Philippians 2:5–11

The Letter to the Philippians states "that at the name of Jesus every knee would bend." Represent this scene with a simple sketch or more elaborate drawing.

Ongoing Assignments

1. Design a symbol or logo that teaches that Jesus is the Light of the World.
2. Research and report on the topic of the knowledge Jesus had. Do an Internet search for "the knowledge of Jesus" or "What did Jesus know?" Or, locate and read the article "Jesus' Knowledge" by Fr. William G. Most: www.ewtn.com/faith/teachings/incaa2.htm.
3. Create a small booklet of favorite sayings of Jesus. Select at least ten passages that are especially meaningful to you. Use appropriate artwork downloaded from the Internet to illustrate your booklet.
4. Read Exodus 12 focusing on the instructions offered about the Passover meal. Note at least five specific regulations the Israelites had to observe while preparing for and celebrating this feast.
5. Record the following statements that are heresies or false statements about the faith. Research why each statement is a false teaching. Use Church documents to contradict the false statement with a true one.
   - Jesus became God's Son at his baptism.
   - God the Father created God the Son.
   - It was impossible for Christ to really suffer pain.
   - Because Jesus has a divine nature, he can do what God does. Because Jesus has a human nature, he could do what humans do.
6. Create a PowerPoint presentation on symbols of Jesus Christ in art. Alternately, create a poster of five common symbols with a brief explanation of each.
7. Using a digital camera, take photos of symbols for Christ in local churches and religious institutions. If you're not sure what some of the symbols mean, interview priests or staff members at that church, school, or shrine to discover their significance. Using computer design techniques, create a poster or booklet presenting and explaining these local Christian symbols.

8. Visit a Catholic cemetery or a cemetery with the graves of many Catholics and Christians of other denominations. Use a digital camera to take photos of the symbols of faith that are often featured on tombstones. Develop a PowerPoint presentation on your findings.
9. Create a question-answer style catechism with twenty-five questions about Jesus. Write and format the catechism so that it would be appropriate for fourth-grade readers. Present it as a booklet with images and symbols downloaded from the Internet.
10. Do a short report on any one of the following topics: an early heresy about Jesus Christ; an early ecumenical council; a Church Father.

Prayer

Recite the *Agnus Dei*, "Lamb of God," that we pray together at Mass, slowly and reflectively.

> Lamb of God, who takes away the sin of the world, have mercy on us.
> Lamb of God, who takes away the sin of the world, have mercy on us.
> Lamb of God, who takes away the sin of the world, grant us peace.

- *Reflection*: What in your life needs Christ's mercy and peace right now?
- *Resolution*: Plan to receive the Sacrament of Reconciliation during the coming month. Celebrate the loving Lord's invitation to forgive your sins and help you grow in friendship with him. It is a Sacrament of great peace.

WHAT JESUS TELLS US ABOUT OURSELVES

For this I was born and for this I came into the world, to testify to the truth. Everyone who belongs to the truth listens to my voice.

—John 18:37

Understood and Loved as We Are

God, our Father and Creator, understands us perfectly and loves us completely and endlessly despite our flaws and shortcomings.

Jesus, Our Model and Guide

Because he is the Son of God and the perfect human being, Jesus is the ideal guide and model for every person in every time and circumstance.

Human Beings Are Made in God's Image

The Book of Genesis reminds us that God created humans in his image; in the divine image, male and female, he created them.

Jesus Saves!

Though all are burdened with the deadly consequences of Original Sin, we are also offered Salvation and happiness by our loving God through Jesus Christ.

The Beatitudes: Lessons for Happiness

The Beatitudes are guidelines for true happiness that were offered by Jesus in the Sermon on the Mount.

Understood and Loved as We Are

One day, a young boy approached a farmer who was selling some puppies. The farmer told him the puppies were a good breed and rather costly. The boy was crestfallen since he did not have much money. He said to the farmer, "I only have three dollars. Is that enough to take a look?"

"Yes,'" replied the man who then whistled for Sedona, the mother dog. She proudly led four small pups out of the barn. A big smile broke out on the boy's face. Then, out of the barn limped a fifth little fur ball. Clearly, it was the runt of the litter. It had a bum hind leg and could not keep up with the other puppies.

The boy ran up to the tiny dog and gathered him up into his arms. He asked the farmer, "Could I please have this one?" The farmer replied, "Son, I don't think you want that puppy. He'll never be able to run and play with you the way normal dogs can."

The boy looked up at the man and reached down to pull up his right pants leg. A shiny steel brace encircled his leg and was attached to a corrective shoe. Looking up to the farmer, the boy said, "As you can see, I can't run too well myself. This little guy will need someone who understands."

The young boy had great insight about the little puppy with the injured leg. He knew that the puppy would need someone who understood its limitations but loved it all the same. In a similar way, human beings need this kind of understanding and love as well. We all need someone who understands and loves us just as we are. And just like that small puppy, none of us is perfect. We all have flaws, shortcomings, handicaps. Yet, we are precious. How blessed we are if we find someone who truly understands, accepts, and loves us—no questions asked.

Fortunately for us, Jesus Christ is that someone. Jesus does know us through and through, and Jesus loves us perfectly. As both God and man, he knows not only who we are but also what we can be and become. Jesus is our model and our guide for living.

The Second Vatican Council document *The Church in the Modern World* reminded the world that we find the best model for living in the life of Jesus:

> The Church firmly believes . . . that in her most benign Lord and Master can be found the key, the focal point and the goal of man, as well as of all human history. . . . The truth is that only in the mystery of the incarnate Word does the mystery of man take on light.

The Council Fathers added that Jesus "is the goal of human history, the focal point of the longings of history and of civilization, the center of the human race, the joy of every heart and the answer to all its yearnings."

Jesus *is* our goal and our model. He is the perfect human being who shows us how to become the persons God intends us to be. This chapter focuses on what we can learn from Jesus about being human.

For Reflection

When was an occasion that you felt especially understood and accepted for who and what you are?

Persons Are Gifts

You are special! You are a unique gift, created by God. Read the following poem to yourself. Underline or note phrases in the poem that especially resonate with you. Choose two of the phrases and record them in a notebook or journal. Write two or three sentences explaining how the phrase connects with your life. Share what you wrote with a classmate.

Persons are gifts which the Creator God sends
to us . . . wrapped.
Some come wrapped very beautifully,
some come in very ordinary wrapping paper.
Some persons are very loosely wrapped,
others very tightly.
Sometimes the gift has been mishandled in the mail.
Once in a while there is a special delivery!

Some person-gifts are very easy to open up;
others need to be helped out of their boxes.
Is it because they are afraid?
Do they think it might hurt to be opened?
Maybe they have been opened up before
And thrown away!
Could it be that their gift is not for me?

I am a person. Therefore, I am a gift, too!
a gift to myself, first of all.
God my Creator gave myself to me!
Have I every really looked inside the wrapping?
Am I afraid to?
Perhaps I've never accepted the gift that I am.
Could it be that there is something else
inside the wrappings than what I think is there?
Maybe I could never see the wonderful gift that I am.
Could God's gift be anything but beautiful?
I love the gifts which those who love me give to me.
Why not the gift of me?
And I am a gift to other persons.
Am I willing to be given to others?
to be a person for others?
Do others have to be content with the wrapping,
never permitted to enjoy the gift?
Every meeting of persons is an exchange of gifts.
Love is a relationship between persons
who see themselves as they really are:
Gifts given by God to be given to others.

—Author Unknown

Jesus, Our Model and Guide

Pope John Paul II's first encyclical, *The Redeemer of Man*, opens with this line: "Christ is the center of the universe and of human history." In a talk he gave to American youth at New York's Madison Square Garden in 1979, he further explained what he meant about Jesus being the ultimate model for us. "When you wonder about the mystery of yourself," he said, "look to Christ who gives you the meaning of life. When you wonder what it means to be a mature person, look to Christ who is the fullness of humanity." Jesus Christ is the focal point of human history. He is the crucified but resurrected Son of God. He is God's image who entered into human history. We live in a sinful world, but in Jesus we see what we are meant to be. Conversely, we learn from Jesus what God is really like. St. Paul called Jesus the Second Adam. At the Incarnation, Jesus appeared as a "New Adam" in history. Jesus was giving the human race a brand-new start.

From all eternity, the Father intended to send his Son to us. Jesus is the perfect model of God's creation. He is the perfect human being whose words and example teach us about humanity and our eternal destiny. Jesus teaches us how to be holy, how to be fully human, and how to be what God intends us to be.

In the Letter to the Colossians, St. Paul wrote about Jesus:

> He is the image of the invisible God, the firstborn of all creation. For in him were created all things in heaven and on earth, the visible and the invisible, . . . all things were created through him and for him. He is before all things, and in him all things hold together. (Col 1:15–17)

What this means is that Jesus Christ is indeed the absolute center of the universe. Everything is created through him. And he holds everything together. It is Jesus who brings ultimate meaning and purpose to our lives.

Jesus Presents God's Plan

So what is it that Jesus taught us about our purpose for life? We learn an important lesson from Jesus in this passage:

> The Pharisees approached and asked, "Is it lawful for a husband to divorce his wife?" They were testing him. He said to them in reply, "What did Moses command you?" They replied, "Moses permitted him to write a bill of divorce and dismiss her." But Jesus told them, "Because of the hardness of your hearts he wrote you this commandment. But from the beginning of creation, 'God made them male and female. For this reason a man shall leave his father and mother (and be joined to his wife), and the two shall become one flesh.' So they are no longer two but one flesh. Therefore what God has joined together, no human being must separate." In the house the disciples again questioned him about this. He said to them, "Whoever divorces his wife and marries another commits adultery against her; and if she divorces her husband and marries another, she commits adultery." (Mk 10:2–12)

The setting for this passage involves some Pharisees who wished to challenge Jesus and his teaching authority. Probably like other teachers of their day, they permitted men to divorce their wives under certain circumstances. Jesus, however, taught differently. Referring to two passages in Genesis (Gn 1:27 and Gn 2:24), Jesus taught about the sacredness of marriage. Jesus said that God does not want people to separate what he has joined together.

We can see that Jesus really wants us to go back and study God's revelation in the Old Testament and to live as God intended us to before the Original Sin. We should look, for example, in the Book of

Genesis to see exactly what God has to say about human beings. Jesus wanted the Pharisees and everyone else to learn some important lessons from this important passage.

For Review

1. What basic message did Pope John Paul II want to give the world about Jesus in his first encyclical, *The Redeemer of Man*?
2. Why did St. Paul describe Jesus as the Second Adam?
3. What is the lesson on the purpose of life revealed in Jesus' answer to the Pharisees about whether or not to allow divorce?

For Reflection

When was a time you received help and courage to be the person God wants you to be? Did that help come through prayer or the Sacraments? From a faith-filled friend or priest? From a parent or someone in your family?

Human Beings Are Made in God's Image (CCC, 355-384, 1701-1703)

Jesus, as the New or Second Adam, intended for us to look back at creation prior to Original Sin and to consider how God first desired for people to live. The first creation story in the Book of Genesis, particularly the verses (see Genesis 1:26–31) that center on the creation of humans and the responsibilities God endowed them with, reveal much to us about how we are to live and about the Father, who with the Son and Holy Spirit, created us. Some of the lessons and truths of this passage are explored in more depth in the sections that follow.

God Is Creator

Sometimes humans forget that God did not *have* to create us. But he did so out of his infinite goodness and love. God remains our Creator whether we think about him or not. He keeps us in existence whether we think about this truth or not. History has often shown that when humans forget about God, or make themselves into gods, sinfulness abounds. They wreak havoc on themselves and the rest of creation. We must always keep in mind our place in God's creation and always acknowledge God as Creator of all.

God Gives Human Beings a Privileged Place in Creation

Human beings are uniquely precious to our Creator. We are the living masterpieces of his creation. God created everything that exists, but he made human beings stewards of creation. We are given awesome gifts but awesome responsibility as well. Though God is the Creator, it is our duty to love and serve his creatures and creation. Jesus summed up our responsibilities when he taught these two commandments:

> You shall love the Lord, your God, with all your heart, with all your soul, and with all your mind. This is the greatest and the first commandment. The second is like it: You shall love your neighbor as yourself. (Mt 22:37–39)

An important way to show love for God and our "neighbors" all over our world is to respect and responsibly use what we have been given. Our world belongs to all of God's children. Its resources, beauty, and potential are a heritage for each people and each nation. When we fail to share the goods of the earth, we permit great injustices. Overconsumption, for instance, negatively affects all human beings as well as all living creatures on the planet.

God Creates Us in the Divine Image (CCC, 1701, 1704-1706, 1711-1713, 1731)

Humans are unique because God made us in the divine image, enabling us to share in his own life. God, who is a pure Spirit, does not possess physical or material qualities. He is the Supreme Being who possesses infinite knowledge and Truth. He is a Trinity of Persons. God is all-good and a community of perfect Love: Father, Son, and Spirit. By making us in the divine image, God endowed us with important spiritual qualities like the abilities to think, to choose, to love, and to relate to others in community. These traits enable us to share, through knowledge and love, in God's own life.

God has created us with a body and an immortal soul. As the *Catechism of the Catholic Church* puts it, "It is in Christ, 'the image of the invisible God,' that man has been created 'in the image and likeness' of the Creator" (*CCC,* 1701). We are not just "somethings," but "someones." We are people who can know and give themselves in relationships to others and to God. We can also share in God's life and have capacities that separate us from any other earthly creatures. Because we are made in God's image, we were made out of love for love. Through God's special grace, we can also enter into a covenant, a loving relationship with our Creator, and respond to God in faith and in love. Because only human beings are created in the likeness and image of God, no other creature can do what we can do. Each of our special human abilities is described in more detail below.

- *We can think.* Because we have intellects, human beings are rational and can reason and think. We can discover the meaning of life and death. We can learn things and pass on our knowledge to future generations. Most importantly, we can discover truth. We can use our minds to discover the eternal, objective, and universal laws that God implants in his creation. We can also use our human reason to recognize God's voice. God urges us to do good and avoid evil. We each have a conscience that enables us to choose God's will. We also have a duty to form that conscience properly and then follow it.
- *We can choose.* God gave us free wills, that is, the ability to choose from among alternatives. "Freedom is the power, rooted in reason and will . . . to perform deliberate actions on one's own responsibility" (*CCC,* 1731). Because we are free, we can determine our own lives and our futures. We can change, for example, from children who might have been taught prejudices to more loving and tolerant adults. The Church teaches that the power of "authentic freedom is an exceptional sign of the divine image within man" (*Pastoral Constitution on the Church in the Modern World*, 17). Free will empowers men and women to use the talents God gave them for others. We are also able to cooperate with all the graces of the Holy Spirit.
- *We can love.* A good definition of love is choosing to do good for others even if it's painful or difficult. Jesus teaches that love is the fundamental requirement: "I give you a new commandment: love one another. As I have loved

you, so you also should love one another" (Jn 13:34). Once again, Jesus is our guide, our model for learning how to love.

- *We are responsible.* Because we are endowed with **free will** and intelligence, we have the ability to respond to God and to others. This makes us accountable for our choices—whether they are good or evil. Evil choices, of course, will turn us away from God and the persons we are meant to be. The choices we make help to form our identities. For example, a person who regularly helps others is letting Christ shine through him or her. This person is becoming more like Christ. On the other hand, a person who habitually lies or cheats is sinning, but is also transforming his identity, as well. When we turn away from the Truth, we actually distort the image of God within us.
- *We can change.* The abilities to think, to choose, and to love give us the power to change and to grow. Both as individuals and as communities, we humans can learn from our experiences—both good and bad. For example, as we become more mature, we can reject childish self-centeredness and begin to think more about the needs of others. For instance, communities can examine how they live. They might decide to adopt simpler lifestyles that will help protect creation for future generations.
- *We have tremendous dignity.* Because we are made in God's image, every human being possesses profound **dignity**. We have this dignity from the first moment of conception until natural death. Dignity is "inherent," meaning it is an essential quality of being human. It is "inviolable" because no one has the right to violate or profane it. It is "inalienable" because it cannot be taken away by anyone. Even if we commit sin, and thus distort God's image in us, we still have dignity and are worthy of respect. God's grace can always call us back to be the beautiful creatures he made us to be. Our human dignity has nothing to do with our accomplishments, roles, wealth, talents, and so forth. God loved us so much that he sent his Son to befriend us and save us. Jesus died for every human being because every single person is a child of God. The important lesson that Jesus teaches us is that we must respect all people as an "other self" even if they themselves lack self-respect.

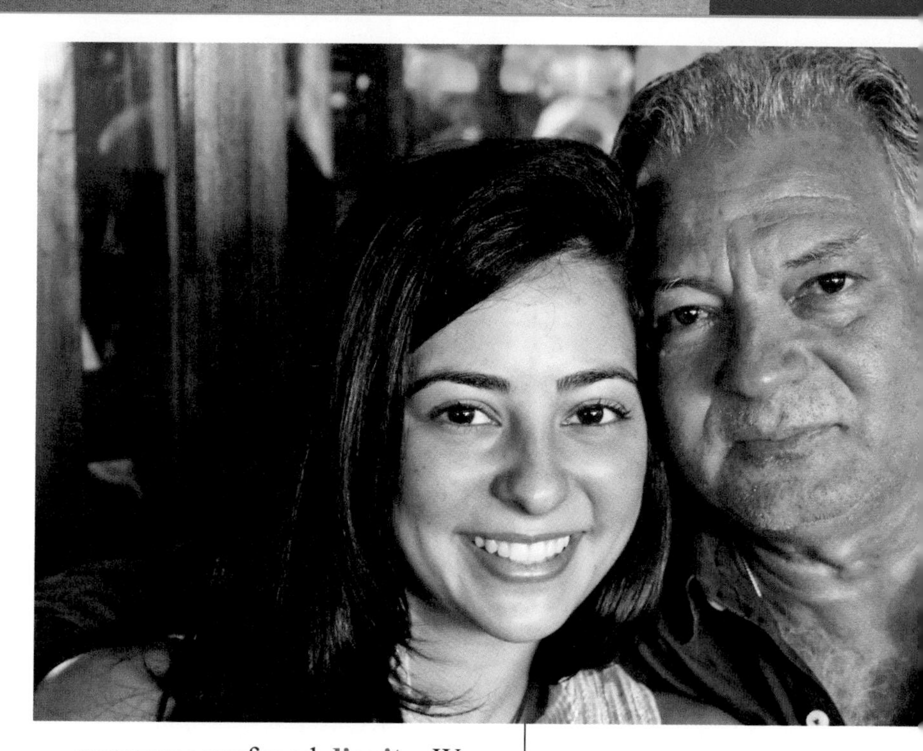

free will
The capacity to choose among alternatives. Free will is "the power, rooted in reason and will . . . to perform deliberate actions on one's own responsibility" (*CCC*, 1731). True freedom is at the service of what is good and true.

dignity
The quality of being worthy of esteem and respect.

Jesus Taught Respect

Read and summarize each of the following passages. Explain how Jesus taught or exemplified respect for others.

- Mark 1:40-42
- Mark 5:1-20
- Mark 9:36-37
- Luke 7:36-50
- Luke 23:32-34
- John 8:1-11

Original Sin
The fallen state of human nature into which all generations of people are born. Christ Jesus came to save us from Original Sin.

sin
An offense against God through a violation of truth, reason, and conscience. It is a deliberate thought, word, deed, or omission against the eternal law of God.

dominion
The role of caretaker and faithful steward given by God to our first parents, Adam and Eve. All human beings inherit the responsibility to be good and loving caretakers of the world, its resources, and its creatures.

The second creation account in Genesis (2:4–25) reveals that human beings are not only created in God's image, but that God is a friend. We read that our first parents were in complete harmony with God, with each other, and with the rest of creation.

Adam and Eve were in an original state of holiness and justice. In this way, they shared in God's life. He placed them in the Garden of Eden "to cultivate and care for it" (Gn 2:15). This shows their familiarity with and closeness to God. Their work was not hard, exhausting labor but a sort of collaborative effort with God, their Creator. Together, they worked to perfect God's good creation.

So, Genesis asserts the fundamental goodness of human beings who were created for friendship with God. However, through the **Original Sin** of Adam and Eve, the original harmony was lost. Human beings became subject to suffering and death. Yet, despite the effects of Original Sin and the **sins** we commit, humans are good because God created us in his image to share divine life and friendship with us. The proof of our fundamental goodness is that God loved us so much that "he gave his only Son, so that everyone who believes in him might not perish but have eternal life" (Jn 3:16).

God Has Made Us Male and Female

Genesis tells us that God created humans as complementary beings, male and female. "Complementary" means "making up for what is lacking in another." Humans need each other in many different ways. We complete and fulfill each other. God builds interdependence into our very nature, creating man and woman to be helpmates, a communion of persons *(CCC,* 372).

God also created man and woman equal in dignity. Neither male nor female is superior or inferior to the other. Both are beautiful creatures of God who need and complete each other:

> Man and woman are both with one and the same dignity "in the image of God." In their "being-man" and "being-woman," they reflect the Creator's wisdom and goodness. (*CCC*, 369)

Recall that God declared what he made to be good, very good. That includes, of course, our sexual identities as males and females. Sexuality is indeed good and beautiful. Because we have bodies, we are part of God's material universe. The human body shares in the dignity of the image of God for two reasons: our body is to be a temple of the Holy Spirit and it is to rise up on the last day. We are created in the image of God. Our whole human person—body and soul—gains knowledge through our five senses in collaboration with our intellect and will. We express our humanity and experience reality through our emotions and feelings, passions and drives, preferences and dislikes. What's more, each individual has a unique, one-of–a kind genetic makeup. There's only one of you. You are an unrepeatable creation of our gracious God.

God Created Humans as Stewards of the Earth

The first creation account in Genesis also reveals that God made human beings stewards of the earth. Men and women have a special dominion over the earth and its resources. But that does not mean that we have the right to selfishly exploit our world. When God placed Adam and Eve in the Garden of Eden, he told them "to cultivate and take care of it" (Gn 2:15). **Dominion** over creation requires us to cultivate God's creation and care for it by preserving "the beauty, diversity, and integrity of nature, as well as . . . fostering its productivity." Sinfulness in the form of greed has led to abuses that have seriously threatened our physical world.

Jesus left an example of care for the environment. He showed his love of the environment by using many beautiful images from nature in his teachings. He also taught the meaning of good stewardship in a Parable of Ten Gold Coins in Luke 19:11–17. There we learn that good stewardship means wise use of what God has given. It also means sharing resources for the benefit of all people.

We Are Social Beings (CCC, 1877-1948)

Because we are created in God's image, we humans are social beings. We live in various societies or groups that are bound together by principles of unity. Among these communities are our families, schools, and parishes.

Our God-given vocation is to reflect the divine image. One way we do that is by relating to and loving others. Another way we do that is by sharing our gifts in and for the world. God is a Trinity of relationships—Father, Son, and Holy Spirit. The three divine Persons in this relationship relate to each other by giving, receiving, and loving. The Trinity created human beings and angels out of love to share divine life.

How Can "Good" Human Beings Do Evil Things?

Though we know Genesis says that human beings are basically "good" in God's eyes, it's hard to explain why some do evil things. At one point in William Shakespeare's famous play, *Macbeth*, the forlorn king says he is disenchanted with life and has a pessimistic view of it. In contrast to his negative judgment is the Biblical view. It says that human life is good and that we are precious sons and daughters of a loving God.

Use a tape recorder or a video camera to record an interview with a person whom you greatly admire. Ask the person to talk about his or her philosophy of life. Be sure to also ask your interview subject what he or she thinks about the basic goodness of human beings. Summarize your interview in a short one-page essay, or play a key portion of the recorded interview for the whole class.

Because God is love and we are created in his image, we are most human when we love. We learn about love most directly from Jesus. He teaches us how to care for one another with respect, equality, and mutual self-giving. We are made to lovingly treat each other as sisters and brothers. We are also made to establish communities that benefit and bring a fuller life for each person.

Humans are relational, that is, social, by nature. We belong to each other, to our world, and to our Trinitarian God. God made us to be one with each other and with him for eternity. We exist with and for others. In the Parable of the Good Samaritan, Jesus taught us that everyone is our neighbor, even our enemies whom we must forgive. We must respect each person because he or she has been created by God and endowed with great dignity. Therefore, we must respect and work for the basic human rights of all people.

Because we have been created to be with and for others, we must use our gifts and talents to help other people. We must work with those in civil authority to build up the communities in which we live in a spirit of truth, justice, solidarity, and freedom by working for peace and justice. We must work to eradicate sinful inequalities that weaken and destroy justice, peace, and human dignity. Furthermore, we must promote the **common good**, that is, "the sum total of social conditions that allow people, either as groups or as individuals, to reach their fulfillment more fully and more easily" (*Pastoral Constitution on the Church in the Modern World*, 26).

The common good requires us to develop and use our talents. St. Irenaeus said that "the glory of God is man fully alive." We are fully alive, that is, fully human, when we are most like the perfect human, Jesus Christ. When we are "fully alive," we are becoming the person God created us to be. We each

EXPLAINING THE FAITH

How can we say God is good when he allows evil in the world?

We should remember that God is supremely good and has proved his love in so many ways. For example, God did not have to create the world and its creatures. But he did so out of love. Sacred Scripture also tells the story of God's love through human history. It reached its climax when God sent his Son, Jesus Christ, to suffer and die for his sinful creatures. Suffering and evil are a sad part of the human story. But, we can't say that God causes or sends them. The *Catechism of the Catholic Church* summarizes the dilemma this way:

> Faith gives us the certainty that God would not permit an evil if he did not cause a good to come from that very evil, by ways that we shall fully know only in eternal life." (*CCC*, 324)

The Old Testament Book of Job confronted the question of evil. Job was a good man who lost all his children and property and then contracted a horrible disease. Despite his setbacks, Job continued to trust God. In fact, good came from Job's sufferings. God restored his family, his flocks, and his wealth. Job also became a holier man. He admitted that God's ways are mysterious. We are not God, and we don't see things from God's perspective. We need to know that we are totally dependent on God and not in control. Therefore, we can never adequately explain all the evil that befalls us.

Another point to consider is that God created a world that is in a process of becoming. It is *not* yet perfect. The more perfect exists alongside the less perfect. "With physical good there also exists *physical evil* as long as creation has not reached perfection" (*CCC*, 310). And finally, we need to see that the misuse of freedom is the cause of much evil. God created humans and angels as intelligent and free creatures, not as mindless robots or unthinking puppets. The gifts of intellect and free will give us tremendous dignity. But these two gifts must be used responsibly. We must freely choose to love God and others. When we refuse to love, we sin. That sin brings about incredible evil and suffering.

have special gifts that we must use to reflect God's goodness. We must develop our minds (intellects), engage our hearts (love), and use our hands to develop our unique talents so that we can bring God to other people.

Recognizing that we are social beings and being fully alive persons leads us to exercise the virtue of solidarity. **Solidarity** is the Christian virtue of social charity and friendship. Solidarity can mean visiting the sick, reaching out to the lonely, and responding to the needs of the poor. It is Jesus who teaches us the value of each human life. Through the Incarnation, God is united in solidarity with each person. Solidarity gives us the courage and generosity to share our money and possessions as well as our spiritual gifts. Solidarity recognizes that we are all members of the human family and that we must go out of our way to help one another.

For Review

1. What book of the Bible confirms that God had a plan for every creature but especially for the first human beings?
2. What is meant by the words "in our image" and "after our likeness"?
3. What words in Genesis 1 tell us that God gave human beings a special place among the creatures of the earth?
4. Name some of the spiritual qualities that God gave to human beings.
5. What is meant by "free will"? Give one example of how a person might use free will.
6. What is the fundamental requirement or expectation that God places on all human beings?
7. What do the Bible and the Church mean by *dignity* as it relates to human beings?
8. How are men and women "complementary"?
9. What is *Original Sin*? How does it affect human beings today?
10. Explain, in simple terms, what the Church means by the *common good*.

For Reflection

- Share a recent experience of solidarity (social charity or friendship) you have had. How did you feel about reaching out to someone who needed your friendship and help? Will your experience make it easier to do it again?
- Recall a movie or book that deeply impressed you with a powerful message about a person's ability to change and grow.
- What are some ways that your friends and fellow students really do recognize and honor the God-given dignity of other individuals? How do their words show it? How do their actions show it?

common good
The sum total of social conditions that allow people, either as groups or as individuals, to reach their fulfillment more fully and more easily.

solidarity
A Christian virtue of charity and friendship whereby members of the human family share material and spiritual goods.

Jesus Saves! (*CCC*, 1264, 1846, 1849, 1707-1709, 1714-1715)

There are two vital messages for us in the Incarnation. The first is that we are created fundamentally good. Why else would God bother to send his Son Jesus to become one of us? The other message, however, is that we clearly needed to be saved. Jesus, the Son of God, would not have come to live, suffer, and die for us unless there was no other solution. Jesus Christ, our Savior, rescued us from sin and death so that we could have a life of eternal joy with the Blessed Trinity.

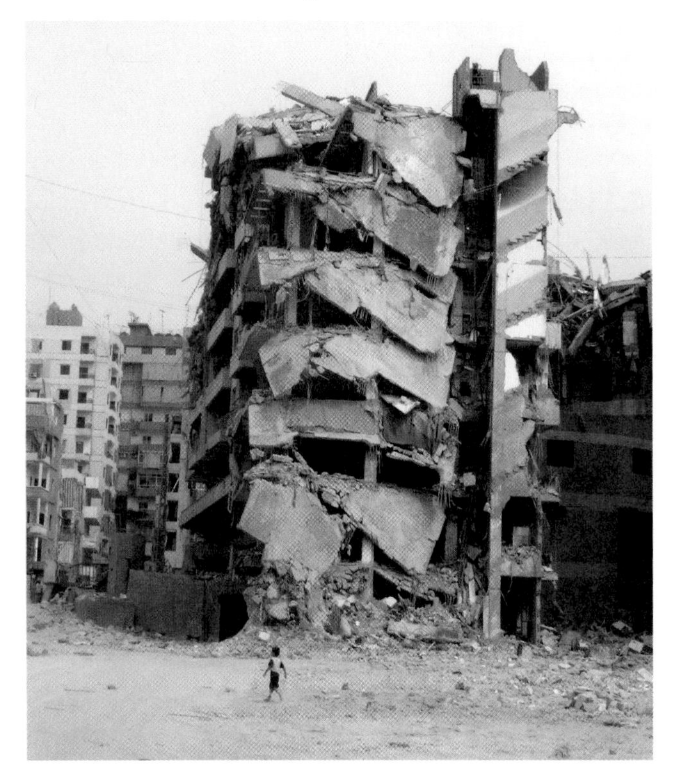

From the beginning, human beings were wounded by sin and inclined toward evil and selfish mistakes. Genesis 2:15–3:24 reports that Adam and Eve chose to follow their own desires and ignore God's plan for them. Pride led to their downfall and expulsion from the Garden. There were many consequences. They were alienated from God and became subject to suffering and death. In addition, the children of Adam and Eve—the whole human race—became infected by sin. Every human being who would ever live would suffer the consequences of that Original Sin.

One of the consequences of Original Sin is that both individuals and communities of people must cope with **concupiscence**. *Concupiscence* is the weakness or inclination in human beings to sin, individually and collectively. This sin, of course, can take many shapes. It could be cowardice, selfishness, deceit, anger, violence, jealousy, and a host of other tragic and destructive evils. We often have the best intentions to do the right thing. But, we are weak and inclined to commit sin. It is as if we are at war with ourselves. We are so prone to sin because we are often weak-willed. We fail to do what we know is right.

Salvation History verifies that what we sense is, as well, the moral battle of every person. Within each of us wages a battle between good and evil, between light and darkness. Though we are beautiful creatures of a loving God, we are also sinners. Sin wounds human nature and hurts human solidarity. When we sin, we fail to show true love for God or for our neighbor. What we do show is that we choose to put our own wills and desires above everything else. At least at that moment in time, we are willing to disobey God. We refuse to follow Jesus and his teaching. Obeying God and following Jesus are keys to our Salvation. St. Paul understood this sad human weakness and the tendency to choose our own will over the will of the Father:

> What I do, I do not understand. For I do not do what I want, but I do what I hate. . . . For I do not do the good I want, but I do the evil I do not want. Now if [I] do what I do not want, it is no longer I who do it, but sin that dwells in me. (Rm 7:15, 19–20)

St. Paul recognized what each of us recognizes as we move through life. We are weak and can't rescue ourselves from this inclination, the magnetism of sin. We need a Savior to rescue us from this hopeless situation.

We Are Saved Sinners

The *Catechism of the Catholic Church* summarizes the lot of humans so well: "The Gospel is the revelation in Jesus Christ of God's mercy to sinners" (1846).

The Paschal Mystery—the Passion, Death, Resurrection, and glorification of Jesus Christ—has delivered humans from the clutches of sin and from the Evil One. The sacrifice Jesus made saves us from eternal death and wins for us eternal life with the Triune God. In short, Jesus gave up his life so that we might live. Jesus showed us how to love by making the ultimate sacrifice. God the Father accepted the self-surrendering gift of Jesus but later rescued him from death. Jesus rose from the dead to superabundant life at the right side of God the Father. Together, the Father and the Son sent us the Holy Spirit who releases power and grace to us. The Holy Spirit comes so that we might live wholesome, holy, and loving lives for others. Jesus has continued his work of Salvation in his Body, the Church. The Holy Spirit guides, enlightens, and strengthens the Pope, bishops, priests, and all those who minister in the name of the Church. We also benefit from the Seven Sacraments given to the Church by Jesus. These Sacraments are fountains of grace that continue the saving work of Jesus through time.

We Are Children of God (CCC, 1226, 1262-1274, 1279-1280, 1391-1397, 1468-1470)

Before his Ascension into Heaven, Jesus instructed his Apostles to preach the Gospel to the ends of the earth. He also instructed his followers to make disciples of all nations and to baptize them "in the name of the Father and of the Son, and of the Holy Spirit" (Mt 28:19). From the very beginning, the Church obeyed Christ's command. On Pentecost St. Peter told the crowd:

> Repent and be baptized, every one of you, in the name of Jesus Christ for the forgiveness of your sins; and you will receive the gift of the holy Spirit. (Acts 2:38)

What Peter promised in Jesus' name was a wonderful gift—the forgiveness of sin and gifts of the Holy Spirit. Those gifts restore and renew us. They enable us to live holy, happy, full lives. Peter followed the instructions Jesus gave his Apostles. He called for repentance, just as Jesus did. Jesus had proclaimed:

> This is the time of fulfillment. The kingdom of God is at hand. Repent, and believe in the gospel. (Mk 1:15)

Repentance means to reform our hearts, minds, and wills. It also means turning from sin and avoiding anything that might lead to sin. The call

concupiscence
The weakness or inclination in human beings to sin, individually and collectively.

that Jesus made for repentance is sometimes called ***metanoia***, a Greek word that means "turning away" or "changing directions." Jesus knew that this new direction would be necessary if God's love was to find room in our hearts. We have to let go of anything that enslaves us, anything that leads us away from God. We have to convert and welcome the graces of the Holy Spirit. These graces would help us to combat sin and would help us to look at the world from Christ's point of view.

Repentance and the Sacrament of Baptism are linked in the teaching of the Church. If we think about it carefully, it's easy to see that Baptism is a Sacrament of conversion. Through Baptism, we gain a new life in the Holy Spirit. In Baptism, the Holy Spirit showers many graces on us, including:

- *The forgiveness of sin*. Baptism forgives Original Sin and personal sin—as well as the punishment due sin. However, some consequences of sin remain, like suffering, weakness of will, the inclination to sin, and, ultimately, death.
- *Sanctifying grace.* This type of grace heals fallen human nature and gives us a share in the divine life of the Blessed Trinity. Sanctifying grace is a habitual, supernatural gift that makes us perfect, holy, and Christ-like.
- *Initiation and incorporation*. Baptism, along with Confirmation and Eucharist, is one of the Sacraments of Initiation.
- *Sealing*. The Sacrament provides us with an indelible spiritual character that marks us as belonging to Christ.
- *Birth into a new life in Christ*. Through Baptism, we become children of God and a temple of the Holy Spirit. Baptism is necessary for our Salvation as is the Church herself.

In summary, Baptism brings us into God's own family. That means that we are no longer simply God's creatures. Now, as a baptized Christian, each one of us becomes an adopted child of God the Father. We also become brothers or sisters of Jesus and, of course, of one another. St. Paul wrote:

> As proof that you are children, God sent the spirit of his Son into our hearts, crying out, "Abba, father!" So you are no longer a slave but a child, and if a child then also an heir, through God. (Gal 4:6–7)

This is Good News indeed! God has been so gracious to give us Jesus as our Savior. He has adopted us into his family, and given us the gift of the Holy Spirit so that we can live Christ-like lives and become his disciples. As we will discuss further in the next chapter, Jesus also calls us his friends. We are friends that he asks to continue his work here on earth. Jesus calls us to help lead others to him.

EXPLAINING THE FAITH

If we inherited the inclination to sin, do we really have free will?

The Church teaches that the Original Sin of Adam and Eve has been transmitted or passed down to all of their descendents. So, each person is born in a "condition of sin" but can be freed from that through Baptism and the merits of Jesus Christ. Nonetheless, much of the pain and sorrow in our world is not due to Original Sin but to our continued and deliberate sins. Unlike Original Sin, these are actual sins. They are offenses against God that we personally choose to commit. But, our sinning is not inevitable. We are not programmed to say "yes" to temptation. We do have free will; we can say "no."

God has honored us with the ability to choose because he knows that love needs freedom. In the First Letter to the Corinthians, St. Paul reminds the Church in Corinth that God "is faithful and will not let you be tried beyond your strength"(1 Cor 10:13). St. Paul is also referring to grace. If a temptation is too strong for us, it is not too strong for God who will strengthen us if we ask for help. God also gives us sufficient wisdom to choose to do the right thing.

Being a disciple of Jesus is a lifelong commitment. In fact, it's really an endless process of repenting for our sins and failings, and turning more and more to God. However, Jesus offers us powerful assistance for this tough journey. One support is the Sacrament of Penance, a Sacrament in which we can confess our sins, receive God's loving forgiveness, and be reconciled with the Church. What's more, in the Sacrament of Penance, we receive graces to help us live more faithfully in the future.

The Fathers of the Second Vatican Council called the Eucharist "the source and summit of the Christian life" (quoted in *CCC*, 1324). In this Sacrament, we receive Jesus himself. Holy Communion is a spiritual food that "preserves, increases, and renews the life of grace received at Baptism" (*CCC*, 1392). The Body and Blood of Jesus also separate us from sin. The Eucharist strengthens love within us and unites us more closely to the other members of Christ's Body. In receiving Jesus, we are more able to be like him and more ready to take him and his message into the world. In particular, Jesus asks us to serve the poor and suffering and those who desperately want to hear the Good News about God's love for us.

For Review

1. What are two important messages we can learn in the mystery of the Incarnation?
2. Name several consequences of Original Sin.
3. Define *sin*. How does sin affect our relationship with God and with our neighbors?
4. Define and give an example of *concupiscence*.
5. What is *metanoia*? How is it a good word to describe what Jesus asks of all people?

For Reflection

- What things are most effective in your own life for resisting sin?
- Many people do not see evil events as a direct result of sin. How does this attitude reject a basic Christian teaching?

The Beatitudes: Lessons for Happiness (*CCC*, 1716-1729)

We were created by a loving God to know, love, and serve him. Of course, the goal of knowing, loving, and serving God is happiness in heaven. In a sense, God programmed us with a desire for eternal happiness. Nothing in this world can really satisfy the hungry heart that every human being possesses. Not wealth, not straight As, not getting into the best college, not athletic success, not fame, not power, not a huge bank account or awesome good looks. None of those things are

metanoia
A Greek word for "repentance" or a turning away from sin with the intention of living a life of virtue and holiness.

evil, but they can't really satisfy us for the long run. Only God's goodness and love satisfy our deepest hunger for true and lasting happiness.

In fact, God wants us to be happy in this life, as well as in heaven. This is why he left us with a blueprint for happiness, the **Beatitudes**. Jesus presented these eight guidelines and approaches to happiness in the Sermon on the Mount. In fact, the word *beatitude* means "happy." In the Beatitudes, Jesus teaches how we must think and act to find true happiness. They order us no longer to possession of *things*, but to the Kingdom of God, to participate in God's nature, to be children of God, and to love.

Beatitudes
Beatitude means "supreme happiness." The eight Beatitudes preached by Jesus in the Sermon on the Mount respond to our natural desire for happiness.

Living the Beatitudes

The Beatitudes show us the heart of Jesus. They also invite us to become partners with God in establishing his Kingdom here on earth. Being able to live the Beatitudes, however, is a gift from God. The Beatitudes ask so much more of us than our human nature might see as reasonable. But God grants us the graces we need if we ask for them. The Beatitudes appear at the beginning of the Sermon on the Mount (Mt 5:3–12). They are also found in the Sermon on the Plain in Luke 6:20–26. The Beatitudes complete the promises that God made to Abraham, the father of the Jewish faith. They show us how to fulfill our desire for happiness and teach us how we should live in order to reach our eternal destiny of union with him. The Beatitudes also explain how we should love God and neighbor in a Christ-like way. The Beatitudes are summarized below.

"Blessed are the poor in spirit, for theirs is the kingdom of heaven."

Being "poor in spirit" means that we recognize that everything we have is a gift from God. So, we depend totally on a good and loving God who is in charge of the universe. We should not hoard what we have been given. Rather, we should use our talents, intelligence, possessions, and whatever we have to help others.

"Blessed are they who mourn, for they will be comforted."

Those who mourn know how close God is. In their sorrow, they are ultimately comforted as they see that God's love will never end. They see and believe that "love is stronger than death." Suffering a deep loss also sensitizes people to others who are wounded, suffering, sick, or dying. A shared bond of suffering helps people to reach out and help where they can. And those who mourn remember the lesson of the Paschal Mystery. After suffering and death, God will surely bring new life and new joy.

"Blessed are the meek, for they will inherit the land."

The blessed "meek" are gentle people. They have an inner strength that isn't always easy to see. They meek aren't pushy, self-centered, or controlling.

BLESSED FREDERICK OZANAM

When Frederick Ozanam was a college student at the University of the Sorbonne in Paris in the 1830s, he was often offended when some of his teachers made fun of the Catholic Church. Ozanam, who had once had his own doubts about the faith, politely but brilliantly defended the faith. His fellow students and even the professors took notice. They were impressed with his eloquence.

During those years, France was still settling and healing after the collapse of the French Empire that had been created by Napoleon. Years of war and destruction had left people cynical and poor. To help defend Catholicism even further, Frederick soon founded a discussion club at the university. One night, after he had just finished a talk about the contributions of Christianity, one student raised his hand and criticized Frederick. "All you do is talk about faith," he said. "Is your faith good for anything besides talk?" That comment stung Frederick deeply because he felt it was accurate.

Soon after hearing that remark, however, Frederick and a friend began to visit and take food to the poor in the apartment houses all over Paris. They founded a small group under the patronage or special help of St. Vincent de Paul, a sixteenth-century priest who had served the poor. These groups quickly spread throughout Paris, and eventually throughout Europe. Those who joined the groups lived and worked in the spirit of the Beatitudes, especially the Beatitude that asks us "to hunger and thirst for righteousness."

Frederick Ozanam and his friends knew that they were simply doing what Jesus would do—serving and comforting the poor and the needy. Frederick continued his studies and received doctorates both in law and in literature. In 1841, he married Amelié Soulacroix. They became parents of a daughter, Marie. Frederick continued to teach at the Sorbonne where students flocked to his classes. But Frederick's health began to decline. In 1858, he died at the age of forty on a journey back to France from Italy. Frederick's young family was shattered by their loss. But Amelié Ozanam knew that her husband's work and ministry would live on. Today, the St. Vincent de Paul Society that Frederick founded has hundreds of thousands of members and serves the poor in 131 countries around the world. Frederick Ozanam was beatified in 1997 by Pope John Paul II. Blessed Frederick Ozanam's feast is celebrated on September 7.

The meek understand that they are followers of Jesus. They treat others with deep respect, understanding, and compassion. They don't complain or make scenes even if they have a reason to. They don't hide when they're ridiculed for their behavior or for their beliefs. Instead, the meek identify with Jesus who suffered wrongs patiently. The meek are good stewards of God's good earth, treating creation with joyful and gentle gratitude. They will inherit the earth.

"Blessed are they who hunger and thirst for righteousness, for they will be satisfied."

Disciples of Jesus must have high ideals and goals. They cannot be satisfied with mediocrity. The highest goal we can have is to help establish God's justice in our world today. With God's will in mind, we must work hard to give our brothers and sisters what they need. That's what it means "to hunger and thirst for righteousness." And all the while, those seeking righteousness should recall the advice of St. Thérèse of Lisieux who said, "Remember that nothing is small in the eyes of God. Do all that you do with love."

"Blessed are the merciful, for they will be shown mercy."

When we pray the Our Father, we petition God to "forgive us our trespasses as we forgive those who trespass against us." God created us out of love and sent his Son, Jesus into the world to redeem us. As grateful children of God and as followers of Jesus, we must forgive others—even our enemies. We must do it without conditions and without grudges against those who have hurt us. We must genuinely care for others by showing true compassion as Jesus did. If we are merciful, God will show mercy to us in turn.

"Blessed are the clean of heart, for they will see God."

The clean of heart are people who are undivided in their loyalties. They are honest, truthful, and

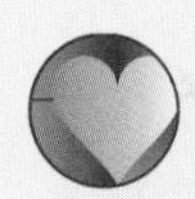

Are You a Beatitude Person?

Reflect on an answer "yes" or "no" to the following questions connected to the Beatitudes. Then, write short answers that reflect on how you might begin to or further develop that Beatitude in your own life.

- **Poor in Spirit:** Do I recognize God as the source of everything in my life? Do I share my gifts with others?
- **Mourn:** Do I empathize with others? Do I do anything to help those less fortunate than I am?
- **Gentle:** Am I a gentle and kind person? Do I respect others?
- **Righteous:** Do I really want to be Christ-like? Do I do anything to grow in holiness?
- **Merciful:** Do I forgive others when they hurt me?
- **Clean in heart:** Am I an authentic, trustworthy, and trusting person?
- **Peacemaker:** Do I go out of my way to solve conflicts?
- **Persecuted:** If it was a crime to be a Christian, would there be enough evidence to convict me for it?

EXPLAINING THE FAITH

Is it really possible to live the Beatitudes as Jesus asks us to do?

At first glance, the eight Beatitudes announced by Jesus seem impossible to take seriously. How can it be a blessing to mourn, to be meek, or to be persecuted for the sake of righteousness? In asking us to live according to the Beatitudes, is Jesus asking something that human beings can't honestly accept or believe in? The answer is "No." Because Jesus began his public life by teaching the Beatitudes to a crowd, he must want his followers to take them to heart. In many ways, all of the Beatitudes say, "Because I have come, everything is different." The logic of life is turned upside down. Because Jesus is ushering in the Kingdom of God, the heartaches and tragedies that used to grieve and burden us are no longer painful or burdening. In the Beatitudes, Jesus calls for a new mind-set. Happiness (or Beatitude) is found in living in a new way, the Kingdom way. Although it may not seem possible to fully abide by the Beatitudes, we can surely learn to trust that God's way, not the world's ways, will surely lead to happiness.

genuine. This Beatitude refers to people who "put on the mind and heart of God" and put God before all other priorities. That is, they look at others with the eyes of Jesus. They accept them as brothers and sisters, as people of great beauty and value. The pure of heart know what is important. They know that it is only God who satisfies the deepest human longings for love and understanding. The clean of heart will not be distracted. They see goodness and the face of God all around them.

"Blessed are the peacemakers, for they will be called children of God."

By definition, Christians are peacemakers. As God's children, it is wrong to fight, quarrel, and cause dissension. This tears apart the human family. Rather, we are called to join the Prince of Peace in settling disputes, avoiding violence, forgiving others, and showing compassion. We are to unite, not divide. We are to cooperate, not compete. We are to build bridges, not erect walls. The Risen Lord says, "Peace be with you" (Jn 20:19). His followers must share the same message.

"Blessed are they who are persecuted for the sake of righteousness, for theirs is the kingdom of heaven."

Star athletes know the truth of the expression, "No pain, no gain." The Quaker founder of Pennsylvania, William Penn, had something similar in mind when he said, "No cross, no crown." To stand up for what is right, especially in the face of mockery, rejection, and abuse, is to stand with Jesus Christ. These are the Christians who are persecuted for the sake of righteousness. Jesus never promised his followers an easy path. He did promise, however, that we could have eternal happiness united with the Blessed Trinity. Jesus said, "My yoke is easy, and my burden light" (Mt 11:30). For Christians, the cross is not a sign of defeat. It is the ultimate sign of victory and of life with our Savior Jesus. His love for us is never-ending:

Blessed are you when they insult you and persecute you and utter every kind of evil against you (falsely) because of me. Rejoice and be glad, for your reward will be great in heaven. Thus they persecuted the prophets who were before you. (Mt 5:11–12)

For Review

1. Define the word *beatitude*.
2. Where and how did Jesus teach the Beatitudes?
3. Explain what it means to be "clean of heart."
4. What will be the reward of those who are persecuted for the sake of righteousness?

For Reflection

Finish a necessary and new Beatitude for the world today: "Blessed are . . ."

Main Ideas

- Because Jesus is fully human and fully divine, he is the perfect ambassador to the human race. (pp. 190–193)
- More than anything or anyone, Jesus shows us God's perfect plan for creation and for all of us. (pp. 190–193)
- Jesus used the issue of divorce to explain that God really intends for people to live as they were first created prior to the Original Sin. (p. 192)
- The Book of Genesis confirms the essential goodness of everything God created, including human beings. (pp. 193–199)
- All human beings are made in the divine image and likeness of God. (pp. 193–199)
- God gave human beings a privileged place in creation; he gave them dominion over other creatures and over creation. (pp. 193–194)
- Of all creatures on earth, only human beings can enter a love relationship with our Creator. (p. 194)
- Because we are made in God's image, human beings have wonderful and unique capacities. We can think, choose, love, accept responsibility, and change. (pp. 194–196)
- Every human being has tremendous inherent dignity from the moment of conception. (pp. 195–196)
- God created human beings as complementary beings, male and female, so that we make up for what is lacking in each other. (pp. 196–197)
- Men and women are equal in dignity and in rights. (pp. 196–197)
- Jesus taught us to be good stewards, using wisely what God has given to us. (p. 197)
- Because we are created in the Trinitarian image, we are naturally social beings. (pp. 197–199)
- God intends for us to promote the common good—social conditions that answer everyone's needs and allow all people to fulfill their potential. (pp. 198–199)
- Solidarity is the Christian virtue of social charity or friendship. (p. 199)
- Through the Original Sin of our first parents, the perfect justice and harmony of creation was fractured. (pp. 200–201)
- Concupiscence is the inclination of all human beings to sin, either as individuals or collectively. (pp. 200–201)
- *Metanoia*, a word with Greek roots, means repentance, a turning away from the things that enslave us and lead us away from God. (pp. 201–203)
- At the beginning of the Sermon on the Mount, Jesus offered guidelines for achieving true happiness in the Beatitudes. (pp. 203–208)

Terms, People, Places

Use all of this chapter's ten vocabulary terms to write a three- to four-paragraph essay about the challenges of living as a Catholic in the twenty-first century.

Beatitudes
Common good
Concupiscence
Dignity
Dominion
Free will
Metanoia
Original Sin
Sin
Solidarity

Primary Source Quotations

Salvation and Free Will

He who created us without our help will not save us without our consent.

—St. Augustine of Hippo

Chapter 8 Quick View

Jesus Is the Beloved Son of God
He [Jesus] it was, and he alone, who satisfied the Father's eternal love, that fatherhood that from the beginning found expression in creating the world, giving man all the riches of creation, and making him "little less than God" in that he was created "in the image and after the likeness of God." He and he alone also satisfied that fatherhood of God and that love which man in a way rejected by breaking the first Covenant and the later covenants that God "again and again offered to man."

—Pope John Paul II

The Meaning of the Beatitudes
The Beatitudes are at the heart of Jesus' preaching. They take up the promises made to the chosen people since Abraham. The Beatitudes fulfill the promises by ordering them no longer merely to the possession of a territory, but to the Kingdom of heaven. . . .
—*Catechism of the Catholic Church*, 1716

The Power of the Meek and Humble
The most powerful weapon to conquer the devil is humility. For, as he does not know at all how to employ it, neither does he know how to defend himself from it.

—St. Vincent de Paul

Ongoing Assignments

1. Research several presentations of the Beatitudes in film, art, PowerPoint, and other online media. Using these for inspiration, create your own PowerPoint presentation on the Beatitudes.
2. Focus your research on a single Beatitude. Research the Beatitude that interests you most. Report on the meaning of any one of the eight Beatitudes.
3. Read Luke 6:20–23. Note two differences in Luke's version of the Beatitudes compared to Matthew's.
4. Watch the PBS documentary *Merchants of Cool*. The documentary shows how advertisers create and sell popular culture to teens. After viewing it, write a report about the way popular culture contradicts the teachings of Jesus on what is "the good life" and the true meaning of happiness. If possible, view the documentary online.
5. Exercise the virtue of solidarity by doing one of these projects as an individual or group:

- Research an area of the world that is suffering from a current crisis. Create a portfolio of newspaper, magazine, or Internet stories on this hot spot of trouble.
- Design a poster on the theme of global solidarity. Display it in the school hallways.
- Sponsor a needy child.
- Sponsor a fund-raising drive at your school. Consider encouraging classmates to abstain from a snack one day each week for a month. Then donate the proceeds to the Catholic Relief Services (CRS).

6. Check news sites to find articles that deal with the consequences of human sin—both for individuals and for communities. Select one article and identify the sin or sins involved. Comment on how the situation described would have been different if the parties involved had acted like children of a loving God and as brothers and sisters to Christ and other people.
7. Read the Parable of the Prodigal Son, Luke 10:25–37. Then write an essay about the meaning of this parable. What connection does it have to the virtue of solidarity? Or, rewrite this parable in a modern-day setting. For the robbery victim, substitute a

person in today's society who is often mistreated and ignored by important people. Share your story.

8. Do one of the following projects focused on stewardship:

- Photograph some favorite nature scenes. Include some contrasting pictures of places where natural beauty has been disfigured or destroyed. Create a presentation to depict the contrast between God's beauty and human folly.
- Visit the Catholic Conservation Center online. Read and report on its introduction to Catholic Environmental Justice.
- Discover how much productive land and water you need to support what you use and what you discard. Then compare what you use to what is available on our planet. After you see your results, investigate what individuals, communities, and schools can do to act as better stewards of God's good earth. Map out an action plan for the coming semester.

Prayer

Spend some quiet time in prayer before a crucifix. Try to embrace the silence as a time free of distractions and noise. Your spirit really needs some quiet time to connect with God. Slowly and carefully read these words from the Letter to the Hebrews:

> Let us rid ourselves of every burden and sin that clings to us and persevere in running the race that lies before us while keeping our eyes fixed on Jesus, the leader and perfecter of faith. For the sake of the joy that lay before him he endured the cross, despising its shame, and has taken his seat at the right of the throne of God. Consider how he endured such opposition from sinners, in order that you may not grow weary and lose heart.
>
> —Hebrews 12:1–3

- *Reflection*: What burdens and sins "cling" to you right now? Take them to Jesus and ask him to send the Holy Spirit to help you. You want to be the beautiful person God intends you to be. What made you really happy as a small child? How did those ideas of happiness evolve and change as you grew older?
- *Resolution*: Make a three-step plan for happiness. What will you do to enact the plan in the next week? In the next month? In the next year?

FRIENDS AND DISCIPLES OF JESUS

No one has greater love than this, to lay down one's life for one's friends. You are my friends if you do what I command you. I no longer call you slaves, because a slave does not know what his master is doing. I have called you friends, because I have told you everything I have heard from my Father. It was not you who chose me, but I who chose you and appointed you to go and bear fruit.

—John 15:13-16

The Heart of a True Friend

The heart of a true friend is filled with endless love and compassion; it is the love that Jesus modeled in his life and ministry.

What It Means to Be a Disciple of Jesus

To be a disciple of Jesus means becoming his pupil, making a commitment to Jesus, and, finally, helping to spread his message.

Growing in Friendship with Jesus

In the Gospel of John, Jesus invites his followers to an even closer relationship; he invites them to be his friends.

Committed Disciples Help to Spread the Gospel

The committed disciples of Jesus become just like Jesus by imitating his actions, sharing his love, and spreading the Gospel throughout the world.

St. Paul: Apostle and Dedicated Disciple

Though not one of the original Twelve Apostles, St. Paul became one of the greatest thinkers of the Church, the Apostle to the Gentiles, and one of the Church's most dedicated disciples.

The Heart of a True Friend

This chapter explores the meaning of friendship and especially how it relates to our friendship with Jesus Christ. As the passage from the Gospel of John verifies, Jesus invited his followers to be his friends. Put another way, the Son of God, Second Person of the Holy Trinity, and Creator of the universe calls us *his* friends. Since we have many human friends, we have a concept of what friendship means. But it's important to consider the subject deeper in preparation for its context as a friendship between God and humans.

George Gordon Byron (1787–1824) came from a wealthy family and was sent off to boarding school. One day when he was a teenager, he saw an older student beating up his friend. Unfortunately, Byron had a clubfoot that made it hard for him to move and defend his friend. But Byron made up in courage what he lacked in physical agility. He went over to the bully and demanded to know how many times he planned to hit his bloodied friend. "What's it to *you*?" sneered the bully. "Because," answered Byron without hesitation, "I'll take half of them." Byron was living proof of the saying, "A true friend is one who walks in when everyone else walks out." He saw that real friendship meant self-sacrificing love and generosity. It meant being willing to step into a challenging and dangerous situation to help a friend.

Friendship: What People Say It Is

Here are a few cited and anonymous quotations about friendship. Read through the list. Which one speaks most clearly to you about the meaning of friendship? Ask a friend or classmate to add his or her own quotation about the meaning of friendship. Add your own quotation as well.

> There is nothing on this earth more to be prized than true friendship.
>
> —St. Thomas Aquinas

> A friend knows your faults but loves you anyway.

> Friendship is born at that moment when one person says to another, "What! You, too? I thought I was the only one."
>
> —C. S. Lewis

> Be slow in choosing a friend, slower in changing.
>
> —Benjamin Franklin

> Friendship is a single soul dwelling in two bodies.
>
> —Aristotle

> A sometimes "friend" finds time on her calendar for you; a true friend does not even look at her calendar.

> A Christian should never complain of the tough times he is having while he knows that Jesus Christ is his friend.

> A friend is a person who listens attentively while you say nothing.

> The best vitamin for developing friends is B1.

The Gospels show us that Jesus was completely filled with this kind of compassionate love. Christ shed his blood on the cross and won for us the forgiveness of our sins and the chance for eternal life. Not only was Jesus willing to take half the blows coming to his friends; he was ready to take them all.

 For Reflection

How do you find this statement accurate: "A true friend is one who walks in when everyone else walks out"?

What It Means to Be a Disciple of Jesus

Though the invitation comes from Jesus himself, it is the Holy Spirit who makes it possible for us to become devoted disciples of Jesus Christ. The Holy Spirit gives us the courage, wisdom, understanding, and knowledge to accept Jesus, his way of life, and his mission. That's the short definition of discipleship. More concretely, there are three steps to being a disciple, explained in the sections that follow.

Learning All We Can from Jesus

The word ***disciple*** comes from the Latin word *discipulus* that can be translated as "a pupil." In this case, however, *pupil* means "one who grasps intellectually and analyzes thoroughly" the teaching of another. This definition comes from the two smaller Latin words: *dis* ("apart") and *capere* ("to take").

Jesus was known as a "teacher" or "rabbi," and was often addressed that way in the Gospels. The friends of Jesus called him rabbi because they truly wanted to learn from him. But his opponents also called him rabbi when they were challenging Jesus. For example, in Matthew 8:19 "a scribe approached and said to him, 'Teacher, I will follow you wherever you go.'" In Mark 4:38 the frightened Apostles, buffeted about in their boat by a violent wind, woke the sleeping Jesus. The terrified disciples said to Jesus, "Teacher, do you not care that we are perishing?"

There are several other references to Jesus as rabbi or teacher in the Gospels. In Luke's Gospel, an anonymous stranger who had been quarreling with his brother also addressed Jesus in this way: "Teacher, tell my brother to share the inheritance with me" (Lk 12:13). And in John's Gospel, Nathaniel (1:49), Nicodemus (3:2), the disciples (4:31, 6:25, 9:2, 11:8), and Mary Magdalene (20:16) all referred to Jesus as rabbi. Nicodemus spoke the truth when he realized that Jesus was a special teacher, worth listening to: "Rabbi, we know that you are a teacher who has come from God, for no one can do these signs [miracles] that you are doing unless God is with him" (Jn 3:2).

disciple
A follower of Jesus. The word comes from a Latin word that means "learner."

Making a Commitment to Jesus

Because Jesus was brilliant in his role as teacher, people approached him to hear his lessons about how to live. While most of those who heard Jesus were ready to follow after him, the Gospels tell of one occasion when someone who learned from Jesus was not ready to make a commitment to him. This is described in Mark's Gospel when a rich man (identified as a young man in Matthew's Gospel) approached Jesus and posed an important question, "Good teacher, what must I do to inherit eternal life?" (Mk 10:17).

Precepts of the Church
Rules Catholics follow to help them become good and moral people. They include attending Mass on Sundays and holy days of obligation, confessing sins at least once a year, receiving Communion at minimum during the Easter season, observing days of fasting and abstinence, and providing for the needs of the Church.

Jesus told the young man that he should keep the commandments. The young man replied to Jesus,

> "Teacher, all of these I have observed from my youth." Jesus, looking at him, loved him and said to him, "You are lacking in one thing. Go, sell what you have, and give to [the] poor and you will have treasure in heaven; then come, follow me." At that statement his face fell, and he went away sad, for he had many possessions. (Mk 10:20–22)

Here was a case of someone being attracted to the message of Jesus. But, somehow this young man could not apply the message any further. This was a good person, one Jesus looked on with great love. The young man saw that Jesus could tell him how to live so that he might gain eternal life. Jesus looked into this young man's heart and saw that he was preoccupied by his possessions. They were keeping him from being truly free. They were preventing him from giving himself to God. So, Jesus asked him to sell his things and give the money to the poor. Moreover, he invited this youth to become one of his disciples. However, this young man simply could not let go of his things; he walked away in sadness.

The most important lesson we can glean from this incident is that nothing is more important than the love of God and following his ways. Oppositely, it is a human weakness and often sinfulness to hoard one's wealth and set it up to be the top priority in life. With worldly riches often comes the belief that one is in control, that we do not need anyone, not even God. Wealth can make us feel like we are in charge. We begin to think that money can buy happiness. Jesus asks us to put our faith in God, not in our possessions, talents, or achievements. Everything we have is a gift from God. We must not hoard our gifts but offer thanks for them and use them for others.

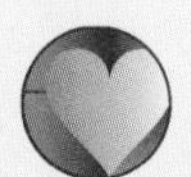

A New Ending for the Rich Man Who Went Away

Read the story of Jesus' encounter with the rich man in Mark 10:17-31. Then create a scenario in which the rich man changes his mind and returns to Jesus. Write an introduction to the scene and some dialogue between the rich man and Jesus. Choose a classmate and exchange scenes. Take turns acting the new endings for the rest of your class.

EXPLAINING THE FAITH

Is it wrong to be rich?

In the Gospels, Jesus never specifically condemned wealth though he made it clear that in the journey to God, it could be a burden. To illustrate how burdensome, he used the analogy of a camel not being able to move through the eye of a needle. In this story about the camel, many Scripture scholars suggest that Jesus was actually referring to one of the gates of Jerusalem, a gate called "The Needle's Eye." To help protect the city, this gate was built so low that a camel could only enter on its knees and without baggage strapped to its back. Since being on one's knees is a sign of submission, Jesus was also apparently saying something about the attitude or disposition of a wealthy person's heart.

In describing wealth as a burden, Jesus questioned traditional Jewish teaching. In the mind of the Jews, great wealth had long been seen as a sign of God's favor. So, the Apostles and others who heard Jesus talking about the "burdens of wealth" were shocked. Today, the Church echoes this Gospel teaching of Jesus. In itself, wealth is not evil. But excessive attachment to it and affluent lifestyles are. They violate the mandate Jesus issued in Matthew 25. Those who do not answer the needs of the hungry, the thirsty, the naked, and the imprisoned will be judged harshly, Jesus warned. To share wealth, the Church points to one of the Precepts of the Church. This precept or law requires Catholics to help provide for the needs of the Church and its outreach to the needy. And in Christianity and in Judaism, believers have also been advised for centuries to give away a tithe or a tenth of what they have to those in need. "Love for the poor is incompatible with immoderate love of riches or their selfish use," the *Catechism of the Catholic Church* states clearly (*CCC*, 2445).

When the man walked away, Jesus, the Teacher, turned to those around him. He said that it was very difficult for wealthy people to enter God's kingdom. In one of his most vivid images, Jesus said, "It is easier for a camel to pass through [the] eye of a needle than for one who is rich to enter the kingdom of God" (Mk 10:25). This teaching astonished the Apostles. The Apostles then asked Jesus who could be saved. Jesus answered them by saying, "For human beings it is impossible, but not for God. All things are possible for God" (Mk 10:27).

Helping Jesus to Spread His Message

Jesus did not ask all of his disciples to give up their wealth. For example, Joseph of Arimathea was a wealthy disciple of Jesus and a member of the Sanhedrin, the supreme court of Israel. It was Joseph who provided a tomb for Jesus after his Death. So, why did Jesus ask the rich young man to sell his belongings and give the money away? Jesus knew that the young man was too attached to his wealth and the things his money could provide. For this man, wealth was literally keeping him from following Jesus.

The story of the rich man points out that there is much more than just listening to and agreeing with Jesus in our words. We must put his teaching into action. We must follow Jesus and do what he tells us. Much of what he instructs us to do involves our role in spreading the Good News, the Gospel.

This point is emphasized toward the end of the Sermon on the Mount. Jesus warned, "Not everyone who says to me, 'Lord, Lord,' will enter the kingdom of heaven, but only the one who does the will of my Father in heaven" (Mt 7:21). Then, Jesus told a story to drive home the point: The true disciple not only learns from the teacher, but he *acts* and builds on what he has been taught. Jesus said:

> Everyone who listens to these words of mine and acts on them will be like a wise man

who built his house on rock. The rain fell, the floods came, and the winds blew and buffeted the house. But it did not collapse; it had been set solidly on rock. And everyone who listens to these words of mine but does not act on them will be like a fool who built his house on sand. The rain fell, the floods came, and the winds blew and buffeted the house. And it collapsed and was completely ruined. (Mt 7:24–27)

More on Being a Disciple

Read and compare Matthew 7:15-23 with 7:24-27. How are these lessons the same? How are they different? Check a biblical commentary to help you complete this assignment.

For his disciples, the teachings of Jesus are like the house built on rock—solid and true. Today, we continue to learn about the message of Jesus through the Church. For twenty centuries, the Church has passed on the teachings of Jesus and his call to evangelize. The Pope, bishops, priests, teachers, and many inspired spiritual writers help us to understand, live out, and then share the teachings of Jesus.

For Review

1. What does the word *disciple* mean?
2. What is the first step to discipleship?
3. Explain what's involved in the second step to discipleship?
4. How did Jesus test the commitment of the man who came to ask how he could earn eternal life?
5. Why did Jesus think that wealth often gets in the way of making discipleship commitments?
6. What is the third step to discipleship named in this section?

For Reflection

What do you think Jesus is trying to say in the Gospels about riches and wealth? Would most people agree with his teaching today? Do you agree with his teaching? Why or why not?

Growing in Friendship with Jesus

In the first step to discipleship, followers of Jesus focus on learning from his teaching. At this stage, discipleship is primarily an activity of the intellect. Disciples gather knowledge about what Jesus taught and who he is. This first step is very important. Knowing someone well can lead to a lasting personal relationship. The true disciples are those who get to know Jesus so well that they want to be with him. The disciples of Jesus wish to imitate him, to be his friends, and to love him. This "head knowledge" of Jesus leads to heart knowledge. That is, knowing Jesus leads to loving him.

It is Jesus himself who invites the second step of discipleship—a deeper and loving commitment. He takes the initiative by inviting us to be his friends. In John's Gospel, Jesus says, "I call you friends. . . . It is not you who chose me, but I who chose you and appointed you to go and bear fruit" (Jn 15:15–16).

Jesus Shared His Heart with His Friends

The Gospels tell us that Jesus had many friends. His Apostles were certainly counted among his friends. With these Galilean men, Christ traveled dusty roads, shared meals, and talked and slept under the open sky. Jesus also shared his heart with the Twelve. Once, after seeing a poor widow put a small copper coin in the treasury, he was deeply moved. Because of her spirit of generosity, he told the Apostles, she had donated "more than" had any of the rich people. This woman gave from her heart, not just from her surplus (see Mark 12:41–45).

Jesus also comforted his friends. At the Last Supper, they were grieving because Jesus said that he would soon die. With tenderness, Jesus said, "Do not let your hearts be troubled" (Jn 14:1). Later, in the Garden of Gethsemane, he confessed to Peter, James, and John, "My soul is sorrowful even to death. Remain here and keep watch with me" (Mt 26:38). He also forgave them for their shortcomings. Jesus forgave Peter who denied knowing him, and Thomas who doubted his Resurrection. Jesus was a faithful friend to his Apostles.

The Gospels verify that the friendships of Jesus ran deep. John Zebedee, for instance, was a particularly close friend. He was called "beloved" or "the disciple Jesus loved." As he was dying on the cross, Jesus entrusted the care of the Blessed Mother to this close friend, saying, "Behold, your mother" (Jn 19:27).

John's Gospel also tells of the close friendship Jesus maintained with Mary, Martha, and Lazarus of Bethany. One of the most emotional scenes in the Gospels describes how Jesus arrived at Bethany four days after the death of Lazarus. Martha went out to meet him and complained, "Lord, if you had been here, my brother would not have died" (Jn 11:21). Her sister Mary echoed the same lament to Jesus. John's Gospel says:

> When Jesus saw her weeping and the Jews who had come with her weeping, he became perturbed and deeply troubled, and said, "Where have you laid him?" They said to him, "Sir, come and see." And Jesus wept. So the Jews said, "See how he loved him." (Jn 11:33–36)

Jesus then brought his friend Lazarus back to life, showing that he, Jesus Christ, is the Resurrection and the Life.

Among the other friends of Jesus was Mary Magdalene. She was the one he appeared to first after his Resurrection. Also included in his circle of friends were tax collectors and sinners, including prostitutes. Jesus was criticized for associating and eating with them, an ancient sign of friendship. He even invited Matthew, a despised tax collector, to follow him.

Friendship, as everyone knows, also carries the risk of betrayal. And that is what happened to Jesus. Judas, one of the twelve Apostles, betrayed Jesus, turning him over to be arrested by Roman soldiers in the Garden of Gethsemane. When Judas approached Jesus to identify him with a kiss, Jesus said, "Friend, do what you have come for" (Mt 26:50). Jesus still loved his betrayer, just as he still loves us when we sin and turn against him.

philia
A Greek word that describes brotherly love, or a lifelong affection between friends.

storge
A Greek word that describes love among family members.

eros
A Greek word that describes sexual love and attraction.

agape
A Greek word that describes a self-sacrificing sort of love; the love Jesus showed to all.

In all his friendships, Jesus exhibited the many qualities of friendship listed in this chapter's opening exercise. He was loyal to them to the point of death. He was warm, affectionate, understanding, and dependable. Jesus gave his friends everything he had. He shared his life and his heart with them. Jesus was the perfect friend.

A Closer Look at the Qualities of Friendship

It's helpful to reflect a bit more on some qualities of friendship that Jesus calls us to. First of all, note that friendship is a kind of love. The Greeks used the word ***philia*** to distinguish it from several other kinds of love. For example, philia is a different sort of love than ***storge*** (the love among family members), ***eros*** (the sexual love between a man and a woman), and ***agape*** (the self-sacrificing love exemplified in the expression "to give and not to count the cost"). There is an interesting connection between being a friend of Jesus and agape love. Because we are his friends, Jesus expects us to love others in a self-giving way, even to the point of forgiving and loving our enemies. Our friendship with Jesus makes it possible to obey him and then love others with agape love.

By definition, a friend has a personal attraction, affection, and high regard for the person who is seen as a friend. This special relationship is marked by many different qualities. Among those are the ability to keep confidences, loyalty, understanding, dependability, and patience. Other critical friendship traits include the following:

- *Availability.* Availability has two aspects: exterior and interior. Exterior availability means making time for friends. "We make time for our friends and excuses for others," reports one popular maxim. This means that we might turn down an invitation from an acquaintance to hang out instead with a special friend. Interior availability means that when we are with our friends, we are able to emotionally and verbally connect with them. For example, we listen attentively to those we know well. We pick up on nonverbal communication and are sensitive to moods. For example, we can easily recognize if a good friend is sad and can respond to him or her with sympathy.
- *Generosity.* Friends give and receive time, affection, and gifts from each other. True friendships are reciprocal; they are a two-way street. If you are the only one giving in a relationship, then it probably is not a true friendship. A true friendship is a relationship from which you can expect to gain something. This is not a selfish response; it is the beauty and gift of this special kind of love.
- *Common interests.* Friendships are often "born" when two people discover that they like to do things together. It is important for friends to have plenty of things in common. Then, they will have

EXPLAINING THE FAITH

What's the connection between Eucharist and friendship with Jesus?
"I have called you friends," Jesus told the Apostles at the Last Supper "because I have told you everything I have heard from my Father. It was not you who chose me, but I who chose you and appointed you to go and bear fruit that will remain . . ." (Jn 15:15-16). These words directed to his Apostles are also directed to us. At that same meal Jesus also chose to give us the Eucharist, his Body and Blood. The two are connected: friendship and the Eucharist. In establishing the Eucharist, Jesus gave all generations to come the same uniting Bread of Life and the same Cup of Salvation. Down through the ages, the Eucharist gathers in people from every culture and language. It unites the followers of Jesus with him and with each other through the Church, the Body of Christ. As the *Catechism of the Catholic Church* teaches:

> The principle fruit of receiving the Eucharist in Holy Communion is an intimate union with Christ Jesus. Indeed, the Lord said: "He who eats my flesh and drinks my blood abides in me, and I in him." Life in Christ has its foundation in the Eucharistic banquet. (*CCC*, 1391)

Through this same Eucharist, our bonds within the Body of Christ are sustained and strengthened.

a basis for sharing. But, it is also important for friends to allow each other the freedom to develop their own interests. Whatever enriches one friend ultimately enriches the other.

- *Openness.* Friends do not have to be "fake" or play roles with each other. They can and should be themselves. Friends should be able to accept each other without the need to play games. Openness means that friends communicate on a gut level. That is, they share our feelings as well as our ideas. With our friends, we are willing to laugh and cry, rejoice and express anger, praise and correct. Friendship relies on sincerity.

One expert on friendship promotes the theory that best friends or close friends are special because they have traits that we'd like to have ourselves. There is something in them that we want to imitate. As a result, we are drawn in friendship to certain people in order to become more like them. Interestingly, this attraction is typically subconscious.

However, this is only part of the friendship story. Our friends see something special in us, as well. It could be an inner beauty, a talent, a great sense of humor, or the ability to listen well. Friendship is reciprocal; it works both ways. Our friends cherish us because they see someone whom they want to imitate. Your friend wishes to be you.

On the spiritual level, what happens to one friend happens to the other. If your friend grows, you also grow. And vice versa. The poet John Donne wrote, "No man is an island." How right he was when talking about friendship. If you have even one friend, you are never alone.

Friendship between You and Jesus

We can apply some of these insights about human friendships to our friendship with Jesus. On the topic of availability, Jesus is always present to us. He always has us in mind. He would never forget us.

The words of the prophet Isaiah are essentially the same message that Jesus communicated to us:

> Can a mother forget her infant,
> be without tenderness for the child of her womb?
> Even should she forget,
> I will never forget you.
> See, upon the palms of my hands I have written your name. (Is 49:15–16)

Our names are written on the heart of Jesus. Do we take time for him? Do we turn to him in prayer, tell him about the day, express regret for our sins, and thank him for his gifts? Do we receive him in the Eucharist? Not making time for a friend risks destroying the relationship. Jesus has said, "You are my friends if you do what I command you." And here are eight important aspects of the command that Jesus gives us.

1. *Believe in Jesus.* "I am the resurrection and the life; whoever believes in me, even if he dies, will live, and everyone who lives and believes in me will never die. Do you believe this?" (Jn 11:25–26).
2. *Invite Jesus into your life.* "Behold, I stand at the door and knock. If anyone hears my voice and opens the door, (then) I will enter his house and dine with him, and he with me" (Rv 3:20).
3. *Love God and others.* "You shall love the Lord, your God, with all your heart, with all your soul, and with all your mind. This is the greatest and the first commandment. The second is like it: You shall love your neighbor as yourself" (Mt 22:37–39).
4. *Make Jesus your best friend.* "Whoever loves father or mother more than me is not worthy of me, and whoever loves son or daughter more than me is not worthy of me" (Mt 10:37).
5. *Love deeply.* "Love one another. As I have loved you, so you also should love one another. This is how all will know that you are my disciples, if you have love for one another." (Jn 13:34–35).

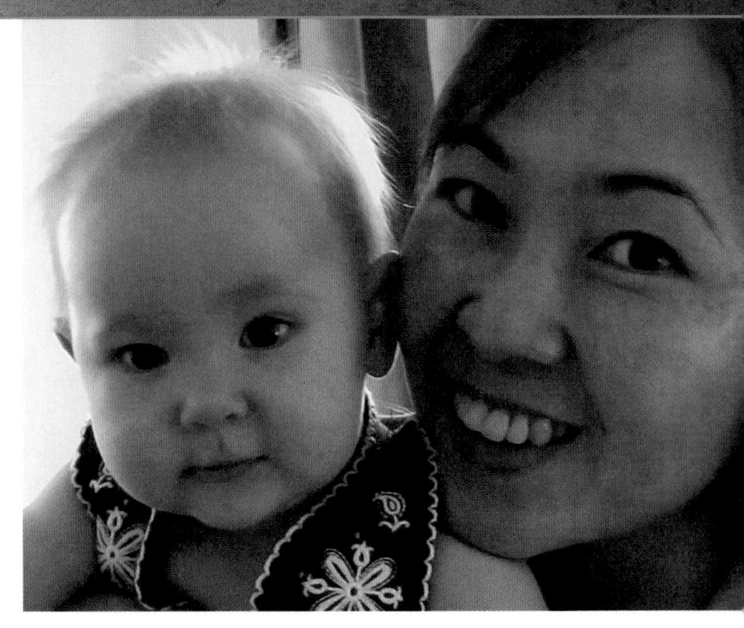

6. *Serve one another.* "If I, therefore, the master and teacher, have washed your feet, you ought to wash one another's feet. I have given you a model to follow, so that as I have done for you, you should also do" (Jn 13:14–15).
7. *Forgive one another.* "Then Peter approaching asked him, 'Lord, if my brother sins against me, how often must I forgive him? As many as seven times?' Jesus answered, 'I say to you, not seven times but seventy-seven times'" (Mt 18:21–22).
8. *Witness Jesus to others without fear.* "Even the hairs of your head have all been counted. Do not be afraid. You are worth more than many sparrows. I tell you, everyone who acknowledges me before others the Son of Man will acknowledge before the angels of God" (Lk 12:7–8).

Recall another trait of friendship: sharing common interests and openness. Jesus cares very much about what you are interested in, whether it's sports, music, drama, or whatever. Who, after all, put those interests and desires in you? In return, Jesus wants us to use and develop those talents. When you do, you are praising God and drawing others to him. Jesus responds by giving himself in the Eucharist. He enters our life and enables us to enter his.

It only takes a moment to see why we would want to call Jesus a friend. Here is God's Son, the perfect teacher who is understanding, patient, and kind. Here is the one who loves perfectly, the one who gave his life for his friends so that we might have abundant eternal life with him. "But God proves his love for us in that while we were still sinners Christ died for us" (Rm 5:8). The friendship of Jesus offers us the inner life of the Blessed Trinity. He offers us eternal happiness, everything our hearts desire.

For Review

1. Which Gospel tells us most about the invitation from Jesus to be his friends?
2. Describe four times in which Jesus treated others as friends.
3. Tell how Jesus took risks in offering his friendship—relating to people who were usually rejected or hated by most people.
4. What are four friendship traits that are needed for any healthy friendship?
5. What does it mean to say that friends need to be "available" to each other?
6. What does the trait of "openness" mean to a friendship?
7. Name three of the eight important requests that Jesus makes of those who wish to be his friends.

For Reflection

- What are the qualities of friendship of one of your best friends that makes him or her attractive to you?
- Review the eight requests that Jesus makes of those who wish to be his friends. Which request would be the most difficult for you to fulfill?

Committed Disciples Help to Spread the Gospel

Following Jesus is not a passive exercise. Disciples of Jesus must do much more than simply follow their Master. They must share the Gospel with others. In the first steps toward discipleship, we give our minds and hearts to Jesus. Later, however, we must put our faith into action.

The first disciples took seriously Jesus' great commission at the end of Matthew's Gospel (Mt 28:16–20). Jesus sent his followers out to the ends of the earth to make even more disciples. They went to baptize and teach everything that Jesus commanded them: to repent for sins; to believe in Jesus; to forgive others; to love God above everything and one's neighbor as oneself; to serve; and to proclaim Jesus' message of peace, justice, and mercy to everyone.

The tasks of discipleship are awesome, both in a difficult and rewarding sense. Jesus himself told us that discipleship will not be easy:

> Whoever wishes to come after me must deny himself, take up his cross, and follow me. For whoever wishes to save his life will lose it, but whoever loses his life for my sake and that of the gospel will save it. What profit is there for one to gain the whole world and forfeit his life? What could one give in exchange for his life? Whoever is ashamed of me and of my words in this faithless and sinful generation, the Son of Man will be ashamed of when he comes in his Father's glory with the holy angels. (Mk 8:34–38)

Jesus will not require most of his disciples to die physically for him. However, he does ask us to die to our own self-centeredness. When we love, we die to selfishness. We are saying "no" to ourselves as we reach out to others. Jesus assures us that through the process of dying to selfishness, we

works of mercy
Charitable actions that remind us how to come to the aid of a neighbor and his or her bodily and spiritual necessities.

will truly live. Death to self is the first step to loving others, that is, putting their needs ahead of our own.

What also makes following Jesus more difficult is that we live in a "faithless and sinful generation." Those are the words of Jesus used to describe his own generation (see Mark 8:38). Although he was speaking about people living two thousand years ago, it applies to people in every generation. Consider our own times. Advertising, for example, constantly pushes the idea of self-gratification. We are told that we have the right to satisfy our every need and desire—whether it is the latest in technology or the latest whitening toothpaste. The idea of self-sacrifice and generosity obviously does not sell products.

In our day, the media also promotes the "beautiful people"—glamorous Hollywood stars, exorbitantly paid athletes, Fortune 500 CEOs, and self-indulgent musicians who often "sing" lyrics that are degrading, most often to women. They are held up as the people we should admire and emulate. Their lifestyles, however, are often far from what Jesus asks of his followers. He wants us to be men and women for others, to give and not to count the cost, and to wash the feet of others. In other words, the disciples of Jesus are asked to imitate the Master at the Last Supper.

Jesus tells us that following him takes discipline. In the Sermon on the Mount, he tells us to be careful on our way:

> Enter through the narrow gate; for the gate is wide and the road broad that leads to destruction, and those who enter through it are many. How narrow the gate and constricted the road that leads to life. And those who find it are few. (Mt 7:13–14)

In commenting on this passage, Pope Benedict XVI said that Jesus reminds us that everyone has an equal chance to enter through the narrow gate, "but it is 'narrow' because it is demanding; it requires commitment, self-denial, and mortification of one's own egoism." Jesus wants everyone to go to Heaven, "but with one and the same condition: that of making the effort to follow him and imitate him, taking up one's cross, as he did, and dedicating one's life to the service of our brothers." In our world today, this message often seems to be unfashionable. However, Jesus makes it the very basis of our judgment at the end of time. In the parable of goats and sheep, Jesus tells about the Last Judgment. The sheep will be placed on the right and will inherit the Kingdom of Heaven; the goats will be placed on the left and will suffer eternal punishment. The basis for our own judgment will be what we did, or did not do, for others. Our goal as Christian disciples is to hear these words from Jesus on the last day:

> Then the king will say to those on his right, "Come, you who are blessed by my Father. Inherit the kingdom prepared for you from the

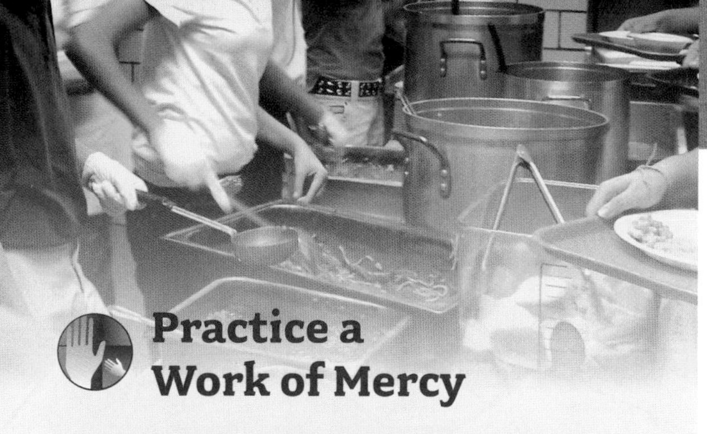

Practice a Work of Mercy

The *Catechism of the Catholic Church* teaches that the "works of mercy are charitable actions by which we come to the aid of our neighbor in his spiritual and bodily necessities" (*CCC*, 2447). See a list of the works of mercy on page 272. Offered below are some suggestions for projects that can help you (either individually or with others) to practice the works of mercy. Choose at least one of these projects to work on. Write a report of the experience, expressing how it helped to connect you more deeply in your friendship with Christ.

- Sponsor a "gently used" clothing drive at your school. Donate what you collect to a local shelter.
- Visit a sick classmate, elderly neighbor, or a nursing home.
- Organize a class "get-well-soon" project or card for a sick classmate.
- Collect recent magazines for donation to hospitals.
- Write a note of consolation to a neighbor or friend who has had a recent death in the family.
- Tutor a younger student.
- Volunteer in a soup kitchen.
- Write letters to legislators to ask them to sponsor bills to help the homeless or to support measures for affordable housing for poor people.
- Interview a member of your parish's St. Vincent de Paul Society. Ask how you can help in the work this organization does to serve the poor.

foundation of the world. For I was hungry and you gave me food, I was thirsty and you gave me drink, a stranger and you welcomed me, naked and you clothed me, ill and you cared for me, in prison and you visited me." Then the righteous will answer him and say, "Lord, when did we see you hungry and feed you, or thirsty and give you drink? When did we see you a stranger and welcome you, or naked and clothe you? When did we see you ill or in prison, and visit you?" And the king will say to them in reply, "Amen, I say to you, whatever you did for one of these least brothers of mine, you did for me." (Mt 25:34–40)

For Review

1. What is the "great commission"?
2. What are some of the specific things Jesus told his Apostles that he wanted them to do in the great commission?
3. What was Jesus really talking about when he told his followers that they would have to "enter through a narrow gate"?
4. What is the criteria of judgment Jesus speaks of in the Parable of the Goats and Sheep?

For Reflection

How would you respond to questions St. Ignatius of Loyola asked to Christians of his day: "What have you done for Christ? What are you doing for Christ? What will you do for Christ?"

St. Paul, Apostle and Dedicated Disciple

St. Paul is a model of faith and a Christian disciple worth emulating. St. Paul was one of the greatest teachers and missionaries of Christianity. His original name was Saul. He earned his living as a tentmaker. Born around AD 10 in Tarsus in modern-day Turkey, he studied to be a Pharisee in Jerusalem under Gamaliel, a famous rabbi of his day. Because of Saul's zeal as a Pharisee, he joined in the persecutions of the early followers of Jesus. For example, he took a leading role in the stoning of St. Stephen, the first Christian martyr.

When Saul was traveling to the city of Damascus to persecute and arrest Christians, Jesus appeared to him. In a blinding vision, Jesus asked, "Saul, Saul, why are you persecuting me?" (Acts 22:7). By persecuting Christians, members of Christ's Body, the Church, Saul was persecuting Christ himself. This life-changing encounter with the Risen Lord converted Saul to Christianity. It convinced him to preach the Gospel to Gentiles, that is, non-Jews.

The Pharisee Saul soon became the great Apostle Paul. After arriving at Damascus, he was baptized by Ananias and then retreated to Arabia where he spent three years in prayer preparing for his future missions.

When Paul eventually went back to Jerusalem, the Apostles at first feared him. But Barnabas judged that Paul was indeed a changed man. Thus began Paul's tireless and courageous life as a missionary and evangelist for Jesus Christ. He embarked on three missionary journeys that took him to Antioch, Cyprus, Asia Minor, Greece, Ephesus, Macedonia, Achaia, and eventually Rome. During his various travels, Paul wrote epistles, that is, letters to his new converts. The letters dealt with various problems that individual congregations were having. These letters included theological reflections concerning Jesus Christ and instructions on ways to deal with false teachers and heresies. Paul also shared advice on practical matters and gave excellent instructions on how to live the Christian life.

Thirteen of the New Testament's letters are attributed to St. Paul, though modern scholars think that he only wrote seven of them—Romans, 1 and 2 Corinthians, Galatians, Philippians, 1 Thessalonians, and Philemon. Many scholars consider Romans and 1 Corinthians to be his greatest epistles. The other six letters attributed to St. Paul—2 Thessalonians, Ephesians, Colossians, 1 and 2 Timothy, and Titus—were probably written by his disciples.

On Paul's last return to Jerusalem, his opponents attacked and imprisoned him. Paul appealed to the authorities, firmly claiming that because he was a Roman citizen he should be tried in Rome. His wish was granted. On the dangerous journey across the Mediterranean Sea, he was shipwrecked on the island of Malta. When he finally made it to Rome, he was kept under house arrest for two years waiting for his trial.

Paul was probably set free when he went to trial and then resumed his missionary work. One tradition holds that he preached in Spain and may have

DISCIPLESHIP IN BRIEF

In John's Gospel, there is a one-sentence description of discipleship: "This is the way we may know that we are in union with him: whoever claims to abide in him ought to live as he [Jesus] lived" (1 Jn 2:5-6). Or, to put John's point in another way once popularized by initials on a bracelet: "What would Jesus do?" Create a short role-play that is based on a common moral dilemma teens face each day. Resolve the dilemma by having the main character in the story act like Jesus would. Arrange to perform the skit for your class.

returned to the East. Eventually, though, Paul was martyred by beheading in Rome in either AD 64 or 67 by the emperor Nero in one of his persecutions of Christians.

St. Paul is one of Christianity's greatest thinkers. His theological themes treated the role of faith, justification, the Holy Spirit in the life of the Christian, Jesus Christ as God's eternal Son, the centrality of Christ's Resurrection, and the Church as the mystical Body of Christ. Moreover, even though Paul was not among the original Twelve Apostles, he is called "the Apostle to the Gentiles." At a council held in Jerusalem in AD 49, Paul convinced Church leaders like St. Peter that Gentiles could become Christians without having to become Jews first. He preached that Jesus Christ came to save all people, Jews and Gentiles alike. Paul also wrote many practical instructions on how to live a loving life in union with Jesus Christ by power of the Holy Spirit. It is a life that will eventually result in the Resurrection in Christ of all believers.

For Review

1. How did Paul make his living?
2. Where was Paul going and what was he doing when Jesus appeared to him?
3. What happened to Paul right after his life-changing encounter with Jesus?
4. Name two kinds of messages that Paul's epistles or letters to Christian churches often contained.
5. Why is St. Paul called the "Apostle to the Gentiles"?
6. How and where did Paul die?

For Reflection

- What gifts do you have that can help to build up the Church?
- Peruse the epistles of St. Paul. Write or share a passage that encourages you to be a better disciple of Jesus Christ.

Main Ideas

- There are three steps toward discipleship: learning from Jesus, making a personal commitment to Jesus, and helping to spread the Gospel. (pp. 215–218)
- The word *disciple* comes from the Latin word *discipulus* that means "pupil" or "student." (p. 215)
- Jesus was known as and called "rabbi," both by those who followed him and by those who disagreed with him. (p. 215)
- Many people approached Jesus for instruction on how to best live their lives. Included among them was the rich man who was not willing to sell his things and give the proceeds to the poor. (pp. 216–217)
- Jesus taught that people with riches often believe that they are in control and do not need God. (pp. 216–217)
- Jesus compared the difficulty of following him as a faithful disciple to entering "through the narrow gate." (p. 217)
- Jesus did not ask everyone to give up their wealth and all of their possessions, only people who were too attached to their wealth. (pp. 217–218)
- In the Gospel of John, Jesus invited those who followed him to also be his friends. (p. 218)
- Throughout the Gospels, it is clear that Jesus cultivated deep friendships and shared his life and his heart with his friends. (pp. 218–220)
- Jesus befriended many people who were socially rejected in his culture. (p. 219)
- Qualities that must characterize any true friendship are availability, generosity, common interests, and openness. (pp. 220–221)
- Eight expectations that Jesus has of his friends include believing in him, inviting him into our lives, loving God and other people, serving one another, and forgiving one another. (pp. 221–223)
- Jesus said that it is necessary to die to self in the midst of a "faithless and sinful generation," a moral climate that describes his own day as well as ours. (pp. 223–225)
- The kind of friendship Jesus showed throughout his ministry was agape love, a type of love that the Greeks defined as self-sacrificing love. (p. 220)
- Though not one of the original Twelve Apostles of Jesus, St. Paul was one of the greatest Christian teachers of the Church. He was also known as the "Apostle to the Gentiles." (pp. 227–228)

Terms, People, Places

Use five of the seven vocabulary terms for this chapter to help you complete the following sentences. Review the terms carefully before completing the sentences.

Agape
Eros
Works of mercy
Disciple
Philia
Precepts of the Church
Storge

1. ________________ is a Greek word that describes brotherly love or lifelong affection between friends.
2. ________________ is a listing of works of practical charity that includes instructing the ignorant, comforting the sorrowful, and bearing wrongs patiently.
3. A Greek work that describes sexual love and attraction is ____________.

   ______________ is the love among family members.

4. A pupil or one who intellectually grasps and thoroughly analyzes the teachings of another defines a ____________.
5. ____________ is a Greek word that describes a self-sacrificing type of love, the love that Jesus exhibited throughout his life and ministry.
6. ______________ are rules that Catholics are to follow, including participating in Sunday Mass.

Primary Source Quotations

Thinking about Discipleship

It is not hard to obey when we love the one whom we obey.

Teach us to give and not to count the cost.

—St. Ignatius of Loyola

Called to Follow Jesus

The transmission of the Christian faith consists primarily in proclaiming Jesus Christ in order to lead others to faith in him. From the beginning, the first disciples burned with the desire to proclaim Christ: "We cannot but speak of what we have seen and heard." And they invite people of every era to enter into the joy of their communion with Christ.

—*Catechism of the Catholic Church*, 425

Deepening Friendships

The better friends you are, the straighter you can talk, but while you are only on nodding terms, be slow to scold.

Take care not to frighten away by stern rigor poor sinners who are trying to lay bare the shocking state of their souls. Speak to them rather of the great mercy of God . . . sometimes people are helped by your telling them about your own lamentable past.

—St. Francis Xavier

The Risk of Discipleship

If you follow the will of God, you know that in spite of all the terrible things that happen to you, you will never lose a final refuge. You know that the foundation of the world is love, so that even when no human being can or will help you, you may go on, trusting in the One that loves you.

—Pope Benedict XVI

Ongoing Assignments

1. Disciples of Jesus want to live simply based on needs and not selfish desires. They also want to preserve God's beautiful creation. Do one of the following:
   - Find ten advertisements that appeal to instant gratification. Prepare a PowerPoint presentation that discusses how each ad either appeals to a real human need or just simply to a superfluous "want."
   - Report on five different ways to resist consumerism and shop differently.
   - Visit the Catholic Migrant Farmworker Network online. Report on the connection between the food we eat and the workers who provide it.
2. In various surveys and opinion polls done on friendship over the years, certain qualities or traits appear over and over. Ten of the top traits appear below. On a scale of 1 (the lowest) to 5 (the highest), rate how much each quality is evident in your relationship with two of your closest friends. Total your score for each friend. Then, conclude the activity by writing a paragraph about how Jesus had all these friendship traits.

   Traits
   - Ability to keep confidences
   - Loyalty

- Warmth and affection
- Understanding
- Good listener
- Sense of humor
- Patient
- Generous
- Common interests

3. Locate the lyrics to any two songs on friendship. Analyze these questions:
   - What qualities of friendship do the songs emphasize?
   - Identify and explain how some verses could apply to a friendship with Jesus.
4. Read the following Gospel passages in which Jesus is called "Teacher" or "Rabbi." Then answer the questions that correspond with each.

   Matthew 22:15–22
   - Who addresses Jesus?
   - Do they respect Jesus or not? Explain.
   - How does Jesus answer them?

   Mark 9:14–29
   - Who makes the request of Jesus and what does he want?
   - What does Jesus say in Mark 9:23? What do you think he means?

   Mark 9:38–41
   - Who addresses Jesus as Teacher?
   - What point is Jesus making in verse 39?

   Luke 7:36–50
   - Who addresses Jesus?
   - Is the man sincere? Why or why not (offer proof)?
   - What is the point of the parable told by Jesus?

   Luke 20:20–26
   - Who addresses Jesus? Are they sincere? Explain.
   - What brilliant response does Jesus give?

   John 1:43–51
   - What does Nathaniel originally think about Jesus?
   - Why does he change his mind?
   - What does he proclaim about Jesus?
5. The Gospel of Luke has some of the most challenging things to say about money. Read the following passages. Summarize them and reflect on them in a short two-page theme.
   - Rich fool: Luke 12:13–21
   - On almsgiving and watchful servants: Luke 12:33–53
   - Right use of money: Luke 16:9–13
   - Rich Man and Lazarus: Luke 16:19–31
   - Zacchaeus: Luke 19:1–10
6. Read and report on "What Is Mercy?: 14 Ways to Show You Know," an article by Jim Auer, a noted teen catechist. Search for the article on the Internet.
7. Report on a religious order that has as one of its ministries the corporal or spiritual works of mercy.
8. Read Galatians 3:1–29. Imitate St. Paul's fiery style by writing a letter to a group of young Catholics who have stopped going to Mass. Use persuasive language to convince them that the Church needs them.
9. Construct a one-page biography of St. Paul based on his own writings. Do an Internet search for Catholic sites on St. Paul, the Apostle to the Gentiles.
10. St. Paul's letters give much practical advice on how Christians should act as worthy disciples of Jesus. Read and report on the following:

- *Romans 12–13.* List three specific behaviors expected of Christians.
- *Ephesians 4–6.* Name four types of behavior redeemed Christians should avoid. What does St. Paul say about drunkenness (5:18)? How should parents and children relate to each other (6:1–4)? Describe the images Paul uses in 6:13–17.

Prayer

The following prayer is attributed to St. Francis of Assisi. It outlines several great ways that disciples of Christ can put their faith into action. Commit the prayer to memorization.

Prayer for Peace
Lord, make me an instrument of your
peace.
Where there is hatred, let me sow love;
where there is injury, pardon;
where there is doubt, faith;
where there is despair, hope;
where there is darkness, light;
where there is sadness, joy.
O Divine Master,
grant that I may not seek so much to be
consoled as to console;
to be understood, as to understand,
to be loved, as to love.
For it is in giving that we receive,
it is in pardoning that we are pardoned,
and it is in dying that we are born to
eternal life.
Amen.

- *Reflection*: How has the Lord given you peace? How have you been an instrument of his peace and love to others?
- *Resolution*: Collaborate with another to bring joy to someone's life this coming week. Resolve to do some specific act to spread Christ's joy to a special person or group.

JESUS TEACHES US TO PRAY

Whatever you ask for in prayer with faith, you will receive.

—Matthew 21:22

- ## Prayer Means Talking to and Listening to God

  When we make time for God in prayer, we learn that God answers our prayers in many ways and in his own time.

- ## Prayer Is God's Gift to Us

  Because God first approaches us, we can seek, approach, and build a living relationship with him through prayer.

- ## Jesus Is Our Best Guide to Prayer

  Through his words and his own prayer life, Jesus offers a model for many different kinds of prayer.

- ## The Lord's Prayer

  To teach us how to praise God's name and how to ask for our needs, for forgiveness, and for protection from evil and temptations, Jesus taught us the Our Father, the perfect Christian prayer.

- ## A Prayer Primer

  Using traditional Catholic prayers and practices, we can develop our own unique life of prayer, a life of talking to and listening to God.

- ## Living the Mission

  Jesus Christ calls us to share the Good News with others with our words and actions.

Prayer Means Talking to and Listening to God

An old story is told about the effects of prayer and about how God answers prayers. It goes like this:

> After a hurricane, a man was trapped in his home due to flooding. The waters came up to his front door, so he decided he had better start to pray. "Lord, please rescue me." Fifteen minutes later someone in a canoe came by and offered to take the man to safety. "No thanks," said the man, "God will save me."
>
> The floodwaters soon came into the house, forcing the man upstairs. Again he prayed, "Lord, please help me." Ten minutes went by and a motor boat came, but the man declined help, saying, "God will save me."
>
> Finally, the floodwaters drove the man to the roof of his house. Desperately the man begged God, "Please help me Lord." Within minutes he looked up to the sky and saw a helicopter. He waved the pilot away saying, "I don't need your help. God will save me."
>
> A half-hour later, a monstrous wave rushed over the top of the house and carried the man off. Sadly, he drowned, and when he met God in heaven, he told him how confused he was. Even though he'd prayed, he had not been saved. God replied, "That puzzled me, too. I sent you a canoe, a boat, and a helicopter. Yet, you still drowned!"

What this man forgot was that **prayer**—simply defined as "communication with God"—must go both ways. Prayer does mean *talking to* God and asking for what we need. But prayer also involves *listening to* God and the many ways God speaks: sometimes directly to our hearts, sometimes through the Church and its Sacraments, sometimes through events, and sometimes through other people. The man on the roof didn't remember to listen to God.

Prayer is essential for Catholics because all relationships between friends need communication. So it is with a friendship with Jesus. Disciples of Jesus pray because Jesus asks us to pray. God promises that he will answer our prayers. However, that answer may come in three different ways. God may answer our prayers with: "Yes," "No," or "Wait awhile." The man in the story actually had his

prayers for help answered. But, he was so locked into his own ideas about prayer that he didn't realize that God uses other people to accomplish his will!

Sometimes, God will say "No" to something we ask for because it is not ultimately good for us. His "No" might close one door. But, as we often discover, it opens another. Finally, the Lord answers our prayers in his own time—not in ours. Jesus' advice about prayer is to not be concerned about how or when the prayer will be answered, but rather to continue to pray without ceasing.

For Reflection

When was an occasion that prayer really helped you to cope with a difficult situation or relationship? How did you pray at that time? How did the prayer help?

When and How You Pray: A Quick Survey

Blessed Mother Teresa of Calcutta said, "Prayer enlarges the heart until it is capable of containing God's gift of himself." Teenagers often say that they pray in the following times:

- to thank God for favors granted
- after Holy Communion
- when I need something
- before going to sleep
- while jogging or walking
- to ask for forgiveness when I've hurt someone
- when I'm in trouble
- before and after meals
- when I'm alone
- in the morning
- when I see a beautiful sunset or rainbow

Answer the following questions about your own prayer life:

1. What is your own definition of prayer?
2. Where is the best place for you to pray?
3. When is the best time for you to pray?
4. On what occasions do you usually turn to God in prayer?

Prayer Is God's Gift to Us (*CCC*, 2558-2567, 2590, 2623-2649)

The Holy Spirit enables us to pray to God the Father. This means that the only reason that we can pray is because God approaches us first. In fact, our hearts are made to seek him. We desire Jesus Christ and his gift of Salvation. Prayer is our way of responding to God who first seeks us. It does take humility to pray because we are admitting that we can't go it alone. We need God. We need and want to say "Yes!" to his great love for us. We want to ask the Father for many good things. And he is happy to give them to us through his Son, Jesus Christ.

There are, as you have already seen, many ways of defining or looking at prayer. St. John Damascene defined prayer as "the raising of one's mind and heart to God." When we pray, therefore, we consciously pay attention to God. We direct our thoughts to the loving God who calls us. St. Thérèse of Lisieux described prayer as "a surge of the heart; it is a simple look turned toward heaven, it is a cry of recognition and of love, embracing both trial and joy." This means that we can take everything to the Lord when we pray—what troubles us and what we are happy about.

Prayer Is Relationship with God

The *Catechism of the Catholic Church* defines prayer as "the living relationship of the children of God with their Father who is good beyond measure,

prayer
Conversation with God; lifting of one's mind and heart to God or requesting good things from him; joining one's thoughts and love to God in adoration and blessing, petition, intercession, thanksgiving, and praise.

spontaneous prayer
A form of personal prayer in which the person prays to God in his or her own words.

praise
A form of prayer whereby we acknowledge God and his goodness and glorify him for who he is.

petition
A form of prayer where we ask for something.

thanksgiving
A form of prayer that involves expressing gratitude or thanks to God for all that he gives to and for us.

contrition
A form of prayer in which we ask God, our merciful Father, to forgive our sins.

intercession
A prayer of petition for the sake of others.

with his Son Jesus Christ, and with the Holy Spirit" (*CCC*, 2565). Prayer is a relationship, a two-way street with God the Father who is our "Abba" or Daddy. It is also a relationship with Jesus Christ, our Savior, brother, and friend. And, it is a relationship with the Holy Spirit who is our Comforter and Helper. Prayer connects us with our loving Triune God. Interestingly, the first place of education for prayer is also in relationship—in the relationship of the Christian family.

Because prayer is "conversation with God" as St. Clement put it, we can assume that it will take time to develop. St. Teresa of Avila also thought of prayer this way. She said to think of prayer as a journey with an invisible Friend, a companion who walks next to us along the path of life. We turn to this Friend in an ongoing conversation. Human friendships thrive on similar dialogue. Prayer deepens our friendship with God and gives us the strength to live according to God's plan for us.

The Many Ways to Talk to God

Honesty is important in how we express our prayer. Like any good friend, Jesus wants to hear about our dreams and hopes as well as about our fears and disappointments. Nothing we take to him is unimportant. Friends are like that too; they want to hear about the really important things in our lives, not just the day-to-day events. Talking to God in everyday language about what is really important to us is known as **spontaneous prayer**. We don't come with an agenda. We simply become aware of our Lord's presence and share our thoughts and feelings with him.

There are many types of prayer. Sometimes we use our own prayer words; at other times, we use or recite the words of others. The main types of prayer are described below.

Praise

Prayers of **praise** are also called blessings or adoration. We bless God because he first blesses us. That is, God showers his graces on us. When we bless God in return, we adore and praise him. We adore God because he is the Creator and we are his creatures. We praise God and give him glory because he is so good, gracious, loving, and compassionate. He deserves this response from us. The Holy Spirit helps us to praise God, enabling us to have faith in Jesus Christ and allowing us to call God "Abba." True praise of God is free of selfish motives because we take joy in loving

God alone. Many of the psalms in the Old Testament praise, adore, and bless God. The opening verse of Psalm 8 praises God for his marvelous creation:

> O Lord, our Lord,
> how awesome is your name through all the earth!
> You have set your majesty above the heavens!
> What are humans that you are mindful of them,
> mere mortals that you care for them?
> Yet you have made them little less than god,
> crowned them with glory and honor.
> (Ps 8:2, 5–6)

Petition

To **petition** is to ask for favors. Prayers of petition are also called prayers of supplication. We ask God to provide what we need. Jesus himself tells us to ask God for the most important gift of all—the Holy Spirit. Jesus gave this instruction when he taught about the need for persistence in prayer (see Luke 11:9–13). Psalm 17 is an example of a prayer of petition:

> Keep me as the apple of your eye;
> hide me in the shadow of your wings
> from the violence of the wicked.
> (Ps 17:9)

Thanksgiving

Prayers of **thanksgiving** offered to God are very natural. God has given us so much. We have our lives (including our health, families, talents, and so forth). God has also given us Jesus and Salvation. And we have been given the Holy Spirit who lives within us. Thanking God in prayer shows that we owe him everything. He deserves our gratitude. The Psalmist tells us, "Give thanks to the Lord who is good, whose love endures forever!" (Ps 107:1).

The Eucharist is the greatest prayer of thanksgiving. In fact, all types of prayer are gathered at Mass: we bless, adore, praise, and thank God for all the blessings he has given to us. We also express our sorrow, ask for forgiveness, and petition God for the good things that we need to live our lives fully. When we receive Holy Communion, our Savior Jesus Christ lives in us and unites us to God. This Sacrament also unites us with our Christian brothers and sisters by the power of the Holy Spirit.

Contrition

Contrition is a type of petition prayer. We ask our merciful Father to forgive us for our sins. In this type of prayer, we also express sorrow or regret for failing to do God's will.

Intercession

Intercessory prayer is prayer we offer to God on behalf of others. Whenever people ask us to pray for them, they trust that we will approach God on their behalf. Prayer for others is a wonderful example of Christian mercy and love in action, especially when we pray for those people who are in extreme need. Christian saints who live with God in eternity offer **intercessions** on our behalf. We, too, offer intercessions for our loved ones who have died.

The Many Ways to Listen to God

A conversation with God also requires moments of silence. We need quiet time and space in order to "hear" God speak. Of course, God speaks to us in many ways, but distractions often keep us from hearing what he says. For example, he speaks to us in the beauties of creation—sunsets and sunrises, gentle rains, and cooling breezes. He addresses us in the events and people who come into our lives. For example, God can (and often does) speak through the love and direction of our parents and friends. He sometimes speaks to us through a disappointment, steering us in another direction. God the Father always addresses us through his Son. Jesus also speaks to us through Scripture and in the Sacraments, especially the Eucharist.

God may also speak to us in our dreams or in the thoughts and ideas he places into our minds. We often call that kind of an idea an "inspiration," a word based on the Latin word *spiritus* for "breath" or "life." Listening to the Lord can also help to calm our troubled emotions, as he reminded his listeners in the Sermon on the Mount:

> Therefore I tell you, do not worry about your life, what you will eat (or drink), or about your body, what you will wear. Is not life more than food and the body more than clothing? Look at the birds in the sky; they do not sow or reap, they gather nothing into barns, yet your heavenly Father feeds them. Are not you more important than they?" (Mt 6:25–26)

The Lord can strengthen our wills to do the right thing when we face temptation. And he can heal the bad memories that might be troubling us. Jesus can just as easily boost our self-esteem or remind us of all the good things he has done for us. When we put ourselves in the presence of Jesus, quiet down, and wait in silence, we might hear him speaking to our minds, or through our feelings, imagination, will, or memory.

The key to hearing the Lord is to be still and let him speak. The payoff for true conversation—listening as well as talking to God—is that a real encounter takes place.

Many Expressions of Prayer (CCC, 2700-2719, 2221-2724)

Heartfelt Christian prayer has always been expressed in a variety of ways. Sometimes, it is the prayer of just one person; at other times, it is prayer raised collectively by a group, such as the People of God at the Liturgy of the Eucharist. Consider some of the ways that Christians pray in the sections that follow.

Vocal or Spoken Prayer

Our prayers can be said mentally or out loud. When we express our feelings in words, we are doing what Jesus himself did when he taught and prayed the Our Father. When we say our prayers aloud within our families or at Mass with our Christian brothers and sisters, we strengthen our spiritual relationship with them and with God.

Meditation

Meditation is a "tuning in to God," thinking about him, and trying to be aware of his presence. Meditation involves actively using our thoughts, emotions, imaginations, and desires to think about how God is in the world and in our lives. We meditate to gain a greater knowledge and love of the Lord so that we may better serve him. Great Catholic saints like St. Teresa of Avila, St. Ignatius of Loyola, and St. Francis de Sales have suggested using the Bible, especially the Gospels, for **meditation**. We can also meditate on the writings of the saints, the events in our world, and the action of God in our own lives.

Mental Prayer

This kind of prayer usually centers on Jesus. In our minds, we "talk" with him or reflect on one of the mysteries of his life. For example, we might spend time thinking about how hard it was for Jesus to endure all of the physical pain of his scourging and crucifixion when he had no comfort from anyone. All of his friends had abandoned him.

Contemplation

Sometimes, mental prayer can lead to **contemplation**, a form of silent, wordless prayer where we simply rest in the presence of our all-loving God. St. John Vianney, a nineteenth-century French parish priest, told of a simple peasant who perfectly described what contemplative prayer means. The peasant sat each day in front of the Blessed Sacrament reserved in the tabernacle. "I look at God and he looks at me." What the peasant meant was that he "looked at" God with such devotion and love that no words were needed. And, he felt God "looking upon" him with such devotion and love that no words were needed.

When praying this way, we empty our minds of thoughts and images and simply allow the divine presence to fill us. We don't have to do anything at all. If you are already able to pray in this way, you really have been given a great gift from God.

Dom John Chapman, an English Benedictine monk (1865–1933), once advised, "Pray as you can; don't pray as you can't." In other words, people should feel free to find prayer expressions that best suit them. For some it might be vocal or spoken prayer; for others it might be contemplation. It could also be that different prayer expressions will work for us at different times of day or in different circumstances. No matter how we pray, God wants to hear us. And he wants to speak to us!

For Review

1. What are two different ways of defining prayer?
2. What is spontaneous prayer? Give an example of how it might be used.
3. Define a prayer of petition.

The Psalms: A Timeless Treasury of Prayer

The Book of Psalms, a collection of hymns sacred to Jews and Christians alike, is a great resource. Reading a Psalm can help you to begin a conversation with God. Jesus himself prayed the Psalms, including Psalm 22, while on the cross. The Psalms capture every human emotion, from sadness and fear to joy and awe. Many Psalms are also prayers full of confidence and trust in a loving God. Others pour out grief or deep contrition for sin or personal failings like fear or the failure to reach out to the poor. The Psalms are also recited or sung at every Mass as a response to the Scripture readings.

- Locate and read the following six Psalms:
  Psalm 30
  Psalm 38
  Psalm 51
  Psalm 96
  Psalm 104
  Psalm 148
- Next, identify the type of prayer in the Psalm: praise, petition, thanksgiving, contrition, or intercession.
- Write down a key verse or line from the Psalm that particularly appeals to you.

meditation
A form of prayer where the mind and imagination focus on Christ or some truth of Divine Revelation with the purpose of applying the lessons we learn to our lives.

contemplation
A form of silent wordless prayer in which mind and heart rest in God's goodness and majesty.

4. What are two different kinds of thanksgiving prayer that a Christian might say?
5. Name and explain four prayer expressions.

For Reflection

- Reflect on Dom John Chapman's advice on prayer on page 239. How would you explain this advice in your own words?
- Which kind or kinds of prayer expressions best fit you, your lifestyle, and your personality at this time of your life?

Jesus Is Our Best Guide to Prayer

Savvy travelers know the value of consulting atlases, travel guides, and Internet mapping sites in planning travel. These resources help to guide us on the way. It usually is much more difficult to travel alone than it is with relying on guides of many kinds. It is easy to travel the road of prayer with a guide as well. As the title to the section points out, Jesus is our best guide to prayer. We can learn from him by reading the Gospels and meditating on his words.

We can learn what we need to know about prayer from Jesus. What's more, through the power of the Holy Spirit, Jesus will pray alongside of us. We can be confident that our prayers are heard because Jesus constantly intercedes for us. At the Last Supper, Jesus prayed his great priestly prayer of intercession to the Father:

> I pray not only for them, but also for those who will believe in me through their word, so that they may all be one, as you, Father, are in me and I in you, that they also may be in us, that the world may believe that you sent me. And I have given them the glory you gave me, so that they may be one, as we are one, I in them and you in me, that they may be brought to perfection as one, that the

EXPLAINING THE FAITH

Is it possible to petition God too often?

Sometimes we feel guilty that too much of our prayer falls into the "gimmee" category; that is, "God, give me this," "God, give me that." Should we balance our prayers of petition with prayers of blessing? It's true that blessing, as the *Catechism of the Catholic Church* puts it, "expresses the basic movement of Christian prayer" (*CCC*, 2626). In blessing prayer, there is a dialogue, a loving exchange that acknowledges the very existence, being, and goodness of the other. The *Catechism* also reminds us, "Because God blesses, the human heart can in return bless the One who is the source of every blessing" (*CCC*, 2645). Truthfully, our prayer life often needs to deepen and grow. But that is not a reason to keep from constantly asking God for favor. Remember, Jesus taught about a persistent person who knocked on the door of a friend at midnight looking for three loaves of bread. Though the friend inside the house may not have got out of bed to give him the bread out of friendship, "He will get up to give him whatever he needs because of his persistence" (Lk 11:8). Jesus went on to say:

> And I tell you, ask and you will receive; seek and you will find; knock and the door will be opened to you. For everyone who asks, receives; and the one who seeks, finds; and the one who knocks, the door will be opened. (Lk 11:9)

So, while you should expand your prayer form to other expressions, don't feel guilty about petitioning God for all that you need.

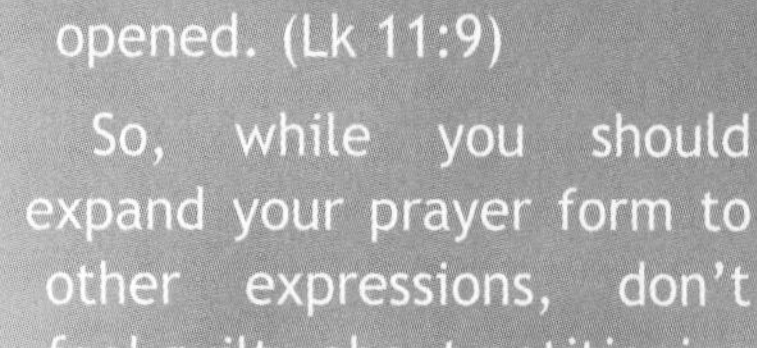

world may know that you sent me, and that you loved them even as you loved me. Father, they are your gift to me. (Jn 17:20–24)

Clearly, Jesus prayed for unity among his followers so that others would be attracted to him who is one with his Father. Prayer brings us into union with Jesus. Then, this union with him helps attract others to God the Father. Jesus called each of us a gift. Consider the power in that statement—that we are his Father's gift *to him*! This is why we can say, "What a friend we have in Jesus!" He is the Friend who promises,

And whatever you ask in my name, I will do, so that the Father may be glorified in the Son. If you ask anything of me in my name, I will do it. (Jn 14:13–14)

When Jesus Prayed

It can be said that Jesus always "walked the walk" and "talked the talk." This is true in the area of his own prayer life. For example, after his baptism in the Jordan River, Jesus went to the desert for a forty-day retreat to pray in preparation for the beginning of his ministry. Jesus also prayed before making other important decisions. He prayed the whole night before selecting the Apostles. After performing his first miracles of healing, Jesus also withdrew to pray. Likewise, after performing the miracle of the loaves and fishes, Jesus dismissed the crowd and his followers and withdrew to a hill to pray. And the night before Peter confessed Jesus to be the Messiah, Jesus could be found praying.

Jesus' Transfiguration was also an occasion for prayer. That's when Peter, James, and John were privileged to see the glory of the Risen Lord. After the Last Supper, Jesus took the Apostles to the Garden of Gethsemane where he prayed as he suffered great mental anguish. He knew that great suffering and Death were upon him. Jesus, like anyone of us, was afraid of pain and death. Yet he prayed, "Father, if you are willing, take this cup away from me; still, not my will but yours be done" (Lk 22:42). This prayer led to a prayer of submission, of following the will of his Father.

Jesus also prayed prayers of praise. For example, Jesus *praised* the Father for revealing his will to the humble and lowly:

At that very moment he rejoiced [in] the Holy Spirit and said, "I give you praise, Father, Lord of heaven and earth, for although you have hidden these things from the wise and the learned you have revealed them to the childlike. Yes, Father, such has been your gracious will." (Lk 10:21)

On another occasion, at the raising of Lazarus from the dead, Jesus *thanked* God:

Father, I thank you for hearing me. I know that you always hear me; but because of the crowd here I have said this, that they may believe that you sent me. (Jn 11:41–42)

And like we often do, Jesus *petitioned* his Father for many things. For example, he prayed that Peter would not be tempted. Jesus petitioned for all of his followers at the Last Supper. Jesus hoped that we would remain in the truth and stay united to him.

As a pious Jew, Jesus also celebrated various religious festivals important to Jewish worship. He would have prayed in the morning when rising, at noon, and in the evening before going to sleep. He would also have recited prayers before and after eating his meals. Additionally, Jews participated in the synagogue services each week. There were three major prayers recited at these services. The first, known as the *Shema* ("Hear") confessed faith in God as "one." It came from three biblical passages and the blessings before and after them (Dt 6:4–5; 11:13–21; Nm 15:37–41). The second prayer was the *Eighteen Benedictions* that asked God for wisdom, forgiveness, and help. The third prayer, known as the *Kaddish* ("Hallowed") asked that people hallow and glorify God's name throughout the world and that God would fully establish his kingdom soon. Jesus would have been familiar with all of these Jewish prayer rituals.

Jesus also knew and frequently recited the 150 Psalms, those powerful hymns that were already one thousand years old by that time. Many of these Psalms were used in worship services in the Jerusalem Temple and played an important part in the life of the Chosen People. Jesus sang these prayer-songs with his Apostles, for example, on the way to the Garden of Gethsemane after the Last Supper. As mentioned, he even recited Psalm 22 on the cross, a Psalm that begins with a lament of abandonment but ends with a confident belief that God will rescue the tormented, innocent victim.

The Death of Jesus is also a prayer lesson. Jesus prayed even to his last breath. In the midst of his own great and agonizing suffering, he prayed for sinners. "Father, forgive them, they know not what they do" (Lk 23:34). And, in his last moments, Jesus prayed with great confidence and faith, "Father, into your hands I commend my spirit" (Lk 23:46). Every part of the life and Death of Jesus teaches us that prayer was vital to him. The sections that follow offer other suggestions from the life and ministry of Jesus for how to pray.

Pray with Sincerity

Jesus spoke out against prideful displays of religious devotions: "When you pray, do not be like the hypocrites, who love to stand and pray in the synagogues and on the street corners so that others may see them" (Mt 6:5). Jesus was not against public prayer, because he himself often prayed in public. What he objected to was the attitude of pompous people who were seeking praise from human beings, not the approval of God.

To counteract any temptation to hypocrisy, Jesus told people to "go to your inner room, close the door, and pray to your Father in secret" (Mt 6:6). There is much wisdom in this advice from Jesus. First, separating ourselves to a place alone—both literally and figuratively—gets us away from the distractions of a busy day. In a quiet room, we can spend some time in peace with our God. Second, it purifies our motives. When we are away from others, we can be ourselves before God. There will be no temptation to try to impress others. Praying with the right intention—that of pleasing God alone—is very important. A person's character is often measured by doing the right thing whether someone is watching or not. This applies to our prayer life too.

Pray with Childlike Simplicity

Heaping up a lot of words does not make prayers any more effective. Wordiness or the eloquence of a polished speaker is not necessary to communicate with God. The Lord can read our hearts as well as hear our lips. Jesus said:

> In praying, do not babble like the pagans, who think that they will be heard because of their many words. Do not be like them. Your Father knows what you need before you ask him. (Mt 6:7–8)

Rather, Jesus teaches us to pray with the confidence of little children approaching their loving parents. God's love far surpasses any earthly love we have ever known. God always hears our petitions and will provide for us. Jesus reminded us:

> Which one of you would hand his son a stone when he asks for a loaf of bread, or a snake when he asks for a fish? If you then, who are wicked, know how to give good gifts to your

children, how much more will your heavenly Father give good things to those who ask him? (Mt 7:7–11)

Pray with Persistence

When Jesus tells us to ask, to seek, and to knock, he is giving us a command. The present tense used in the Greek in the quoted passage from Matthew 7:7–11 suggests that Jesus wants us to keep on asking, seeking, and knocking. Simply put, Jesus does not want us to give up when we pray. To underscore this point, Jesus told the story about prayer and patience in Luke 11:5–8.

Another story in Luke's Gospel involved a widow and a judge (Lk 18:1–8). The judge, as we hear in the story, was self-centered and an opportunist. The widow was powerless and defenseless, with no social influence. You would think that the judge would have decided against her because he had nothing to gain by ruling for her. Certainly, she had no standing or power to influence the judge, and he certainly was neither honorable nor compassionate. But this judge finally did give her the justice she sought. Why? Simply because the widow kept badgering him, refusing to take no for an answer to her case. The judge finally caved in simply to get her out of his courtroom.

These parables teach important lessons. If a powerless widow can win over a dishonest judge, how much more will our persistence pay off with our infinitely merciful, just, compassionate, and loving God?

Pray with Faith

A progression of increased faith should accompany our perseverance in prayer. Jesus told his Apostles that "If you have faith the size of a mustard seed, you would say to [this] mulberry tree, 'Be uprooted and planted in the sea,' and it would obey you" (Lk 17:6). Jesus reiterated that we must believe that our heavenly Father will answer our prayers:

> Amen, I say to you, if you have faith and do not waver, not only will you do what has been done to the fig tree, but even if you say to this mountain, 'Be lifted up and thrown into the sea,' it will be done. Whatever you ask for in prayer with faith, you will receive. (Mt 21:21–22)

Pray with Others

Jesus wants us to pray with others as well as to pray privately. He said that he would be present whenever a community gathered in his name. This group could be as small as two people together:

> Again, (amen,) I say to you, if two of you agree on earth about anything for which they are to pray, it shall be granted to them by my heavenly Father. For where two or three are gathered together in my name, there am I in the midst of them. (Mt 18:19–20)

Think of the power of that last statement. Jesus is always with us when we gather in his name.

Pray with a Forgiving Heart

Jesus does not want us to approach God full of anger and hate. He wants us to present a calm heart and a loving spirit when we address our loving God in prayer. More concretely, we are to approach God only after settling any grievances with another person: "When you stand to pray, forgive anyone against whom you have a grievance, so that your heavenly Father may in turn forgive you your transgressions" (Mk 11:25).

SEEK YOUR OWN SOLITUDE

The public life of Jesus was absolutely filled with preaching, healing the sick, and traveling dusty roads of Palestine. Jesus never stopped inviting people to seek God the Father's will in all things. But Jesus also knew the importance of solitude. He never hesitated to take time to prayerfully reflect on his mission. Read the following passages from the Gospels. Then answer the three questions that follow:

- Luke 4:1-11
- Luke 6:12-13
- Matthew 14:13-33
- Mark 1:35-37
- Luke 5:15-16
- Mark 14:32-42

1. What happened when Jesus went off to pray?
2. Tell about a time when you longed to be alone to think or pray.
3. What is the difference between "being alone" and "being lonely"?

For Review

1. Name four different occasions when Jesus set aside extra time to pray.
2. What were prayer practices that Jesus followed as a Jew?
3. Define the *Shema*.
4. What was the *Kaddish*? What was the purpose of the prayer?
5. Name several ways that Jesus prayed the Psalms.
6. Name four instructions Jesus gave his followers on how to pray. Explain how we should put these instructions into practice today.

For Reflection

Describe an inner room or sanctuary that you might use for prayer.

The Lord's Prayer (*CCC*, 2759-2865)

Jesus taught the Our Father, the perfect Christian prayer. Church Father Tertullian called the Lord's Prayer "the summary of the whole gospel" (quoted in *CCC*, 2761). The Our Father appears in both Matthew's and Luke's Gospels.

Matthew's version (6:9–13) appears in the Sermon on the Mount where Jesus instructed his followers to be authentic, to pray with trust in God and with forgiveness in their hearts.

Luke wrote his Gospel for Gentile-Christians, people who didn't have a strong tradition of prayer. Luke's version (Lk 11:2–4) portrays Jesus giving his disciples this model prayer—also called "the Lord's Prayer"—Luke then added those stories from Jesus about the need for persistence in prayer and trust. God will give us what we need to live a holy life, Jesus reassures us. (See Luke 11:5–13.) The following short sections offer synthesis of the parts of the Our Father, the Lord's Prayer.

ST. THÉRÈSE OF LISIEUX

Even as a very young child, St. Thérèse of Lisieux had a sense that prayer is simply a reflection of our friendship with God. Thérèse was the youngest of the five daughters of Louis and Zelie Martin, a faith-filled couple who lived and worked in Alençon, France. There's little doubt that Thérèse, as the baby of the family, was pampered and spoiled. Even her doting mother wrote that "Thérèse flies into frightful tantrums when things don't go just right . . ." But Zelie also saw how intelligent, loving, and good-hearted her youngest child was. Sadly, Zelie died of cancer in August 1877 when Thérèse was only four years old.

Losing her mother wounded Thérèse deeply, but it also shifted her attention to Heaven and the Kingdom of God. Prayer, she began to see, is not a series of memorized words to be recited. "You don't have to be kneeling or in church to be praying," Thérèse would say. Like her older sisters, Thérèse believed she had a religious vocation. In 1888, she joined the Carmelites, a religious order devoted to prayer. Soon, it was clear that Thérèse had insights and ideas about prayer that shocked many of her fellow nuns. For instance, Thérèse often fell asleep during the long hours spent in chapel. She reasoned that God loved her while she slept, just as parents love their children just as much asleep as awake. Thérèse also made all the events of her day part of her prayer. She called it her "Little Way to God," and wrote about it in her best-selling autobiography, *Story of a Soul*. Thérèse died at twenty-four from tuberculosis. She was canonized in 1925, twenty-eight years after her death. She was named a Doctor of the Church in 1997. Her feast day is October 1.

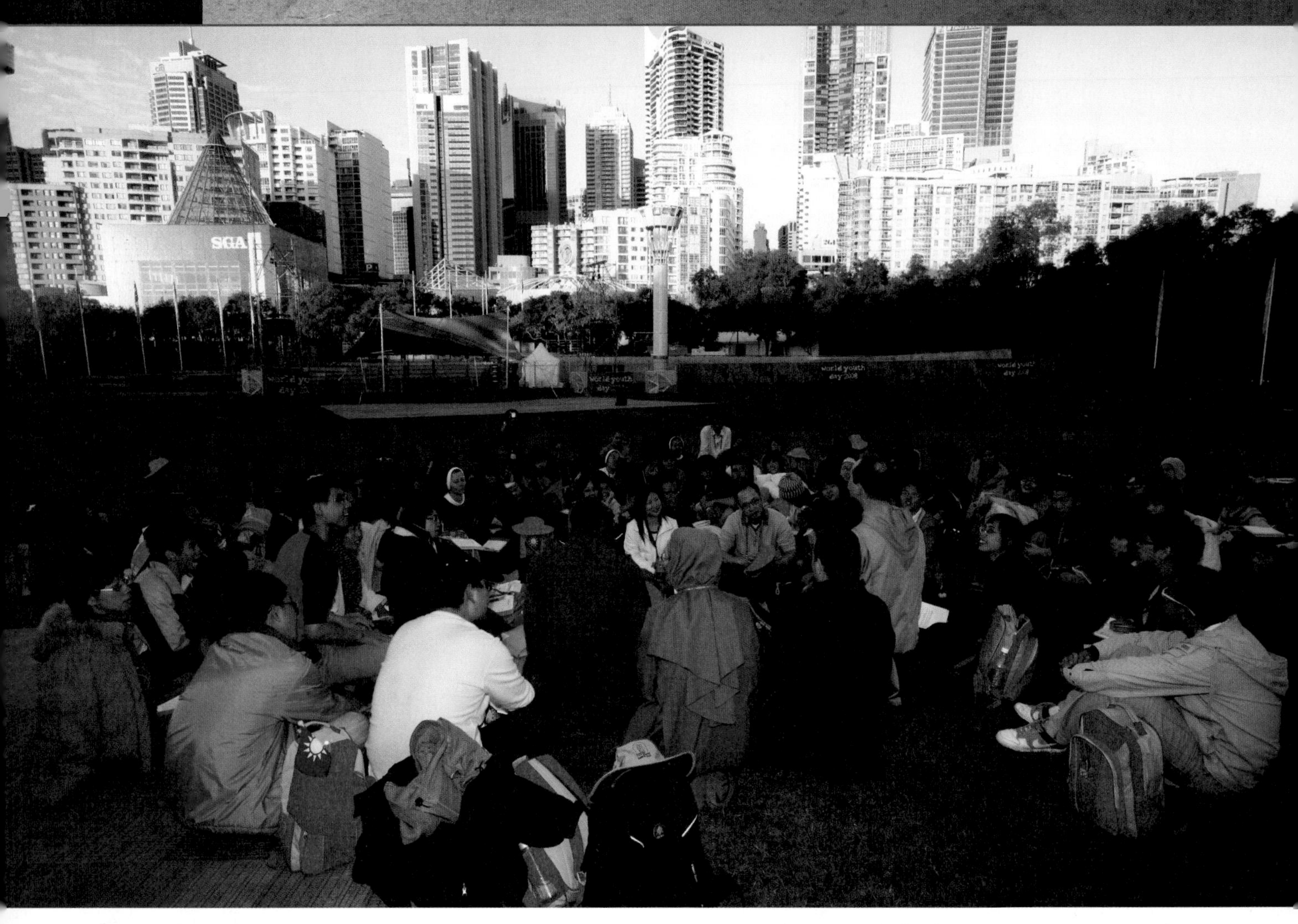

Our Father Who Art in Heaven

Jesus invites us to address God as "Our Father," and even as "Abba" or "Daddy." Our Father is a good and gracious Father, a loving Father whom we can address with confidence. We have been adopted into the divine family. God is *our* Father, which means that we are all brothers and sisters, and should treat each other with understanding, compassion, and love. If we believe what Jesus teaches us by this prayer, we commit ourselves to understand, love, and respond to *everyone* who comes into our lives. We are all related to our heavenly Father.

"In heaven" refers to God's transcendence, his way of being, and his majesty above all his creatures. Through Jesus, God lives in the hearts of the just. We profess that we are God's people and that we are united to Christ in Heaven. We wait for the day when a heavenly reward will be fully ours.

Hallowed Be Thy Name

Your personal name calls forth your uniqueness. Jesus wanted Simon to be the leader of the Apostles, so he renamed him Peter, which means "rock." Peter was to be the solid foundation on which Christ would build the Church. Our personal names carry special meanings: David means "beloved," Jennifer is "gentle spirit," Christopher is "Christ bearer."

For many in the ancient world, the name of the person *was* the person. When we pray for the "hallowing of God's name," we pray that the Father may be regarded as holy by all people on earth (as God is already regarded in Heaven).

God is the source of all holiness. We "hallow" or "make holy" God's name when we accept God's love and act like his Son, Jesus Christ. When we live up to our name as "Christians," we lead others to come to know and praise God because they can see God's image reflected in us.

Thy Kingdom Come; Thy Will Be Done on Earth as It Is in Heaven

With the coming of Jesus Christ, God's rule—which is firmly established in Heaven—has broken into our world. Peace, justice, truth, community, and mutual love reign in Heaven. Jesus inaugurated this Reign through his own ministry and his Paschal Ministry. He preached the Good News to the poor, brought liberty to captives, wholeness to those who were broken, and healing and Salvation to all people.

However, God's kingdom will be fully established only at the end of time. Until that day, under the guidance of the Holy Spirit, we should live, experience, and work for it right now. We pray for Christ's return and the final coming of God's Kingdom when there will be perfect righteousness, peace, and joy. Until then, we ask God the Father to join our will to his Son's and to his ongoing work of Salvation by loving others and responding to the least in our midst.

Give Us This Day, Our Daily Bread

When we ask for bread, we are asking for all the things that bread represents—the material and spiritual goods and the blessings that are necessary for life. When we pray for our daily bread, we are praying for a number of things. We are praying for the necessities (not luxuries) for physical life: food, shelter, clothing; for psychological life: friendship, love, companionship; and for spiritual life: grace, goodness, and integrity. We concretely receive our daily bread in our reception of Holy Communion at Mass.

Praying for *our* daily bread also challenges us to remember the needs of others, especially those of hungry and poor people. This petition also reminds Christ's followers of their duty to share the Bread of Life (Christ) by preaching the Gospel to others in both word and deed. In this petition, we are also praying for the fullness of God's material and spiritual blessings that will be ours in Heaven.

The word *daily* in the original Aramaic spoken by Jesus may have also meant something like "for tomorrow, today." When we pray for our daily bread, we are praying for the fullness of God's material and spiritual gifts, which will be ours in Heaven. We dare to ask God to give us a taste of these gifts today.

And Forgive Us Our Trespasses as We Forgive Those Who Trespass Against Us

Here, we humbly acknowledge that we are sinners and that we need the Holy Spirit to help us to repent of our selfishness and to turn to a life of love and service. We need the help of Jesus and forgiveness on our way to the Father.

Jesus teaches that for God's forgiveness to penetrate our hearts we must, in turn, forgive others, even our enemies. When we forgive those who have hurt us, we are communicating love and understanding, thus encouraging them to respond to us in love. The gift of God's forgiveness must be shared with others. Extending forgiveness is an invitation to love.

And Lead Us Not into Temptation

We pray that God will not allow us to take the path that leads to sin. We pray to remain in his grace until the very end of our lives. Prayer helps us to resist what leads us to sin. It also gives us strength to overcome difficulties in living a Christian life. We ask the Holy Spirit to shower us with gifts like fortitude, watchfulness, and perseverance. We also ask for hearts that can tell the difference between trials that strengthen us spiritually and temptations that lead to sin and death.

The petition also calls us to remove the temptations that keep other people from knowing our loving Father: the subhuman conditions that keep people impoverished, the culture that encourages pornography and reduces people to objects, the laws that permit the taking of innocent human life, and the policies that squander limited resources on destructive weapons that can reduce humanity to shambles.

Second Coming
The final judgment of all humanity when Christ returns to Earth. It is also known by its Greek name, *Parousia*, which means "arrival."

But Deliver Us from Evil

In union with the saints, we ask God to extend the victory that Christ has already won over Satan. We pray that the Father will deliver us from Satan's snares and from all the world's temptations. We beg God to keep us from the evil of accidents, illness, violence, and natural disasters. We also pray that God will help lead us to reject injustice, prejudice, or selfishness. Finally, we pray with the Holy Spirit and all God's people—the Communion of Saints. We pray for the Lord's **Second Coming** when we will be free forever from the snares of the Evil One. Last, we pray that we will never be put into a situation where we might be tempted to deny our loving Father. That would be the greatest evil of all.

Amen

When we say "Amen" at the end of the Our Father, we are professing our belief and agreement with everything that we prayed. This word means "I believe," or "I agree." Adding this final word indicates that we are saying this prayer with personal conviction.

For Review

1. What do the words "Our Father" tell us about relationships in the Kingdom of God?
2. How is God's name made holy?
3. What are we asking for when we pray for "our daily bread"?
4. What are two things we pray for when we say the phrase "lead us not into temptation"?

For Reflection

- What are the most common temptations that confront high-school-aged people today? Share your ideas about what it is that "leads" many of them into or toward temptations. What helps to strengthen many young people in resisting these temptations?
- What is the most memorable experience you've had of forgiveness? It could be an experience of being forgiven yourself, or of offering forgiveness to someone who hurt or offended you.

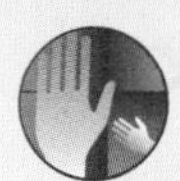

Making the Lord's Prayer Your Prayer

Do one of the following activities to express your commitment to living out the words of the Our Father.

- Create a PowerPoint presentation to illustrate the petitions of the Lord's Prayer. Choose appropriate visuals to accompany the text of the prayer.
- Rewrite each petition of the Lord's Prayer in your own words.
- Read and write a summary of the meaning of the Lord's Prayer verse by verse as gleaned from a biblical commentary.

A Prayer Primer

When we pray, we should address our prayers to the Father, our loving Abba who is the source of our life. We should also pray to Jesus and invoke his name often. For example, many Christians love to pray the famous Jesus Prayer: "Lord Jesus Christ, Son of God, have mercy on me, a sinner." We should also invoke the help of the Holy Spirit who lives within us and teaches the lessons of Christian prayer.

Through the ages, Catholics have also found it valuable to pray in union with Mary, the Blessed Mother of Jesus. In her life, Mary showed us how to cooperate with the graces of the Holy Spirit. She was a model disciple of her son Jesus and showed us how to live a Christ-like life. The Hail Mary praises God for his goodness shown to Mary. It also petitions our Blessed Mother to pray for us to her beloved Son.

Many of us learned how to pray from our parents or grandparents, but also from teachers, priests, and others who have made prayer an important part of their lives. Throughout the history of the Church, many saints have taught different ways to approach God in prayer. They share many points in common on how to pray.

Where, When, and How to Pray

Of course, you can pray anywhere, but it is good to find a special place where you can slow down, relax, and focus your attention. Others have found praying in their bedrooms, at the school chapel or parish church, or taking a walk with the Lord outdoors to be good places for prayer.

You can pray at any time of the day. However, it is good to get in the habit of choosing a special time each day to pray. We learn to pray by praying. Good times to pray include when rising in the morning or before going to bed, as a break between homework assignments, before and after meals, for ten minutes during a free period at school, and so forth. Participating at Mass and the other Sacraments is a certain grace-filled way to pray.

It is hard to pray if we are tense or distracted. Prayer requires that we be both alert and relaxed. So, breathing exercises that help us drain away the cares of the day can help us to pray. Also important is a comfortable body posture—like sitting upright in a chair, taking a walk outside, or kneeling.

Having a Good Attitude for Prayer

To pray we must be open to God. We should begin our prayer time by recalling that God is present to us, that he loves us immensely, and that he has given us many gifts, including the great gift of life. We should approach God with humble hearts. We should remember that our loving God has invited us to spend time with him in prayer. Therefore, we can trust that the Lord will be with us and will answer our heartfelt desire to be with him.

It can be difficult to pray regularly. Sometimes we are lazy or tired. At other times, Satan tempts us to think that prayer is silly, old-fashioned, or has no practical value in our lives. Even if we are faithful in our prayer, sometimes we feel that God is not there and not much is going on. Add to this the distractions that always seem to come along, making it difficult to focus or hear the Lord in the depth of our hearts.

To persevere with prayer, we need to have faith that God always hears us, even if we do not "feel" anything. When things seem to be going badly, we should pray for the Holy Spirit to come to us. The Holy Spirit is the source of all gifts, especially the gift of love. It is that love that will keep us at prayer and lead us to our Lord who is Love itself.

Distractions in prayer are often caused by a wandering mind, an overactive imagination, or external noises. One way to overcome distractions is to focus on a crucifix, a holy picture or icon, or a lit candle to help keep our attention on God. We can also turn to the Holy Spirit and ask for help. Another good technique is to recite repeatedly a prayer-word or phrase like "Abba," "Savior," or "Jesus help me." This practice can "distract us from the distractions" and refocus our attention on God. No matter what, always remember that God is very pleased with our efforts. Trying to pray is itself a prayer. Jesus, Our Lord, appreciates any effort we make on his behalf.

The Example of the Saints in Prayer

Saints know the value of prayer as a way to stay close to their friend, Jesus. We can learn from their example. Two saints that modeled lives of prayer are St. Maria Goretti and St. Aloysius Gonzaga.

St. Maria Goretti (1890-1902)

Maria Goretti's life was short and tragic, yet ultimately very inspirational. She was the second child of Luigi and Assunta Goretti, born near Nettuno, twenty miles from Rome. When she was six, her impoverished parents had to give up their farm and move to another town. There, the Gorettis were forced to work for others. When she was nine, her father died of malaria and the family had to move again. From then on, Maria cared for her five brothers and sisters while her mother worked in the fields to earn food for the family. Maria was a pious child who was devoted to daily prayer. Though she could not read or write, she was very intelligent and had a strong will. She took to heart her mother's instruction to never commit a sin, at any cost.

By this time, the Gorettis shared a house with the Serenelli family. One of the Serenelli sons, Alessandro, age twenty, became increasingly attracted to Maria. He, like his father, abused alcohol and scorned religion. Two months before her twelfth birthday, Alessandro tried forcefully to molest and rape Maria. She resisted his sexual advances, yelling at him and reminding him that he was sinning. Angry, Alessandro choked her and then stabbed her fourteen times.

Maria survived the brutal attack for twenty hours, but suffered terribly from her wounds. While she lay dying, she prayed for her attacker, forgave him, and told her parish priest that she wanted Alessandro to join her in heaven one day. Shortly after her death, Alessandro was captured and, because he was a minor, was sentenced to thirty years in prison.

Everyone who knew Maria testified to her goodness, her purity of body and soul, her love of her parents and siblings, her devotion to prayer and Jesus in the Eucharist, and the forgiving heart she so generously showed on her deathbed.

For the first few years in prison, Alessandro was bitter and unrepentant and, at times, even close to despair. Then, one night during his eighth year of imprisonment, Maria appeared to him in a dream. She offered him fourteen lilies, representing the fourteen wounds he inflicted on her. Maria instructed Alessandro to take the lilies, which then turned into purifying flames. In the dream, Maria assured Alessandro that he would one day join her in heaven. When he awoke, the hatred in Alessandro's heart had left him. He became profoundly sorrowful for the horrible crime he committed. When he got out of prison after twenty-seven years (three years were forgiven due to the model prisoner he became after his conversion), he begged Maria's mother to forgive him. Assunta did so in a very touching way, following her beloved daughter's own deathbed example. She even called Alessandro "my son" and received Holy Communion with him.

Pope Pius XII canonized Maria as a virgin and martyr in 1950, the youngest saint ever to be canonized. Maria's mother was present at the canonization as were four of her siblings. Remarkably, Alessandro, her assailant and murderer, was also present. He had given moving testimony about her heroic virtue during the canonization process. He became a Capuchin lay brother and worked as a gardener and receptionist until his death in 1970 at the age of eighty-nine. He lived his life in prayer and penance for the crime he committed, often praying to St. Maria Goretti as his protector.

Maria is a wonderful example of great courage and devotion to purity, compassion, forgiveness, and prayer.

St. Aloysius Gonzaga (1568-1591)

Another model of prayer in the Christian life is St. Aloysius Gonzaga. Born to a noble family, Aloysius was raised in a castle in Castiglione delle Stiviere, a town in northern Italy near Mantua. His father wanted him to be a soldier, but Aloysius also received an education in languages and other subjects. He served for a time at the court of the famous Medici family, but fell ill with a kidney disease that troubled him for the rest of his life.

While recuperating, the young Aloysius read the lives of the saints and spent much time in prayer. He was especially devoted to Mary, the Blessed Mother. After returning to his family's castle, he received his first Holy Communion at the age of twelve from St. Charles Borromeo. Soon after that, he read a book about Jesuit missionaries and decided that he wanted to become one himself. He also started to teach catechism classes to the young boys in his town.

For a time, his family moved to Spain where Aloysius became a page at the royal court. He still kept telling his parents that he wanted to be a priest, but his father was angry about this prospect. He wanted his firstborn son to carry on his legacy. But Aloysius would not give up his calling, despite his father's many pleadings for him to head up the noble family. Finally, when he was eighteen and back in Italy, Aloysius renounced all claims to his inheritance. He surrendered his family title to his brother and traveled to Rome where he was received into the Jesuits.

Despite the wealth of his family, Aloysius had lived an austere life, engaging in many penances, including fasting. Later, as a Jesuit, his religious superiors told him to ease up on the severity of his penances. Clearly, the young man's health was very fragile, and his difficulties included diseased kidneys, chronic headaches, insomnia, and a skin condition. He studied for a time in Milan, but returned to Rome where he took the three religious vows of poverty, chastity, and obedience. He continued to live a holy life, much enriched by his prayers and devotion to Christ in the Eucharist. He also threw himself into the chores of his Jesuit house by helping in the kitchen, washing dishes, and distributing food to the poor who came to the house gate. He also tended the sick.

In 1591, a plague broke out in Rome. The Jesuits opened a hospital for plague victims, and the young Aloysius volunteered to minister to them. He himself eventually contracted the disease after carrying a stricken man on his back to the hospital. Although he recovered for a time, the disease seriously weakened his health. He died in June of 1591 at the age of twenty-three. The last word on his lips was the word "Jesus."

St. Aloysius is a model for Catholics today because he lived a holy life amid the many temptations of courtly life to which he was exposed. His prayer life sustained him. His devotion to the Blessed Mother and Jesus in the Eucharist gave him the strength to endure many physical ailments and persevere in living a holy life of service for others.

EXPLAINING THE FAITH

Why do Catholics ask Mary to intercede for them to God?

The Catholic Church teaches that Mary, the Mother of God, is also the Mother of the Church. Catholics ask Mary, the Mother of God, to join them in prayer because she was perfectly faithful to God. The second reason, however, is linked directly to the words of Jesus. Just before his Death, he commended his Apostle John to his Mother Mary. "Woman, behold your son" (Jn 19:26). And, Jesus asked John to take Mary into his home and look after her. Then he said to the disciple, "Behold, your mother" (Jn 19:27). "Ever since," as we read in the *Catechism of the Catholic Church*, "her motherhood has extended to the brothers and sisters of her Son who still journey on earth surrounded by dangers and difficulties" (*CCC*, 2674). Jesus gave us his Mother. As she always has, Mary accepts any request from her Son Jesus with love and joy. Mary can't wait to add her prayers to ours when we ask her to.

Living the Mission

As you complete this semester study of Jesus Christ and his mission, you are called to expand your knowledge of him and your commitment to him to by sharing the Gospel with others. You do this in particular by the way you speak and act. In just a few years you will live apart from your parents and have the opportunity to explore and choose your own life's work and vocation. As you do so, continue to make Jesus the focus of your life. It is Jesus who loves and embraces you for who you are. Come to share in his mission and his ministry. Remember the last words he shared with his disciples prior to ascending to Heaven:

> Go, therefore, and make disciples of all nations, baptizing them in the name of the Father, and of the Son, and of the Holy Spirit, teaching them to observe all that I have commanded you. And behold, I am with you always, until the end of the age. (Mt 28:19–20)

For Review

1. Print the words of the Jesus Prayer and the Hail Mary from memory.
2. What are some important considerations in finding a place for personal prayer?
3. Why is it important to have a relaxed body and mind before beginning prayer?
4. Why is it wise to have regular prayer times during your day?
5. Name two good strategies for resisting distractions during prayer.

For Reflection

- When did prayer help you do the right thing by resisting peer pressure?
- "Fast forward" the story of either St. Maria Goretti or St. Aloysius Gonzaga into your own time and place. Rewrite the story of one saint's courage and virtue as if she or he was living now.

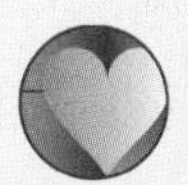

Meditating with Scripture

Meditating on a Gospel passage is a wonderful way to meet the Lord in prayer. This form of prayer engages the faculties of thinking and imagination (our minds) and the love we have for God (our hearts). These, in turn, lead to resolutions that help us live better Christian lives (our hands).

St. Ignatius of Loyola taught a method of meditation that fully engages our imaginations when reflecting on a Bible passage. An important value to his method is that it helps to keep distractions to a minimum. Here are the steps to take:

Preliminaries for Meditation

1. *Select a text*. Pick a passage ahead of time, for example, Luke 17:11-19.
2. *Settle down*. Take a few moments to calm yourself. Assume a comfortable position. Breathe slowly. Let the cares of the day drain from you.
3. *Pray to the Holy Spirit*. Put yourself in God's presence. Feel the warmth of his love. Ask the Holy Spirit to help you pray and to hear the word of God speak to you.
4. *Read the passage slowly and reflectively.* Here is the text:

   As he continued his journey to Jerusalem, he traveled through Samaria and Galilee. As he was entering a village, ten lepers met (him). They stood at a distance from him and raised their voice, saying, "Jesus, Master! Have pity on us!" And when he saw them, he said, "Go show yourselves to the priests." As they were going, they were cleansed. And one of them, realizing he had been healed, returned, glorifying God in a loud voice; and he fell at the feet of Jesus and thanked him. He was a Samaritan. Jesus said in reply, "Ten were cleansed, were they not? Where are the other nine men? Has none but this foreigner returned to give thanks to God?" Then he said to him, "Stand up and go; your faith has saved you."

Steps for Meditation

1. *Observe*. Step into the story and become part of it. What is happening? What kind of day is it? Hot? What is the road like? Dusty? Who is with Jesus? Imagine yourself as one of the disciples traveling with Jesus. You can't wait to get to town to get a drink of water. You notice the

continued on next page

continued from previous page

diseased men, with their sores covering their arms and legs. They cover their faces and ring a bell to warn passersby away. Then, suddenly, you hear them cry out to Jesus. He looks at them. What is his reaction? Do you want him to avoid them for fear of contamination? Are you afraid for yourself? Listen to what Jesus says. What do his words mean? Will the men be cured? What is their reaction? How are the other disciples reacting?

Now imagine that you are one of the diseased persons. You begin your journey to the priest when suddenly your loathsome skin disease disappears. What do you do? Do you come back and thank Jesus? If not, what do you do? Why?

Now focus on the Samaritan. He falls down before Jesus and grabs the Lord's feet. He thanks and praises Jesus. Listen to the response Jesus makes. Is he disappointed with the other cured men? What do you think he means when he says, "Your faith has saved you"?

2. *Reflect.* What does the story mean? Is it just about physical illness? Can it also apply to sickness of the spirit? How does it focus on the mercy of Jesus, his compassion for the ones society rejects? Is it a call to faith? Is it about gratitude? Courage? Obedience to the word of the Lord? What do you think the evangelist Luke is stressing in this story? What strikes you as the main point?
3. *Listen.* What is this passage telling you? Is there something in your life that Jesus needs to touch and cure? Do you have the courage to approach Jesus to ask for his help and Salvation? Are you willing to listen to him? How strong is your faith? Do you need Jesus to strengthen it? Or perhaps he is telling you to say thank you for all your gifts. Will you be like the Samaritan who came back to offer thanks? Or will you be like the ungrateful ones? Prayerfully ask, "What, Lord, are you saying *to me* in this reading?"
4. *Resolution.* After spending ten to fifteen minutes with the Lord in your mediation, resolve to do something about the insights you have gained. Perhaps you will simply need to acknowledge that not all is well in your life and that you need the Lord's forgiveness or help to overcome a bad habit. Perhaps you will decide to thank the Lord for everything he has done for you. Perhaps you will think of a person who has done something for you, and that you need to thank him or her. Whatever "fruit" you take from your time with the Lord, thank him for being with you.

Meditation Follow-up

Repeat the exercise above in the coming weeks by meditating on each of the following Gospel passages:

- The Young Jesus (Luke 2:41-50)
- Calming of the Storm (Mark 4:35-41)
- The Woman in Simon's House (Luke 7:36-50)
- Miracle of the Loaves and Fishes (John 6:1-13)
- Jesus and Zacchaeus (Luke 19:1-10)
- Washing the Apostles' Feet (John 13:1-20)
- Jesus in the Garden of Gethsemane (Luke 22:39-46)

Main Ideas

- Prayer means both talkingto and listening to God; it is God's gift to us. (p. 234)
- It is God who creates in us a longing for prayer—communication with him. (pp. 235–236)
- The *Catechism of the Catholic Church* defines prayer as the "living relationship of the children of God with their Father." (pp. 235–236)
- Talking to God in our own words is called *spontaneous prayer*. (p. 236)
- There are many kinds of prayer, including *praise*, *petition*, *intercession*, *thanksgiving*, *contrition*, *meditation*, and *contemplation*. (pp. 236–239)
- Praise is a prayer of "blessing" or calling God holy. It is a prayer of adoration and love for our Creator God, the Creator and source of all blessing. (pp. 236–237)
- Many of the Old Testament Psalms are beautiful and timeless prayers of praise. (p. 237)
- *Petition* is a prayer of asking God for favors or help. *Intercession* is a type of petition and involves asking God to help other people. (p. 237)
- *Thanksgiving* is simply a prayer expressing our gratitude to God from whom we receive every good gift. (p. 237)
- *Contrition* is a prayer expression of sorrow or regret for our sins. In this prayer, we also ask for God the Father's forgiveness. (p. 237)
- Tuning toward God as we focus our thoughts, emotions, and imagination on God is a type of prayer called *meditation*. (p. 238)
- When meditation leads to a silent, wordless prayer of resting in the presence of God, it is called *contemplation*. (pp. 238–239)
- Jesus is the perfect model and guide for prayer; he prayed to prepare for his ministry and before important decisions. (pp. 240–241)
- Jesus prayed in many different ways with different kinds of prayer and different prayer types. (pp. 241–242)
- As a pious and active Jew, Jesus regularly prayed in the synagogue and Temple, and often prayed the *Shema*, the *Eighteen Benedictions,* and the *Kaddish*. (pp. 241–242)
- Jesus taught his followers to pray with simplicity, persistence, faith, forgiveness in our hearts, and in community with others. (pp. 242–243)
- To teach his followers to pray, Jesus presented the *Our Father*, a perfect Christian prayer of praise, petition, and contrition. (pp. 244–248)
- Studying the text of the Lord's Prayer will teach us lifelong lessons about how best to pray. (pp. 244–248)
- Finding or establishing a prayer place, time, position, and attitude will help us to develop a consistent prayer life. (pp. 249–250)
- St. Maria Goretti (1890–1902) and St. Aloysius Gonzaga (1568–1591) are ideal models of holiness and virtues for young people. Both persisted in prayer in difficult circumstances. (pp. 250–252)

Terms, People, Places

Use at least five of the vocabulary words below in a half-page essay. The theme of the essay should involve Jesus and prayer.

Prayer
Contemplation
Spontaneous prayer
Contrition
Second Coming
Intercession
Meditation
Praise
Thanksgiving

Primary Source Quotations

The Life of Prayer

Prayer is the habit of being in the presence of the thrice-holy God and in communion with him. This communion of life is always possible because, through Baptism, we have already been united with Christ. Prayer is Christian insofar as it is communion with Christ and extends throughout the Church, which is his Body.

—*Catechism of the Catholic Church*, 2565

The Way to Salvation

Three things are necessary for the salvation of man: to know what he ought to believe; to know what he ought to desire; and to know what he ought to do.

—St. Thomas Aquinas

Searching for God Is Prayer

The desire [for God] is your prayer; and if your desire is without ceasing, your prayer will also be without ceasing. The continuance of your longing is the continuance of your prayer.

—St. Augustine of Hippo

Nonstop Prayer

To saints, their very slumber is prayer.

—St. John of the Cross

Jesus and the Journey of Life

What really matters in life is that we are loved by Christ and that we love him in return. In comparison to the love of Jesus, everything else is secondary. And, without the love of Jesus, everything is useless.

—Pope John Paul II

Write three goals for increasing and varying your prayer life. Determine how you will meet them.

Ongoing Assignments

1. Research various examples of a "scriptural rosary." Then reference your own Scripture passages for at least one of the mysteries of the rosary using separate references for each bead. Pray and share your scriptural rosary with your classmates.
2. Develop a PowerPoint presentation on the Hail Mary using appropriate pictures and music. Later, present it to your class or perhaps to a group of adults in your parish.
3. Read and reflect on one of the parables Jesus told about prayer. For example: read the Parable of the Parable of the Pharisee and the Tax Collector (Lk 18:9–14). Then, write a reflection on the following:
   - Describe the Pharisee. How was the tax collector different?
   - According to Jesus, what qualities should we have in our heart when we approach God in prayer?
4. Reflect on what Jesus meant when he said that "everyone who exalts himself will be humbled, and the one who humbles himself will be exalted." Discuss a real-life example of this Gospel maxim or truth actually lived out or demonstrated. Alternatively, create a multimedia poster to portray an example of this Jesus saying.
5. Report on the life of a favorite saint to discover what role prayer had in his or her life.
   - www.catholic-pages.com/dir/saints.asp
   - Transcribe the Lord's Prayer from one or more foreign languages. Consider memorizing the Our Father in the language of some of your ancestors. Do an Internet search for the Lord's Prayer in other languages or visit this website for hundreds of languages: www.christus rex.org/www1/pater/index.html

6. Write your own one-page reflection on how you hope to pray to your Father in the future.
7. Further explore and research the life of St. Maria Goretti or St. Aloysius Gonzaga.

Prayer

As you complete this course on *Jesus: His Mission and Ministry*, pray the following with an open heart:

The Grail Prayer
Lord Jesus,
I give you my hands to do your work.
I give you my feet to go your way.
I give you my eyes to see as you do.
I give you my tongue to speak your words.
I give you my mind that you may think in me.
I give you my spirit that you may pray in me.
Above all,
I give you my heart that you may love in me
your Father and all mankind.
I give you my whole self that you may grow in me,
so that it is you, Lord Jesus,
who live and work and pray in me.

- *Reflection*: What is it that you can give to Jesus today?
- *Resolution*: Commit to one specific thing you can do each day for the coming week to give your hands, feet, eyes, tongue, mind, spirit, heart, and self to Jesus.

CATHOLIC HANDBOOK FOR FAITH

A. Beliefs

From the beginning, the Church expressed and handed on its faith in brief formulas accessible to all. These professions of faith are called "creeds" because their first word in Latin, credo, *means "I believe." The following creeds have special importance in the Church. The Apostles' Creed is a summary of the Apostles' faith. The Nicene Creed developed from the Councils of Nicaea and Constantinople and remains in common between the Churches of both the East and West.*

Apostles' Creed

I believe in God,
the Father almighty,
Creator of heaven and earth,
and in Jesus Christ, his only Son, our Lord,
who was conceived by the Holy Spirit,
born of the Virgin Mary,
suffered under Pontius Pilate,
was crucified, died and was buried;
he descended into hell;
on the third day he rose again from the dead;
he ascended into heaven,
and is seated at the right hand of God the Father almighty;
from there he will come to judge the living and the dead.

I believe in the Holy Spirit,
the holy catholic Church,
the communion of saints,
the forgiveness of sins,
the resurrection of the body,
and life everlasting. Amen.

Nicene Creed

I believe in one God,
the Father almighty,
maker of heaven and earth,
of all things visible and invisible.

I believe in one Lord Jesus Christ,
the Only Begotten Son of God,
born of the Father before all ages.
God from God, Light from Light,
true God from true God,
begotten, not made, consubstantial with the Father;
through him all things were made.
For us men and for our salvation
he came down from heaven,
and by the Holy Spirit was incarnate of the Virgin Mary,
and became man.

For our sake he was crucified under Pontius Pilate,
he suffered death and was buried,
and rose again on the third day

in accordance with the Scriptures.
He ascended into heaven
and is seated at the right hand of the Father.
He will come again in glory
to judge the living and the dead
and his kingdom will have no end.

I believe in the Holy Spirit, the Lord, the giver of life,
who proceeds from the Father and the Son,
who with the Father and the Son is adored and glorified,
who has spoken through the prophets.

I believe in one, holy, catholic, and apostolic Church.
I confess one Baptism for the forgiveness of sins
and I look forward to the resurrection of the dead
and the life of the world to come. Amen.

Gifts of the Holy Spirit

1. Wisdom
2. Understanding
3. Counsel
4. Fortitude
5. Knowledge
6. Piety
7. Fear of the Lord

Fruits of the Holy Spirit

1. Charity
2. Joy
3. Peace
4. Patience
5. Kindness
6. Goodness
7. Generosity
8. Gentleness
9. Faithfulness
10. Modesty
11. Self-control
12. Chastity

The Symbol of Chalcedon

Following therefore the holy Fathers, we unanimously teach to confess one and the same Son, our Lord Jesus Christ, the same perfect in divinity and perfect in humanity, the same truly God and truly man composed of rational soul and body, the same one in being (*homoousios*) with the Father as to the divinity and one in being with us as to the humanity, like unto us in all things but sin (cf. Heb 4:15). The same was begotten from the Father before the ages as to the divinity and in the later days for us and our Salvation was born as to his humanity from Mary the Virgin Mother of God.

We confess that one and the same Lord Jesus Christ, the only-begotten Son, must be acknowledged in two natures, without confusion or change, without division or separation. The distinction between the natures was never abolished by their union but rather the character proper to each of the two natures was preserved as they came together in one person (*prosôpon*) and one hypostasis. He is not split or divided into two persons, but he is one and the same only-begotten, God the Word, the Lord Jesus Christ, as formerly the prophets and later Jesus Christ himself have taught us about him and as has been handed down to us by the Symbol of the Fathers.

—From the General Council of Chalcedon (AD 451)

B. Faith in God: Father, Son, and Holy Spirit

Our profession of faith begins with God, for God is the First and the Last, the beginning and end of everything.

Attributes of God

St. Thomas Aquinas named nine attributes that seem to tell us some things about God's nature. They are:

1. *God is eternal.* He has no beginning and no end. Or, to put it another way, God always was, always is, and always will be.
2. *God is unique.* There is no God like YHWH (see Isaiah 45:18). God is the designer of a one-and-only world. Even the people he creates are one of a kind.
3. *God is infinite and omniscient.* This reminds us of a lesson we learned early in life: God sees everything. There are no limits to God.
4. *God is omnipresent.* God is not limited to space. He is everywhere. You can never be away from God.
5. *God contains all things.* All of creation is under God's care and jurisdiction.
6. *God is immutable.* God does not evolve. God does not change. God is the same God now as he always was and always will be.
7. *God is pure spirit.* Though God has been described with human attributes, God is not a material creation. God's image cannot be made. God is a pure spirit who cannot be divided into parts. God is simple, but complex.
8. *God is alive.* We believe in a living God, a God who acts in the lives of people. Most concretely, God assumed a human nature in the divine Person of Jesus Christ, without losing his divine nature.
9. *God is holy.* God is pure goodness. God is pure love.

The Holy Trinity

The Holy Trinity is the central mystery of the Christian faith and of Christian life. Only God can make it known to us by revealing himself as Father, Son, and Holy Spirit. Viewed in the light of faith, some of the Church dogmas, or beliefs, can help our understanding of this mystery:

- *The Trinity is One.* There are not three Gods, but one God in three Persons. Each one of them—Father, Son, and Holy Spirit—is God whole and entire.
- *The three Persons are distinct from one another.* The three Persons of the Trinity are distinct in how they relate to one another. "It is the Father who generates, the Son who is begotten, and the Holy Spirit who proceeds" (Lateran Council IV, quoted in *CCC*, 254). The Father is not the Son, nor is the Son the Holy Spirit.
- *The Three Divine Persons of the Blessed Trinity relate to one another.* While the three Persons are truly distinct in light of their relations, we believe in one God. The three Persons do not divide the divine unity. The Council of Florence taught, "Because of that unity the Father is wholly in the Son and wholly in the Holy Spirit; the Son is wholly in the Father and wholly in the Holy Spirit; the Holy Spirit is wholly in the Father and wholly in the Son" (quoted in *CCC*, 255).

St. John Damascus used two analogies to describe the doctrine of the Blessed Trinity.

Think of the Father as a root,
of the Son as a branch,
and of the Spirit as a fruit,
for the substance of these is one.

The Father is a sun
with the Son as rays
and the Holy Spirit as heat.

Read the *Catechism of the Catholic Church* (232–260) on the Holy Trinity.

Faith in One God

There are several implications for those who love God and believe in him with their entire heart and soul (see *CCC* 222–227):

- It means knowing God's greatness and majesty.
- It means living in thanksgiving.
- It means knowing the unity and dignity of all people.
- It means making good use of created things.
- It means trusting God in every circumstance.

C. Deposit of Faith

"Deposit of Faith" refers to both Sacred Scripture and Sacred Tradition handed on from the time of the Apostles, from which the Church draws all that she proposes is revealed by God.

Canon of the Bible

There are seventy-three books in the canon of the Bible, that is, the official list of books the Church accepts as divinely inspired writings: forty-six Old Testament books and twenty-seven New Testament books. Protestant Bibles do not include seven Old Testament books in their list (1 and 2 Maccabees, Judith, Tobit, Baruch, Sirach, and the Wisdom of Solomon). Why the difference? Catholics rely on the version of the Bible that the earliest Christians used, the *Septuagint*. This was the first Greek translation of the Hebrew Scriptures, begun in the third century BC. Protestants, on the other hand, rely on an official list of Hebrew Scriptures compiled in the Holy Land by Jewish scholars at the end of the first century AD. Today, some Protestant Bibles print the disputed books in a separate section at the back of the Bible, called the *Apocrypha*.

The twenty-seven books of the New Testament are detailed in Chapter 2. The New Testament is central to our knowledge of Jesus Christ.

There are forty-six books in the Old Testament canon. The Old Testament is the foundation for God's self-Revelation in Christ. Christians honor the Old Testament as God's Word. It contains the writings of prophets and other inspired authors who recorded God's teaching to the Chosen People and his interaction in their history. For example, the Old Testament recounts how God delivered the Jews from Egypt (the Exodus), led them to the Promised Land, formed them into a nation under his care, and taught them in knowledge and worship.

The stories, prayers, sacred histories, and other writings of the Old Testament reveal what God is like and tell much about human nature, too. In brief, the Chosen People sinned repeatedly by turning their backs on their loving God; they were weak and easily tempted away from God. YHWH, on the other hand, *always* remained faithful. He promised to send a messiah to humanity.

Listed on the following page are the categories and books of the Old Testament.

The Old Testament

The Pentateuch

Book	Abbreviation
Genesis	Gn
Exodus	Ex
Leviticus	Lv
Numbers	Nm
Deuteronomy	Dt

The Historical Books

Book	Abbreviation
Joshua	Jos
Judges	Jgs
Ruth	Ru
1 Samuel	1 Sm
2 Samuel	2 Sm
1 Kings	1 Kgs
2 Kings	2 Kgs
1 Chronicles	1 Chr
2 Chronicles	2 Chr
Ezra	Ezr
Nehemiah	Neh
Tobit	Tb
Judith	Jdt
Esther	Est
1 Maccabees	1 Mc
2 Maccabees	2 Mc

The Wisdom Books

Book	Abbreviation
Job	Jb
Psalms	Ps(s)
Proverbs	Prv
Ecclesiastes	Eccl
Song of Songs	Sg
Wisdom	Wis
Sirach	Sir

The Prophetic Books

Book	Abbreviation
Isaiah	Is
Jeremiah	Jer
Lamentations	Lam
Baruch	Bar
Ezekiel	Ez
Daniel	Dn
Hosea	Hos
Joel	Jl
Amos	Am
Obadiah	Ob
Jonah	Jon
Micah	Mi
Nahum	Na
Habakkuk	Hb
Zephaniah	Zep
Haggai	Hg
Zechariah	Zec
Malachi	Mal

The New Testament

The Gospels

Book	Abbreviation
Matthew	Mt
Mark	Mk
Luke	Lk
John	Jn
Acts of the Apostles	Acts

The New Testament Letters

Book	Abbreviation
Romans	Rom
1 Corinthians	1 Cor
2 Corinthians	2 Cor
Galatians	Gal
Ephesians	Eph
Philippians	Phil
Colossians	Col
1 Thessalonians	1 Thes
2 Thessalonians	2 Thes
1 Timothy	1 Tm
2 Timothy	2 Tm
Titus	Ti
Philemon	Phlm
Hebrews	Heb

The Catholic Letters

Book	Abbreviation
James	Jas
1 Peter	1 Pt
2 Peter	2 Pt
1 John	1 Jn
2 John	2 Jn
3 John	3 Jn
Jude	Jude
Revelation	Rv

How to Locate a Scripture Passage

Example: 2 Tm 3:16–17

1. Determine the name of the book.

   The abbreviation "2 Tm" stands for the book of Second Timothy.

2. Determine whether the book is in the Old Testament or New Testament.

   The book of Second Timothy is one of the New Testament Letters.

3. Locate the chapter where the passage occurs.

   The first number before the colon—"3"—indicates the chapter. Chapters in the Bible are set off by the larger numbers that divide a book.

4. Locate the verses of the passage.

   The numbers after the colon indicate the verses referred to. In this case, verses 16 and 17 of chapter 3.

5. Read the passage.

   For example: "All Scripture is inspired by God and is useful for teaching, for refutation, for correction, and for training in righteousness, so that one who belongs to God may be competent, equipped for every good work."

Relationship between Scripture and Tradition

The Church does not derive the revealed truths of God from the holy Scriptures alone. The Sacred Tradition hands on God's Word, first given to the Apostles by the Lord and the Holy Spirit, to the successors of the Apostles (the bishops and the Pope). Enlightened by the Holy Spirit, these successors faithfully preserve, explain, and spread it to the ends of the earth. The Second Vatican Council fathers explained the relationship between Sacred Scripture and Sacred Tradition this way:

> It is clear therefore that, in the supremely wise arrangement of God, Sacred Tradition, Sacred Scripture, and the Magisterium of the Church are so connected and associated that one of them cannot stand without the others. Working together, each in its own way, under the action of the one Holy Spirit, they all contribute effectively to the Salvation of souls. (*Dei Verbum*, 10)

Relevant Church Teaching on Reading and Studying Scripture

> If one carefully reads the Scriptures, he will find there the word on the subject of Christ and the prefiguration of the new calling. He is indeed the hidden treasure in the field—the field in fact is the world—but in truth, the hidden treasure in the Scriptures is Christ. Because he is designed by types and words that humanly are not possible to understand before the accomplishment of all things, that is, Christ's second coming.
>
> —St. Irenaeus (second century AD)

> [Christ's words] are not only those which he spoke when he became a man and tabernacled in the flesh; for before that time, Christ, the Word of God, was in Moses and the prophets . . . [their words] were filled with the Spirit of Christ.
>
> —Origen (third century AD)

> You recall that one and the same Word of God extends throughout Scripture, that it is one and the same Utterance that resounds in the mouths of all the sacred writers, since he who was in the beginning God with God has no need of separate syllables; for he is not subject to time.
>
> The Scriptures are in fact, in any passage you care to choose, singing of Christ, provided we have ears that are capable of picking out the tune. The Lord opened the minds

of the Apostles so that they understood the Scriptures. That he will open our minds too is our prayer.

—St. Augustine of Hippo
(fifth century AD)

My dear young friends, I urge you to become familiar with the Bible, and to have it at hand so that it can be your compass pointing out the road to follow. By reading it, you will learn to know Christ. Note what St. Jerome said in this regard: "Ignorance of the Scriptures is ignorance of Christ" (PL 24,17; cf. *Dei Verbum*, 25). A time-honoured way to study and savor the Word of God is *lectio divina* which constitutes a real and veritable spiritual journey marked out in stages. After the *lectio*, which consists of reading and rereading a passage from Sacred Scripture and taking in the main elements, we proceed to *meditatio*. This is a moment of interior reflection in which the soul turns to God and tries to understand what his Word is saying to us today. Then comes *oratio* in which we linger to talk with God directly. Finally we come to *contemplatio*. This helps us to keep our hearts attentive to the presence of Christ whose Word is "a lamp shining in a dark place, until the day dawns and the morning star rises in your hearts" (2 Pet 1:19). Reading, study and meditation of the Word should then flow into a life of consistent fidelity to Christ and his teachings.

St. James tells us: "Be doers of the word, and not merely hearers who deceive themselves. For if any are hearers of the word and not doers, they are like those who look at themselves in a mirror; for they look at themselves and, on going away, immediately forget what they were like. But those who look into the perfect law, the law of liberty, and persevere, being not hearers who forget but doers who act—they will be blessed in their doing" (1:22–25). Those who listen to the Word of God and refer to it always, are constructing their existence on solid foundations. "Everyone then who hears these words of mine and acts on them," Jesus said, "will be like a wise man who built his house on rock" (Mt 7:24). It will not collapse when bad weather comes.

To build your life on Christ, to accept the Word with joy and put its teachings into practice: this, young people of the third millennium, should be your programme! There is an urgent need for the emergence of a new generation of Apostles anchored firmly in the Word of Christ, capable of responding to the challenges of our times and prepared to spread the Gospel far and wide. It is this that the Lord asks of you, it is to this that the Church invites you, and it is this that the world—even though it may not be aware of it—expects of you! If Jesus calls you, do not be afraid to respond to him with generosity, especially when he asks you to follow him in the consecrated life or in the priesthood. Do not be afraid; trust in him and you will not be disappointed.

—Pope Benedict XVI
(twenty-first century AD)

D. Church

The Church is the Body of Christ, that is, the community of God's people who profess faith in the Risen Lord Jesus and love and serve others under the guidance of the Holy Spirit. The Church is guided by the Pope and his bishops.

Marks of the Church

1. *The Church is one.* The Church remains one because of its source: the unity in the Trinity of the Father, Son, and Spirit in one God. The Church's unity can never be broken and lost because this foundation is itself unbreakable.
2. *The Church is holy.* The Church is holy because Jesus, the founder of the Church, is holy, and he joined the Church to himself as his body and gave the Church the gift of the Holy Spirit. Together, Christ and the Church make up the "whole Christ" (*Christus totus* in Latin).
3. *The Church is catholic.* The Church is catholic ("universal" or "for everyone") in two ways. First, she is catholic because Christ is present in the Church in the fullness of his body, with the fullness of the means of Salvation, the fullness of faith, Sacraments, and the ordained ministry that comes from the Apostles. The Church is also catholic because she takes its message of Salvation to all people.
4. *The Church is apostolic.* The Church's apostolic mission comes from Jesus: "Go, therefore, and make disciples of all nations" (Mt 28:19). The Church remains apostolic because she still teaches the same things the Apostles taught. Also, the Church is led by leaders who are successors to the Apostles and who help to guide us until Jesus returns.

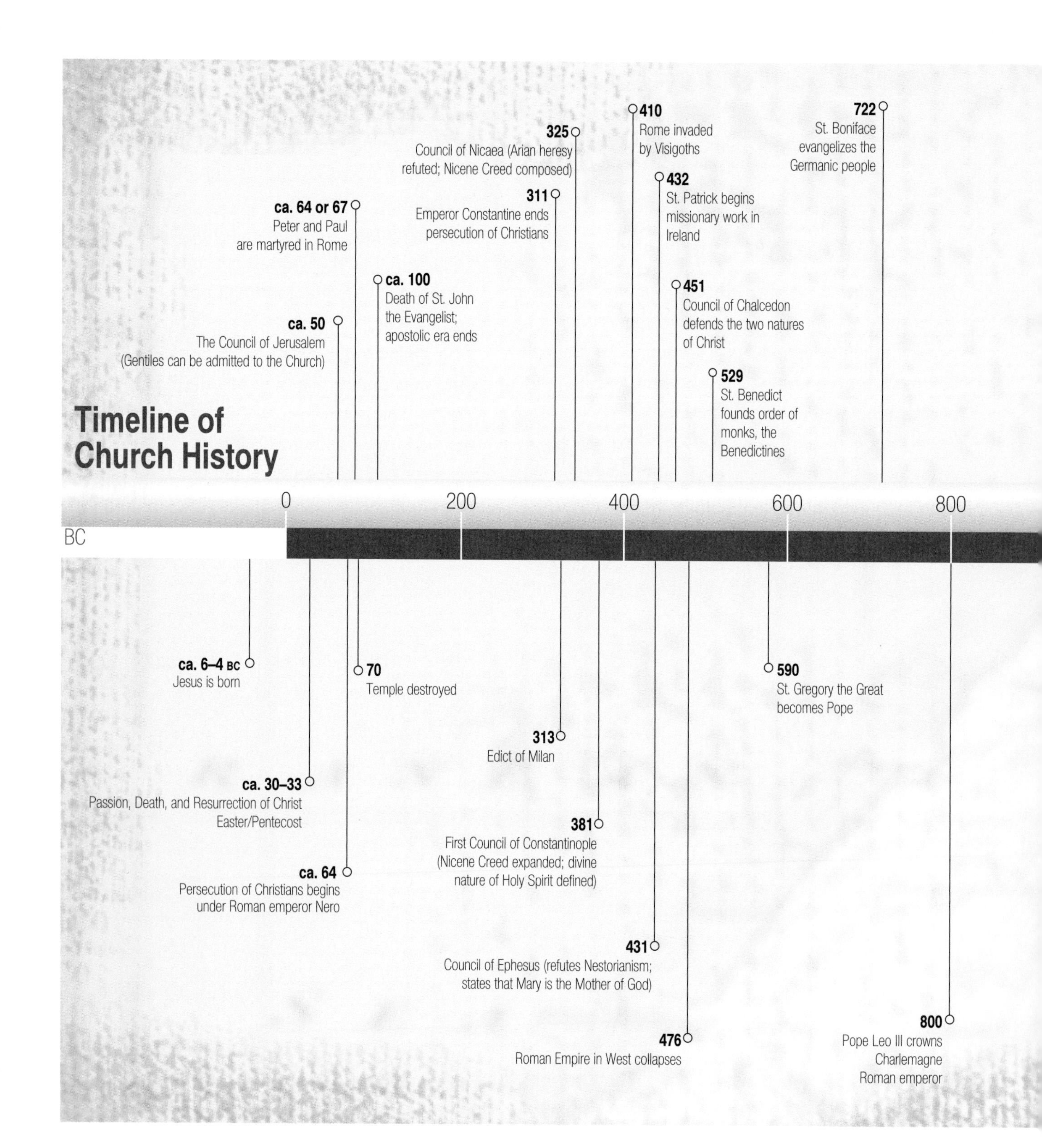
Timeline of Church History
BC
0
200
400
600
800
ca. 6–4 BC Jesus is born
ca. 30–33 Passion, Death, and Resurrection of Christ Easter/Pentecost
ca. 50 The Council of Jerusalem (Gentiles can be admitted to the Church)
ca. 64 Persecution of Christians begins under Roman emperor Nero
ca. 64 or 67 Peter and Paul are martyred in Rome
70 Temple destroyed
ca. 100 Death of St. John the Evangelist; apostolic era ends
311 Emperor Constantine ends persecution of Christians
313 Edict of Milan
325 Council of Nicaea (Arian heresy refuted; Nicene Creed composed)
381 First Council of Constantinople (Nicene Creed expanded; divine nature of Holy Spirit defined)
410 Rome invaded by Visigoths
431 Council of Ephesus (refutes Nestorianism; states that Mary is the Mother of God)
432 St. Patrick begins missionary work in Ireland
451 Council of Chalcedon defends the two natures of Christ
476 Roman Empire in West collapses
529 St. Benedict founds order of monks, the Benedictines
590 St. Gregory the Great becomes Pope
722 St. Boniface evangelizes the Germanic people
800 Pope Leo III crowns Charlemagne Roman emperor

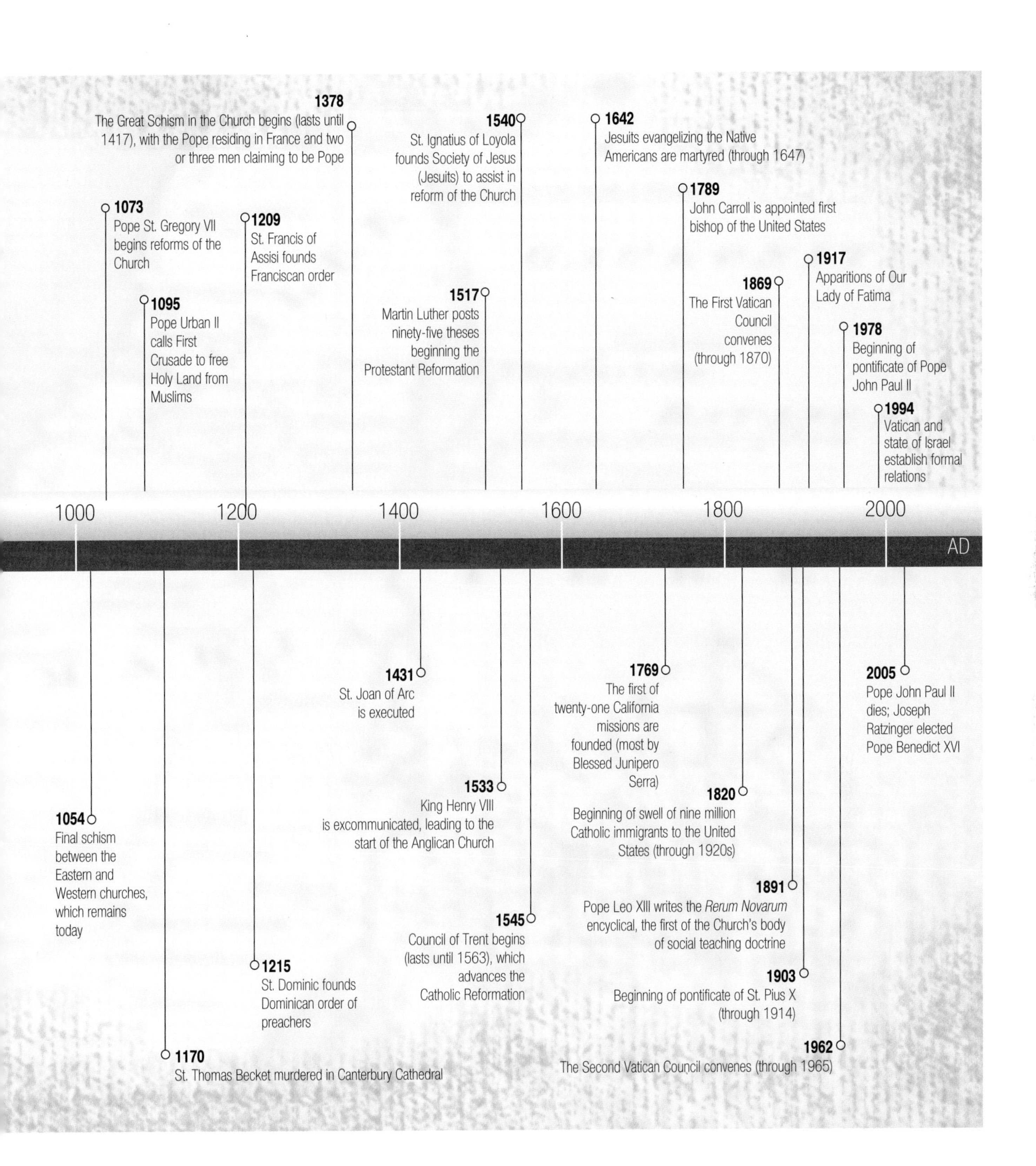
1073
Pope St. Gregory VII begins reforms of the Church
1095
Pope Urban II calls First Crusade to free Holy Land from Muslims
1209
St. Francis of Assisi founds Franciscan order
1378
The Great Schism in the Church begins (lasts until 1417), with the Pope residing in France and two or three men claiming to be Pope
1517
Martin Luther posts ninety-five theses beginning the Protestant Reformation
1540
St. Ignatius of Loyola founds Society of Jesus (Jesuits) to assist in reform of the Church
1642
Jesuits evangelizing the Native Americans are martyred (through 1647)
1789
John Carroll is appointed first bishop of the United States
1869
The First Vatican Council convenes (through 1870)
1917
Apparitions of Our Lady of Fatima
1978
Beginning of pontificate of Pope John Paul II
1994
Vatican and state of Israel establish formal relations
1000
1200
1400
1600
1800
2000
AD
1054
Final schism between the Eastern and Western churches, which remains today
1170
St. Thomas Becket murdered in Canterbury Cathedral
1215
St. Dominic founds Dominican order of preachers
1431
St. Joan of Arc is executed
1533
King Henry VIII is excommunicated, leading to the start of the Anglican Church
1545
Council of Trent begins (lasts until 1563), which advances the Catholic Reformation
1769
The first of twenty-one California missions are founded (most by Blessed Junipero Serra)
1820
Beginning of swell of nine million Catholic immigrants to the United States (through 1920s)
1891
Pope Leo XIII writes the *Rerum Novarum* encyclical, the first of the Church's body of social teaching doctrine
1903
Beginning of pontificate of St. Pius X (through 1914)
1962
The Second Vatican Council convenes (through 1965)
2005
Pope John Paul II dies; Joseph Ratzinger elected Pope Benedict XVI

The Apostles and Their Emblems

St. Andrew

Tradition holds that Andrew was crucified on an X-shaped cross, called a *saltire*.

St. Bartholomew

Bartholomew was flayed alive before being crucified. He was then beheaded.

St. James the Greater

James the Greater, the brother of John, was beheaded by Herod Agrippa. It is the only death of an Apostle mentioned in Scripture (Acts 12:2). The shell indicates James's missionary work by sea in Spain. The sword is of martyrdom.

St. James the Less

James the Less is traditionally known as the first bishop of Jerusalem. The saw for his emblem is connected with the tradition of his body being sawed into pieces after he was pushed from the pinnacle of the Temple.

St. John the Evangelist

John was the first bishop of Ephesus. He is the only Apostle believed to have died a natural death, in spite of many attempts to murder him by his enemies. One attempt included his miraculous survival after drinking a poisoned drink.

St. Jude

Some traditions have Sts. Jude and Peter martyred together. It is thought that he traveled throughout the Roman Empire with Peter.

St. Matthew

Matthew's shield depicts three purses, reflecting his original occupation as tax collector.

St. Matthias

Matthias was the Apostle chosen by lot to replace Judas. Tradition holds that Matthias was stoned to death and then beheaded with an ax.

St. Peter

Simon Peter was the brother of Andrew. The first bishop of Rome, Peter was crucified under Nero, asking to be hung upside down because he felt unworthy to die as Jesus did. The keys represent Jesus' giving Peter the keys to the Kingdom of Heaven.

St. Philip

Philip may have been bound to a cross and stoned to death. The two loaves of bread at the side of the cross refer to Philip's comment to Jesus about the possibility of feeding the multitudes of people (Jn 6:7).

St. Simon

The book with fish depicts Simon as a "fisher of men" who preached the Gospel. He was also known as Simon the Zealot.

St. Thomas

Thomas is thought to have been a missionary in India, where he is thought to have built a church. Hence, the carpenter's square. He may have died by arrows and stones. It is then thought that he had a lance run through his body.

The Pope

The bishop of Rome has carried the title "Pope" since the ninth century. Pope means "papa" or "father." St. Peter was the first bishop of Rome and, hence, the first Pope. He was commissioned directly by Jesus:

> And so I say to you, you are Peter, and upon this rock I will build my church, and the gates of the netherworld shall not prevail against it. I will give you the keys to the kingdom of Heaven. Whatever you bind on earth shall be bound in Heaven; and whatever you loose on earth shall be loosed in Heaven. (Mt 16:18–19)

Because Peter was the first bishop of Rome, the succeeding bishops of Rome have had primacy in the Church. The entire succession of Popes since St. Peter can be traced directly to the Apostle.

The Pope is in communion with the bishops of the world as part of the Magisterium, which is the Church's teaching authority. The Pope can also define doctrine in faith or morals for the Church. When he does so, he is infallible and cannot be in error.

The Pope is elected by the College of Cardinals by a two-thirds plus one majority vote in secret balloting. Cardinals under the age of eighty are eligible to vote. If the necessary majority is not achieved, the ballots are burned in a small stove inside the council chambers along with straw that makes dark smoke. The sign of dark smoke announces to the crowds waiting outside St. Peter's Basilica that a new Pope has not been chosen. When a new Pope has been voted in with the necessary majority, the ballots are burned without the straw, producing white smoke and signifying the election of a Pope.

Recent Popes

Since 1900 and up to the pontificate of Pope Benedict XVI, there have been ten Popes. Pope John Paul II was the first non-Italian Pope since Dutch Pope Adrian VI (1522–1523). The Popes of this era with their original names, place of origin, and years as Pope:

- Pope Leo XIII (Giocchino Pecci): Carpineto, Italy, February 20, 1878–July 20, 1903.
- Pope St. Pius X (Giuseppe Sarto): Riese, Italy, August 4, 1903–August 20, 1914.
- Pope Benedict XV (Giacomo della Chiesa): Genoa, Italy, September 3, 1914–January 22, 1922.
- Pope Pius XI (Achille Ratti): Desio, Italy, February 6, 1922–February 10, 1939.
- Pope Pius XII (Eugenio Pacelli): Rome, Italy, March 2, 1939–October 9, 1958.
- Pope John XXIII (Angelo Giuseppe Roncalli), Sotto il Monte, Italy, October 28, 1958–June 3, 1963.
- Pope Paul VI (Giovanni Battista Montini): Concessio, Italy, June 21, 1963–August 6, 1978.
- Pope John Paul I (Albino Luciani): Forno di Canale, Italy, August 26, 1978–September 28, 1978.
- Pope John Paul II (Karol Wojtyla): Wadowice, Poland, October 16, 1978–April 2, 2005.
- Pope Benedict XVI (Joseph Ratzinger): Marktl am Inn, Germany, April 19, 2005–present

Fathers of the Church

Church Fathers, or Fathers of the Church, is a traditional title that was given to theologians of the first eight centuries whose teachings made a lasting mark on the Church. The Church Fathers developed a significant amount of doctrine that has great authority in the Church. The Church Fathers are named as either Latin Fathers (West) or Greek Fathers (East). Among the greatest Fathers of the Church are:

Latin Fathers	Greek Fathers
St. Ambrose	St. John Chrysostom
St. Augustine	St. Basil the Great
St. Jerome	St. Gregory of Nazianzus
St. Gregory the Great	St. Athanasius

Doctors of the Church

The Doctors of the Church are men and women honored by the Church for their writings, preaching, and holiness. Originally the Doctors of the Church were considered to be Church Fathers Augustine, Ambrose, Jerome, and Gregory the Great, but others were added over the centuries. St. Teresa of Avila was the first woman Doctor (1970). St. Catherine of Siena was named a Doctor of the Church the same year. The list of Doctors of the Church:

Name	Life Span	Designation
St. Athanasius	296–373	1568 by Pius V
St. Ephraim the Syrian	306–373	1920 by Benedict XV
St. Hilary of Poitiers	315–367	1851 by Pius IX
St. Cyril of Jerusalem	315–386	1882 by Leo XIII
St. Gregory of Nazianzus	325–389	1568 by Pius V
St. Basil the Great	329–379	1568 by Pius V
St. Ambrose	339–397	1295 by Boniface VIII
St. John Chrysostom	347–407	1568 by Pius V
St. Jerome	347–419	1295 by Boniface XIII
St. Augustine	354–430	1295 by Boniface XIII
St. Cyril of Alexandria	376–444	1882 by Leo XIII
St. Peter Chrysologous	400–450	1729 by Benedict XIII
St. Leo the Great	400–461	1754 by Benedict XIV
St. Gregory the Great	540–604	1295 by Boniface XIII
St. Isidore of Seville	560–636	1722 by Innocent XIII
St. John of Damascus	645–749	1890 by Leo XIII
St. Bede the Venerable	672–735	1899 by Leo XIII
St. Peter Damian	1007–1072	1828 by Leo XII
St. Anselm	1033–1109	1720 by Clement XI
St. Bernard of Clairvaux	1090–1153	1830 by Pius VIII
St. Anthony of Padua	1195–1231	1946 by Pius XII
St. Albert the Great	1206–1280	1931 by Pius XI
St. Bonaventure	1221–1274	1588 by Sixtus V
St. Thomas Aquinas	1226–1274	1567 by Pius V
St. Catherine of Siena	1347–1380	1970 by Paul VI
St. Teresa of Avila	1515–1582	1970 by Paul VI
St. Peter Canisius	1521–1597	1925 by Pius XI
St. John of the Cross	1542–1591	1926 by Pius XI
St. Robert Bellarmine	1542–1621	1931 by Pius XI
St. Lawrence of Brindisi	1559–1619	1959 by John XXIII
St. Francis de Sales	1567–1622	1871 by Pius IX
St. Alphonsus Liguori	1696–1787	1871 by Pius IX
St. Thérèse of Lisieux	1873–1897	1997 by John Paul II

Ecumenical Councils

An ecumenical council is a worldwide assembly of bishops under the direction of the Pope. There have been twenty-one ecumenical councils, the most recent being the Second Vatican Council (1962–1965). A complete list of the Church's ecumenical councils with the years each met:

Nicaea I	325
Constantinople I	381
Ephesus	431
Chalcedon	451
Constantinople II	553
Constantinople III	680
Nicaea II	787
Constantinople IV	869–870
Lateran I	1123
Lateran II	1139
Lateran III	1179
Lateran IV	1215
Lyons I	1245
Lyons II	1274
Vienne	1311–1312
Constance	1414–1418
Florence	1431–1445
Lateran V	1512–1517
Trent	1545–1563
Vatican Council I	1869–1870
Vatican Council II	1962–1965

E. Morality

Morality refers to the goodness or evil of human actions. Listed below are several helps the Church offers for making good and moral decisions.

The Ten Commandments

The Ten Commandments are a main source for Christian morality. The Ten Commandments were revealed by God to Moses. Jesus himself acknowledged them. He told the rich young man, "If you wish to enter into life, keep the commandments" (Mt 19:17). Since the time of St. Augustine (fourth century), the Ten Commandments have been used as a source for teaching baptismal candidates.

I. I, the Lord, am your God: you shall not have other gods besides me.

II. You shall not take the name of the Lord, your God, in vain.

III. Remember to keep holy the sabbath day.

IV. Honor your father and your mother.

V. You shall not kill.

VI. You shall not commit adultery.

VII. You shall not steal.

VIII. You shall not bear false witness against your neighbor.

IX. You shall not covet your neighbor's wife.

X. You shall not covet your neighbor's goods.

The Beatitudes

The word *beatitude* means "happiness." Jesus preached the Beatitudes in his Sermon on the Mount. They are:

Blessed are the poor in spirit, for theirs is the kingdom of God.

Blessed are they who mourn, for they will be comforted.

Blessed are the meek, for they will inherit the land.

Blessed are they who hunger and thirst for righteousness, for they will be satisfied.

Blessed are the merciful, for they will be shown mercy.

Blessed are the clean of heart, for they will see God.

Blessed are the peacemakers, for they will be called children of God.

Blessed are they who are persecuted for the sake of righteousness, for theirs is the kingdom of Heaven.

Cardinal Virtues

Virtues—habits that help in leading a moral life—that are acquired by human effort are known as moral or human virtues. Four of these are the cardinal virtues, as they form the hinge that connects all the others. They are:

- Prudence
- Justice
- Fortitude
- Temperance

Theological Virtues

The theological virtues are the foundation for moral life. They are gifts infused into our souls by God.

- Faith
- Hope
- Love

Corporal (Bodily) Works of Mercy

1. Feed the hungry.
2. Give drink to the thirsty.
3. Clothe the naked.
4. Visit the imprisoned.
5. Shelter the homeless.
6. Visit the sick.
7. Bury the dead.

Spiritual Works of Mercy

1. Counsel the doubtful.
2. Instruct the ignorant.
3. Admonish sinners.
4. Comfort the afflicted.
5. Forgive offenses.
6. Bear wrongs patiently.
7. Pray for the living and the dead.

Precepts of the Church

1. You shall attend Mass on Sundays and on holy days of obligation and rest from servile labor.
2. You shall confess your sins at least once a year.
3. You shall receive the Sacrament of Eucharist at least during the Easter season.
4. You shall observe the days of fasting and abstinence established by the Church.
5. You shall help to provide for the needs of the Church.

Catholic Social Teaching: Major Themes

The 1998 document Sharing Catholic Social Teaching: Challenges and Directions—Reflections of the U.S. Catholic Bishops *highlighted seven principles of the Church's social teaching. They are:*

1. Life and dignity of the human person
2. Call to family, community, and participation
3. Rights and responsibilities
4. Preferential option for the poor and vulnerable
5. The dignity of work and the rights of workers
6. Solidarity
7. God's care for creation

Sin

Sin is an offense against God.

Mortal sin is the most serious kind of sin. Mortal sin destroys or kills a person's relationship with God. To be a mortal sin, three conditions must exist:

- The moral object must be of grave or serious matter. Grave matter is specified in the Ten Commandments (e.g., do not kill, do not commit adultery, do not steal, etc.).
- The person must have full knowledge of the gravity of the sinful action.
- The person must completely consent to the action. It must be a personal choice.

Venial sin is less serious sin. Petty jealousy, disobedience, and a sarcastic word may be examples of venial sins. Venial sins, when not repented, can lead a person to commit mortal sins.

Vices are bad habits linked to sins. Vices come from particular sins, especially the seven capital sins: pride, avarice, envy, wrath, lust, gluttony, and sloth.

F. Liturgy and Sacraments

The Sacraments and the Divine Office constitute the Church's liturgy. The Mass is the most important liturgical celebration.

Church Year

The cycle of seasons and feasts that Catholics celebrate is called the Church Year or Liturgical Year. The Church Year is divided into five main parts: Advent, Christmas, Lent, Easter, and Ordinary Time.

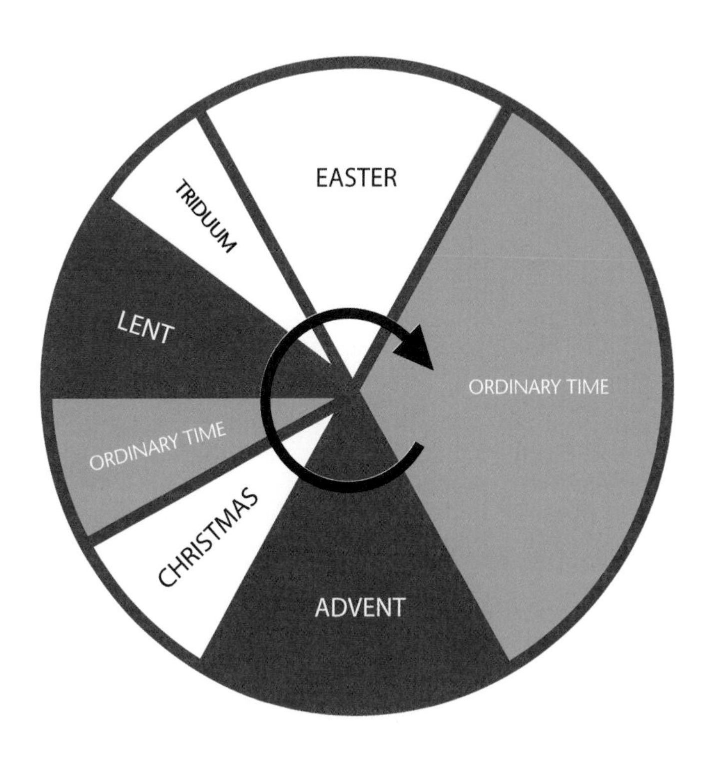

Holy Days of Obligation in the United States

1. Immaculate Conception of Mary
   December 8
2. Christmas
   December 25
3. Solemnity of Mary, Mother of God
   January 1
4. Ascension of the Lord
   Forty days after Easter
5. Assumption of Mary
   August 15
6. All Saints Day
   November 1

The Seven Sacraments

1. Baptism
2. Confirmation
3. Eucharist
4. Penance and Reconciliation
5. Anointing of the Sick
6. Matrimony
7. Holy Orders

How to Go to Confession

1. Spend some time examining your conscience. Consider your actions and attitudes in each area of your life (e.g., faith, family, school/work, social life, relationships). Ask yourself, Is this area of my life pleasing to God? What needs to be reconciled with God? with others? with myself?
2. Sincerely tell God that you are sorry for your sins. Ask God for forgiveness and for the grace you will need to change what needs changing in your life. Promise God that you will try to live according to his will for you.
3. Approach the area for confession. Wait at an appropriate distance until it is your turn.

4. Make the Sign of the Cross with the priest. He may say: "May God, who has enlightened every heart, help you to know your sins and trust his mercy." You reply: "Amen."
5. Confess your sins to the priest. Simply and directly talk to him about the areas of sinfulness in your life that need God's healing touch.
6. The priest will ask you to express your contrition or sorrow and to pray an Act of Contrition. Pray an Act of Contrition you have committed to memory. See page 282 for a prayer of contrition.
7. The priest will talk to you about your life, encourage you to be more faithful to God in the future, and help you decide what to do to make up for your sins—your penance.
8. The priest will then extend his hands over your head and pray the Church's official prayer of absolution:

   God, the Father of mercies, through the Death and Resurrection of his Son, has reconciled the world to himself and sent the Holy Spirit among us for the forgiveness of sins; through the ministry of the Church may God give you pardon and peace, and I absolve you from your sins in the name of the Father, and of the Son, and of the Holy Spirit.

   You respond: "Amen."
9. The priest will wish you peace. Thank him and leave.
10. Go to a quiet place in church and pray your prayer of penance. Then spend some time quietly thanking God for the gift of forgiveness.

Order of Mass

There are two main parts of the Mass, the Liturgy of the Word and the Liturgy of the Eucharist. The complete order of Mass is as follows:

The Introductory Rites

- The Entrance
- Greeting of the Altar and of the People Gathered
- The Act of Penitence
- The *Kyrie Eleison*
- The *Gloria*
- The Collect (Opening Prayer)

The Liturgy of the Word

- Silence
- The Biblical Readings (the reading of the Gospel is the high point of the Liturgy of the Word)
- The Responsorial Psalm
- The Homily
- The Profession of Faith (Creed)
- The Prayer of the Faithful

The Liturgy of the Eucharist

- The Preparation of the Gifts
  - The Prayer over the Offerings
  - The Eucharistic Prayer
    - Thanksgiving
    - Acclamation
    - Epiclesis
    - Institution Narrative and Consecration
    - Anamnesis
    - Offering
    - Intercessions
    - Final Doxology
  - The Communion Rite
    - The Lord's Prayer
    - The Rite of Peace
    - The Fraction (Breaking of the Bread)
    - Communion
    - Prayer after Communion

The Concluding Rites

Communion Regulations

To receive Holy Communion properly, a person must be in the state of grace (free from mortal sin), have the right intention (only for the purpose of pleasing God), and observe the Communion fast.

The fast means that a person may not eat anything or drink any liquid (other than water) one hour before the reception of Communion. There are exceptions made to this fast only for the sick and aged.

Three Degrees of the Sacrament of Holy Orders

There are three degrees of the Sacrament of Holy Orders: the ministries of bishop, priest, and deacon.

The bishop receives the fullness of the Sacrament of Orders. He is the successor to the Apostles. When he celebrates the Sacraments, the bishop is given the grace to act in the person of Christ, who is the head of the Body of the Church.

Priests are ordained as coworkers of the bishop. They, too, are configured to Christ so that they may act in his person during the Sacraments of Eucharist, Baptism, and the Anointing of the Sick. They may bless marriages in the name of Christ and, under the authority of the bishop, share in Christ's ministry of forgiveness in the Sacrament of Penance and Reconciliation.

Deacons are ordained for service and are configured to Christ the servant. Deacons are ordained to help and serve the priests and bishops in their work. While bishops and priests are configured to Christ to act as the head of Christ's body, deacons are configured to Christ in order to serve as he served. Deacons may baptize, preach the Gospel and homily, and bless marriages.

G. Mary and the Saints

The doctrine of the Communion of Saints flows from our belief that we Christians are closely united as one family in the Spirit of Jesus Christ. Mary is the Queen of the Saints. Her role in the Church flows from an inseparable union with her Son.

Mother of God

Mary, the Mother of Jesus, is the closest human to cooperate with her Son's work of redemption. For this reason, the Church holds her in a special place. Of her many titles, the most significant is that she is the Mother of God.

The Church teaches several truths about Mary.

First, she was conceived immaculately. This means from the very first moment of her existence she was without sin and "full of grace." This belief is called the Immaculate Conception. The feast of the Immaculate Conception is celebrated on December 8.

Second, Mary was always a virgin. She was a virgin before, in, and after the birth of Jesus. As his Mother, she cared for him in infancy and raised him to adulthood with the help of her husband, Joseph. She witnessed Jesus' preaching and ministry, was at the foot of his cross at his crucifixion, and present with the Apostles as they awaited the coming of the Holy Spirit at Pentecost. With her whole being, she is, as she stated: "I am the handmaid of the Lord" (Lk 1:38).

Third, at the time of her death, Mary was assumed body and soul into Heaven. This dogma was proclaimed as a matter of faith by Pope Pius XII in 1950. The feast of the Assumption is celebrated on August 15.

The Church has always been devoted to the Blessed Virgin. This devotion is different from that given to God—Father, Son, and Holy Spirit. Rather, the Church is devoted to Mary as the first disciple, the Queen of all Saints, and the Church's own

Mother. Quoting the fathers of the Second Vatican Council:

> In the meantime the Mother of Jesus, in the glory which she possesses in body and soul in Heaven, is the image and the beginning of the Church as it is to be perfected in the world to come. Likewise she shines forth on earth, until the day of the Lord shall come, a sign of certain hope and comfort to the pilgrim People of God. (*Lumen Gentium*, 68)

Marian Feasts throughout the Year

January 1	Solemnity of Mary, Mother of God
March 25	Annunciation of the Lord
May 31	Visitation
August 15	Assumption
August 22	Queenship of Mary
September 8	Birth of Mary
September 15	Our Lady of Sorrows
October 7	Our Lady of the Rosary
November 21	Presentation of Mary
December 8	Immaculate Conception
December 12	Our Lady of Guadalupe

Canonization of Saints

Saints are those who are in glory with God in Heaven. *Canonization* refers to a solemn declaration by the Pope that a person who either died a martyr or who lived an exemplary Christian life is in Heaven and may be honored and imitated by all Christians. The canonization process first involves a process of beatification that includes a thorough investigation of the person's life and certification of miracles that can be attributed to the candidate's intercession.

The first official canonization of the universal Church on record is St. Ulrich of Augsburg by Pope John XV in 993.

Some non-Catholics criticize Catholics for "praying to saints." Catholics *honor* saints for their holy lives but we do not pray to them as if they were God. We ask the saints to pray with us and for us as part of the Church in glory. We can ask them to do this because we know that their lives have been spent in close communion with God. We also ask the saints for their friendship so that we can follow the example they have left for us.

Patron Saints

A patron is a saint who is designated for places (nations, regions, dioceses) or organizations. Many saints have also become patrons of jobs, professional groups, and intercessors for special needs. Listed below are patron saints for several nations and some special patrons:

Patrons of Places

Americas	Our Lady of Guadalupe, St. Rose of Lima
Argentina	Our Lady of Lujan
Australia	Our Lady Help of Christians
Canada	St. Joseph, St. Anne
China	St. Joseph
England	St. George
Finland	St. Henry
France	Our Lady of the Assumption, St. Joan of Arc, St. Thérèse of Lisieux
Germany	St. Boniface
India	Our Lady of the Assumption
Ireland	St. Patrick, St. Brigid, St. Columba
Italy	St. Francis of Assisi, St. Catherine of Siena
Japan	St. Peter
Mexico	Our Lady of Guadalupe
Poland	St. Casmir, St. Stanislaus, Our Lady of Czestochowa
Russia	St. Andrew, St. Nicholas of Myra, St. Thérèse of Lisieux

Scotland	St. Andrew, St. Columba
Spain	St. James, St. Teresa of Ávila
United States	Immaculate Conception

Special Patrons

Accountants	St. Matthew
Actors	St. Genesius
Animals	St. Francis of Assisi
Athletes	St. Sebastian
Beggars	St. Martin of Tours
Boy Scouts	St. George
Dentists	St. Apollonia
Farmers	St. Isidore
Grocers	St. Michael
Journalists	St. Francis de Sales
Maids	St. Zita
Motorcyclists	Our Lady of Grace
Painters	St. Luke
Pawnbrokers	St. Nicholas
Police Officers	St. Michael
Priests	St. John Vianney
Scientists	St. Albert
Tailors	St. Homobonus
Teachers	St. Gregory the Great, St. John Baptist de la Salle
Wine Merchants	St. Amand

H. Devotions

Catholics have also expressed their piety around the Church's sacramental life through practices like the veneration of relics, visits to churches, pilgrimages, processions, the Stations of the Cross, religious dances, the Rosary, medals, and many more. This section lists some popular Catholic devotions.

The Mysteries of the Rosary

Joyful Mysteries

1. The Annunciation
2. The Visitation
3. The Nativity
4. The Presentation in the Temple
5. The Finding of Jesus in the Temple

Mysteries of Light

1. Jesus' Baptism in the Jordan River
2. Jesus Self-manifestation at the Wedding of Cana
3. The Proclamation of the Kingdom of God and Jesus' Call to Conversion
4. The Transfiguration
5. The Institution of the Eucharist at the Last Supper

Sorrowful Mysteries

1. The Agony in the Garden
2. The Scourging at the Pillar
3. The Crowning with Thorns
4. The Carrying of the Cross
5. The Crucifixion

Glorious Mysteries

1. The Resurrection
2. The Ascension
3. The Descent of the Holy Spirit
4. The Assumption of Mary
5. The Crowning of Mary as the Queen of Heaven and Earth

How to Pray the Rosary

Opening

1. Begin on the crucifix and pray the Apostles' Creed.
2. On the first bead, pray the Our Father.
3. On the next three beads, pray the Hail Mary. (Some people meditate on the virtues of faith, hope, and charity on these beads.)
4. On the fifth bead, pray the Glory Be.

The Body

Each decade (set of ten beads) is organized as follows:

1. On the larger bead that comes before each set of ten, announce the mystery to be prayed (see above) and pray one Our Father.
2. On each of the ten smaller beads, pray one Hail Mary while meditating on the mystery.
3. Pray one Glory Be at the end of the decade. (There is no bead for the Glory Be.)

Conclusion

Pray the following prayer at the end of the Rosary:

Hail, Holy Queen

Hail, holy Queen, Mother of Mercy,
our life, our sweetness, and our hope.
To thee do we cry,
poor banished children of Eve.
To thee do we send up our sighs,
mourning and weeping in the valley of tears.
Turn then, most gracious advocate,
thine eyes of mercy toward us;
and after this our exile,
show unto us the blessed fruit of thy womb,
Jesus.
O clement, O loving, O sweet Virgin Mary.

Pray for us, O holy Mother of God,
that we may be made worthy of the
promises of Christ.
Amen.

Stations of the Cross

The Stations of the Cross is a devotion and also a sacramental. (A sacramental is a sacred object, blessing, or devotion.) The Stations of the Cross are individual pictures or symbols hung on the interior walls of most Catholic churches depicting fourteen steps along Jesus' way of the cross. Praying the stations means meditating on each of the following scenes:

1. Jesus is condemned to death.
2. Jesus takes up his cross.
3. Jesus falls the first time.
4. Jesus meets his Mother.
5. Simon of Cyrene helps Jesus carry his cross.
6. Veronica wipes the face of Jesus.
7. Jesus falls the second time.
8. Jesus consoles the women of Jerusalem.
9. Jesus falls the third time.
10. Jesus is stripped of his garments.
11. Jesus is nailed to the cross.
12. Jesus dies on the cross.
13. Jesus is taken down from the cross.
14. Jesus is laid in the tomb.

Some churches also include a fifteenth station, the Resurrection of the Lord.

Novenas

The novena consists of the recitation of certain prayers over a period of nine days. The symbolism of nine days refers to the time Mary and the Apostles spent in prayer between Jesus' Ascension into Heaven and Pentecost.

Many novenas are dedicated to Mary or to a saint with the faith and hope that she or he will intercede for the one making the novena. Novenas to St. Jude, St. Anthony, Our Lady of Perpetual Help, and Our Lady of Lourdes remain popular in the Church today.

Liturgy of the Hours

The Liturgy of the Hours is part of the official, public prayer of the Church. Along with the celebration of the Sacraments, the recitation of the Liturgy of the Hours, or Divine Office (office means "duty" or "obligation"), allows for constant praise and thanksgiving to God throughout the day and night.

The Liturgy of Hours consists of five major divisions:

1. An hour of readings
2. Morning praises
3. Midday prayers

4. Vespers (evening prayers)
5. Compline (a short night prayer)

Scriptural prayer, especially the Psalms, is at the heart of the Liturgy of the Hours. Each day follows a separate pattern of prayer with themes closely tied in with the liturgical year and feasts of the saints.

The Divine Praises

These praises are traditionally recited after the benediction of the Blessed Sacrament.

Blessed be God.
Blessed be his holy name.
Blessed be Jesus Christ, true God and true man.
Blessed be the name of Jesus.
Blessed be his most Sacred Heart.
Blessed be his most Precious Blood.
Blessed be Jesus in the most holy sacrament of the altar.
Blessed be the Holy Spirit, the Paraclete.
Blessed be the great Mother of God, Mary most holy.
Blessed be her holy and Immaculate Conception.
Blessed be her glorious Assumption.
Blessed be the name of Mary, Virgin and Mother.
Blessed be St. Joseph, her most chaste spouse.
Blessed be God in his angels and his saints.

I. Prayers

Some common Catholic prayers are listed below. The Latin translation for three of the prayers is included. Latin is the official language of the Church. There are several occasions when you may pray in Latin; for example, at a World Youth Day when you are with young people who speak many different languages.

Sign of the Cross

In the name of the Father,
and of the Son,
and of the Holy Spirit. Amen.

In nómine Patris,
et Filii,
et Spíritus Sancti.
Amen.

Our Father

Our Father
who art in Heaven,
hallowed be thy name.
Thy kingdom come;
thy will be done on earth as it is in Heaven.
Give us this day our daily bread
and forgive us our trespasses
as we forgive those who trespass against us.
And lead us not into temptation,
but deliver us from evil.
Amen.

Pater Noster qui es in celis:
sanctificétur Nomen Tuum;
advéniat Regnum Tuum;
fiat volúntas Tua,
sicut in caelo, et in terra.
Panem nostrum
cuotidiánum da nobis hódie;
et dimítte nobis débita nostra,
sicut et nos
dimíttimus debitóribus nostris;
Et ne nos inducas in tentatiónem,
sed libera nos a Malo.
Amen.

Glory Be

Glory be to the Father
and to the Son
and to the Holy Spirit,
as it was in the beginning,
is now,
and ever shall be,
world without end. Amen.

Glória Patri
et Filio
et Spiritui Sancto.
Sicut erat in princípio,
et nunc et semper,
et in sae'cula saeculórum.
Amen.

Hail Mary

Hail Mary, full of grace,
the Lord is with thee.
Blessed art thou among women
and blessed is the fruit of thy womb, Jesus.
Holy Mary, Mother of God,
pray for us sinners now
and at the hour of our death. Amen.

Ave, María, grátia plena,
Dóminus tecum.
Benedicta tu in muliéribus,
et benedíctus fructus ventris
tui, Iesus.
Sancta María, Mater Dei,
ora pro nobis peccatoribus
nunc et in hora mortis nostrae.
Amen.

Memorare

Remember, O most gracious Virgin Mary,
that never was it known
that anyone who fled to your protection,
implored your help,
or sought your intercession was left unaided.
Inspired by this confidence,
I fly unto you,
O virgin of virgins, my Mother,
To you I come, before you I stand,
sinful and sorrowful.
O Mother of the Word Incarnate,
despise not my petitions,
but in your mercy hear and answer me. Amen.

Hail, Holy Queen

Hail, holy Queen, Mother of Mercy,
our life, our sweetness and our hope!
To you do we cry,
poor banished children of Eve;
to you do we send up our sighs,
mourning and weeping in this valley of tears.
Turn then, O most gracious advocate,
your eyes of mercy toward us,
and after this exile,
show us the blessed fruit of your womb, Jesus.
O clement, O loving, O sweet Virgin Mary.

V. Pray for us, O holy Mother of God.
R. that we may be made worthy of the promises of Christ. Amen.

The Angelus

V. The angel spoke God's message to Mary.
R. And she conceived by the Holy Spirit.
Hail Mary . . .
V. Behold the handmaid of the Lord.
R. May it be done unto me according to your word.
Hail Mary . . .
V. And the Word was made flesh.
R. And dwelled among us.
Hail Mary . . .
V. Pray for us, O holy Mother of God.
R. That we may be made worthy of the promises of Christ.

Let us pray: We beseech you, O Lord, to pour out your grace into our hearts. By the message of an angel we have learned of the Incarnation of Christ, your son; lead us by his Passion and cross, to the glory of the Resurrection. Through the same Christ our Lord. Amen.

Regina Caeli

Queen of Heaven, rejoice, alleluia.
The Son you merited to bear, alleluia,
has risen as he said, alleluia.
Pray to God for us, alleluia.

V. Rejoice and be glad, O Virgin Mary, alleluia.
R. For the Lord has truly risen, alleluia.
Let us pray.
God of life, you have given joy to the world by the Resurrection of your son, our Lord Jesus Christ. Through the prayers of his Mother, the Virgin Mary, bring us to the happiness of eternal life. We ask this through Christ our Lord. Amen.

Grace at Meals

Before Meals

Bless us, O Lord,
and these your gifts,
which we are about to receive from your bounty,
through Christ our Lord. Amen.

After Meals

We give you thanks, almighty God,
for these and all the gifts
which we have received
from your goodness
through Christ our Lord. Amen.

Guardian Angel Prayer

Angel of God, my guardian dear, to whom God's love entrust me here, ever this day be at my side, to light and guard, to rule and guide. Amen.

Prayer for the Faithful Departed

V: Eternal rest grant unto them, O Lord.
R: And let perpetual light shine upon them.
May their souls and the souls of all faithful departed, through the mercy of God, rest in peace.
R: Amen.

Morning Offering

O Jesus, through the Immaculate Heart of Mary, I offer you my prayers, works, joys, and sufferings of this day in union with the holy sacrifice of the Mass throughout the world. I offer them for all the intentions of your Sacred Heart: the Salvation of souls, reparation for sin, the reunion of all Christians. I offer them for the intentions of our bishops and all members of the apostleship of prayer and in particular for those recommended by your Holy Father this month. Amen.

Act of Faith

O God,
I firmly believe all the truths that you have revealed
and that you teach us through your Church,
for you are truth itself
and can neither deceive nor be deceived.
Amen.

Act of Hope

O God,
I hope with complete trust that you will give me,
through the merits of Jesus Christ, all necessary grace in this world
and everlasting life in the world to come,
for this is what you have promised
and you always keep your promises.
Amen.

Act of Love

O my God, I love you above all things, with my whole heart and soul, because you are all good and worthy of all my love. I love my neighbor as myself for the love of you. I forgive all who have injured me, and I ask pardon of all whom I have injured. Amen.

Act of Contrition

My God,
I am sorry for my sins with all my heart.
In choosing to do wrong
and failing to do good,
I have sinned against you
whom I should love above all things.
I firmly intend, with your help,
to do penance,
to sin no more,
and to avoid whatever leads me to sin.
Our Savior Jesus Christ
suffered and died for us.
In his name, my God, have mercy.

Prayer for Peace (St. Francis of Assisi)

Lord, make me an instrument of your peace.
Where there is hatred, let me sow love;
where there is injury, pardon;
where there is doubt, faith;
where there is despair, hope;
where there is darkness, light;
where there is sadness, joy.
O Divine Master,
grant that I may not so much seek to be
consoled as to console;
to be understood, as to understand,
to be loved, as to love.
For it is in giving that we receive,
it is in pardoning that we are pardoned,
and it is in dying that we are born to eternal life.

GLOSSARY

agape
A Greek word that describes a self-sacrificing sort of love; the love Jesus showed to all.

agnostic
A person who asserts that he or she does not know whether there is a God or not.

Alpha and Omega
A Christian symbol formed with the first and last letters of the Greek alphabet—Alpha and Omega. Together, these letters suggest that Jesus is the beginning and end or completion of all history.

Anno Domini
A Latin phrase meaning "in the year of Our Lord" used in reference to events that took place after the birth of Jesus Christ.

Annunciation
The announcement by the angel Gabriel to the Virgin Mary that God wanted her to be the Mother of the Savior, Jesus Christ.

apocryphal Gospels
A group of writings about the life and teaching of Jesus that do not meet Church criteria for inclusion in the New Testament canon. The term *apocryphal* means "hidden." Most apocryphal writings date from the second through the fourth centuries, many years after the Apostolic era.

Aramaic
A western Semitic language commonly spoken in Palestine, Syria, and Mesopotamia from the third century before Christ until AD 650. Aramaic was later replaced by Arabic.

Arianism
A heresy common during the first Christian centuries that denied that Jesus was truly God; named after Arius (AD 250–336), a priest and popular preacher from Alexandria, Egypt.

Assumption
The dogmatic teaching of the Catholic Church that when the earthly life of Mary was completed, she was taken body and soul into the presence of God. Mary was granted this grace, the Church says, because she is the sinless Mother of God.

atheist
A person who denies the existence of God.

Beatitudes
Beatitude means "supreme happiness." The eight Beatitudes preached by Jesus in the Sermon on the Mount respond to our natural desire for happiness.

blasphemy
Any thought, word, or act that expresses hatred or contempt for God, Christ, the Church, saints, or holy things. It is a grave sin, contrary to the Second Commandment.

Blessed Trinity
The central mystery of the Christian faith. It teaches that there are three Persons in one God: Father, Son, and Holy Spirit.

Body of Christ
A rich image for the Church from St. Paul who wrote that the Church is like a body for which Christ is the head. Paul taught that the members of the Church are like the members or parts of the body, drawing direction from the head and life from the rest of the body.

canon of the Bible
The official list of inspired books in the Bible. Catholics list forty-six Old Testament books and twenty-seven New Testament books in their canon.

charism
A spiritual gift given by God to individuals to help build up and strengthen the Church.

Christ
The Greek term for "Messiah." It means "the anointed one."

Christology
The branch of Christian theology that studies the nature, Person, and works of Jesus Christ.

Church Fathers
Bishops, theologians, teachers, and scholars whose writings have greatly contributed to Church doctrine and practice. Among the Church Fathers of the early Church are Sts. Irenaeus, Athanasius, Cyril of Alexandria, and Pope St. Leo the Great.

common good
The sum total of social conditions that allow people, either as groups or as individuals, to reach their fulfillment more fully and more easily.

concupiscence
The weakness or inclination in human beings to sin, individually or collectively.

consubstantial
The quality "of one being" in the relationship between all the divine Persons of the Trinity—Father, Son, and Holy Spirit. So, the Son and the Holy Spirit have the exact same nature as the Father, the first Person of the Trinity.

contemplation
A form of silent wordless prayer in which mind and heart rest in God's goodness and majesty.

contrition
A form of prayer in which we ask God, our merciful Father, to forgive our sins.

covenant
A solemn agreement or contract of love between God and his people.

creed
A statement of belief; sometimes a collection of creedal statements.

Deposit of Faith
The body of saving truths and the core beliefs of Catholicism that are faithfully preserved by the Magisterium.

didache
A word that means "teaching" that described oral teaching to those who had already accepted Jesus.

dignity
The quality of being worthy of esteem and respect.

disciple
A follower of Jesus. The word comes from a Latin word that means "learner."

divine missions of the Blessed Trinity
The distinctive works of God's saving intervention in the world—creation, Salvation, and sanctification. Although creation is attributed to the Father, Salvation (Redemption) to the Son, and sanctification to the Holy Spirit, all three Persons of the Trinity act as one and are fully present in all the missions.

divine providence
The sovereignty of God over events in the lives of individuals and throughout history.

Divine Revelation
The gift of God's self-revelation by which he makes known the mystery of his divine plan.

Docetism
A first-century heresy that taught that Jesus only seemed to be human.

dogma
A central truth of Revelation that Catholics are obliged to believe.

dominion
The role of caretaker and faithful steward given by God to our first parents, Adam and Eve. All human beings inherit the responsibility to be good and loving caretakers of the world, its resources, and its creatures.

ecumenical council
A worldwide, official assembly of the bishops under the direction of the Pope. There have been twenty-one ecumenical councils, the most recent being the Second Vatican Council (1962–1965).

Epiphany
The celebration of the manifestation of God in human form; the manifestation of Jesus to the Gentiles or non-Jews.

eros
A Greek word that describes sexual love and attraction.

eternal
A term that describes existing without a beginning and forever.

evangelists
The authors of the four Gospels of the New Testament—Matthew, Mark, Luke, and John—and disciples closely associated with them.

faith
One of the theological virtues. Faith is an acknowledgment of an allegiance to God.

form criticism
A type of literary criticism used by Scripture scholars that analyzes and compares different literary forms used in the Gospels.

free will
The capacity to choose among alternatives. Free will is "the power, rooted in reason and will . . . to perform deliberate actions on one's own responsibility" (*CCC*, 1731). True freedom is at the service of what is good and true.

fruits of the Holy Spirit
Spiritual perfections that result from the Holy Spirit living in us. The Church lists them as charity, joy, peace, patience, kindness, goodness, generosity, gentleness, faithfulness, modesty, self-control, and chastity.

genealogy
A record or history of the ancestors or descendants of a person, a people, or a nation.

gifts of the Holy Spirit
Seven spiritual gifts from the Holy Spirit given to the Church and her members, especially at Baptism and Confirmation. The gifts are wisdom, understanding, knowledge, counsel, fortitude, piety, and fear of the Lord or wonder and awe.

Gnosticism
A heresy from the first Christian centuries that taught that Jesus shared secret information or knowledge with only a few people who were guaranteed Salvation. Gnosticism comes from *gnosis,* the Greek word for "knowledge." Gnosticism also distrusted material creation, teaching that the human body was evil.

Gospel
The "Good News," the story of the coming of the Savior, Jesus Christ, and the inauguration of God's Kingdom.

grace
God's gift of friendship and life that enables us to share his life and love.

heresy
An obstinate denial after Baptism to believe a truth that must be believed with divine and Catholic faith, or an obstinate doubt about such truth.

historical criticism
An approach to Scripture analysis that tries to discover what evangelists really wanted to say when they wrote a particular text.

Immaculate Conception
The dogmatic teaching of the Catholic Church that Mary was conceived in the womb of her mother without the stain of Original Sin that all other human beings inherit. This teaching was declared as an infallible teaching by Pope Pius IX in 1854.

immanence
A trait of God that refers to his intimate union with and total presence to his creation, whereby he upholds and sustains all creation in its being.

Immanent Trinity
A focus on the inner life of God as a Trinity of three divine Persons without consideration of God's relationship to human beings or his creation work.

Incarnation
The teaching that God became flesh through the birth of Jesus Christ, the Son of God and the child of the Virgin Mary.

infallible teaching
Catholic teachings, proposed by the Magisterium in union with the Pope, that are declared to be totally free of error. Infallibility is a gift of the Spirit whereby the Pope and the bishops are preserved from error when proclaiming a doctrine related to Christian faith or morals.

infinite
A term that means extending endlessly, having no end or limits.

intercession
A prayer of petition for the sake of others.

Jesus
A word that means "YHWH is Salvation" or "Savior."

justification
The forgiving of our sins in order to welcome us into a right relationship with God through our faith in Jesus Christ.

kerygma
A form of preaching used in the early Church that presumed an audience of unbelievers.

king
A title given to the newborn Jesus by the Magi from the East who came to honor him. Jesus was also called a "king" at the end of his life by Jews seeking to accuse and convict him of sedition.

Kingdom of God or Kingdom of Heaven
The beginning of God's new reign on earth, which was to bring the forgiveness of sins, the healing of the sick, and the establishment of a time of peace and joyful living for all. Jesus, the Redeemer, initiated this new Kingdom.

Lamb of God
An Old Testament title for Jesus that has roots in the Passover celebration. Unblemished lambs were sacrificed for the Passover meal. Jesus gave up his life for the redemption of all humanity and became the sacrificial lamb of the New Testament.

liturgy
The public worship and communal worship of the Church.

Lord
A New Testament title given to Jesus that meant "God." In Greek, the word was translated as *Kurios* and in Hebrew *Adonai.*

Magisterium
The official teaching authority of the Church comprised of the Pope and bishops who are successors of Christ and his Apostles.

martyrs
A Greek word that means "witness," referring to those who were put to death because of their religious beliefs.

meditation
A form of prayer where the mind and imagination focus on Christ or some truth of Divine Revelation with the purpose of applying the lessons we learn to our lives.

metanoia
A Greek word for "repentance" or a turning away from sin with the intention of living a life of virtue and holiness.

miracle
A deed or an event that cannot be explained by ordinary human intervention or known natural forces.

Monophysitism
A fifth-century heresy that promoted the error that Jesus had only one nature—a divine nature. In response, the Church taught that Christ has two natures, one divine and one human; from the Greek words *monos*, which means "one" or "alone," and *physis,* which means "nature."

monotheism
From the Greek words *monos* ("one") and *theos* ("God"); the belief in one, all-powerful God. Christianity, Judaism, and Islam are three great monotheistic religions.

mystery
A truth about God and his saving plan that will always be beyond human understanding.

Nativity
The birth of Jesus Christ, the Son of God and of the Virgin Mary.

Nestorianism
A fifth-century heresy that taught that Christ exists as two persons—the man Jesus and the divine Son of God. The heresy was corrected by Church teaching that stated that Jesus has two natures (a divine nature and a human nature) in one Person. The heresy originated with Nestorius (ca. 386–ca. 451), the Archbishop of Constantinople.

omnipotent
An attribute of God that he is everywhere, unlimited, and all-powerful.

Original Sin
The fallen state of human nature into which all generations of people are born. Christ Jesus came to save us from Original Sin.

orthodoxy
From the Greek word *orthodoxos*, it means having the "right" opinion or thinking; adhering to the accepted or traditional especially in matters of religious faith.

Paraclete
Another name for the Holy Spirit that means advocate, defender, or consoler.

paradox
A figure of speech or statement that *seems* contradictory but actually contains a hidden truth.

Paschal Mystery
The redemptive Passion, Death, Resurrection, and glorious Ascension of Jesus Christ through which Jesus not only liberated us from sin, but also gave us new life through his Resurrection.

petition
A form of prayer where we ask God for something.

philia
A Greek word that describes brotherly love, or a lifelong affection between friends.

polytheism
The belief, in opposition to Christian doctrine, that there are many gods.

praise
A form of prayer whereby we acknowledge God and his goodness and glorify him for who he is.

prayer
Conversation with God; lifting of one's mind and heart to God or requesting good things from him; joining one's thoughts and love to God in adoration and blessing, petition, intercession, thanksgiving, and praise.

Precepts of the Church
Rules Catholics follow to help them become good and moral people. They include attending Mass on Sundays and holy days of obligation, confessing sins at least once a year, receiving Communion at minimum during the Easter season, observing days of fasting and abstinence, and providing for the needs of the Church.

Presentation in the Temple
The presentation of the infant Jesus by Mary and Joseph in the Temple took place forty days after his birth. This ritual observed the Law of Moses and marked the end of forty days of purification for the mother after childbirth. This presentation also completed the "redemption" of a firstborn son with a ritual offering.

priest
A title given to Jesus that meant "a mediator between God and humanity." In the Old Testament, priests offered sacrifices for the Chosen People. Jesus became the priest of the New Testament, offering himself as a sacrifice for all. Today, priests are members of the order of the presbyterate and coworkers with the bishops.

prophet
A title given to Jesus. A prophet is one who predicts the future but is also known as a representative and spokesman for God. Jesus acted as prophet in both ways but chiefly as God's representative because he was God himself.

rabbi
A highly respected teacher of Jewish law or theology.

redaction criticism
A scholarly approach to the study of Scripture that attempts to see how each of the Gospel writers edited, or redacted, materials for that Gospel's audience.

religion
A set of beliefs, values, and practices that binds believers in a relationship with God and with other believers.

Resurrection
The rising of Jesus from the dead on the third day after his Death on the cross. Jesus was able to conquer death because he is God.

ruah
A Hebrew word meaning "wind" or "breath" often used in the Old Testament to refer to God's mysterious and powerful life-giving presence.

Sacred Scripture
The inspired Word of God; the written record of God's Revelation.

Sacred Tradition
The living transmission of the Catholic faith through the teaching, life, and worship of the Church.

saint
A "holy one" of God who lives in union with God through the grace of Jesus Christ and the power of the Holy Spirit and whom God rewards with eternal life in Heaven.

Salvation History
The account of God's saving activity and intervention on behalf of humanity.

Salvific Trinity
The active and inseparable work of the Triune God—Father, Son, and Holy Spirit—in Salvation History.

savior
A title given to Jesus that means "one who protects or saves from present or future danger"; a Messiah.

Second Coming
The final judgment of all humanity when Christ returns to Earth. It is also known by its Greek name, *Parousia*, which means "arrival."

sin
An offense against God through a violation of truth, reason, and conscience. It is a deliberate thought, word, deed, or omission against the eternal law of God.

solidarity
A Christian virtue of charity and friendship whereby members of the human family share material and spiritual goods.

Son of Man
A title Jesus used to refer to himself. It emphasizes both Jesus' humanity and divinity. Its origins are in Daniel 7:13: "I saw . . . one like a son of man coming on the clouds of heaven."

source criticism
The study by Scripture scholars to determine what sources the Gospel writers used to compose their works.

spontaneous prayer
A form of personal prayer in which the person prays to God in his or her own words.

storge
A Greek word that describes love among family members.

Synoptic Gospels
The Gospels of Matthew, Mark, and Luke that have so much content in common that they are often studied side by side. The word *synoptic* comes from the Greek word for "to see together."

textual criticism
Scripture study that looks to the various early manuscripts of the biblical texts.

thanksgiving
A form of prayer that involves expressing gratitude or thanks to God for all that he gives to and for us.

theology
The study of the existence or the attributes of God; a word taken from the Greek words *theos* ("God") and *logos* ("word").

Theotokos
A Greek term for Mary meaning "God bearer" or "birth mother of God" that was first used by the Council of Ephesus in AD 431.

tongues
A term for the practice of "speaking in tongues"; a gift from the Holy Spirit that allows a person to speak in languages that were never learned.

Torah
The entire body of Jewish literature, teaching, and law.

transcendence
The teaching that God, by nature, is beyond this world and beyond the comprehension of human beings.

Transfiguration
The glorious transformation of Jesus that manifested his divine identity for Peter, James, and John on a high mountain, probably Mount Tabor. The event, reported in all three Synoptic Gospels, also involved the appearance of both Moses and Elijah.

virtue
Moral excellence and righteousness; an inclination and habitual preference for the good.

works of mercy
Charitable actions that remind us how to come to the aid of a neighbor and his or her bodily and spiritual necessities.

YHWH
A name for God that God himself revealed to Moses and the Chosen People on Mount Sinai. The word means "I Am Who I Am" and led to Israel's understanding that God is the one, living, and true God.

Subject Index

Scripture Index

CCC Index

Photography Credits

Corbis

page 32, 60, 62, 146, 159, 176, 212

SuperStock

cover, page viii, 2, 9, 28, 35, 37, 39, 40, 42, 44, 46, 49, 50, 58, 63, 70, 71, 78, 79, 80, 82, 88, 93, 101, 105, 106, 112, 117, 119, 124, 131, 132, 140, 142, 147, 150, 153, 164, 167, 171, 173, 188, 193, 214, 219, 220, 224, 226, 232, 236, 241, 243, 245, 246, 248

Art Resource

page 67; 103 Erich Lessing / Art Resource, NY; 125 Bildarchiv Preussischer Kulturbesitz / Art Resource, NY